Recovering the Soul

Recovering the Soul

Aquinas's and Spinoza's Surprising and Helpful
Affinity on the Nature of Mind-Body Unity

G. Stephen Blakemore

PICKWICK *Publications* · Eugene, Oregon

RECOVERING THE SOUL
Aquinas's and Spinoza's Surprising and Helpful Affinity on the Nature of Mind-Body Unity

Pickwick Publications
An Imprint of Wipf and Stock Publishers
199 W. 8th Ave., Suite 3
Eugene, OR 97401

www.wipfandstock.com

PAPERBACK ISBN: 978-1-5326-9812-5
HARDCOVER ISBN: 978-1-5326-9813-2
EBOOK ISBN: 978-1-5326-9814-9

Cataloguing-in-Publication data:

Names: Blakemore, G. Stephen [author].

Title: Recovering the soul : Aquinas's and Spinoza's surprising and helpful affinity on the nature of mind-body unity / G. Stephen Blakemore.

Description: Eugene, OR: Pickwick Publications, 2023 | Includes bibliographical references and index.

Identifiers: ISBN 978-1-5326-9812-5 (paperback) | ISBN 978-1-5326-9813-2 (hardcover) | ISBN 978-1-5326-9814-9 (ebook)

Subjects: LCSH: Mind and body | Philosophical anthropology | Aquinas, Thomas, Saint, 1225?–1274 | Spinoza, Benedictus de, 1632–1677 | Metaphysics

Classification: BD418.3 B53 2023 (print) | BD418.3 (ebook)

01/13/23

To Carolyn—my soul's mate . . .

Contents

Introduction

THIS BOOK HAS GROWN over the years out of my dissertation completed at the University of Tennessee under the supervision of Richard Aquila. While studying there, I came to see that much contemporary philosophy of mind discussion assumes reductionist commitments from the beginning. This imposes a priori strictures on philosophical analyses of our own natures as human beings who experience ourselves as both biological beings and "spiritual" or rational selves, i.e., we are physical organisms who are endowed with an irreducible nonmaterial aspect of our physical existence. There is what Hillary Putnam has described as a methodological dualism of the current approaches, which is a limiting and foundational presupposition which constrains holistic philosophical analysis. Such a methodological starting point needs to be argued for, rather than merely asserted or embraced uncritically. It is my conviction that, if Putnam is correct, such a commitment to methodological dualism is most likely what leads to various reductionist theories in philosophy of mind, because the predominant materialist theories of philosophy of mind presume that they should bow to science in matters of ontology. This, then, relegates mind to, at best, idealist versions of the Kantian variety. Additionally, while a student focused upon historical philosophical arguments and developments in both the medieval and early modern periods, I began to read Thomas Aquinas and Baruch Spinoza, first independently, then in tandem. In the reading of their quite disparate ontologies, I began to believe I was noticing some startling similarities in the way that they conceived of the nature of human beings with regard to the unity of mind and body. The following chapters present you with my own conclusions regarding my original perceptions. Indeed, as you will see in the arguments and interpretations in the book, I am convinced that my original intuitions or observations were and are correct. Spinoza and Aquinas both contend for a kind of unity of the human being that is neither dualistic in flavor nor reductionistic. Rather, they attempt, in their distinct approaches, to describe the unity of mind and body as "one and the same thing," without denying the distinctions inherent in these aspects of our human essence, granting causal priority to one over the other, or positing a distinction of "being" between them. In the case of both, a basically Aristotelian doctrine of hylomorphism is at work.

I deal with a similarity that I see between these philosophers' metaphysics regarding the question of mind-body unity or identity for a twofold purpose. First is the matter of scholarly and historical interest. I want to demonstrate that there is this surprising affinity between the metaphysical doctrine of Spinoza regarding mind-body identity and that of Aquinas's own discussion and analysis of the nature of the relationship between mind and body in human beings. The argument on offer here is that Aquinas's understanding of hylomorphism, in which the human soul is the *form* of a human being's existence—both bodily *and* mentally—is echoed in Spinoza's doctrine of the *conatus.* The mind is not synonymous to the soul, strictly speaking, for either philosopher. Rather, both *anima* in Aquinas's theory and *conatus* as Spinoza presents the issue of human ongoing existence are themselves distinct from the nonmaterial aspect of our being we refer to as *mind,* every bit as much as from the physical body. Each of them conceives and describes by the particular terminology he employs (*animus/ conatus*) a kind of organizational grounding principle in living creatures (and specifically for our purposes human beings) that accounts for life in and the unity of existence in creatures. Neither mind nor body, nor the unity/identity of these dual aspects of our existence could exist, in their views, apart from *anima* (Aquinas) or *conatus* (Spinoza). No dependence by Spinoza upon Aquinas is implied in this comparative study, but merely the argument that their conceptions of the mind-body relationship specifically, and human existence more broadly, have some very interesting parallels that have not been observed sufficiently by other interpretations of their work.

Secondly, this analysis is intended to suggest that the distinct but comparable ways that Spinoza and Aquinas analyze the nature of human existence provide helpful insights that could enrich contemporary philosophy, should it engage and employ them, as it tries to work, in conjunction with modern science, to understand the way that mind and body are present in human beings. This could move the discussions beyond methodological dualism on the one hand, but also undercut the hegemony that the tendency to privilege materialistic scientism as the standard imposes upon philosophical analysis. Instead, I hope to be offering a holistic and rigorous way of contemplating the mystery of human existence, with no presumption to answer all the vexing questions but rather to suggest a reset to the nature of the discussion. This reset will require the rediscovery of the *soul* as a philosophical (and not just theological or religious) analytical concept.

Divided into nine chapters, the argument unfolds as follows. The first chapter introduces the problems related to the subject of mind and body in both Spinoza and Aquinas, establishing the parameters of the research. Chapter 2 looks at the

Aristotelian background of hylomorphism and argues that it is still a philosophically respectable theory. Aquinas's further development of the doctrine of hylomorphism beyond Aristotle's own foundational theory is the focus of the third chapter. Chapter 4 turns to Aquinas's discussion of the nature of mind and body identity, and the fifth chapter further addresses this question by discussing the concept of person and the metaphysical import this category has in his philosophy; it includes a favorable presentation of Aquinas's thought in contrast and dialogue with contemporary theories. The next chapter deals substantively with Spinoza's doctrine of mind-body identity, considering some of the more authoritative commentators' interpretations, and concludes with a preliminary presentation of the affinity he has with Aquinas's doctrine. Chapter 7 points explicitly to their similarities and describes the hylomorphism at work in both philosophies of human nature, showing how this concept undergirds the claims of unity of body and mind and how to understand the "interaction" between them. In the penultimate chapter, the controversial, thorny issue of the immortality of the soul or mind in both philosophers' metaphysics is presented and an argument as to the coherence of each one's thought is on offer. Finally, in chapter nine, I suggest the ways that a recovery of the soul as a serious philosophical category can be of benefit (because it is very likely true) to contemporary philosophical discussions regarding human nature and existence. The persistent and unyielding issue of mind and body ontology and relationship that dualist and physicalist philosophers have yet to resolve is of central concern for the pursuit of wisdom: the soul is the key.

1

On Being Rationally Alive

Why Compare the Doctrines of Thomas Aquinas and Baruch Spinoza?

VERY LITTLE SCHOLARLY ATTENTION has been given to the primary topic this book addresses. Unsurprisingly, the thought that one could compare Thomas Aquinas's and Baruch Spinoza's respective doctrines of the relationship between mind and body might, at first glance, strike many as philosophically fruitless. One might assume that only a collision of jarring opposites could be produced, since Spinoza is often considered, by considerable authorities, a debunker of medieval philosophical thought, a description captured in Dan Levin's subtitle to his biography of Spinoza, "the young thinker who destroyed the past."[1] Many Spinoza interpreters have read him as a kind of super-Cartesian who drove the conclusions of Descartes's definition of Substance to its logical conclusions. Pursuing the implications of Substance monism drove him to declare famously that *Deus sive Natura* is the only Substance. Such pantheism is a thorough rejection of theism and its resulting ontology, so a good many Christian philosophers and theologians have dubbed Spinoza an enemy of the faith—and for good reason.[2] As I focus on the possibility of a Thomistic reading of Spinoza, therefore, I am conscious that mine is a kind of minority report.

A close reading of Spinoza's "geometric method" shows that even with lines of demarcation appropriately drawn between the ontological commitments of the Catholic philosopher Aquinas and the nontheistic Spinoza, a certain affinity can be seen between their theories of the nature of human beings as minded and as embodied. Specifically, the likeness I have in mind is of a hylomorphic theory of human existence. Therefore, I aim to show that Aquinas's particular doctrine of hylomorphism

---

1. Levin, *Spinoza*.

2. Spinoza's *Tractatus Theologico-Politicus*, published anonymously, was a critical appraisal of the Bible and Jewish (and Christian) faith. See Spinoza, *Theologico-Political Treatise*, vol. 1.

is helpful for understanding Spinoza's mind-body identity theory. They share, I will argue, a remarkable conceptual similarity regarding the mind and body as dual aspects of a human being's unified existence, which both view as the result of a formal cause. There is an organizational antecedent that is the actualizing, life-giving principle, which we can call soul (*anima*). Additionally, I intend to demonstrate that a recovery and reconceptualization of their metaphysical concept will enrich modern philosophical reflection on the so-called mind-body problem. Knowing that suggesting a hylomorphic reading of Spinoza will be as controversial as attributing the dual-aspect designation to Aquinas, in this chapter I want to indicate the overall trajectory of my extensive argument that will be exegeted and developed in the later chapters. Before doing so, however, I want to set my "minority report" in the context of other works that have gone before this one.

SECONDARY SOURCE INTERPRETATIONS THAT INFORM THIS PROJECT

The research of others—most notably Henry Wolfson—provides a background for this present work. Wolfson famously, and controversially, argues in his now-classic *The Philosophy of Spinoza: Unfolding the Latent Process of His Reasoning* that Spinoza can best be understood by recognizing he is interacting with and is being influenced by medieval philosophical categories. Wolfson's Spinoza is a kind of latter-day Aristotelian who seized the categories (as did Aquinas) of form and matter and translated them into his concepts: Thought and Extension.[3] Wolfson's interpretation of Spinoza's theory regarding the modes of extension and the ideas of those modes is essentially a restatement of Aristotelian hylomorphism.[4] Such a reading suggests that Thomas's thirteenth century philosophy—also influenced by Aristotle, but developed beyond Aristotle's thought—and Spinoza's views might be fruitfully compared and contrasted as Aristotelian-inspired philosophies of hylomorphism. Perhaps they are "philosophical cousins" at least.

Wolfson also contends that Spinoza's development of the categories *natura naturans* and *natura naturata* result from his engagement with Thomists on the nature of God as cause and the world as effect: "Spinoza's description of these two phrases seems to be a modification of the description given by Thomas Aquinas" and Spinoza's reason for the "modification of [Aquinas's] description can be adequately accounted for."[5] In other words, while Spinoza is developing his metaphysical argument, he is

3. Wolfson, *Philosophy of Spinoza*, 1:234.

4. Wolfson, *Philosophy of Spinoza*, 2:46–48.

5. Wolfson, *Philosophy of Spinoza*, 2:16. Wolfson points out that Spinoza denies the Thomist notion of God as "an intelligent and purposive cause" and that Spinoza also defied the notion of God as only immaterial substance, which allowed him to develop his idea of the modes of substance, both extended and mental. One question, however, to look at is how the Thomists themselves might have departed from Thomas's idea of the analogy of being and his philosophy of participation in God's being.

engaged, per Wolfson, perhaps indirectly but still significantly, in dialogue with the intellectual legacy of Aquinas. This is the background, even where he nuances his concepts in contradistinction.

Very few scholars have taken Wolfson's proposals as a starting point for interpreting Spinoza. Perhaps viewing Spinoza as having any medieval leanings makes him seem less relevant to issues of current philosophical interest. Jonathan Bennett's assessment of Wolfson is exemplary of the general attitude: "[Wolfson's] labor and learning are awesome, but the philosophical profit is almost nil."[6] E. M. Curley, another of Spinoza's more recent respected commentators, agrees with Bennett's assessment, but demurs from Bennett's total disregard of Spinoza's scholastic background.[7] While this project cannot address the question of Wolfson's scholarship, his insights suggest, the above criticisms notwithstanding, that further and more focused analysis of Spinoza's thought in relation to Aquinas such as I offer is worth considering.

Others beyond Wolfson have also charted similar waters. Before Wolfson's work, Dunin-Borkowski in *Der Junge Spinoza* brought attention to the formative influence exerted on Spinoza's theory of the Attributes of Substance by certain seventeenth-century Christian discussions on how to understand the relationship of the "Persons" of the Trinity.[8] From the thirteenth to the seventeenth century, Aquinas's treatment of the Trinity proved mightily influential in Catholic and Protestant theology.[9] While this does not suggest dependence upon Aquinas, much less a commitment to Christian dogma—and Dunin-Borkowski rightly concludes that Spinoza totally rejected the Christian dogma of Trinity—nevertheless he contends that Spinoza paid due attention to the philosophical exposition of the distinction of Persons in the unity of the Trinity that Christian theology offered, and this provided a conceptual framework for Spinoza's doctrine of the unity of the infinite Attributes of Substance. Once again, there are interesting possibilities raised by Dunin-Borkowski's commentary for the thesis of this book that Aquinas and Spinoza might be considered together for philosophical and interpretive purposes.

Even more directly related to my thesis is the work of Efraim Shmueli, who persuasively argues that Spinoza's much-discussed lack of clarity in his theory of Attributes can be adequately understood as Spinoza's endeavor to reconcile the intellectual heritage of debate between medieval subjectivism (nominalism, from Maimonides) regarding attributions made about God and that of medieval objectivist (realist) views. Shmueli contends that Spinoza spans the divide in a way that harkens back (even if unintentionally and independently) to Thomas's basic view of the issue.[10] Aquinas has been called a "moderate realist," because he argued that the distinctions and

6. Bennett, *Study of Spinoza's Ethics*, 16.

7. Curley, *Behind the Geometrical Method* 137n2.

8. Von Dunn-Borkowski, *Der Junge de Spinoza*, 340–41; 451; 489–90.

9. Ury, *Trinitarian Personhood*, 215–24.

10. Shmueli, "Thomas Aquinas' Influence," 71.

similarities that we perceive among things must be real if they have existence in our minds, since our minds are informed by the intelligible forms of primary substances. Applying such epistemic considerations to the distinctions between the Attributes of God (even though God as an abstract object is not perceivable), Aquinas argued that they are real because they are conceivable as "distinctions of reason" (based on natural and revealed theology), but "in their highest form the Attributes are identical with each other and with the simple divine essence."[11] Shmueli concludes that one can discern an influence of Aquinas's reasoning (indirectly) on Spinoza's concept of Attributes, contending that the theory of the Attributes of Substance was a restatement of the medieval debate about the nature of universals, and whether any predication could be made about God. Something akin to Aquinas's notion of "the analogy of being," claims Shmueli, allowed Spinoza to develop a view of the Attributes that was neither fully nominalist nor strictly realist.[12] Thomas viewed the divine Attributes as true aspects of God's essence, but only known in our experience and conceptual framework by analogy. His doctrine of God as the pure Act of Being provided the ontological starting point for Aquinas as he argues that the *being* (act of existing) of creation must *participate* in some sense in the Being of God, since God's power of Being—uncreated, unbounded, independent, and infinite—is a category that would include all other existents via participation in said power. Thus, God's power of Being could not be excluded from any other existence, nor is there any other possible source of the power of being. (Of course, for Aquinas, no creature could be a part of God's Substance *in se*, contra Spinoza's views.)

Seeing an indirect influence of this Thomistic concept on Spinoza's view of the Attributes, Shmueli declares that Spinoza's thought was consonant with a general "Thomistic" analysis, i.e., that Attributes are each real in God but not ontologically independent from one another in God. Our intellect, therefore, conceives the Attributes, in Spinoza's judgment (by Shmueli's lights), as the real features of Reality *in se* that are accessible to our understanding for describing ontologically the nature of the One Substance. They are "forms of God's potency and, thus, aspects of *natura naturans*, not just ways of thinking, not abstractions. They are inseparable in reality, though distinguishable in kind . . . Distinctions are not divisions."[13] Hence, just as in Aquinas's theology neither the divine attributes nor Persons of the Trinity are *constitutive* of God's Being, so the infinite Attributes, per Spinoza's ontology, are not *constitutive* of

11. Shmueli, "Thomas Aquinas' Influence," 68.

12. Shmueli, "Thomas Aquinas' Influence," 68. "In general, it was Thomas's position that terms signify God to the extent that our intellect knows Him. Attributes are predicated of God neither universally nor equivocally but analogically. The divine perfection, like his wisdom or goodness, exists in God in a super-eminent and infinite (i.e., unique and most perfect) degree. The Attributes really exist in God and can be properly predicated of him. The analogical sense, however, does not mean that we have an adequate positive idea of what is objectively signified by the divine attribute."

13. Shmueli, "Thomas Aquinas' Influence," 71. It should be noted as well that the doctrine of God's "simplicity" must be at play.

Deus sive natura naturans. Aquinas denies a constituting role to the attributes of God because, on his view, God is simple, meaning God's unity of essence entails that God is not a composite made of parts, principles, entities, or stuff that could be considered more properly basic than the essence of God itself. However, these attributes of God that we name do indicate something real about God in our experience of God's acting in the world. Observing this about Aquinas's understanding of God, we can see why Shmueli argues for a Thomist background for Spinoza's metaphysics.[14]

THE CONTRIBUTION OF THIS PROJECT

The hypothesis of this present volume is not unprecedented, even if contemporary scholarship has tended to ignore or downplay it. This work is an analysis of the metaphysical views that each of the two philosophers presents regarding the irreducible unity of mind and body, offered in the hope that two distinct, but related, contributions might be made. The first is a demonstration of a metaphysical view about the identity of mind and body that the two share. Both, it will be demonstrated, utilize a *hylomorphic* view of the "constitution" of human beings in order to argue for the fundamental, inseparable, and irreducible unity of the human person. This will be surprising for many regarding Spinoza, but the interpretative work will show that he is quite similar to Aquinas's own theory. Hence, for the former every bit as much as the latter there is at play the dynamics of a uniquely human form (*anima*/soul) that not only enables the instantiated expression of the human body and the human mind but must be conceived as a distinct metaphysical principle at work which cannot be strictly identified with either. Such an approach does not imply that Spinoza is in any way indebted to Thomas's metaphysics as a conscious source in any way or that their larger metaphysical programs are ultimately compatible. The argument is that Spinoza's doctrine of mind-body identity can be legitimately read as a post-Cartesian development that expresses a surprising and significant affinity with a general Thomistic view. This could help us in understanding more readily his mind-body identity claims. If successful, it will not merely be a contribution to Spinoza scholarship, but a new dialogue with Thomistic scholarship might develop. A dialectical engagement such as this could well prove to be quite philosophically fruitful for historic interpretive reasons, but perhaps more importantly on the question of how to understand human nature and existence in the world as a minded and material unity.

Hence, the second motivation behind this project is beyond the purely historical, interpretive focus. Analyzing Aquinas's and Spinoza's conceptions of the question of mind-body identity can and should be treated as part of a larger philosophical

---

14. Shmueli, "Thomas Aquinas' Influence," 71. Although it is quite common to see Spinoza as a nominalist, Shmueli's assessment is convincing. "The basic view, then, of Spinoza [on the Attributes of Substance] is the Thomistic view of the attributes (universals) as extra-mental realities without being distinctly existent on their own, not the [nominalist/subjectivist] view of Maimonides."

issue: what makes *rational life* possible in physical organisms in an essentially material world? Because both present a similar, convincing alternative to the current *methodological* dualism in philosophical analysis, they provide an impetus for a robust recovery of the soul as a metaphysical principle that is necessary to explain mind and body, but distinct from both mental powers and material existence. This recovery could realign the framework of the current discussion in the philosophy of mind that sees the relation of mind and body as a problem to be solved. Yet, the "problem" is only a problem if one views human existence from the wrong vantage point. Furthermore, the approach that is on offer in the renaissance of their doctrines of hylomorphism would also place the philosophical quest to understand mind and body where it most decidedly belongs—the philosophy of Life.

LIFE AS THE PHILOSOPHICAL FOUNDATION

Let us briefly outline each of their metaphysical schemas. In Spinoza's case, the foundation of his metaphysics is that Life is ubiquitous in *natura naturata* as an expression of *natura naturans*. His doctrine that all of reality in *natura naturata*, as modes of the One Substance, is essentially extended and mental is built on this. Life is not per se synonymous with either, for Spinoza and his ontology of ubiquitous life allows for a subtle discrimination about what being alive means. (The "aliveness" of a rock is not identical with the "aliveness" of a slime mold nor the "aliveness" of a slime mold the same as that of a lobster, nor is the lobster's way of being alive the same as that of a simian primate, nor the primate expression of living the same as that of a human.) There is a hierarchy of life based upon a hierarchy of complexity in organization of the body of a particular thing (*res*). And since this omnipresent Life includes both extension and thought, it cannot be *caused by* forces or principles inherent to either. By Aquinas's description, on the other hand, a distinction between animate and inanimate is certainly more clearly drawn. However, Life is also not, for him, a supervening aspect that emerges from or supervenes upon an otherwise inert material world out of material forces. Neither is it simply the *mind*, as though rational consciousness itself is what Life *is*. He sees that being alive is a particular way that many entities are in fact *material* in a unique act; and the presence of Life is what enables the material design and function of their being. All organic, living entities are identified as being alive as specific *kinds* of living things, however, in different ways and with different powers of living. This is so, for Aquinas, because there exists a hierarchy of varying levels and qualities of life (soul) that establishes their existence as the kinds of things they are.

In other words, Life is not a univocal term in Aquinas, any more than for Spinoza, because the concept of soul (*anima*) entails distinctions of souls as the organizing forms that enables distinct things to be alive in differing ways. Hence, there is the *vegetative* soul in which botanical organisms participate and partake, enabling things like being capable of functions that utilize nutrients and respond to the environment.

Then there is the *sensitive* soul—the form and enabler of animal life. It entails the lower powers of the vegetative soul for nutrition but also enables them to be sensible of the environment in which they live to greater and lesser degrees (the awareness of a dog is quite more elaborate than that of a mollusk). Finally, the *intellectual* soul is the form of life that enables human existence alone, and it gives a distinct quality to the vegetative and sensitive powers that are, as well, part of human living existence, in that it guides them. But, most importantly the *intellectual* soul grants to the human being the power of abstract knowledge of the world, understanding of the nature of being, and an engaged consciousness of itself in relation to other things in its world. From this comes the power of deliberation and choice.[15]

For both philosophers, the fact that one is dealing with Life manifest in material things, some of which, at least, have self-consciousness, is a matter of no small consequence.[16] Each of them discusses the reality of self-consciousness and the capacity for rational insight in humans as something that is not alien to our material existence as biological organisms. Rather, this is the way that humans are alive precisely as *material* creatures; and contra the Cartesian mystery of ontological distinction from the materiality of the body, being a "thinking thing" is the way that human beings are *physically* (materially) alive. Furthermore, both Spinoza and Aquinas see conscious and self-conscious rationality in material human beings as a feature of Life that is irreducible to the physical, material explanations and causes and not adequately explained in mechanistic and materialistic terms. For each of them, since Life itself (and rational life in human beings particularly) are inherently a part of the world we experience, the existence of both must be given an explanation; and both perceived that material forces alone were not able to explain the origin, existence, and functions of Life. Their insights are still important, for materialistic explanations have not been shown to be adequate to explain it. It is doubtful that it is possible to give an account on physical reductionist terms.[17] Neither could rationality be reduced to material causes. By allowing the metaphysics of Life-mind-body found in each philosopher to engage the other, philosophical analysis can recast in important ways the larger issue of consciousness as a feature of living things. So, in the subsequent chapters, Aquinas's and Spinoza's ways of arriving at a similar conclusion will be unpacked. Their shared view is that the mindedness of the body and the embodiedness of the mind are the

15. See, *Summa Theologiae,* Prima Pars, Q 78.

16. That Descartes's metaphysics left Western philosophy with a view of the extended world that saw living things mechanistically is well attested. However, much of contemporary philosophical reflection is still captive to Descartes's siren call. Consider, for instance, the options that frame the discussion today: (1) either we must "explain" causality of the mental and physical interaction or (2) we feel we must jettison the nonmaterial altogether. This is the legacy of Descartes's schema but not Spinoza or Aquinas.

17. For an excellent discussion of the history of the failure of materialistic views to be able to account for the origin and functions of life, much less the existence and operations of complex life forms, see Meyer. *Signature in the Cell.*

result of an antecedent cause that is the form of both and the cause of them as distinct expressions (modes) of "one and the same thing." That "one and the same thing" cannot be reduced to either mind or body, for they share an identity that is simultaneously both. As I will argue, the human *person* (of which both are expressions) is the *identity* in question.

The metaphysical structure of human existence they express in their various philosophical schemes is metaphysically helpful and an intellectually defensible concept. Their insights can enable philosophers to pursue understanding of the mystery of human existence without diminishing or erasing the distinctive reality of our consciousness as physicalist reductionism does. As well, it will enable philosophers who take the substance of consciousness and rationality as ontologically foundational to move beyond the confounding problems of substance dualism: interaction between body and mind—as well as the singularity of human existence as *one and the same thing,* rather than an association of ontically disparate things. Focus can be placed instead on conceiving *how* rational thought can come about in physical beings in the first place, for which nonreductive physicalist and emergentist theories fail to give adequate account. As the similitude of their perspectives offers contemporary philosophers an important resource for reflecting on human nature and its singleness of existence in its duality of expression, the recovery of the *soul* as an important principle of analysis and even of existence becomes evident. That is, at least, what I will be arguing in conclusion to this study. Should that be the case, then Bennett's disdain for the "medieval setting" of Spinoza's thought might prove to be shortsighted. Rather than being a philosophical albatross around Spinoza's neck, an affinity for a post-Cartesian "Thomistic" analysis of the mind-body "problem" might prove, instead, to provide him with philosophical wings. As well, it could allow modern philosophy to follow him (and Aquinas) to new heights that could set us free from both materialistic reductionism and methodological dualism.

THE ARGUMENT IN BRIEF

Part of the difficulties faced by contemporary endeavors to interpret Spinoza and Aquinas result from the way that the two philosophers employ the descriptors "body" and "mind" when discussing the metaphysical nature of a human being. Neither the Angelic Doctor nor the "young thinker who destroyed the past" utilize these terms primarily as *substantives*. Rather, they are designators of irreducible *modes* or aspects whereby a singular entity's specific and definite existence, namely the human person, is *expressed* (to utilize Spinoza's terminology). Body and mind are dual aspects of human existence, but they are not themselves *things* that have any independent being apart from the existing human person.

In Aquinas's metaphysics, this notion of singular existence, resulting from the essence that enables a human being to exist in these dual ways, is expressed via the phrase *rational animal*. The adjective *rational* describes the unique powers inherent in the human being as a biological, material organism. These powers exist because of the organizing and potential property-giving principle that is distinct from either the matter of the body or the powers of the mind, i.e., the rational soul, the *form* of the body. It is the intrinsic, defining reality for our bodily existence (our animality). The modifier "rational," it must be realized, does not merely describe the *ability* for rationality that the body evinces—nor just its exercise—as though the rational mind is something supervening upon or emerging out of a preceding biological causal state of affairs. Much less does it suggest a power of thought that is self-sufficient and self-contained, as with Descartes's metaphysics, that "relates" to the physical. Rather, his description of human beings as the rational animal points out the unity in existence and action of the material and mental aspects of a human being who exists biologically as a reasoning entity and rationally as a biological one. Something, therefore, must be a prerequisite subsistent principle that metaphysically accounts for the fact that bodily organisms that self-consciously know and reason exist in the first place as one and the same thing in action. When Aquinas insists that rationality is the *subsistent* form of the human body, he is not embracing any kind of straightforward dualism, contra some interpreters, in which the soul is thought of as an independently existing thing that is instantiated in its own right and considered synonymous with the mind. In his doctrine *rational soul* is an operative, necessary principle of existence, but not a thing-in-itself.

The necessity of the soul as a logically prior *and* causally antecedent principle is embraced by Aquinas because he realized that nothing inherent in matter or simply material stuff—physical elements and energy—explain *how* matter or physical principles and energies become organized and combined so as to operate as specific and living material things. In the case of human beings, the existent human person is the resultant effect of the informing principles of the soul united with the material elements of the body. This person is the locus of all the living properties of body and mind, so the rational soul is a principle different from the mind per se, because the exercise of rationality in a human person is only possible because of the organizing influence of the *rational soul*. In like manner, the rational soul is the causal source of the shape, function, powers, and limitations of the human body that enables the human body to be suited to accommodate (but not produce) the power of self-knowledge, rational thought, and insight (the mind). These nonmaterially caused intellectual powers are features that the human person manifests as a physical living organism. Thus, Thomistic hylomorphism means that the essence of the rational soul is to be the form of the human being, enabling both bodily organismic life and rational thought *in* and *as* the particular person.

Similarly, Spinoza expresses a view of the body and what he calls "its idea" as not two things, but one coextensive reality (Aquinas's "rational animal"). Treating the extended body and the mental awareness that attends the body as distinct expressions of the singular and identical state of affairs that is a human being's existence, Spinoza does not utilize the medieval term soul. Rather, in his metaphysics he utilizes a rather ambiguous term to explain and describe this unity. The term is *conatus*. In Spinoza's era this was most often used in an ethical sense, but he employed this term and developed its use in his metaphysics in unique way in the mechanistic Newtonian and Cartesian world of his day. While many have noted the importance of *conatus* in Spinoza's thought for expressing the oneness of the act of a thing's striving to continue in existence *post facto* its actual existence, careful analysis of his conceptual framework demonstrates that his use of *conatus* to describe the ongoing active striving to sustain their existence that entities manifest raises the question what causes their existence and orients their striving. To answer this requires and presupposes, I shall demonstrate, an additional view of *conatus* at work (although implicit and not developed). Spinoza must have had a working assumption in his metaphysics that views *conatus* not only as a *post facto* manifestation of the innate act of striving to maintain existence of an actualized entity, but as a kind of *ex ante* organizing principle of the entity's existence. This additional meaning can account for how "mind and body are one and the same thing" in the first place in an individual thing that is striving to maintain its existence in the modes of extension and thought that it is as "one and the same thing." In this secondary sense, *conatus* is an essence—an antecedent principle that enables the concrete drive toward continuation of existence (its striving) of an entity. Each individual thing is made to be the very thing that it is as a striving entity by a particular essence specific to itself; and *conatus* is a good term to employ in capturing the nature of this essence (which is distinct from the thing's concrete existence strictly speaking). *Conatus* as *ex ante* essence and *post facto* striving is identified as instantiating and maintaining a singular entity that is not only extended and physical, but rational regarding the material existence it has. Distinct *conatic essences*, as well, are organizational principles that involve the reality of Life and make everything alive (*animata*) to some higher or lower degree. Hence, the act of striving is the product of the organizing principle (*conatus*), which establishes the essence of and informs the drive of a particular thing to strive to continue in its essential existence. *Conatus* must be, therefore, a much larger concept in Spinoza's thought than has been noted by his interpreters and can be seen as the essence of a thing that makes it to be—and therefore be alive—in a particular way.[18] Through this reading of Spinoza's theory, *conatus* is both a cause qua "form" that enables the actual concrete and unique existence of a thing and a process of striving (*conatus*) to maintain the existence it has as the essence it is.

This interpretation is not only consistent with but may actually be required to make sense of his larger theory of *how* any and every particular thing that is *both* an extended mode and a thinking mode exists as a singular entity. Spinoza's description of *conatus* in III, 7 lends itself to this interpretation: "The striving *by which* each thing

18. Miller, "Spinoza's Axiology," 152.

strives to persevere in its being is nothing but the *actual essence of the thing.*"[19] For Spinoza, all existing entities have attributed to them dual modes (the mental and the extended) which are involved in the *striving* to continue in existence. And if he is to be consistent, these two modes must be *striving* as ultimately one and the same thing. Here his use of the concept *animate* will prove helpful. While the term *animata* is rarely used in the *Ethics*, where it is used it plays a strategic role in his metaphysics. Conceptually *animata* is related to *mens* in his philosophy, but for things to be living realities expressed in or by the two modes of extension and thought requires that there is a *something*—the actual essence of an entity—that enables the existence of minded and bodied singular things in living existence. This essential something, required by Spinoza's metaphysics, for which *conatus* is the logical candidate, will be shown to be analogous in many ways to the sort of thing that Aquinas calls the *anima*. It is further most probable, as my reading suggests, that being *animata* means more for Spinoza than simply having *mens*. Specifically, the concept of an organism *being* animated or living can be taken to mean, in Spinoza's *Ethics*, being *actualized* by an organizing principle (*conatus* in the secondary sense described above) in such a way as to be "minded" in a way that is consistent with the complexity and capacity of the living material that it is. So, each thing is a mode of extension *and* a mode of thought, but not as by a kind of Leibnizian preestablished harmony. Rather, the singular and unified identity its existence has is *expressed by* a mode thought and a mode of extension. The reading that this present work offers, regarding how to interpret Spinoza's cryptic language, has the further advantage of showing that the mind does not just attend the body in parallel fashion. Spinoza sees mind and body as "one and the same thing" expressing the essence of the singular entity that a human being *is*.

Neither Spinoza nor Aquinas discuss metaphysically the psychophysical phenomenon that is a human being in such a way that considers either the physical body or the mind as more fundamental than the other causally or ontologically. Hence, no kind of epiphenomenalism, either ancient or contemporary, nor any theory of emergentism or idealist projectionism of the body will work in their philosophies. But neither will dualism or parallelism (as with Leibniz). For both philosophical schemes, the ultimate cause of both mind and body in regard to the active life of human persons is the antecedent organizational principle that Aquinas calls soul/form and Spinoza assumes and what I am calling "conatic essence." This is the property or influence that enables the concrete actual and particular existence of an entity in the world whose ways of being—mind and bodily life—are the acts of a single living entity.[20] Spinoza would find a point of agreement with Aquinas where the latter writes that we do not strictly speak

19. Emphasis mine. Throughout this work all references to Spinoza's *Ethics* will be from Shirley's translation, unless otherwise noted.

20. At this point the fact that Aquinas calls human beings "primary substances" and Spinoza considers them to be "modes" of the One Substance is not an issue. For both, the particular human we might refer to as mental and physical is a specific entity of some specific essence *qua* entity regardless of the wider, divergent ontological commitments.

accurately of the mind knowing something, rather the person is the knower, just as the arm does not lift a weight, but the man. Spinoza's no less than Aquinas's metaphysics is, therefore, dependent on a hylomorphic view of reality, since every living physical thing is made to be a *particular* and unique living thing because of its essence—an organizing dynamic process that cannot be reduced to purely physical description.

A FURTHER SUMMARY OF THE ARGUMENTS

The affinity I claim exists between these two philosophers and will unpack and describe in the analysis of the following chapters is not immediately apparent, so careful exegetical and interpretive work will be essential. Each philosopher must be allowed to speak on his own terms, so that what he says can be expounded within the larger context of his ontological commitments. By this, important interpretive questions regarding each of their doctrines of the relationship between mind and body that are perennial issues in Aquinas and Spinoza studies respectively must be addressed in ways that prove integrative and reconciling. In order to lay the foundation for the extensive exegetical work on their respective theories and the critical comparative analysis that follows, allow me to sketch further the arguments in the later chapters.

Aquinas

Let us begin with Aquinas. He describes what he calls the "intellectual principle, which is called mind or intellect," as incorporeal and "a substance, that is, something subsistent" (*Summa* I a, Q 75, a 2). Aquinas argues further that this intellectual *principle*—the human soul—is the *form* (in the Aristotelian sense) of the human body. This concept is deeply significant for Aquinas, since he sees the intellect as a power or ability that an existing biological person exercises not by virtue of anything *caused* by the nature of matter itself or biological functions of the body. *Knowing* and achieving rational insight are quite distinct things from any actions associated with material principles and forces, hence, the act of knowing cannot ultimately depend upon any bodily mechanism. And yet, the unity of human existence in Aquinas's philosophy necessitates that the mind cannot be conceived of as a separate entity from the bodily existence of the human person. The organizational principle—the form—which gives specific functions and powers and potentialities to the matter that is the human body, Aquinas contends, is the self-same principle that enables the distinct capacity for insight and knowledge that human beings as otherwise merely material things exercise. This principle that is responsible for the structure of the physical body and the mental powers present in a human person must, he reasoned, have a kind of reality of its own, what he calls a *subsisting* form or a substantial form.

To call this form substantial might suggest a straightforward substance dualism, but his analysis does not stop there. He argues that once one recognizes that a human is a *rational animal*, then the bodily animality and the rational mind must both be considered essential when considering the unique existence of a human person (I a, Q 76, a 3). They are, in a sense, "one and the same thing." Aquinas would seem to be offering a medieval theory of mind-body metaphysics that can be described as a version of dual-aspect identity theory, where a human being's body and mind are essentially expressions of the same entity—the human being who evidences these twofold characteristics. Mind and body are radically distinct ways of being but are both essentially descriptors of the concrete singular and unified existence of a human person.

There is no shortage of commentators who claim that such a way of describing the human soul is self-contradictory in Aquinas's basic Aristotelian metaphysics. How can the intellectual soul be the form of the body, it is asked, if it is itself an entity in some way? Contra Platonism, forms do not "exist" (except conceptually) apart from the physical things that are *informed* by them. Absent the thing so *formed*, the essence itself cannot be thought of as being in existence. Hence, how could a self-professed student of Aristotle claim the form of rationality—the human soul—could be described as having any metaphysical status apart from the body? Aristotle certainly seems to have denied such a possibility. Moreover, it is claimed that the notion of a *subsistent* soul not only raises questions about the cogency of Aquinas's theory of the nature of the soul, but also presents the analytical problem of how human beings can be considered as essentially one if a substantial soul is, metaphysically speaking, a prerequisite reality with its own subsistent being in the hylomorphic entity. While the first critique expresses doubt about the Aristotelian coherence of Aquinas's claim that soul is a substantial form, the second concern suggests that Aquinas loses what he is attempting to prove, namely the ontological oneness of a human being's physical existence. Despite his remonstrations, Aquinas is, so his critics claim, a substance dualist *simpliciter* and, thus, a bad Aristotelian, because as many contend either one can conceive of an intellectual soul as a form (Aristotle) or as a subsistent entity (Plato/Descartes), but it cannot be both. I will argue that with a careful and proper reading one can make sense of Aquinas's claim about the subsistent nature of the soul as a form, as well as find his consistency even convincing. For that to happen, though, we must unpack the meaning of his description of the soul as an *intellectual principle*.

Essentially, *anima*, described as a principle, must be understood in Thomistic terms, as the life-giving, essence-establishing, function-granting, and informing source of the active and unified being of the component parts and properties of the human person (formal cause in the Aristotelian sense). *Anima* as a source or cause of the organization, function, and interrelatedness of matter in a body is not itself physical, although it has a relationship to the physical thing that it establishes in concrete living essence as it organizes that thing's corporeal, organic existence as a physical entity capable of rationality. This formal principle, organizing a dizzying complexity of components and enabling intricate functions to the human body as the source of its animate life, while not itself material, is nonetheless only actualized in existence (given specificity) in the particular entity that is enabled to exist because of it. Furthermore, the animate body so informed by the soul is made amenable to rationality. Hylomorphism of the Thomistic variety, when discussing human beings, simply denotes *rationality* as describing the nature of the particular organizing form which is an antecedent "cause" that enables the exercised power of rationality in a physical human person. While not a physically describable or dependent property, the form itself and the nonmaterial powers it produces are concretely existent and exercised only as features of the bodily life of the biologically material creature called human. It exists in the same "natural" world as the body and is neither supervening nor merely attendant. Let me emphasize this point: for Aquinas, this intellectual form in action, once a human being is given existence, enables the exercise of knowing and rational insight as functions of the material human person. While not reducible to some biological or chemical or physical cause, mental powers are functions of the *biological* human being, distinct, strictly speaking, from the physical nature of the organism that is capable of mind because of the intellective soul. Hence, "the thinking thing" is not merely attendant to the body but is part of the bodied existence of the human person.

As an antecedent organizational influence and cause in the world of matter, the human *anima* is conceived as a necessary cause and a subsisting entity because it has the formal causal powers described above. It is, nonetheless, a real feature of the same world as the material human body. The label, "subsisting entity," recognizes that this principle or power that organizes the matter of the body has prior independent reality from the actual organism it enables to exist as a rational animal. This priority is not merely logical because even if, as Aquinas argues, it only has *actual existence* in the life of the concrete organism, the form must be antecedent to that organism, since the organism is dependent upon it for not only its functions and shape and potentialities, but its actual life. Aquinas's reasoning on this matter will be extensively described and analyzed in chapters 4 and 5 to demonstrate two things regarding Aquinas's doctrine of the soul. The first is that it functions as a *necessary* concept, in his metaphysics, with real explanatory power, designating a real subsistent feature of the world. Following that, it will be shown that Aquinas does not promote a self-contradictory theory. Without this preliminary explication, analysis, and defense of his metaphysics as consistent and instructive, his hylomorphism will prove to be no help at all in considering the puzzle of Spinoza's own purported obscurity in his claim that the human mind and the human body are "one and the same thing." Properly interpreted, however, Aquinas is self-referentially coherent and therefore a helpful lens through which to read Spinoza. Showing these things to be the case, I can develop the second aspect of my thesis and argue that their metaphysical affinity provides us good philosophical reasons to reconsider hylomorphism and recover this concept of the soul in the philosophy of mind (and body).

Spinoza

Spinoza has similarily provided no small challenge for his best interpreters. Recognizing his oft cited and confounding definition of the *identity* of mind and body, Michael Della Rocca speaks for many where he describes this claim as "one of the most famous and puzzling claims in the *Ethics*."[21] In *Ethics* III, P 2, sch. where he defines body and mind as "one and the same thing, conceived now under the attribute of Thought, now under the attribute of Extension," Spinoza describes a numerical identity between a mode of extension and its idea (the mode of thought) or between the body and mind.[22] Given the causal and conceptual barrier that Spinoza famously insists is a feature of Attributes in *Deus sive natura*, one must then ask how a Spinozistic metaphysics allows for such identity? Those who accept the idea that Spinoza is promoting numerical identity have offered hypotheses including dual-aspect theories, parallelism, and Curley's fact-proposition interpretation. More recently, Della Rocca has offered a semantic reading of Spinoza in which the concept of the referential opacity of specific contexts and Spinoza's own parallelism are the under girding of his identity theory.[23]

Many interpretations of Spinoza on this matter seem to imply a functional dualism in Spinoza's metaphysics, which is inherent in those who describe him as embracing parallelism between the distinct modes of thought and extension. Parallelism, it is argued, allows for what Jonathan Bennett calls a "mapping" of the mental with the physical.[24] Yet, if Spinoza holds to parallelism in his view of mind and body relations, it must be noted that Spinoza's modes, understood along the lines of parallelism, end up being conceivable only as closely related realities on the metaphysical map, but not "one and the same thing" that is differently expressed or conceived. Thus, either Spinoza is woefully unaware he is inconsistent with his own metaphysics or a better explication is demanded for Spinoza's encumbering description—"one and the same thing." Prima facie, he seems to be claiming something robust; and parallelism strikes me as weakening the essential singularity of the living essence that an individual thing *is* and the concept of a singular *striving* to maintain existence that he depicts. Only if the modes are seen from the perspective of a third, singular entity that is neither strictly mental or physical, but essentially both simultaneously and continually, can something like parallelism work.

---

21. Della Rocca, *Representation*, 118.

22. Aquila, "Identity of Thought and Object," 271–72. "Spinoza defends a form of the 'identity theory' with respect to mind and body." Aquila contends Spinoza's conception of said identity is "unique in the history of philosophy" and that this uniqueness is what makes Spinoza's doctrine "incredible." Cf. Della Rocca, *Representation*, 119–20 for another interpretation of Spinoza as holding a numerical identity theory. Cf. Allison, *Benedict De Spinoza*, and Delahunty, *Spinoza* for interpretations of Spinoza that deny he sees this relation in terms of numerical identity.

23. Della Rocca, *Representation*, 118–40.

24. Bennett, *Study in Spinoza's Ethics*, 127–53.

Parallelism can only invoke Spinoza's description of mind and body as "one and the same thing" in a *weak* sense. The interpretation I am offering, on the other hand, takes Spinoza's description of these modes as "one and the same thing" in a *strong* sense. This seems to be how he meant it. A single striving, as Spinoza insists is the reality of each "one-and-the-same-thing," requires that a singular *res* be recognized as striving to continue in existence, not parallel modes simultaneously striving in a mapping process.

Since Books III and IV of the *Ethics* are meant to follow from Books I and II in Spinoza's strategy, the functional dualism that parallelism leaves us with cannot be his view. There he can legitimately argue that emotions, desires, and volition are really the mental expression of bodily needs and encounters in the world, if and only if a human's mind and body (though distinguishable as expressions) are together a singular entity that is "one and the same thing." Otherwise, the *idea* of the body (the *thoughts* reflecting the affections and changes and experiences of the body) and the body along with its affections, since changes in the body's condition cannot *cause* the idea, are only conceivable as two different things functionally, not "one and the same thing." By his insistence that the living human organism is a specific and single *conatus* in the regular sense in which he employs the term, namely a striving to maintain existence, Spinoza's metaphysics demands a sense of identity of the modes in the strongest possible sense. Without this, there is the life of the body and there is the mapped life of the mind, both of which strive, but it is not a *single life* in the most full-blown ontological sense. Parallelism gives no explanation for how the oneness could be conceived.

Parallelism misses Spinoza's intention in II, 7, I shall argue in chapter 6, because what he is analyzing is not the existence of parallel orders (ideas and things), but the essential "sameness" of the orders themselves. In other words, Spinoza is arguing that when we speak of *things* (here Spinoza gets sloppy in his terminology, equating things and modes of extension) and ideas of those things, we are not speaking of two distinct and parallel *somethings*. Rather, we are speaking of a singular reality that is only and always adequately designated in terms of two distinct and necessary descriptors—the body and its *idea*. These descriptors are the modes by which the one single entity's essential (conatic) life is expressed. That, at least, seems to be the implication that Spinoza draws out in Books III and IV of *Ethics*. If the doctrine of parallelism could be made consistent with this ontological unity, then one might be able to embrace it. However, parallelism seems to imply a distinction of existence that is unspinozistic.

Those interpretations that describe Spinoza's understanding as a dual-aspect theory of mind-body identity, therefore, are probably much more consistent with the intent of his metaphysics. However, dual-aspect expositions of Spinoza's doctrine in my view fail to give an adequate explication of the ontological foundation for the essential unity in distinction for which Spinoza's doctrine of mind-body unity seems to call. Dual aspect models of Spinoza's metaphysics generally take these aspects purely as descriptions of phenomena. Thomas Nagel is representative in this regard.

Defending himself against Searle's treatment of his position on mind and body, Nagel writes: "Searle identifies me as a defender of property dualism. I prefer the term 'dual aspect theory,' to express the view deriving from Spinoza that mental phenomena are the subjective aspects of states that *can also be described* physically."[25] This move, of course, intends to solve the ontological and functional unity problem that, as I am contending, parallelism does not solve. Yet, dual-aspect descriptions seem to do so without providing an adequate explanation for *how* Spinoza might theorize the unity of an entity that possesses truly distinct dual aspects, much less how such distinct aspects could be actually "one and the same thing." As Nagel interprets Spinoza, for example, one could be forgiven for thinking that the dual descriptions on offer are not much removed from parallelist interpretations with one "description" being interposed on another.

When an account of the unity of the distinct aspects is offered in dual-aspect interpretations of Spinoza, the question of the ultimate *unity and identity* of the individual finite modes (minds and bodies) is most often presented as only resolvable in *Deus sive Natura*, where the ultimate unity of the Infinite Attributes (Thought and Extension) is grounded. The unity of finite modes as the "one-and-the-same thing" they manifest, therefore, is pushed back into the realm of the indecipherable. Hence, dual aspect interpretations do not typically adequately account theoretically for how the things of which these double aspects can be predicated are in *natura naturata* "one and the same thing." It may well be that Spinoza is simply unclear on this matter himself and creates this ambiguity, as well as the necessity to regress into the unity of all things in *Deus sive Natura*. Perhaps his pantheism led him to be unconcerned with the unity of particular entities *qua* the particular *res* that each particular in fact is. However, given the import that the identity doctrine obviously plays for Spinoza in the latter part of the *Ethics,* we owe it to ourselves to see if his philosophy provides us with resources for understanding how he might indeed envision the unity issue in finite things.

In this pursuit, we cannot avoid putting the questions to Spinoza regarding both the "real distinction" of the Infinite Attributes and the "real distinction" of the Modes of those Attributes. At issue is whether the Attributes and their Modes are ultimately objective states (and if so how) or are instead only subjective expressions of our mental thought processes. This is a debate of no small consequence and controversy in Spinoza studies.[26] Unsurprisingly, traditional dual-aspect theories do not help us at this point. If dual-aspect theory sees the Attributes as truly identical only *in God* and distinct from one another only in our *ways of considering* God or Nature—as *perceived* aspects thereof—then it creates a further problem for adequately interpreting Spinoza. Not addressing the question of what provides the constitution in function and existence of a particular *res* (individual entity) in the first place, the dual-aspect

25. Searle, "Searle," 105n6, my emphasis.

26. Cf. Sprigge, "Spinoza," 149–58 for a discussion of the various approaches taken to this issue and the implications that they have for interpretation.

description of Spinoza's ontology is superficial. In this project it will be shown that, for Spinoza, the Modes of Thought and Extension that we posit about the world are *real* features of things and are distinct from one another in *natura naturata* even while being ontologically united in *Deus sive natura naturans*. Here, as will be shown, the Spinozan doctrine of *conatus* provides us with a Spinozistic category as the singular immediate, formal cause of the essence of an entity that has truly distinct dual aspects to its *singular* identity.

Since dual-aspect theory currently comes closest to portraying Spinoza's thought, what I hope to offer is a greatly enhanced version, in order to more adequately illuminate Spinoza's view of mind-body identity. As already suggested, the focus on *conatus* will provide what dual-aspect theory requires, i.e., an accounting for the constitution of the singularity and unity of the entity that Spinoza says is one and the same thing (*res*) that is expressed via mind and body as the dual aspects. In chapters 6 and 7 we will see that his concept of *conatus* as the *post-facto* act of striving to maintain existence of a singular "one and the same thing" presupposes an additional assumed concept of an essence that enables the striving to be a single striving of a human being. There it will be demonstrated that the concept *ex ante* essence can and should be interpreted in Spinoza's thought as related closely to *conatus*. In Spinoza's philosophical system, antecedent to the human being, a "conatic essence" with *form*-like function orders, establishes, and drives the unity of a human being in striving to continue in existence. The application of the geometric definition of essence in Part I of *Ethics* requires in the latter parts, therefore, a metaphysical function in regard to *conatus*. The dual aspects are the two modes by which one and the same thing *qua* a human being expresses its singular existence made possible by its conatic essence.

On this issue in Spinoza's thought, Hans Jonas's observations are relevant. Recognizing that Spinoza's central concern in *Ethics* is "a foundation for psychology and ethics," Jonas rightly observes that the metaphysics of Spinoza enable him to produce what other modern philosophers up to his time had not, namely, a theoretical construct in which "an organic individual is viewed as a fact of *wholeness* rather than of mechanical interplay of parts."[27] Even more, Jonas contends, Spinoza's metaphysics allowed him to continue to provide the modern period a great paradigmatic gift: "For the first time in modern speculation, a speculative means is offered for relating the degree of organization of a body to the degree of awareness belonging to it."[28] In other words, Spinoza offers, according to Jonas, a conceptual framework in which mental states are features of a physical organism and the physical states of said organism are conditions (but not causes) of mental awareness.

Building upon Jonas's claims, we can begin to understand a bit more clearly how to translate what Spinoza means by the Latin verb *expressa* (to which intimation has been made above in the recurring use of "expressed") when he says in II, P 7, sch. that

27. Jonas, "Spinoza and the Theory of Organism," 269, my emphasis.
28. Jonas, "Spinoza and the Theory of Organism," 271.

mind and body as the same thing (*res*) that is simply differently *expressed* via respective reference to either the Attribute of Thought (of which minds are the finite modes) or the Attribute of Extension (of which bodies are the finite modes). Many of Spinoza's interpreters attribute to *expressa* in this scholium something equivalent to the word *described*. What has been greatly under analyzed, however, in Spinoza studies concerning this "puzzling claim," as it has been called, is the relationship that such a statement has to his more basic concept of physical organisms as living entities. Ironically, this issue of being alive is the foundation upon which Spinoza builds his theory of mind in II, 13. Taking Jonas's observations into consideration, we see Spinoza's use of the term *expressa* in more than nominalist terms. *Expressa* can be taken to refer not primarily to the act of our describing (expressing) something we observe but seen as a function of the essence of the thing (*res*) itself. As an entity exists in and out of the *essence* that enables it, it gives *expression* of its "whatness" or essence (objectivism) in the two distinct modes involved in manifesting the complexity—but singularity—of the existing entity. Spinoza's theory, as I will demonstrate, sees the unity of any distinct entity as the product of a specific and unique *conatus* that first *establishes* (in the sense of a formal cause) and then *maintains* (as the immanent functioning) that entity as a unified, distinct finite particularization of the One Substance. It exists as "one and the same thing," and does so in the real distinction between the modes of the Attributes of Substance.

In the strictest technical terms for Spinoza, a particular mode that is a body and the particular "idea of that mode" which is its mind are ways that the singular entity (the *res*) exists in the world. What is *expressed* in the Modes of Extension and Thought is the existential complexity of an entity that is capable of thought as a physical entity and a whose thought is inextricably part of its physicality (extendedness). And the greater the complexity of the physical organization *qua* extended, the more capable, in Spinoza's view, is the organism of higher-level thought *qua* idea of the extended body, even though said physical complexity has no causal role to play in the capacity for thought.[29] The living organism that exists with the modal features of mind and body is itself the one-and-the-same *thing* that we must put under consideration, because thought and extension are features of its life expressed via the two Attributes of *Deus sive Natura* of which human rationality can be cognizant.[30] Whereas Descartes saw

29. Spinoza's panpsychism is not counterintuitive regarding our common understanding that all things are not alive. There is room in his doctrine to account for different definitions of the equivocal term "alive."

30. Miller (see note 18) observes the import of *conatus* in Spinoza's thought in a way that complements the concerns of this present thesis. He contends: "The introduction of *conatus* and the emphasis on the power of acting necessitates the introduction of another factor into the discussion. It may be that something is useful if it furthers (or at least does not inhibit) our ability to act so as to preserve our being. Spinoza thought, however, that we have *two* radically different powers of action and as a result, he thought there were two radically different orders of value. To explain this—that is, to explain why he thought that we have two different powers of action and, consequently, that there are two different orders of value—a digression into his metaphysics is necessary" (Miller, "Spinoza's Axiology,"

an ontological separation between himself as a "thinking thing" and his body so that in some sense his mind is "cut off" from the material world,[31] it made no sense to Spinoza to talk this way. Since there is only One Substance there can be no ontological distinction between body and mind.

Hence, mind cannot be a different substantial reality from the body. They are different only as particular modes of distinct Attributes. Given that we can encounter the existence of the One Substance (Reality) in just two of the infinite Attributes of God, our understanding can experience and describe all the entities that we name only as physically extended (a body) and/or as mental (a mind). So, mental Modes describe only phenomena that fit within the general Attribute of Thought. And a similar rule follows for bodily Modes and the Attribute of Extension.[32]

Jonas's interpretation of the significance of Spinoza's conceptualization of the relationship between organizational complexity and the degree of awareness (thought) of which an organism is capable is certainly consistent with Spinoza's discussion in II P 13, where Spinoza intends to bolster, by way of a metaphysical demonstration of the nature of "bodies," his earlier claim (I, P 7, sch.): "a mode of extension and the idea of that mode are one and the same thing, expressed in two different ways." In the Scholia, Lemmas, Proofs, Corollaries, and Axioms that Spinoza introduces for the purposes of demonstrating how to conceive of "the union of mind and body" he seeks to define the underlying principle(s) that account for the *enduring identity* of individual entities. It is quite significant that he does this in a proposition that is interested in the relationship between mind and body. He informs us, however, that he is prompted to do this because of his conviction that "nobody can understand [the union of mind and body] adequately or distinctly unless he first gains adequate knowledge of the nature of the body."

153, emphasis original). But Miller ultimately embraces parallelism uncritically in his interpretation of Spinoza's metaphysics. "As the metaphor of parallelism suggests, the two orders—the mental and the physical—run parallel to one another without ever intersecting. A thought can lead to another thought but it can never produce or otherwise affect a body, and vice versa. It is true that substance is changing (or: appears to our intellects as though it were changing); and since we perceive substance under the attribute of thought and the attribute of extension, the changes happen simultaneously. But there is an insurmountable conceptual barrier between the thinking and the extended realms, such that interaction between them is impossible" (Miller, "Spinoza's Axiology," 154). Hence, we are again left with a lack of explanation as to how such parallel tracks are *one and the same*. The reading offered in this project can allow for Miller's notion of dual axiological realms within the human being but can underscore better than parallelism how the values after which humans "strive" because of their *conatus* are ultimately united as human values, rather than values of the body and values of the mind simply manifesting themselves as substance changes.

31. Cottingham et al., *Philosophical Writings of Descartes*, 2:18–20.

32. This is the epistemic counterpart of the ontological foundation for the so-called causal boundary between Extension and Thought and their various Modes. See Della Rocca, *Representation*, 121–29 for a discussion of the causal boundary, especially in the light of the opaqueness of contexts in which we experience events and things.

Spinoza contends straightforwardly in this proposition that bodies are distinguished from one another not as primary substances as they are in Aristotle (and Aquinas), but on a distinction of motion and rest. The motion or rest of any specific individual body is determined by a prior body, ad infinitum. Yet, when he speaks of what he calls "composite bodies," i.e., those that are made up of many different components, in order to argue for their identity and duration of existence, Spinoza must be assuming the concept of *conatus*, although he does not introduce it as a term until much later in the work. I am suggesting that he must have in mind here in this proposition, at the least, some metaphysical reality analogous to *conatus*, even if he does not use the term, because he is analyzing how composite bodies—or as he says, "individual things"–*preserve* their own natures. He is focused on complexly organized living entities when describing composite bodies. Spinoza's philosophy must have some principle that could account for the identity of a thing over time, since he denies because of his monism that individual entities are in any way substantial in their existence. Instead, they are products or "effects" of interactions with other modes, i.e., determinations established by changes in motion or rest between bodies and between complex organisms. Again, Jonas's observations are instructive and consistent with my own view:

> The continuity of determinateness [of a thing's identity] throughout such interactions (a continuity, therefore, not excluding change) bespeaks the self-affirming '*conatus*' by which a mode tends to persevere in existence, and which is identical with its essence. Thus, it is the *form* of determinateness, and the *conatus* evidenced by the survival of that form in a causal history, i.e., in *relation* to co-existing things, that defines an individual.[33]

Spinoza and Aquinas

What Jonas fails to note when he describes Spinoza's appreciation of organizational complexity as "the first time," however, is that such a conceptual framework was offered centuries before in the philosophy of Thomas Aquinas. It is articulated in his own development of a doctrine of hylomorphism building on what he received from Aristotle. Hence, he is a potentially helpful archetype by which one might better understand the intent of Spinoza's much and variously interpreted claim. Building upon Aristotle's definitions, but going beyond them, Aquinas contends that *anima rationale* (the soul or life-giving principle that enables both our biological existence, organizational complexity and functionality, as well as our rationality) is the formal essence that causes (in the Aristotelian sense of an essential or formal cause) a human body to be a body capable of interacting with rational thought and self-consciousness. Human mindedness is an inherent feature of our particular kind of biological and material

---

33. Jonas, "Spinoza and the Theory of Organism," 265.

existence, distinct from the body but not ontologically separate from it. While form and matter as technical metaphysical concepts are alien to Spinoza's ontological vocabulary, a careful reading of Aquinas will show that, although in different terms and based on a distinct ontology, the great medieval doctor of the church discussed a human being's minded physical existence in a manner that anticipates Spinoza's analysis of the mind and body as "one and the same thing, conceived under different attributes." John O'Callaghan comments on the general orientation in Aquinas's thought that this present project will demonstrate in the course of its own exploration and analysis:

> . . . for Aquinas we live but *one life*, the life of a rational animal . . . Aquinas argues that the principle of rational life just is "one and the same thing" as the principle of animal life in the human being. Thus, the life of the mind or intellect is identically the life of the animal that is human . . . Aquinas leaves no doubt about his desire to emphasize the absolute unity of human life in all its manifestations; animal could not be included in the definition of man, *if the principle of animal life were not "one and the same thing" as the principle of rational life in man."*[34]

The description of mind and body as "one and the same thing" that is modally expressed and therefore conceptually understood in two distinct ways, based on the metaphysical but not ontological difference between the attribute of Extension and the attribute of Thought, is rhetorically a Spinozistic novelty. It is not, however, a philosophical innovation altogether. Aquinas, as O'Callaghan suggests, contends in his essential definition of a human being as a rational animal for a similar sense of identity between the mind and body of a human person when he, in the *Summa,* argues that *anima rationale* is the *form* that causes a particular person's body to be what and to be all that it is. "Rational soul" is not in Aquinas's thought a term that refers to the mind or to our power of thought strictly defined or to the mental "aspect" of a human being. Instead, it is a term that denotes some essential ordering principle (an essence) that accounts for the human body being the kind of body that it is—a body capable of the expression of rational life. For Aquinas, the mental aspect of human existence cannot be *caused* by the physical/material forces, nor is the body qua physical *caused* by or dependent upon the mind. And they both are expressions in the same substantial reality. Therefore, human nature must be described philosophically in such a way that the material and the mental phenomena of our existence are understood as inhabiting the selfsame world, but without succumbing to the temptation of reductionism (either physicalist or idealist). This is essentially Spinoza's position.[35]

---

34. O'Callaghan, "Aquinas Rejection of Mind," 49, my emphasis.

35. In Spinoza's case he argues in *Ethics* III, 2 based on II, 7 that "the body cannot determine the mind to think, nor can the mind determine the body to motion or rest." He intends to help his readers see that neither of these modes can determine the other, because they are not distinct from one another on a more fundamental level, i.e., the existing human being who is the source of activity as a single *conatus.*

Aquinas and Spinoza both conceive of the actual existence of human beings in terms of active agency and passive receptivity. By active agency I mean that both Spinoza and Aquinas begin with the empirically confirmed idea that humans are self-conscious actors in the world they perceive. Our mental activities are our consciousness of the material world and our material existence, not some Cartesian presence that "interacts" with the body. Nor is our mental life in relationship to our physical existence dependent upon some preestablished harmony of the Leibinitzian variety.[36] Instead, a human being is an entity that is active, self-consciously and world-consciously so simultaneously with all material conditions in which he or she lives. The concept of passive receptivity gives expression to their conviction that human beings both physically and *mentally* are acted upon by features or entities of this same perceived world. And they are acted upon in both modalities by the very same world (reality), even if the physical world cannot *cause* changes in the mental knowledge. This focus on agency and receptivity, I contend, means for Aquinas *and* Spinoza that, from an even more fundamental metaphysical commitment on their part, when one is philosophically analyzing human beings in the real world as bodily and minded things, the real issue for them is not how manifestly distinct expressions of human existence relate, but what it means to be a *living* agent in the world whose singular existence in that world entails both body and mind as a singular existence of "one and the same thing."[37] Recognizing this affinity between their analyses leads to the first part of the proposal I present and defend in this book: a more adequate interpretation of Spinoza's view of how a thing's conatic essence organizes its very being in the world can be discovered by seeing how it is quite similar to Aquinas's notion of "soul" as subsisting form which is responsible for the material and mental function and existence of a human person. Thus, I shall exegete both to show that soul in Aquinas functions in a way that is analogous to the notions of essence and/or *conatus* in Spinoza.

RECOVERING *ANIMA*

The second part of my project is of contemporary relevance: to show that this affinity between these two quite different philosophers is not only surprising and interesting

36. See Kulstad and Carlin, "Leibniz's Philosophy of Mind," sec. 2.

37. This way of envisioning the state of affairs that is a human being's existence is what undergirds both Spinoza's and Aquinas's epistemologies. They are not worried about whether or not one can have adequate knowledge about the world. Instead, both argue that epistemological certitude is possible about the fundamental nature of reality. This certitude is possible for them without reference to the concurrence of God or the veracity of God (as in Descartes and, in some ways, Augustine in his doctrine of divine illumination of the mind). Instead, certitude is possible because in the world an action upon the body is ultimately an action experienced by the embodied knower. The act prompts, but does not cause, reflection leading to knowledge. While their epistemological commitments are beyond the scope of this present analysis, and are quite discreet in their particulars, nonetheless both of them can contend for adequate knowledge of the world on the basis of their monism regarding the relationship between mind and body.

in the history of philosophy, but even more importantly their hylomorphism is a helpful framework for current discussions and philosophy of human nature. Because the Angelic Doctor and the great rationalist are not troubled with trying to account for the presence of mindedness in an otherwise materialistic world, they not only avoid Cartesian pitfalls, but also the decidedly contemporary tendency to account for the existence of mind reductionistically as produced by some physical process of biochemistry and physics. Comparably, dualism nor epiphenomenal emergentism nor metaphysical supervenience as philosophical problems do not concern them. While dualism and various forms of physicalism are often seen as the two mutually exclusive options in contemporary philosophy, Hilary Putnam's evaluation is informative, I think, where he describes present-day philosophy of mind as methodologically Cartesian.[38] The metaphysical schemes of Aquinas and Spinoza avoid the dilemmas that such a tacit approach creates, because in their philosophical anthropologies a concept of the soul (*anima* for Aquinas and *conatus* for Spinoza) play the critical role. Both employ a metaphysical framework of hylomorphism. Aquinas does this in an obvious and conscious manner and Spinoza implicitly. Each endeavors to express his metaphysical understanding of the relationship of the body and the mind in terms of what it means to be an "ontological" unity—a human being. Aquinas, no less than Spinoza, presents human existence as irreducibly mental *and* physical, neither being more ontologically foundational, existentially primary, or causally prerequisite in relation to the other. In so doing, they point us to the more profound question: how is this harmonious unity and singularity to be accounted for philosophically? Those who are willing to give up methodological Cartesianism and who recognize the failures of reductionism will find their affinity is not only surprising but helpful for philosophical discussion.

When one considers the length of time that philosophers have contemplated, discussed, and offered various theories to "solve" the mind-body problem, a reintroduction of hylomorphism should be welcome. Strenuous and laudable philosophical efforts notwithstanding, the relationship of mind and body in human beings remains a conundrum in contemporary philosophy. At least one philosopher has outright argued that "we cannot solve the mystery."[39] Colin McGinn contends that understanding how biology and conscious thought (or consciousness of thought for that matter) are related might be beyond the mental ability of human beings, just as other perceptual and conceptual issues are "closed" to certain mental systems. Our mental awareness and capacity to form explanatory concepts, as features of our biological make-up, might be (and most likely is) thus cognitively closed to our understanding.

> The invisible parts of the electromagnetic spectrum are just as real as the
> visible parts, and whether a specific kind of creature can form conceptual

38. Putnam, *Threefold Cord*, 110, 170.
39. McGinn, "Can We Solve?," 543.

representations of these imperceptible parts does not determine whether they exist. Thus cognitive closure with respect to P does not imply irrealism about P. That P is (as we might say) noumenal with respect to M does not show that P does not occur in some naturalistic scientific theory T—it shows only that T is not cognitively accessible to M. Presumably monkey minds and the property of being an electron illustrate this possibility. *And the question must arise as to whether human minds are closed with respect to certain true explanatory theories.* Nothing, at least, in the concept of reality shows that everything real is open to the human concept-forming faculty—if, that is, we are realists about reality.[40]

Putnam's observation that the philosophy of mind operates methodologically from a Cartesian starting point might seem at first glance to be at odds with the assessment of Jaegwon Kim who notes that most of the current debate in philosophy of mind operates on the presumption of "the ontological primacy or priority of the physical in relation to the mental," so that the physical properties of things are regarded as "*basic* and what mental features *they* have is wholly dependent on their physical nature."[41] But, it is not, when one ponders what "methodological Cartesianism" means for philosophical analysis, namely that since body and mind are present and seem so alien from one another at least phenomenologically, if not ontologically, there is a problem to be solved about how these are related. So, if one is a physicalist *simpliciter* (as is Kim) the problem is essentially the same as it is for substance dualists, namely how are these aspects of our existence related to one another. Furthermore, how do we avoid asserting a divide in human existence (dualism) or diminishing the reality of the mental experiences of our lives (physicalist reductionism). Those philosophical perspectives that assume and are committed to the ontological priority of the physical still find the mind a strange presence in the philosophical analysis of ourselves. For most who concur that a materialistic causal description adequately expresses the situation regarding our minds, the recognition that things such as *qualia* are not the same as brain states creates a troublesome point of contention. It is this: if one rejects the ontological priority of the physical then one is saying "that there are things in the spacetime world other than physical things, like Cartesian souls, or at least that some things in the world have certain properties that are independent of their physical nature."[42] However, such a boggle is only confounding if one starts from the assumption that the physical is all that comprises the *natural world* and thinks that mind is some sense a feature that does not fit in that world. Such a starting point cannot but conceive of them as utterly disparate if not radically different and a problem to be explained or explained away. On the other hand, if one can start from a different point of departure for the process of analysis and recognize that even for the variety of

40. McGinn, "Can We Solve?," 544.
41. Kim, *Philosophy of Mind*, 11.
42. Kim, *Philosophy of Mind*, 12.

physicalist theories that exist something besides material forces are needed to account for *why* human beings' bodies are able to "produce" or "emanate" or have "supervene" upon them mental experiences and powers. Happily, there is an alternative—hylomorphism of soul and body.

As Kim further observes, the quandary of the mind-body relation continues to challenge us to resolve two issues that present themselves in our lived experience.

> If we are prepared to embrace reductionism, we can explain mental causation. However, in the process of reducing mentality to physical/biological properties, we may well lose the intrinsic, subjective character of our mentality—arguably the very thing that makes the mental mental. In what sense, then, have we saved "mental" causation? But if we reject reductionism, we are not able to see how mental causation would be possible. But saving mentality while losing causality doesn't seem to amount to saving anything worth saving. For what good is the mind if it has no causal powers? Either way, we are in danger of losing mentality. That is the dilemma . . . .
>
> . . . It is not happy to end a book with a dilemma, but we should all take it as a challenge, a challenge to find an account of mentality that respects consciousness as a genuine phenomenon that gives us and other sentient beings a special place in the world and that also makes consciousness a causally efficacious factor in the working of the natural world. The challenge, then, is to find out what kind of beings we are and what our place is in the world of nature.[43]

Discovering what kind of beings we are and what our place is in the world of nature is precisely the question. The difficulty in answering it for some no doubt resides in the very nature of the way things are conceptualized. Is the mind-body "problem" really a problem in the way that some think it is? Does causality and interaction really present us with an insoluble puzzle? Is the concept of soul simply another term for the conscious rational mind? Perhaps the very starting point of our consideration is wrongly placed, and we are trying to "solve" a problem that should instead be a hint that we should be looking for some antecedent and more fundamental instantiating property. Conceiving of mind and body rather as modal expressions of a single entity's unified life, that is itself the product of an essence giving principle, is a better way to approach the subject, as the treatment of Aquinas's hylomorphism as an interpretive framework for understanding the post-Cartesian Spinoza will show. It will, at least, consider issues that drop off the table of discussion, to our philosophical impoverishment, in much of contemporary philosophy's "methodologically Cartesian" approach. The approach of Aquinas and Spinoza is to look beyond the phenomena of mind and body and to contend that there is a cause of the profound unity of the mental and the physical that does not diminish either or conflate the uniqueness of each. It is their hylomorphism that enables this. Just because they might have an internally consistent

43. Kim, *Philosophy of Mind*, 237.

doctrine in their metaphysics of mind-body (as I shall show in later chapters), that does not mean hylomorphism is the correct view of reality. But as the next two chapters will help to demonstrate, it might very well be!

2

Hylomorphism
The Principles That Enable Beings to BE

As a FIRST STEP into our critical comparison of Aquinas's and Spinoza's philosophical analysis of the nature of the mind-body, we must be clear about what the Aristotelian-Thomistic doctrine of hylomorphism entails. In doing so, we not only get clear about their doctrines but will also set the stage for one thesis of this book, i.e., Thomas's hylomorphism, as a theoretical construct, can help us understand the meaning of Spinoza's assertion that mind and body are one and the same thing, expressed in two different modes. This will allow us room for the argument that supports the claim that the respective conceptual schemes of the medieval Angelic Doctor and the young thinker who destroyed the past do indeed offer descriptions regarding the unicity of the human person as a psycho-physical entity that are philosophically quite similar. Furthermore, careful consideration of Aquinas's metaphysics of mind and body, as a development dependent upon Aristotle's, will allow us better to judge how his theory may also differ from Spinoza's.

In this chapter, attention is given to the seminal development of the doctrine of hylomorphism that one finds in Aristotle's metaphysics, where we engage a theory that takes seriously a view of all individual physical particulars as metaphysically composite in their natures, having more than only a physical or materialistic "cause" of and principle to their existences. This general exposition of the Aristotelian background of Aquinas's doctrine will thus help us understand more completely in the next chapter what motivates Aquinas to contend that a human being is a *compositum*, i.e., a unitary entity produced by the union of matter and a substantial and subsistent form—a soul/*anima*. Understanding this, then, we will be able to show in the following chapters what Aquinas's doctrine of mind-body relation and interaction really involves. By this, we will be able to correct some misinterpretations of Aquinas on this point. Considering the importance of Aristotle's foundational role in the thesis and analysis on offer in this book, and given that the Aristotelian background of the doctrine of hylomorphism being considered is regarded as suspect by many philosophers, quaint by others, or of only historical interest, this chapter will provide an account of Aristotle's reasoning that led him to conclude that all particular things (primary substances) are composed of both the matter of which they are made and the form that makes them a particular kind of thing. Doing this allows us room for the suggestion to be made later that hylomorphism is still a helpful concept in contemporary analyses of mind-body. At least it will help establish that such a claim for hylomorphism is a coherent doctrine. Also, by considering Aristotle's development of this theory in this chapter, we will be able to demonstrate how Aquinas nuances hylomorphism in very important ways that go beyond and even part company with Aristotle. This clarity will be an important bridge for our latter forays into Spinoza's doctrine of *conatus* to argue that it is strikingly similar to Aquinas's understanding of the form or essence of an individual entity.

ARISTOTELIAN BACKGROUND

Substance and Accidents

Aristotle develops his understanding of the essential singularity of each primary substance as a result from his view that individual concrete entities we experience—what he calls primary substances—are ontologically foundational and have epistemological priority. That he considered these ontologically foundational and epistemically prioritized could be a point of contention among philosophers, but for Aristotle's monistic view of the cosmos the objects of the sensory world directly act upon our senses and cognition by the intermediary of intelligible form in relationship to the human sensory organs and mind and make actual knowledge of their essences comprehendible. Kantian-style epistemic concerns did not trouble him, because he saw no need to posit a noumenal "thing-in-itself" that was unknowable. Furthermore, he was not Leucippian or Democritean in his view of the material construction of things. We experience the world as the world is present to us, hence what we experience is true about the essences of the things we experience, even if our sensory experience of them is not exhaustive of their natures under every possible analytical framework or other perspective. So, he develops his epistemology out of his logical analysis of the ways that our sense faculties are acted upon by the intelligible forms of things in the world. Thereby, our minds are provided data from sense experience; and our language that gives description to the world out of our immediate experience is informed by this apprehension. Our minds, then, reflect and abstract the essential natures of things. For Aristotle, language follows thought, which follows our experience of the world via the intelligible forms from which we can abstract knowledge of universals. As Frederick Copleston has said of Aristotle's theory of the relationship between language and thought, language is "built up as an expression of thought and this is especially true of philosophical terms."[1]

The objects of our awareness present us with things whose existence can and must, by virtue of the logic of our language, be analyzed in terms of "categories" or "topics" of being. By Aristotle's analytics, we predicate of each item in our catalogues of experience either that they are a determining feature of something or, alternatively, an existent entity that undergoes such determination: for example, the color of a person's skin considered as a color versus the skin in which the color exists. The technical expression Aristotle gives to this analysis of what our experience of the world requires of us takes the following form:

For some X that we describe with reference to another thing B:

1. X is understood to exist as a feature of B

2. B does not exist as a feature of anything but is simply itself.

3. X has no existence except as a feature of B

4. B can exist in the absence of X

5. X, therefore, (by 2 & 4) is not essential to the definition we have of B

6. B gives existence to X (by 3)

7. X, therefore, (by 2 & 6) we could never call a particular substantial entity

8. X, furthermore, (by 3) is not reducible to B essentially

9. Hence, X, truly exists as X, but only in B and not in X per se.

10. B, therefore, exists as B but not in anything else (by 2 & 4).[2]

In *The Categories*, the examples Aristotle gives are knowledge (X) and the soul/ mind (B) or the color white (X) and a body (B). He contends that knowledge is real when it is in a knower, but there is nothing called "knowledge" that has any existence on its own. Only when predicated of a knowing subject can it be said to be real. Similarly, a white body can exist as qualified by the whiteness of it, but that qualifying whiteness does not exist as a subject of discussion anywhere except in that body (or another body in which whiteness is instantiated). Hence, "whiteness" has no substantial reality. On this basis, Aristotle reasoned that we are correct to describe some items in our catalogues of experience as the "substances" in which other states of affairs exist. The other states are called accidents (things in substances that are not necessary to the substance). These substances cannot, in Aristotle's view, be thought of as existing

1. Copleston, *History of Philosophy*, 2:280. For Aristotle's development of his logic see: *Categories* and *Topics*, where he posits a tenfold linguistic division of predicates. But in *Posterior Analytics*, A 22, 83, a 21–22, b 15, the tenfold division is reduced to eight. Here *cheisthai* and *echein* are relegated to items of other categories.

2. Ackrill, *New Aristotle Reader*, 5–11.

in anything more properly basic than their own actual existence.[3] These individuals that provide the locus for the states of affairs (accidents) that depend upon them for existence are *protai ousiai* (primary beings).[4] Such primary beings are, by definition, one and the same thing with themselves regardless of the accidents that accrue to them.

Actuality and Potency

In the actual existence of each *prote ousia* one observes changes, development, or even alterations physically in the act of its being what it is essentially. Because of this Aristotle posited that there is a distinction in the act of existing of a primary being that we must mark between what he called the "actuality" and the "potency" of these ontologically foundational entities. Noting this, Aristotle provides a philosophical theory about the nature of the world that is filled with beings that are substantial but not static in their existence. As he reflected on the intractable nature of our sensory awareness that presents us a world of individual entities for which change is the rule, Aristotle wanted to understand and define via metaphysical analysis the ontological status of change.[5] Although this will be detailed in a later section, we can outline his thought. In his view, the actuality of a primary being's state of being, as it is at any given moment in its "act of being," always includes, attending the actual state of being, a further potentiality inherent in entities to become other things. However, the potential to become some other actuality is not unlimited in any primary being under consideration but is a "potency"—a power or capability—that is real to that being's essence but is limited by that essence. This potency is, therefore, in one sense part of the *essential being* of the actual existence of the entity, for this potential to become different and change is an element of what it is *now*. And yet, the potential state is not in a part of the being of the entity in its current actualized existence in the world. (An egg is potentially a chicken, but it is in its actuality an egg.) What accounts for the potential rearrangement of the material stuff into a different actuality? The basic material stuff, he reasoned, is always the same material stuff and does not have an organizational power of its own. This ultimately led him to formulate his understanding of the way that "form" and "matter" function as descriptors of the ontological reality of change in

3. On this point, we will see in the third chapter how Aquinas's thought is distinguished from Aristotle's, as Aquinas deals with the question of what it means for a thing to "have being" and be able to exist.

4. Generally, *protai ousiai* is translated "primary substances." This translation is not incorrect, but it misses some of Aristotle's metaphysical impetus, which was to discuss the activity of existing. Aristotle is endeavoring to describe what has existence and how. So, "primary being" is an activity, i.e., a *being* in the sense of an existing (or act of existing).

5. Owens, *Doctrine of Being*, 403. "Change, as found in sensible things, serves therefore as the basis for the study of act and potency. The goal of the investigation, however, lies beyond the order of change."

protai ousiai. Form enables actuality, but also always contains or entails some potency, whereas matter can only express an actuality as a result of the functioning of the form/essence; but the form and matter are united in one primary being.

THE PRE-SOCRATIC BACKGROUND OF
ARISTOTLE'S METAPHYSICS

The conceptual parameters of philosophical discussion that Aristotle inherited had been established in pre-Socratic philosophy by the juxtaposed theories of Heraclitus and Parmenides. Placing the logic of Aristotle's metaphysics in its historical philosophical context will help explain why his logical analysis led to his theory. This exercise will, in turn, allow for a more adequate assessment of what hylomorphism might provide contemporary discussions of the relationship between mind and body when we turn to Aquinas and Spinoza.

At one pole of Aristotle's philosophical world stood Heraclitus and his doctrine of change as the *only* real feature of the cosmos. For Heraclitus, the "flux" is what really exists and all discussion about constancy of entities is an abstraction, since the constant movement from what is to what is not yet is the only reality that there is.[6] This universal flux is ontologically enabled, Heraclitus contended, by a cosmic order (*Logos*), which he conceived as the essential harmony that the tension of becoming and ceasing to be manifests in the sensible world. "The cosmos works," he proclaims, "by harmony of tensions, like the lyre and bow." Reginald Garrigou-Lagrange has characterized Heraclitus's ontology: "in the process of becoming, which is its own sufficient reason, being and nonbeing are dynamically identified."[7] Since for Heraclitus "becoming" is the ontological basic reality, there can be no ultimate differentiation between things, because a constant reordering is the only essence that really exists ultimately. Change is all there is and, therefore, there is no ordinary particular thing we could experience or conceive that is ontologically real.

When considering the physical world, Heraclitus would reject the distinction that Aristotle would later develop between *act* (what is actual) and *potency*, that which is possible, but not yet existing as an actuality. Such differentiations are nothing, by Heraclitus' lights, but a human conceptual imposition on the ever-changing flux. Our minds alone are the source of the ideas of *specific* things or values. He argued, therefore, "that the principle of contradiction is not a law of being, not even of the intelligence. It is a mere law of speech, to avoid self-contradiction."[8] (This applies, as well,

6. Heraclitus, *Fragments*, 25. "By cosmic rule, as day yields night, so winter summer, war peace, plenty famine. All things change. Fire penetrates the lump of myrrh, until the joining of bodies die and rise again in smoke called incense."

7. Garrigou-Lagrange, *Reality*, 38.

8. Heraclitus, *Fragments*, 39. Heraclitus stands, as does Parmenides, in the philosophical tradition that sees human intelligence as not a part of the world as it is. Aristotle, as will be shown, conceived of the human mind as part of the natural world, hence, the metaphysical basis for his realist epistemology.

to the realm of human moral value judgments: "While cosmic wisdom understands all things are good and just, intelligence may find injustice here and justice somewhere else."[9]) If the process of becoming is Reality, then no particular state of affairs in the flux of the process is real *qua* the particular state of affairs that it is. Rather, the only "reality" it enjoys is its part in the flow of the flux—the "war" of now-being and coming-being. Change, for Heraclitus, then is all we can affirm—so we must—as ultimately real. The genius of Heraclitus's perspective on the ontologically foundational role that change has in the world is that he offers a theory for change—the flux, and the necessary "conflict" that is the flux—that is ontological, rather than simply subjective and empirical. He conceived of our world as unity *because of* the infinite diversity presented to our senses. As Copleston comments, "For him the conflict of opposites, so far from being a blot on the unity of the One, is essential to the being of the One . . . . the One only exists in the tension of opposites."[10] Because he denies any principle of continuity of essences between moments of existence, fire is the perfect elemental metaphor for Heraclitus's metaphysics.

Parmenides, on the other hand, contended, based on his attention to the logic of linguistic expressions, that a radical counterproposal had to be affirmed. In his view the descriptions of the act of being our language reflects leave us only one conclusion: that Being "is" and, therefore, non-Being "is not." Contra Heraclitus, this draws us irresistibly, he argued, to the logical hypothesis that *change* itself is the illusion: necessarily the One—i.e., Reality—is identical with itself. This law of identity and the law of noncontradiction together mean our intellects wrongly attribute becoming and passing-away to the nature of the One Reality. This notion we have of change, therefore, is a mere fiction that our senses cause us to posit. But philosophical analyses allow us to get beyond our sensory experience and understand the absolute, impassible oneness that is Reality. Analytical honesty demands, Parmenides concludes, we affirm this analysis of being: "For thou couldst not know that which is-not (that is impossible) nor utter it; for the same thing exists for thinking and for being" (Fr. 2).[11] Furthermore, Parmenides contended that the force of "true belief" will not "allow that, beside what is, there could arise anything from what is not."

> How could what is thereafter perish? And how could it come into being? For if it came into being, it is not, nor if it is going to be in the future. So coming into being is extinguished and perishing is unimaginable. Nor is it divisible, since it is all alike; nor is there more here and less there, which would prevent it from cleaving together, but it is all full of what is. . . . Wherefore all these are mere names which mortals laid down believing them to be true—coming

---

9. Heraclitus, *Fragments*, 39.

10. Copleston, *History of Philosophy*, 40.

11. Allen, *Greek Philosophy*, 45.

into being and perishing, being and not being, change of place and variation of bright and color" (Fr 8).[12]

Parmenides offered the philosophical discourse of his day a logical deconstruction of our illusory notions about the reality of ordinary particular items.

ARISTOTLE'S COUNTERPROPOSAL

The Logic of Change and Unity

In both Heraclitus's and Parmenides's doctrines we are presented with the long-standing question of the ontological status of change and individuation in the sensible world. One could say that they struggle with the relationship our minds (our knowledge and ideas) have to the extra-mental world: a world of ordinary particulars and the relationships that exists between the myriad of ordinary particulars, yet which we experience in the world we intuit as one reality. They provide starkly divergent answers, even as they agree that the ideas we have about the world based on empirical data are mere conventions, even illusions. Their agreement is grounds for skepticism that our experience of the world is founded on some feature of the world. This is where Aristotle's assessment had to begin.

On his view, the fact that either of these pre-Socratics asserted any philosophical claims at all about the nature of the world belied their conclusions that language is merely conventional and not, at its philosophical best, correspondent to some extra-mental reality. When he began to address the issues as laid down in the polarities offered by this inherited dichotomy, he embraced two assertions as starting points for philosophical inquiry. The first was epistemological: namely, the experience we have of change in the world is a feature of reality to be granted a large measure of significance, even if we later find reason to qualify it in order to clarify and expand our understanding. At this point, he seems to have taken Heraclitus seriously. Yet, with his second starting assertion, which entailed a claim about logic, he seems to have sided with Parmenides against Heraclitus's radical nominalism. His second assertion was that the principle of noncontradiction is a logical principle that is objectively true. There is no obvious or inherent reason, in Aristotle's view, why this logical principle could not coexist concurrently with his epistemological allowance of the import of sensory experience which entails the experience of things coming to be and ceasing to be. We will consider the work done by this second assertion in Aristotle's philosophy as he engaged the Heraclitan doctrine of nonconstancy, before we look at the way he addressed and critiqued Parmenides's theory based on the first assertion that sensory experience ought to be afforded tremendous significance in philosophical reasoning.

12. Allen, *Greek Philosophy*, 46.

Based on the logic of the law of noncontradiction, Aristotle argued against Heraclitus and his disciples as follows. "We shall reply to this theory that although that which is changeable supplies [Heraclitus and his followers], when it changes, with some real ground for supposing that it 'is not,' yet there is something debatable in this; for that which is shedding any quality retains *something of* that which is being shed, and *something of* that which is coming to be must already exist."[13] Aristotle saw in "the flux" more than Heraclitus could (at least from what we know from his extant writings). In fact, the reality of constant change that the Ionian pre-Socratic noted implied, for Aristotle, there had to be continuity in the process of change. He argued that since we can recognize a *process* of change and becoming, the principle of noncontradiction is a logical corollary, because our observations of the empirically perceived process of change entails logically and in reality that what is now is *not* what was. Thus, noncontradiction as a principle necessarily has some epistemic function even in the development of Heraclitan knowledge. The Stagirite thought it self-contradictory to say that change (this is now *not* that) is all that there is and then to contend that our language about change (the law of noncontradiction) is simply a convention imposed on us by our language. To recognize that particulars are (even momentarily as part of the flux) identical with themselves, which pass away and some other particular in the next moment exists where that particular had existed is to acknowledge that there was a thing that both was and now is not. Since that something was the predecessor of the state that followed it, even belief in the ontological *flux* requires this recognition.

As Garrigou-Lagrange says, "Aristotle, against Heraclitus, holds that the principle of noncontradiction and the further law of identity are laws of reality, not merely of the inferior reason and of speech, but of the higher intelligence, and primarily of objective reality."[14] We cannot posit anything about reality without acknowledging the role this principle plays for our language and thought—even that "change" is all there is, in Aristotle's analysis.

> Generally those who argue in this manner overlook both the being (*ousia*) and what it means to be; for it is necessary for them to assert that all attributes are accidental and that there is no such thing as "being a man" or "being an animal." Now, if there is such a thing as "being a man," it will not be "being nonman" or "not being a man" (its negatives): for it has one meaning, namely, to define the being of something. And to signify its being means that its being [what it is] means it is not something else. But, if "being a man" means "being nonman" or "not being a man," then a man's being will be something else. Hence they must argue that there cannot be such a definition of the being of anything . . . . But if all statements merely predicate accidents, then there will be no first point of reference since accidents always are predicated about

---

13. Aristotle, *Metaphysics*, bk. V 1010 A, 311, my emphasis.
14. Garrigou-Lagrange, *Reality*, 39.

something as a subject. It would be necessary, accordingly, to proceed thus to infinity; but this is impossible.[15]

Since the reality of change per Heraclitus's assertions implies some recognition of the law of noncontradiction, the ultimate metaphysical conclusion that there are entities that change *and* become is unavoidable; it also suggests that there may be something that remains, as well. Entities that are involved in the change must be acknowledged and a definition of their essences as things that are and then are not is involved unavoidably. A definition implies, by its very nature, the awareness that the thing defined is "not-this-other-thing" in its own existence. Therefore, Aristotle argued that Heraclitus's idea that only change is real and not the changing things, thereby, collapses. Further, because Heraclitus could only see the essences of things as accidents in motion, no one could ever attain for our thinking a "first point of reference since accidents always are predicated about something as a subject."

Without this first principle, thought is impossible, Aristotle reasoned, "it would be necessary to proceed to infinity." Such an infinite regress must ultimately undercut any claim to philosophical certitude about the ontological nature of things. Heraclitus cannot argue for change as the foundation of reality if change is really all there is, because he has no epistemic warrant for such a claim. Any epistemic warrant for claiming that change is real in the world must rely on some true *ousia* of the things that are undergoing change. Aristotle considered that the *logos* posited by Heraclitus could not do this. Instead, he insisted that logic demands we recognize the *continuity of being*, conceived as a unified whole in which modification and change within and between individuals occurs and not merely a flux of discrete moments. This is, Aristotle argued, a foundational doctrine of first philosophy; without this recognition and intellectual commitment, philosophy cannot proceed. What Aristotle had to account for and define is the feature of reality that enables there to be continuity of existence for the changing things in the midst of the process of change. To this we will return below, but before that we must consider Aristotle's second metaphysical obstacle, Parmenides's monism.

Heraclitan ontology had exacted from its detractors an account of constancy in the sensible world, but the Parmenidean pole of Aristotle's philosophical context demanded a response to its own radical conclusion. An adequate explanation of change and individuation as real features of an essentially unitary and continuous reality had to be provided. While Aristotle's teacher, Plato, had attempted to answer Parmenides's challenge by positing an unchanging realm of intelligible *Ideas* (Forms) that is unified by the Good as the ultimate Form of all reality, Plato's peripatetic student found this wanting. The radical ontological dualism of Plato removes the essence of a thing from the thing itself, thereby creating a logical confusion and metaphysical nonsense.[16] It

15. Hope, *Aristotle's Metaphysics*, 72.

16. Hope, *Aristotle's Metaphysics*, 24–26. For a good discussion of Aristotle's treatment (and possible misunderstanding of Plato) see Copleston, *History of Philosophy*, 292–301.

also failed, in Aristotle's view, to correct the very weakness of Parmenides's theory that Plato wanted to undercut.

Parmenides and his school, Aristotle believed, inflated the consequences of their version of the law of contradiction: "what is cannot come to be, since it is already, and nothing can come to be out of what is not, since there must be something underlying."[17] Their foundational principle, taken as first philosophy, fails to draw significant linguistic distinctions, Aristotle concluded, about the ways in which continuity and concurrence work in the sensible world. Not-being, as a negation, he argued, can simply be the acknowledgement of the finitude of a particular entity under consideration. In this regard, to posit "not-being" is not a denial of Being itself (as Parmenides concluded); rather it is simply a notation of lack in the particular item under consideration. "We too say that nothing comes to be simply out of what is not; but that things do come to be in a way out of what is not namely by virtue of concurrence. A thing can come to be out of the lack, *which in itself is something which is not*, and is not a constituent."[18] The notion of lack, therefore, points to a state of affairs—an absence of something else. An absence, when considered per se, for Aristotle, is nothing in an existential sense, but not ontologically, because the idea of *the lack* itself entails the idea of a concurrent already-existing reality that is constituted by this lack as part of its essence. As Copleston comments on the implication of Aristotle's logic at this point, "If Parmenides were to object that [this doctrine of privation] is tantamount to saying that a thing comes into being from not-being, Aristotle would answer that it does not come into being from its privation merely (i.e., from bare privation), but from its privation *in a subject*."[19] To speak of a lack of being in existence is not the same thing, therefore, as speaking of Nonbeing. Privation (lack) is not itself some ontic principle, by Aristotle's lights. That would posit an absurdity. From nothing, nothing comes. So, *nothing* is not the source for the coming-to-be of other things. Aristotle called his students to realize that the very concept of lack entails recognition of something that could lack, or something that is also *not* something else. Each thing that exists in actuality is simultaneously *not* something else. The very identity it has requires that it lack some essential feature so that it is what it is. This means that by having the essence of existence in its being, the existing entity is the source of anything that arises out of its being, which suggests that any new states that come from the *lack* are not per se arising from already existing being: "it does not come into being from being precisely as such, but from being which is also not-being, i.e., not the thing which comes to be."[20]

---

17. Aristotle, *Physics*, Bk I, Ch 8; Ackrill, *New Aristotle Reader*, 90–91.

18. Ackrill, *New Aristotle Reader*, 90–91, my emphasis.

19. Copleston, *History of Philosophy*, 311.

20. Copleston, *History of Philosophy*, 311. Aristotle is not here completely refuting Parmenides's epistemological foundations. Zeno, for instance, might attempt to assert that Aristotle is avoiding the real issue, i.e., that our experience of change is just an illusion, and therefore not reliable. However, the extent to which Aristotle refutes Parmenides's logic that EVERYTHING either "is or is not" *simpliciter* destroys much of the analytical motivation for embracing his subsequent radical doubt about the

Foundations of Act and Potency

Therefore, not all language of *nonbeing* implies a "violation of the principle that everything either is or is not" in Aristotle's logical analysis.[21] Existence and the logic of language, which was the foundation of Parmenides theorizing, requires even Parmenides to acknowledge that existence (what *is*) is not nonexistence (what is *not*). Parmenides's own linguistic negation (the "is-not") posits a *concept* of nonexistence as part of the order of knowledge of the world. Because both concepts are critical components in our way of speaking of reality, why would one privilege the "is" over the "is not." Flipping his critique of Heraclitus, Aristotle argues, contra Parmenides, if every specific thing *in our experience* is present to us as a specifically determined entity, it follows that each entity we perceive is what it is by concurrently not being something-else. Coterminous, for Aristotle, with this dialectical analysis is his view that something which *is*—yet which *is not* something else—can be the source of the coming to be of another, if the other that comes to be does so as a result of being in *potential* as an aspect of the already existing entity. (Ex: the oak tree *in* the acorn potentially.)

An example Aristotle offers in *The Physics* Book I, chapter 8 is a doctor and the medical acts performed that lead to healing. A doctor heals, paraphrasing Aristotle, out of his *actualized* doctor-ness. Such a defined, existent identity entails by its very nature certain possibilities. But the state (or thing) we could call the health of sick person X—before it is brought about through the art of healing—is nonexistent and not an actual feature of the world in X's mode of existence. Healing, however, neither arises from nonbeing precisely per se, nor from the present realized actual state of the doctor or the patient. Rather, the act of healing comes to be out of the possibilities inherent in the state of affairs we call healing knowledge and medical practice. These are actual and existent in the doctor, as "healableness" is in *potentia* in the patient. Garrigou-Lagrange illustrates Aristotle's position on the reality but nonactuality of potentiality in things by referring to sculpture. "For Aristotle, that which is in process of becoming cannot arise from an actual being, which already exists. The statue, in process of becoming, does not come from the stone [qua what it is] that already exists. But the thing in process of becoming was at first there in potency, and hence arises from unterminated being, from real and objective potency, which is thus *a medium between* the existing being and mere nothing."[22]

By acknowledging that potentiality is real and distinct ontologically (not just conceptually) from actuality, Aristotle eludes the trap Parmenides had seen in some of

---

world of the senses and its relationship to Reality. Of course, Aristotle does not suggest that nonbeing is itself something or a reality. Rather, he merely demonstrates that Parmenides's own logic posits "not being" as an epistemological corollary to the being that Parmenides insists is all that there is. Hence, Parmenides's logic has to entail something that his ontology denies, which is self-refuting since he was trying to demonstrate that the order of knowing demanded that being be understood to be one.

21. Aristotle, *Physics*, Bk I, Ch 8, Ackrill, *New Aristotle Reader,* 90–91.

22. Garrigou-Lagrange, *Reality,* 39.

the ancient discussions of becoming and of change and avoids falling into the pit that Parmenides had dug for himself, i.e., where *all* our perceptions are only illusory. Aristotle's metaphysics allows him to acknowledge Being as the ontological starting point but not deny, he thought, the ontological status of individual existents and change that our encounter with the world suggests to us: "being is used in various ways, but always with reference to one principle."[23] In fact, Aristotle thought he could account for the ontological reality of these changing particulars in a way that Parmenides's own logic suggested but did not pursue.

In his defense of the legitimacy of his metaphysics, Aristotle gives at some length a demonstration that Being, understood as a unity that exists in the dynamic interplay of actuality and potency, is the true first principle. If that is the case, then it follows that a Parmenidean notion of unchanging unity of Being is not a fundamental ontological concept. It also follows that Heraclitus' flux is not an adequate theory of reality, for the Heraclitan "war" cannot account for what unity there actually is in the midst of change occurring. A different basis for the unicity of reality from those proclaimed by these two pre-Socratic theorists must be provided. Aristotle argues the point based on Parmenides's logical/linguistic analysis of statements.

> For some things are said to "be" because they are substances; others because they are modifications of substance; others because they are a process towards substance, or destructions or privations or qualities of substance, or productive or generative of substance or of terms relating to substance, or negations of certain of these terms or of substance. (Hence we even say that not-being *is* not-being.) . . . Hence the study of all the species of Being *qua* Being belongs to a *science which is generally one*, and the study of several species of Being belongs to the specific parts of that science. Now if Being and Unity are the same, *i.e.*, a single nature, in the sense that they are associated as principle and cause are, and not as being denoted by the same definition (although it makes no difference but rather helps our argument if we understand them in the same sense), since "one man" and "man" and "existent man" are the same thing.[24]

Being is, for him, the ontological homogeneity of the *acts* of existing we see in the world. In that sense, then, the *activity* of beings existing is the unity of reality. Reality is singular in the sense that everything that exists are just *being* (existing in existence). On this basis, then, Aristotle contends, with Parmenides, that Being is the starting

23. Aristotle, *Metaphysics* VI (III). G. E. L. Owen's reading of Aristotle's semantics has been quite influential; and it runs counter to the reading of Aristotle's metaphysics of "being" offered here. In Owen's view, Aristotle does not intend for us to understand the "science of being *qua* being" as a demonstrative endeavor that can establish theorems that correspond to the objective composition of entities. Rather, in Owen's mind, Aristotle is providing us with a linguistic turn that inquires about our own semantics in order to clarify for ourselves the meanings of the conceptual term "being." Owen, "Logic and Metaphysics." For a critique of Owen, see Fraser, "Aristotle on the Separation of Species-Form."

24. Aristotle, *Metaphysics*, VI, (III).

point of philosophy and that the one reality we have is a unity, contra Heraclitus. However, *Being*, for Aristotle, is a verbal descriptor, not a substantive, as seems to be the Parmenidean standard. Therefore, Aristotle contended, Being need not and should not become the basis for a doctrine of unity that denied a plurality of beings and the modifications that exist among all the members who participate in Being. In the same sense, neither could potentiality of being in any actualized member of that plurality be disallowed.[25]

Aristotle was motivated by a further first principle of his monism, i.e., that thought and knowing are part of the very same reality of Being that we are analyzing in philosophical inquiry. In other words, thought is not ontologically alien from the objects which are the contents of thought—both are parts of what *is*. There is no absolute dualistic separation epistemologically (as Plato's ontology requires), even if there is a distinction to be drawn, between mind as an activity and the material world in which and about which the activity is exercised. Therefore, our experience wedded to the law of noncontradiction, he argued, presents us with the real features of primary beings that, considered epistemologically, establish for our thinking the essential identities of unique beings, all of which share Being. In our understanding of the world, statements about the identity of things in the realm of Being entail definitions, because to identify any entity is to define it. (This is as true for nominalists as much as realists.) Such definition, as already noted, entails nonidentity also, i.e., each thing is also—by its definition—*not* something else. The nonidentity principle is the foundation upon which Aristotle builds his metaphysical view that a lack (privation in actuality) is a real feature inherent in things that have being. This wed to the presumption that our minds perceive reality (not impose on it) becomes the framework by which Aristotle avoids Parmenides's critique of the ontological reality of change, namely, that being cannot come from what is not, nor can being come from what is already actually in being. Since "coming-to-be" arises not out of nothing, but from the potentiality inherent in each primary being by way of the privation (the lack of other defining features) that is inherent to the definitional and existential essence of that primary being, change is, therefore, a real feature of the world, but only possible, contra Heraclitus, because continuity of being is also real. What is left, for Aristotle, is to demonstrate conceptually how possible being, or potency, is present as a feature of the world, located in *protai ousiai*, as well as how that potential, unrealized being would be related to the actual existence of *protai ousiai*.

---

25. The true import of Aristotle's analysis can be lost if we do not keep in mind that his discussion of being (*ousia*) and not-being is treating this issue in terms that do not easily translate into English. As with Aquinas later, Aristotle's designation *being* should be conceived of as a gerund-like description of action in the existence of an entity. He does not consider *not-being* to be some actual feature of reality. This is obvious, it would seem, from his famous rejection of the possibility of a vacuum in nature.

Form and Matter

In accounting for both continuity and possible change in the oneness of Being, Aristotle knew he required more qualification of the nature of potency and actuality in his metaphysics. Regarding the metaphysical foundation of an entity's essential identity (its actuality), Aristotle embraces Plato's category *form* as the property or principle by which existent things are established in existence and known by us to be the particular things that they are by making every being the kind of *prote ousia* that it is.[26] Form is the translation given to Aristotle's Greek term *eidos*, which means literally "idea." *Idea*, however, must not be thought of in Humean or Kantian terms. Rather, it is for Aristotle a much more dynamic term that names the what-it-is of a particular existing thing. Diverging from Plato's epistemological (and metaphysical) scheme, which posited an independent existence of *Form(s)*, Aristotle contended that the individual being we experience through sensory data is the substantial primary subject with which philosophy works in the task of understanding, not Platonic ideas. (We know these things because of our participation and existence in the singular world of being which includes material things and minds.) "It is because the *protai ousiai* are subjects for all the other things and all the other things are predicated of them or are in them, that they are called substances most of all."[27] Although we only experience directly the primary beings which are always specific unitary things, the similarities that primary beings share with others that are like them are also real. For example, horses share qualities that make them all horses and we experience these in each horse we come across. These similarities are items of knowledge that we first experience in *each and every* horse, but as similarities we recognize them as species distinctives that make them horses. So, these are "secondary" items of our catalogues of understanding, but nonetheless real because our minds recognize them in material beings. Therefore, these shared, real similarities enable us to identify the reality of *secondary substances* (ways of being). This has ontological implications.

These apperceptions about primary and secondary beings (substances) mean that in Aristotle's philosophy *form* functions in two ways. The first is epistemological and the second ontological. It is epistemic, of course, in an *a posteriori* fashion in that it is known to us by experience. The knowledge of the true nature of any primary being is the knowledge of it as a particular thing in itself, which we subsequently realize by reflection and abstraction is part of a species form. This epistemological centrality of form is expressed in the *De Anima*, where Aristotle begins to consider what it means to call the soul the form of the body. There he says that form is the concept or principle "in virtue of which [any object we are considering] is then spoken of as a particular [a this]."[28] Understanding the significance of form this way Aristotle

26. Aristotle, *De Anima*, II, 412a 8–9; Ackrill, *New Aristotle Reader*, 165.

27. Aristotle, *Categories*, 5, 15–18; Ackrill, *New Aristotle Reader*, 8.

28. Aristotle, *De Anima*; Ackrill, *New Aristotle Reader*, 165. See Owens, *Doctrine of Being*, 388–95

contends that "*protai ousiai* are subjects for all the other things and all the other things are predicated of them or are in them." But the first-order epistemological function is only part of the meaning of form in Aristotle's thought.

When we recognize that a "*this* thing" of our experience shares similar qualities to other things that are also part of our experiences, we realize that the principle, as Aristotle says, "in virtue of which" we *speak* of a particular entity is also an ontological cause of any particular entity about which we predicate existence. Specific particulars are the means, as was described above, by which we begin our knowledge of the world, for by or in them we engage a particular *this* thing. However, more experiences and reflection enable us to realize that the particular *this* thing is in its essence also a particular *kind* of thing. This, also, expands the definition of any primary being, i.e., that it is in its essence part of a kind. He is no nominalist about universal kinds (forms), because, in his reasoning, something must account for the reality that each *this* is a part of a larger *these*, because the similarities of essence among things that share those similarities require our understanding to account for the sharing. As we have noted, a *prote ousia* is the substantial entity in which other predicated categories exist. However, Aristotle describes the form that makes any primary being what it is as having a reality that is more than simply the primary being *simpliciter.* He also claims, controversially among some of his interpreters, that the form that is the essence of a primary being must be described as substantial in a secondary and derivative sense. Since primary beings share features of being with others that are like them, Aristotle contends that the species, general description is the object of science; it is *deutrai ousia*—being in the secondary sense. On this basis he contends that form is an ontological or metaphysical principle that is not simply predicated tautologically of an entity but must have a reality of its own in some way, because it is, at least partially, explanatory of how a thing comes to be what it is.[29]

The reality that form is not reducible to the primary being's essence alone is seen in manufactured artifacts, in an obvious way.

> It is evident, accordingly, that the form, or whatever we want to call the shape of the perceived object, is not produced; nor is there ever any production of it; no intrinsic nature is ever made. For an intrinsic nature comes to be *in something else* made by art or by nature or by some power. It is a bronze sphere that is made out of bronze and 'sphere,' since one makes a form enter into this matter, and thus the result is a bronze sphere . . . . It is evident, therefore, from what has been said, that what we have called the form or essential being is not

where he drives home the epistemological function of form in Aristotle's philosophy. He points out the difficulty involved when describing what form presents us with. He contends that in Aristotle's metaphysics the form of an entity is what we recognize as the "this" of a thing's identity. "The form, then, as separate at least [as a notion in our thinking about the material object in question] from the matter, is in Aristotelian terminology a 'this' though not a 'singular'" (388).

29. This is the impetus of Aristotle's use of the well-known "four causes." Form is necessary to account for why any particular existent is the particular existent that it is.

produced, but *that it is the combined form-in-matter that is produced, and that in everything that is produced there is matter, and that any object is, on the one hand matter and, on the other hand, form.*[30]

And in a parallel way, this predetermining nature of form is also predicable of things in nature, i.e., entities that are endowed with life.

> All things begin in their primary being, as syllogism begins by stating what a thing is; so from being come all becomings. Natural growths follow this same pattern. For *the seed is productive* in a manner analogous to art, *since it has the form potentially; and that from which the seed comes is somehow like its offspring* . . . . For, as it is the bronze sphere that is produced, not 'sphere' or bronze, and likewise in the production of the bronze itself there must always be present both a material and a form in the production of any primary being . . . . However, we may note a peculiarity of the production of primary beings: another primary being, the producer, must preexist in complete realization for example, an animal, if an animal is to be produced.[31]

Form, in Aristotle's view, is more significant in its ontological sense than its epistemological sense. It is a principle of being (cause) that accounts in significant part for the existence of the primary being since it is the determining actuality of a particular entity's way of being—its *whatness*. While it would be meaningless to ask why or how a particular man is the person (man) that he is ("It is pointless to ask why anything is itself"[32]), one can wonder what causes a primary being to be the *kind* of entity it is. Since every material entity exists in the world as a particularized reality, and because the principles of matter themselves do not explain how it becomes specifically organized to be something particular, a principle beyond the mere material/physical elements must be the cause of these being the thing it is (and kind of thing) it is rather than another. Matter per se can be many different things, but primary beings are definite in identity. As Joseph Owens observes, for Aristotle "a Being is a 'what,' i.e., something definitely determined by its form and so distinguished from all other kinds of things." Owens continues, "The form causes that 'definiteness' in the matter and is therefore the cause of its Being. 'Being' evidently means [for Aristotle] 'being so and not so.'"[33] This is what Aristotle means by *formal cause.*

The matter that is organized is also an explanatory principle (cause) in a different sense, because it gives a thing real individuated existence in the world qua physical. So, it is the material cause. By "causes" Aristotle means something much more than we mean when speaking of cause and effect. Causes are antecedent determinants that fundamentally are necessary to explain the existence of primary being. (Formal

30. Hope, *Aristotle's Metaphysics.* Z, 8, my emphasis.
31. Hope, *Aristotle's Metaphysics,* 9. 1034 a, 30–1034 b, 21, my emphasis.
32. Hope, *Aristotle's Metaphysics,* 17. 1041a 13–14.
33. Owens, *Doctrine of Being,* 376, my emphasis.

and material causes function in concert with efficient and final causes). Because form is the particularizing cause giving specific identity to a primary being, Aristotle assigned, reasonably enough, the potentiality of change to the material stuff that is given specific functions and properties (its essence), and hence its identity, by the form. The material existence one is considering when analyzing a primary being is, as Owens points out regarding Aristotle's metaphysics, both a "being so and not so." Matter is always capable of being something else, therefore, there is always something that a material being is not. This passive power of being capable of being made into any kind of primary being is the essence of matter—prime matter. Matter as cause is a necessary antecedent (for all physical things are made of matter), but it only actually exists, in the most precise sense, when it is *formally* organized to be a particular being. Since all physical things are made of the same principle—matter—but are distinct in existence and nature from one another, matter must be, Aristotle reasoned, a real thing but only in the sense of pure potentiality to be formed. Not being another thing is obviously part of the definition of an entity. (An oak tree is *not* a maple tree, even though the material of them both is quite the same.). So, matter becomes an actual nature when informed by form, but it also entails a lack in actual existence that is part of the definition of the nature of the material being (which implies a potentiality). As was described above, Aristotle conceived of change in entities as produced in a subject—a *prote ousia*—because change comes from the potentiality that is inherent in the subject, whose essence entails a lack, i.e., something that the primary being is not, but is apt to become because of the nature it has. Matter informed to be a primary being is the source of the capacity of change, but the form determines the parameters of the change that is possible for any primary being.

The lack, upon which potentiality depends, is not strictly *nothing*, (nonbeing per Parmenides) but is an aspect of the subject's existence which allows for certain kinds of potency to be true of the subject. Physical things exist as particular entities with specific essences, yet we observe that these particulars are also capable of two kinds of change of existence. While remaining within their own essence (as when the acorn transforms into an oak tree), a material change has occurred, but not a change of essence (form), because the acorn is a phase of the oak tree's living existence. An acorn has its own identifying form, but that identifying form is subsumed under the large category of "oak treeness." A second essential radical change, however, into other kinds of things—as when the acorn eaten "becomes" part of the pig that ate it—is also a part of the existence an entity. This aspect of the primary being's essence is *in* its essence only as a potentiality of the matter that is so formed. Aristotle's philosophy describes the dynamic that accounts for the capacity to maintain essence while undergoing the first kind of material change as well as the potential to become *essentially* a different kind of material thing.

Since he thought he had established philosophically that one is justified in the believing three things, namely, (1) that nothing can come from *nothing*, (2) that modifications of existence and of existent things are real, and (3) that change could not be so radical as to lack any continuity with precursor states, Aristotle continued to analyze how to understand the continuity of being of changing primary beings when new states of existence change them dramatically. The paradigmatic case is our example of the change and development of an oak tree from acorn to mighty arboreal giant, which requires one type of metaphysical explanation. Further compounding the issue, however, is the reality that acorns do not always or only become large trees. Wild pigs eat acorns; and when this is done the acorn ceases to exist not only qua acorn, but qua vegetative entity altogether. As pigs eat many acorns, more pig is produced; the wonderment is how this would be so. While matter may be the source of the potentiality for change, what mechanisms are at work as this change into actuality occurs? Because Aristotle reasoned that the material stuff that was the acorn(s) is pure potentiality as the essence of its nature, the physical stuff that received the form of acorn has the capacity of losing, under certain conditions, the form of being an acorn and can be incorporated into the physical make-up the gormandizing swine. When this occurs, the matter of the acorn is radically transformed (one might even say the matter is re-formed) into something that it was not prior to the consumption. Yet, because of the influence of the form in union with the matter, limits are established on the amount of material change possible in a primary being. (Ex: the matter of those same acorns cannot "become" tiger flesh, due to the formal nature of the tiger and the acorns.[34])

Form, Matter, and Immanent Teleological Striving

If the acorn is not eaten, however, then under the right efficient conditions the form of "oak treeness" will impel the acorn stage of existence to end, be transcended, and become the *telos* specific to the essence of which "acorn-ness" was but a phase. This innate telic drive to continue in existence is first manifested by the "intention" to become what it is intended to be and then, secondly, to flourish in its organized, realized essence. Aristotle called this an *energeia* or "entelechy,"[35] which is determinative of and directive toward the actual being of the final *telos* of an essence, even when not exercised or operative at any given time. This theory that the inherent striving is a power that is always real, even if not being manifested, placed him in direct opposition to another school of thought on the meaning of "act." Aristotle observes, "There are some, such as the Megarians, who say that there is a power only [when actively

34. Obviously, Aristotle could not have known about the intricacies of digestive systems, but his assessment fits informally with what is now known.

35. *Energeia* is the Greek word Aristotle uses for "act" or actuality. At times, he uses another word, closely associated with *energeia* in his metaphysics, *entelecheia,* which implies fulfillment or fullness of the act or activity under consideration. Cf. Owens, *Doctrine of Being,* 405. Owens calls this "a peculiarly Aristotelian word."

operating] and that there is no power apart from its operation: that when not engaged in building, a person is not able to build, and that he is a builder only when he is in the act of building, and so forth."[36] Aristotle sees such thinking leads to absurdities. Distinguishing between the actual performance of a capacity and the actual *possibility* of performing it, he notes in both instances a power is present. Otherwise, we cannot account for how change would occur as a reality, if the power does not exist unless it is actively in operation. How else does it begin to be? "These doctrines [those denying any potential, unexercised power associated with essence of a thing] take away all possibility of change and of coming into being."[37]

Aristotle demonstrates that change in the condition of an entity or its relationship to things around it is real and concludes that we must acknowledge that "power and act differ; hence, those doctrines which present power and act [as identical concepts], are trying to deny a difference that is far from trivial."[38] Therefore, "something may be *capable* of being without actually being, and of not being, yet be."[39] Critically important here is his already discussed idea that only things that have actual existence are capable of producing change in themselves or in other things. For this reason, he closely associates the concept of "act" (*energeia*) with the term *entelechy*. But for Aristotle *entelechy*, in its close association with *energeia*, qualifies its verbal counterpart, allowing him to qualify *energeia*, in contradistinction to the "Megarians," to mean more than movement, i.e., powers in operation. He concludes: "The word 'actuality,' which is associated with 'fulfillment' (*entelechy*), has been derived from movements, though it can be applied in other ways . . ."[40]

This concept, then, means that the *actuality* (the formal cause that acts qua *energeia*) of things that "are or come to be naturally," gives to the primary beings in their actualized existence the possibility of future states of being that more fully express the essence of that existence. They have a capacity, whether exercised or not, to strive to express their own specific natures in the most fully adequate and flourishing way. A living entity's nature is "also its form or primary being or the culmination of its becoming"; or we might say, "the nature of anything is," for Aristotle, "in some sense its primary being."[41] From within the essence of a natural (living) being, the source of its growth and "the processes of becoming" arise from within its very nature. And in its life cycle development and change is an expression of the natural, living being's essence, "because this source is inherent in them, either potentially or completely."

36. Hope, *Aristotle's Metaphysics*, 184.

37. Hope, *Aristotle's Metaphysics*, 185.

38. Hope, *Aristotle's Metaphysics*, 185.

39. Hope, *Aristotle's Metaphysics*, 185, my emphasis.

40. Hope, *Aristotle's Metaphysics*, 185.

41. In this definition we see the ontological primacy of *protai ousiai* and the distinction that Aristotle will labor to draw between nature or form or essence and primary being later in the *Metaphysics*. There is some logically necessary distinction that entails a likely ontological distinction, but existentially there can be no distinction.

This is the *entelechy*-act that is an organization and orientation toward *energeia*-act that will, under proper conditions, allow for the thriving of these things in their own natures, because they strive to maintain their existence and to flourish as the things that they are.

Because of this inherent nature and capacity for directed, teleological change Aristotle reasoned the matter of an actualized being is enabled to undergo the specific changes formally possible—the possibility for growth, movement, sustaining, and flourishing. This potentiality is inherently part of the entity's nature by the form in union with the material element(s). Matter receives form as the principle that accounts for the fact that a primary being is "a definite abiding something—flesh, bones, a syllable, or anything else." And, for the Stagirite, "to be a definite abiding something' is simply *to be*."[42] But simply "to be" is to be endowed with the property of potentiality. Statements about being are then statements about a particularity of being—what a thing is *being*. Aristotle concluded that if form is the essential definition of a thing epistemologically, this must be because it is what a thing is ontologically. The material component of its existence, when considered *per se* must, therefore, be nothing else but a principle of existence that is best understood as the capacity to become something particular.[43] This is what he meant by describing Prime Matter as a kind of ultimate substratum which has no definite characteristics of its own.[44] And a third principle—the immanent entelechy present because of the form—"guides" the process of enduring and becoming.

42. Owens, *Doctrine of Being,* 376 shows how the concept of form works its way throughout the "Metaphysics" so that by the close of book *Zeta* "Being is reduced to the formal cause, the primary instance of Entity within the sensible [material] thing" (Owens, *Doctrine of Being,* 376)

43. Copelston, *History of Philosophy,* 1:307n1. "One might also approach prime matter from this point of view. Take any material substance and think away all its definite characteristics, . . . color, shape, etc. You are ultimately left with a substratum that is absolutely formless, characterless, that cannot exist by itself, but is logically presupposed."

44. It might not be readily discernible that this is a coherent notion. Yet, if one takes Aristotle to mean by prime matter something like a principle of physics that is the physical basis for any and all existing particular entities, but it is itself not definable except as this underlying principle, his theory begins to sound much more like the discussions in contemporary particle physics. In the vast array of physical theories of the subatomic world, a kind of consensus might be achievable if one could say that, in some ultimate sense, all matter is in the final analysis the result of physical energy. Energy is a physical feature, but it is surely not conceivable as a particular thing. If Prime Matter is conceived, then, as a principle of physicality and extension materially that can be formed via some other principle that accounts for a particular arrangement of this physical field of energy (prime matter) into some specific manifestation called matter, then the purported absurdity that some see in the idea of Prime Matter might very well disappear. This would be consistent, arguably, with a popular theory among physicists today. See Bennett, *Study of Spinoza's Ethics,* 91–92, 106, for an argument that Spinoza held to a theory similar to this view of fields (of energy) as the ultimate constituents of the extended world.

HYLOMORPHISM AS COHERENT AND COMPELLING

Admittedly, the hylomorphic metaphysics of Aristotle's considerations about potency and actuality have been subjected to serious criticism by some of his commentators and by modern scientific principles.[45] Something as occult sounding as an *entelechy* in the biological (animal or plant) nature of a thing or a substantial form that literally shapes an entity in its physical appearance and orients that entity toward a particular function or end, has struck many as an unnecessary postulation if not an implausible construct. "Of the Aristotelian four causes, the formal cause has been the subject of the greatest attack. Modern science has, of course, always made use of material and efficient causality. And the notion of final causality, although criticized by the founders of modern science as well as contemporary scientists, has never been subject to the same kind of critique as the notion of substantial form."[46]

His conceptual framework of the formal cause is the background in Aristotle's thinking for his additional analysis in what we can call, in contemporary terms, his philosophy of mind. We shall have greater chance to defend hylomorphism as a philosophical attempt to describe the existence of the mind when we turn our attention to Aquinas's mind-body philosophy in chapter 4. But at this point we should note that for many of his interpreters, Aristotle's hylomorphism, when transferred to his anthropological theories becomes problematic, even incoherent for some. A thorough defense of Aristotelian hylomorphism is not possible in the limits of this book, but it should be noted that Aristotle's hylomorphism when thinking about mind in human beings does not imply an ontological dualism of the physical and the mental. Nor does it imply a theory of supervenience. And in chapter 4 it will be argued that on the most fundamental level neither does Aquinas's Aristotle-inspired hylomorphic doctrine imply the kind of dualism that troubles many philosophers.[47]

Bernard Williams represents one philosopher who appreciates and yet has big reservations about Aristotle's hylomorphism. For Williams hylomorphism gets especially troublesome when one begins to consider how to analyze human beings in light of the doctrine. When one allows that "soul" is the "form" of the individual human being, Williams gets worried. Thus, he critiques Aristotle's doctrine and contends:

45. Goyette, "Substantial Form," 520.

46. Goyette, "Substantial Form," 519.

47. This is not a denial that Thomas's doctrine of the survival of the soul after death is not a problem for contemporary philosophy or his doctrine of the resurrection. Rather, it is a claim that what Owen Flanagan has called the "manifest image" of the soul in its Cartesian perspective is not Aquinas's (cf. Flanagan, *Problem of the Soul*). Hence, the problems that beset dualism are not problems that Aquinas has to face, because his hylomorphism does not suggest the kind of dualistic view that Descartes holds. We shall have to address the "solution" to the issue of personal survival after death that Aquinas holds, as well as the idea of the resurrection, but those issues must be discussed in Aquinas studies in terms that go well beyond the familiar boundaries that Cartesian dualism suggest.

[It] earns its reputation as everybody's moderate metaphysics of mind, I believe, by in fact wobbling between two options. In one of them, soul does basically appear only adjectivally, and while the doctrine is, so far as I can see, formally consistent, it is only a polite form of materialism, which is cumbrous, misleading, and disposed to point in the wrong direction from the point of view of deeper theoretical understanding. It also has precisely this disadvantage of readily sliding into the other view, in which soul tries to transcend its adjectival status, and become the bearer of personal proper names: in that form, it yields us a notion of person which is a type-notion . . . . One last point. A strength of hylomorphism, particularly in its more materialistic version, is that it does point to human being as a basic concept in the philosophy of mind, and, consequently, in ethics.[48]

Williams's assessment of hylomorphism fails to see that there is a third way of understanding hylomorphism, especially when it comes to discussing it in terms of the traditional notion of the human soul (*anima*). The choices do not lie between "polite materialism," on the one hand, wherein the soul is simply a way of describing the human being as a "basic concept in philosophy of mind and ethics," and the soul-as-bearer-of-proper-names version of what *anima* entails, on the other. Given that Aristotle's hylomorphism uses the concept *being* primarily in a "verbal" sense of a metaphysical activity, and that the formal principle is a cause of being (*enabling* actual being), there is a third way, beyond the adjectival and substantive senses Williams describes to understand his use of the term *anima* (soul). The cogency and appropriateness of this third way is illumined for contemporary philosophy, I believe, by studies over the last seven decades in genetics and biochemistry, which addresses the "polite materialism" evaluation that Williams offers. (His concerns about soul becoming "the bearer of personal proper names" that yields "a notion of person which is a type-notion" will be addressed later in chapter 4.)

It is now acknowledged that the DNA molecule is a simply a medium of "communication" by which genetic *information* provides organization and functional life to the material stuff of living creatures. Such a discovery in contemporary science has tremendous implications for the heart of Aristotle's theorizing for us, because whatever *information* is it is not a material/physical reality. Recognizing this, the third way of understanding *soul* in hylomorphism would see this term as a descriptor which acknowledges that there is indeed some enabling "cause" at work responsible for the organizational complexity of an organism. This is distinct from the material that is organized and caused to be alive in the particular and specific way that the organism is, just as the information carried by the DNA molecule is not the material constituents of that material molecule. Far from being a courteous materialism, especially when applied to human beings, hylomorphism is Aristotle's recognition that something other than materialistic explanations are necessary for understanding complex life.

48. Williams, "Hylomorphism," 218–19.

Anticipating modern scientific discovery and explanations, hylomorphism is Aristotle's attempt to name the process that is inherently involved in the material world and hence recognizable and describable, but that is not a material cause strictly speaking. Soul names how a human being, as a material creature, is organized (formed) materially into the biologically unique entity that a human being is. (By unique I simply mean having species differences that include rationality.)

To further the comparison, we can say that contemporary science—physics, chemistry, and biology—raises questions about the nature of the relationship between the material entities that populate the universe and the energy or forces that enable them to be what they are. In physics, the "Big Bang Theory" implies that at the beginning of the universe an energy of some kind was unleashed that continues to produce all the forces that then enables material entities (atoms, molecules . . . stars, planets, living beings, and humans) to form.[49] In quantum mechanics the distinction between particles (matter) and waves (energy) is blurred, when one begins to perform calculations and observe phenomena. The question, however, is whether the quantum world can explain the rest of reality. There is good reason to take seriously a hylomorphic understanding of reality even when one takes the quantum realm into account. Robert Koons notes, "A quantum [per the Copenhagen interpretation] doesn't typically have any position or momentum at all . . . ; it has merely the *potential* to interact with macroscopic systems *as if* it had some definite position or momentum . . . at the moment of the interaction. Thus, the quantum world (so understood) can be neither metaphysically fundamental nor a complete basis for the macroscopic world."[50] More directly to our current study, biologically, the discovery of DNA as an "information" bearing molecule enables and requires that one distinguish between the matter that is the molecule, including its chemical compounds, and the *information* that is contained within that chemistry and that molecule. It is just begging the question, it seems to me, simply to posit that the information being conveyed is simply the material properties that are doing the conveying of the code that organizes a particular being to be the kind of being it is. The DNA molecules of all living entities are all similar materially

49. By this "energy" I am not positing the existence of God, but rather observing what physicists themselves have concluded. Something precedes matter, at least as we conceive it. And the forces that originally begin to draw the material universe into a cohesive and coherent organization are themselves describable as physically measurable, but not strictly quantifiable in material or extended terms. In fact many theories of the "force" that preceded the bang acknowledge that the current laws of the universe do not apply prior to the bang. Those particular physical laws do not account for themselves. See Zukav, *Dancing Wu Li Masters* for a clear discussion on the level of a nonexpert regarding this way of looking at the physics of the universe.

50. Koons, "Against Emergent Individualism," 389. "Hylomorphism offers a ready answer to this puzzle. The microscopic constituents of macroscopic objects have (at the level of actuality) only an indirect relation to space and time: they are located (roughly) somewhere at a time only *qua* constituents of some fundamental, micro- or mesoscopic substance (in the Aristotelian sense)" (Koons, "Against Emergent Individualism," 389). Cf. Koons, "Multi-Sacle Realism and Ontological Escalation" and Koons, "Forms Are Not Structures."

but convey remarkably different "instructions" and enable profoundly different life forms, because of the difference in information that they convey.[51] The difference, in other words, between biological beings is not simply a material or even a chemical or physical difference. Nancy Pearcey argues a position very similar to the one I am suggesting where she observes, "Encoded messages are independent of the physical medium used to store and transmit them. If we knew how to translate the message in a DNA molecule, we could write it out using ink or crayon or electronic impulses from a keyboard. We could even take a stick and write it in the sand—all without affecting its meaning."[52]

What Pearcey observes about the material medium not *affecting* the meaning of the DNA "message" is true unless one thinks that the information conveyed by the amino acids and proteins does not carry "instructions" that cells and lesser building blocks are determined by. This would not, however, seem to be consistent with what a growing number of scientists have to say at present about DNA.[53] Genetic science seems to be driving us to the point that we not only have to contend that the material medium not only does not *affect* the meaning of the "message," but neither does it *effect* the "message" in the particular instance of any specific biological creature. The difference between the message and the medium suggests that the idea of a "hylomorphic" interplay between the *matter* of a living organism and its cellular structure information that the DNA molecule carries and communicates to the cellular operations of a living entity is not far afield. Genetic in*form*ation seems quite analogous to Aristotle's *form,* as it organizes the matter that becomes the material being whose existence expresses a particular shape, function, actual powers, and potentialities in a concrete specific and incommunicable entity. Robert Sokolowski argues for the import of this, as well: "it is the plant or animal form that encodes itself in the DNA, and that the form is what the DNA serves to communicate. The form is both speaker and message in DNA."[54] John Goyette agrees with this conclusion.

> . . . the information contained in the genetic material is a kind of expression of the form that is analogous to human speech and serves as a kind of intermediary between form and matter. This may seem somewhat farfetched, but it is worth noting that Aristotle frequently refers to a thing's form as its *logos*— speech, formula, definition. When Aristotle calls the form a *logos* he is not simply referring to the form as it exists in the mind of the knower; rather, he is indicating that human speech is itself a reflection of the intelligibility of the form that is in the matter . . . . the discovery of DNA lends greater credibility

51. The DNA information is not the source of the life, however, because the information is of no use except in the living processes that utilize them. This will be explored in the final chapter.

52. Pearcey, "DNA," 13–14. Pearcey's way of phrasing is loaded, as the concept of message might imply a message-sender. Also, see Meyer, *Signature in the Cell,* 461–64.

53. For instance, Collins, *Language of God.*

54. Sokolowski, "Formal and Material Causality in Science," 64.

to Aristotle's notion of form by showing that it is not merely a projection of the human mind . . . . To the extent, then, that contemporary science has shown that DNA is a "genetic code" or "blueprint," for a living organism, it reveals the inadequacy of a purely mechanical explanation of life and seems to point instead towards the Aristotelian notion of substantial form.[55]

Materialistic presuppositions, with their tendency toward a mechanistic explanation of existence, cannot reduce biological reality down to causes that are simply material and efficient. John Peterson notes the difficulties faced by all reductionism that would too hastily dismiss the complexity involved in the existence of the material universe. He helpfully critiques any theories that decry the necessity to posit some dynamic interplay of forces—some material and some nonmaterial—to account for the physical world. His argument can assist us to gain appreciation for Aristotle's attempt to describe the complexity of the world. Peterson observes that reduction of any kind is a "mistake in logic," which cannot be avoided by any sort of monistic reductionism in the realm of physics or metaphysics.

> Materialists say that all is matter, idealists say that all is mind, and neutral monists say that matter and mind are appearances of some more basic stuff into the definition of which neither matter nor mind enters. But any philosopher who says that all is G, regardless of what G stands for, identifies G with the highest genus. Otherwise, he says that G falls under a wider genus, H. And then he countenances that possibility that H has some species besides G. . . . Put generally, if it is true that all is G then all difference within G must be due to something besides G. No genus explains its own differences, because difference is outside the definition of genus and anything that is implied by genus. No sooner, then, do philosophers who say that all is G recognize difference in their world than they admit features about the world that fall outside of G.[56]

Reductionism is, by Peterson's lights, an equal opportunity fallacy. Materialists cannot be nominalists in their explanation of difference in the world, without positing that something (a knower that discriminates about matter) is also present in the world. "Then they are dualists and not materialists." Similarly, Idealists cannot explain difference simply by mind, "otherwise differences in mind explain differences in mind"; but this conclusion must allow for difference to be part of the purportedly unified and totalizing genus, mind. But if they suggest that something else (matter) explains differences among mental things, they are admitting something besides mind. "They then abandon idealism in favor of dualism." In like manner neutral monists fail "to have their cake and eat it, too." While philosophers like James and (the early) Russell might remonstrate that their monism allows for the diverse appearances of our experience to

---

55. Goyette, "Substantial Form," 528.

56. Peterson, "Reductionism in Metaphysics," 301–2.

be grounded in neutral being, rather than matter or mental naming, Peterson retorts that the difference they might endeavor to argue for really makes no difference.

> If the various appearances have a foundation in reality, then neutral being is no bare identity but itself contains *differences*, quite apart from any differences that are introduced by us. But since difference is not due to genus, it follows that some *real thing* besides neutral being causes these differences within neutral being. And then neutral monism [as with materialism and idealism] fails again.[57]

Contemporary philosophy needs something like hylomorphism for our thinking about the complexity of the material world in general and human nature specifically, even if that doctrine haunts us with an idea that Williams finds troubling. Positing soul and body hylomorphism in human beings and then seeing what it helps us account for phenomenologically is not an unreasonable idea, because it provides an (admittedly ancient) description of the dynamic interplay of "causes" that must be a part of every living being. As the brief discussion of DNA and its information offered above shows, formal causes and material causes are both necessary.

But what about the other of Williams' concerns, namely the potential in hylomorphism for the soul to become the bearer of personal properties? The interpretation of Aquinas's mind-body metaphysics, offered in chapter 4, will go a long way toward addressing this question. At this point, however, we can make a preliminary observation. On Aristotelian and even Thomistic terms, the soul as an analytical and metaphysical concept, when understood properly as a principle that enables a primary being/substance to exist qua human, does not necessarily entail that the soul strictly speaking is itself a bearer of personal properties. It might, of course, be called such in a *highly* qualified way, as Aquinas does when he says that the entire soul is named by the highest "act" of which it is capable (which would be rational self-consciousness). The soul, as the informing, life-instantiating and organization producing information that enables the existence of the human composite (the person who is soul and body together), could be conceived loosely by the personal names and properties of the person (the human composite) whose specific living existence is made possible by the soul's formative influence on the human body. However, if the soul is, instead, conceived as the formal cause (the "information" and life-giving process) that makes a human being human, then the comparison offered above to DNA helps us begin to quell some fears that Williams and others might have. It is the person whose existence is enabled by the soul who becomes the bearer of personal names and properties. There is a self that is enabled to *be* by the organizing principle of the soul, but the self or person, strictly speaking" is categorically distinct from the soul that makes the human being's personal life possible. So, the property-bearing person or self is not exactly synonymous with the soul that precedes the self's existence, even if one might, speaking broadly, utilize the term soul in a personally property-bearing sense, given that the

---

57. Peterson, "Reductionism in Metaphysics," 303–4.

existence of the self is only possible because of the *informing* power of the soul. (Just as the human body is only the kind of body it is because of the same informing power.) Aquinas, who saw the issue of personhood more clearly than Aristotle, would have no problem allowing for this usage. However, he would insist that to speak this way is not to speak of the soul proper. Hence, he says, "the person knows, not the soul."

SUMMARY

To summarize Aristotle's intellectual motivations that have been discussed above, we can observe that in his estimation the nature of change and identity across change necessitates the doctrine of form and matter. Without the reality of the relationship between form as the locus of actuality and matter as the ontic seat of potentiality, one could only be left with the absurdity that all ordinary particular things had arisen from nothing. Furthermore, in his mind, since these ways of being (form and matter) are through analysis distinct from each other, one ought to, for the sake of the most adequate explanation, conceive of them as discrete principles. But both are required to give an adequate account of how concrete particular things exist. In an Aristotelian metaphysics of hylomorphism, every individual primary being is analyzable only and necessarily as a composite being—existing as a result of the material stuff that makes it up and the form that accounts for the particular arrangement of the material stuff. "The composite Being is not just the sum of its material parts. The form cannot be conceived as just another material part."[58] This is not just an ancient way of conceiving things, but as modern research into the nature of and process of genetically informed life shows, it is quite adequate even for contemporary thought.

58. Owens, *Doctrine of Being*, 376.

3

Aquinas's Version of Hylomorphism

THE INFLUENCE OF ARISTOTLE's thought on Aquinas's philosophical theology is well-established. However, the extent to which Aristotle's philosophy is a "source," rather than a mere backdrop, for the latter's own philosophy is debated.[1] While it is beyond the scope of this project to engage the scholarly debate as to the best way to understand Aristotle's contribution to Aquinas's thought, it is impossible to ignore the fact that the reintroduction of Aristotle to medieval Christian Europe was a profoundly significant development. As with many Christian theologians of the Middle Ages, Thomas considered himself to be interpreting and developing further the philosophical insights of Aristotle. Evaluating this expansionist/developmental agenda of Aquinas shows, while engaging Aristotle's metaphysics and using it as a springboard, he does produce a theory of hylomorphism that is distinguishable from his peripatetic tutor. Understanding him at this point of distinction is critical for understanding how to read and interpret, as we will in chapter 4, the specifics of the Angelic Doctor's doctrine of mind and body identity. We now turn our attention to Thomas's utilization of Aristotle and his development of the insights afforded by the latter's hylomorphism.

---

1. Etienne Gilson contends that Aristotle's philosophy is not technically a source for Aquinas, because Aristotle has no doctrine of the distinction between being and essence and, therefore, lacks a doctrine of Creation, which Aquinas defends and demonstrates. Furthermore, Aristotle's God is, in Gilson's view, not the Act of Being, as Aquinas describes God, but is, rather, merely the Act of Thought. Gilson, therefore, represents the thought that Aristotle was less a source and more of a template for Aquinas's philosophical project. However, Lawrence Dewan critiques this way of viewing Aristotle's import for Aquinas in "Aristotle as a Source for St. Thomas's Doctrine of *esse*." Dewan sees Aristotle's development of the distinction between potency and act as a very significant development upon which Thomas advanced. Dewan argues that just such a distinction allowed for a "causal hierarchy and a causality of being as being" (para. 74). This, in turn, allowed for "the distinction between *esse* and essence in later philosophy, St. Thomas's in particular," which was, in Dewan's view, "an appreciation of the implications of causal hierarchy for the doctrine of the primacy of being in act" (para. 75).

ESSENCES, IDENTITY, AND BEING

Analyzing the world in terms of the complementary distinctions between form/matter and act/potency as concepts necessary to provide an adequate account of the existence of individual primary being illuminates a distinction Aristotle did not note. Aquinas claims that behind these concepts there is an even more basic metaphysical distinction, i.e., the distinction and relationship between *esse* (Being, or the act/fact of being in existence) and an *ens* (a particular being) or any *essentia* (identifying essence).[2] This refinement in Aquinas's philosophy is based on his reasoning that the *act* of being (existing) in the world as some particularized essence and *being* that essence are different metaphysical realities and require distinct conceptual analysis. He builds on Aristotle's distinctions in *Categories*, wherein a substance is something in which other things inhere, as a starting point for his own views. Thomas reasons philosophically as follows: in the same way that *essentia* is a derivative of *esse*, the activity of existing is metaphysically different from the essence; and any essence that exists concretely depends upon something other than itself to explain and enable its existence. A primary being (ens) is our epistemic starting point and is the locus of the essence, but the *fact* (the actuality) of a primary being's existence is distinct from its essence, since the *ens* is a contingent thing. Further, an *essentia*—what a thing is—must be considered different analytically from the primary being (*ens*). We shall attend to the metaphysical distinction between *essentia* and *esse* in a subsequent section of this chapter. At this point we must look at how the notion of *essentia* as the act of *esse* informs Aquinas's metaphysical understanding of the nature of an individual, composite primary being (*ens*).

Ens, Aquinas notes, has two meanings in an Aristotelian framework: "Taken in one way it is divided by the ten categories [of Aristotle]; taken in the other way it signifies the truth of propositions" (*De Ente*, 1, 2). The difference between these two uses can be understood in the following way. The first notion defines for us two categories of things in our catalog of experiences, about which we may make predicate statements. Those taxonomies are, first, primary specific entities and, second, the features we encounter in those entities. "In the first way nothing can be called a being unless it is something positive in reality . . ." (*De Ente*, 1, 2). In this sense of *ens*, Aquinas is describing existence as extramental and the foundational necessary condition by which we know and name things that have attributes posited about them. The second way that *ens* is used is as a proposition, which is when we speak affirmatively about states of affairs which may or may not be or have in themselves any truly positive essence. In the first sense of *ens*, the act of seeing (having sight) is a "positive" feature in that it is an active power we encounter. Alternatively, we may speak (in the second sense) of blindness as a feature of our experience in the world as "being the case that."

---

2. The following analysis of Thomas's thought in *De Ente et Essentia* comes from Maurer, *On Being and Essence*. Although this is a relatively early work in Aquinas, he never moved fundamentally from the arguments set forth in this work in a systematic fashion.

However, our statement only names a state of privation of the act of seeing. Paradoxically, we can apply the term *ens* predicatively (in this second sense) to that which has no properties of its own. So, to say that the Rhythm and Blues musician Stevie Wonder is blind is to posit a true state of affairs since he does *lack* sight. We posit "the blindness of 'Stevie Wonder'" as a true aspect of our world. Many people, furthermore, are blind; hence, blindness can be called, in a way, a feature of the world. However, blindness as absence of sight is not an entity or reality (or a "being") except and only in the most qualified sense. Yet, we name it as "having existence," because it is present to us as a feature of the real condition of some primary beings, although really it is merely *not*-sight. The same could be said of all privative designations. Hence, Aquinas says, ". . . in the second sense [*ens* as propositional], anything can be called a being if an affirmative *proposition* can be formed about it, even though it is nothing positive in reality" (*De Ente*, 1, 2). So, conceiving something as an *ens*—as a predicable state or condition—need not involve an actual positive nature. *Essentiae*, on the other hand, can only be properly and adequately understood to have being in the first of the two above-described senses—it names something that positively exists (*De Ente, 1, 5*).[3] A privation has no *essentia*, therefore, but only derivatively "exists" as a lack.

Aquinas's reasoning is both semantic and analytic. The semantic assertion is about the meaning of *essentia* and how, as a derivative of the *esse*, it is related to the (also derivative) noun *ens*. A being (*ens*) is a concrete particular entity; and yet as something that positively exists, it does not entail necessarily the *fact* of its existence (*esse*) as a property of its identity, i.e., its actual existence is not a contained in its identity metaphysically. Furthermore, *essentia* names, Aquinas continues, not the concrete particular entity (*ens*) per se, but something *about* that concrete entity that constitutes the actual existing identity and nature of the primary being (*ens*). Essence does not entail the *thatness* of the primary being, only its *whatness*. Thomas's argument is that *ens* most properly names items that are present as either real *actual* entities or *conditions* of actual entities but can also be used as a kind of shorthand reference for true propositions about states of affairs that are in themselves only privations. *Essentia*, in the most precise sense, names items in our catalogues of experiences about which we may provide a positive description of their powers, properties, and potentialities that signify what they are. Again, neither of these concepts, as we consider their actual existence, explains how the *essentia* that is the *ens* has real *esse*. Without this qualification and distinction that *essentia* can only be used in the first sense of what it is to be (something positive), we might attempt to use it in the second sense and reify negations, which would be absurd, for Aquinas. Essence may, loosely speaking, name states of affairs that are in themselves ontological negations, but such states are not definable except derivatively as *not-being* something else. So, even privative states really exist in the world, but they are "real" only as an absence of some other active power, property or activity that is actually present in the world, e.g., blindness is simply *not*-sight.

3. Maurer, *On Being and Essence.*

Such semantic clarity serves epistemically and logically in Thomas's metaphysics to illuminate that *essence* in the strictest sense names the *whatness* of an entity that has positive existence and/or active power in the world, but he seems to mean more beyond purely nominal designation. When he considers the *essentia* of an *ens*, as Thomas E. Dillon says of Aquinas's argument in this section of *De Ente*, ". . . 'nature' is another name for the essence of a thing, since, as he explains, it is the essence of a thing which makes it intelligible. In short, then, essence is something that is *possessed* by all real beings and only real beings, and it is the principle of their intelligibility."[4] Aquinas's own argument is as follows:

> And so the Philosopher says in V *Metaphysicae* cap. 4 (1014b36) that every substance is a nature. But the term nature used in this way seems to signify the essence of a thing as it is ordered to the proper operation of the thing, for no thing is without its proper operation. The term quiddity, surely, is taken from the fact that this is what is signified by the definition. But the same thing is called essence [*essentia*] because the being [*ens*] has existence [*esse*] through it and in it. (*De Ente*, 1)

The last sentence above indicates the metaphysical import of *essentia*. Looking at the Latin text helps make it clear. Aquinas asserts: *Quiditatis uero nomen sumitur ex hoc quod per definitionem significatur. Sed **essentia** dicitur secundum quod per eam et in ea **ens** habet **esse**.* The relation between *essentia, ens* and *esse*, as well as *quiditatis* is a complex one in this passage. Here Aquinas is contending that the *quiditatis*—the incommunicable what-it-is-*ness*—of a specific, particular entity is the existent reality that is captured linguistically in its unique being and is synonymous with the *ens*, e.g., Socrates or the third bird on the telephone wire outside my window. This definite identity as a material thing is its essence. But *essentia*, for Aquinas, is more than merely an epistemic component of a true designation, because there must be some enabling and instantiating ontological principle of existence *by which* a particular being has its specific being as a definable and knowable contingent entity in our world. This means that *essentia*, by which we know something to be itself, also has a metaphysical priority beyond or "behind" the *ens*. Etienne Gilson reminds us that this does *not* entail, in Aquinas's metaphysics, that the essence is the *source* of the being of the thing under consideration. Aquinas's position is that essences are real principles of being present in the world as the organizing forces by means of which individual things are made particular beings as part of a species.[5]

> Thus in *Metaphysicae* V, com. 14, the Commentator explains the cited text from Aristotle by saying that being, in the first sense, is what signifies the *essence* of a thing. And since, as said above, being in this sense is divided into the ten categories, essence signifies something common to all natures *through*

4. Dillon, "Real Distinction," 121, my emphasis

5. See Gilson, *Christian Philosophy of St. Thomas Aquinas*, 448n30.

which the various beings are placed in the various genera and species, as humanity (human nature) is the essence of man, and so on (*De Ente*, 1).[6]

Because the primary, material beings of our experience are all specific in their essences, something must cause them to be particularized and individuated, he contends. Since material essences, by their material component, only have potentiality to become specified things through (as was argued in chapter 2) the nature of prime matter as pure receptivity, this means nothing about the essence of matter itself explains how it is organized into specific things. That something is the form of the thing, which is metaphysically distinct from the matter that is organized and formed. However, the full essence of all material beings must include the matter that is passively organized in the definition of the being, because only in combination with matter can the formal essence have *actual* existence. It may be described apart from matter as having "subsistence," since it is necessary as an organizing and informing cause of a thing's particular existence. But even though the form is the organizational force in matter that enables the primary being to exist as a material entity with a specific essence, the essence of the concrete particular being is the co-inherence of matter and form. Hence, the particular what-ness of a specific being (*ens*) is not merely a mental description (as nominalism would argue) imposed upon an entity by our minds which conceive of it as a particular essence. Since any *ens* can only have its being (*esse*) as a particular *essentia*, by Aquinas's theory, our minds recognize the essence of the thing that makes it what it is concretely, because its objective essence has been encountered by our senses and understood by our power of abstraction. In so doing, the human mind discovers that the form of the thing so actualized in matter is its necessary and essential determiner. And just as form in union with matter gives a thing an identifiable nature, the matter so formed particularizes its existence as a *quiddity*. The essence of an entity is this union, not merely the form that gives the purpose, function, and shape by which we can know it.[7]

The metaphysical significance given to the concept of essence is tied to Aquinas's contention, quoted above, that essence also entails the concept of the proper operation of a thing (*res*).[8] Since something beyond the material stuff of the complex organism

6. Emphasis mine.

7. His epistemological theory grows out of Aquinas's commitment to a fully hylomorphic metaphysics in which essences are part of the world of human experience, but only *in* the specific entities of our acquaintance.

8. On the difficulty of translating the Latin term *res*, which can be translated as "thing," "event," "business," "fact," "cause," or "property," see Haecker, *Vergil*, 131–32. He considers *res* to be one of the *Hertzworter*, heart-words, for the Latin tongue, in which is concentrated something of the genius of the language. *Res* must be considered a term of some ambiguity, almost a placeholder, but not necessarily indicating itself a metaphysical commitment as to the nature of the entity for which it holds a place. *Res* need not name items of our experience that we could think of in atomistic substantialist terms. This is especially important when considering Aquinas's account of the "participation" of all *ens* as things (*res*) in Being. The same can apply for Spinoza's usage in the light of his discussion of modes of substance.

itself must account for how it exists as what it is, Aquinas tells us that essence is "also called *form,* because it signifies the *determination* of each thing, as Avicenna says" (*De Ente,* 1).[9] He is using the term *form* here in a specialized way, namely as the whole nature or essence of the thing under consideration. This is not his usual way of speaking of form, but he is applying it much more broadly in this context, as we later will see. This is obvious, since Aquinas in the context of this portion of *De Ente* says that the term form can be utilized as a kind of synonym for essence, only because form signifies the determination (*certitudo*) of each thing, i.e., it speaks of the concrete specific, unique truth that can be predicated of a *res.*[10]

In chapter 2 of *De Ente,* however, he is unambiguous in his description. There he details that in composite substances form and matter are found together *as the essence* of the particular entity. Here he returns to his more careful, technical, and usual concept of form.

> But it cannot be said that either one of these [form or matter] is called the essence. That the matter alone of a thing is not its essence is evident, for through its essence a thing is knowable and fixed in its species and genus. But matter is not a principle of knowledge, and a thing is not placed in a genus or species through it but through that by which a thing is actual [specified in its existence]. *Neither can the form alone of a composite substance be called its essence,* though some want to assert this. It is evident from what has been said that the essence is what is signified through the definition of a thing. Now the definition of natural substances includes not only form but also matter; otherwise there would be no difference between definitions in physics [physical sciences] and in mathematics. Nor can it be said that the definition of a natural substance includes matter as something added to its essence, or as something outside its essence. This is the kind of definition proper to accidents; not having a perfect essence, their definition must include their subject, which is outside their genus. It is evident, therefore, that essence embraces both form and matter. (*De Ente,* 2 [1])[11]

A particularized entity, what he calls a natural substance, cannot be adequately defined without inclusion of the concrete physical existence that it has. The material component(s) of the entity is its natural substantiality, and hence inherent to its essence as an existing being. Aquinas is emphasizing that matter is essential to the definition of natural substances, even if matter's properties do not instantiate and organize

9. Note the similarity here to Spinoza's definition of "essence" in *Ethics* II, def. 2: "that without which the thing (*res*) can neither *be* nor be conceived, and, vice versa, that which cannot be or be conceived without the thing."

10. "*Certitudo.* The Arabic term which the mediaeval translator rendered [from Avincenna] by this Latin word has the meaning of perfection or complete determination. On the one hand it signifies the objective truth of a thing, on the other the precise and clear knowledge of it" (Goichon, *La Distinction de l'Essence et de l'Existence,* 34n7, as referenced in Maurer, *On Being and Essence,* 31n8).

11. Emphasis mine.

the specificity of being—the species and genus—of a thing (*res*). While matter is the necessary principle of physical, perceptible, and potentially measurable reality, it is not, Aristotle argued at length, a sufficient cause because nothing about matter shows that it is self-organizing or operation-giving. Therefore, the physical organization of a material entity must be enabled to have an operation proper to it by something distinct from the matter. It is not, however, Aristotle and Aquinas contend, existentially separable from it. Hence, the essence is the *composite* being.

When conceived of as this organization-giving property or cause of the material being that exists, form alone, absent the informed matter, cannot be the definitional essence of an individual material substance, because natural substances have as a part of their definition the material stuff which is organized by form. Form gives it a "proper operation," but since form's operation-granting power only exists in the fullest sense *in union* with the material stuff to which it informs an actual, specified physical existence, it does not itself have an operation per se. So, the essence of primary beings must involve matter and form, because only in matter does form exist as actualized, and an actualized form in matter is an essence in existence (*esse*). This means that matter needs form, but the form that "informs" is not strictly speaking the essence of a thing any more than matter. It is a more fundamental cause of specific existence, but the matter makes that specificity possible. "The essence, according to which a thing is called a being (*ens*), cannot be either the form alone or the matter alone, but both, though form alone is in its own way the cause of this being" (*De Ente*, 2 [3]).[12]

Essences exist because matter *and* form are co-inhering in, and therefore *as*, the primary being—the co-operational relationship of actualizing (the form) and receiving (the matter). This union in act causes the primary being or natural substance to be the particular thing it is by giving it a proper and unified operation in its existence.[13] To speak of an *ens* having its proper operation "in actuality" does not mean that an

12. The Latin text reads: Quia esse substantiae compositae non est tantum formae nequetantum materiae, sed ipsius compositi; *essentia* autem est secundumquam res esse dicitur: unde oportet ut essentia qua res denominator *ens* non tantum *sit forma, neque tantum materia, sed utrumque*, quamuis huiusmodi esse suo modo sola forma sit causa.

13. Here we should recall the "four causes" of Aristotelian metaphysics. These "causes" are not causes in the sense that we often think of them in the analysis of cause and effect. Rather, the "causes" are principles necessary to describe and account for the actual existence of a particular being or entity. The formal and material "causes" are the analytically necessary descriptions of the aspects of the entity's own being. Of course, the "efficient cause" is Aristotle's recognition—and Aquinas after him—that substances are dependent upon other substances for their own existence as embodied forms in the physical world. The "final cause" points to, as is well known, Aristotle's convictions about the teleological way the substances function. While a full-blown analysis of Aristotle's final cause is not possible here, it can be observed that final causality does not need to entail a commitment to any sort of theological assessment about the origins of substances nor of the universe itself. (Aristotle's "Unmoved Mover" is not a creator.) Instead, the final cause can be considered in terms of the ends toward which entities tend in sustaining their existence and that the idea of a species's essence has within it its own particular strivings for survival and flourishing. This would be an analytical distinction that Aristotelian metaphysics could make between the formal cause as instantiating and the final cause as sustaining in accounting for the existence of any natural substance.

"essence" ceases to be usable as a truthful *predication* of a being without regard to its concrete existence. Hence, essence could be said to have a proper function merely *in concept*, as well, as e.g., when we discuss the species concept "horse" in isolation from actual horses.[14] This means that *universals* or secondary substances can be considered as having essence, so long as we remember that our abstracted concepts are dependent upon the actual entities (primary beings) that we encounter. Things that have similarities of function, shape, and potentialities fall under the *concept* of a same universal essence. The essence we name in all things that share such similarities is not only nominal, because some principle must be the cause of the similarities particular entities share. *We* must, therefore, consider more precisely the roles matter and form play in this respect, for Aquinas.

MATERIA SIGNATUM/DESIGNATUM

Speaking of a particular being's essence as the union of matter and form, Aquinas refers to it as a composite being. These principles, in Aquinas's theory, are what Copleston describes as "the primary co-constituents of a material thing."[15] They are the irreducible *principia entis* (principles of actual existence) required to account for the existence of any individualized entity. Neither form nor matter in general (primary matter) are existing "substances" in the strict sense. The formal (forming) element and the material element in an entity are necessary elements of an entity, but as we have noted they do not in isolation from each other define or determine the essence of the entity so described. For example, to be Socrates is to be something more than either the specific human body in question or to be generically human. To be Socrates is to be a *particular* human body "informed" by the substantial form of rational soul. Socrates's particular essence is, as Aquinas views it, not some idealistic essential nature (as a Platonic metaphysics might have to argue) nor merely materialistic. He is a particularized essence as a material entity, who is more than simply the physical elements of his existence. Matter is essential to the definition of Socrates, as is a *substantial form* that causes the physical Socrates to be the kind of thing that he is—a human being. Informed by the substantial form of human rational soul, the matter makes Socrates an individualized, specific, and incommunicable human being. The concept substantial form, for Thomistic thought, takes the place of the concept of immanent entelechy that one finds in Aristotle's terminology. The substantial form is the particularizing information that gives to any being its structure, functional potentialities, and the particular operations that define its material existence. It also instantiates in material

14. Kant's statement that "existence" adds nothing to the concept of 100 thalers, is true when thinking about the essence of 100 thalers solely *qua* definition. However, an existent 100 thalers is quite distinct from the concept of 100 thalers, if one is engaged in the activity of paying a bill.

15. Copleston, *Thomas Aquinas*, 89n1.

beings a drive toward a telos specific to it; this drive causes a "striving" to maintain its existence and to develop the fullness of its essence.

The matter that is informed in a particular entity, Aquinas further reasoned, cannot be, therefore, prime matter (*materia prima*), as Aristotle claimed. Aquinas perceived that since *material prima* is not an existent thing per se, but is purely passive and completely and only potentiality, it does not qualify as being able to be qua *prime* matter part of an entity's essence. If prime matter is truly and only in potentiality to become something specific, then it does not exist strictly speaking. Its reality must be posited as a substrate for the concrete existence of specific material entities, but only existing material things are the primary beings that are the essences of our experience. As Aquinas puts it, "matter cannot be said to be [*esse*]; it is the substance [the particular, essential thing] itself which exists."[16]

This has important implications for Aquinas's ideas about the nature of matter as the physical stuff out of which things are composed. Having ruled out prime matter as a candidate for individuation of substances because it is only and purely the potential to become something specific, he introduces a second concept *designated matter* as the immediate "principle of individuation" for physical entities.[17] In *De Ente*, he says, "matter is the principle of individuation," but it must be realized "that the matter . . . is not just any matter but only designated matter." Admittedly, this is a bit confusing. By designated matter Aquinas means "that which is considered under determined dimensions" (*De Ente*, 2 [4]). In order to grasp his meaning, we must be clear about what he does not mean. He does not envision a dualism that our world participates in of pure form versus pure matter. This, in fact, is precisely what he does not want to posit. He is clear in *De Ente* that the *essentia* of an *ens* as a physical particular is the identity of a being that is informed matter or materialized form. But his way of articulating this dipolar operation "must not be taken to mean that the form [of an *ens*] existed with some kind of universal status before the tree came into existence."[18] The universality of the form that beings of a similarly definable nature share, while real, is not existent apart from the individual primary being to which the form applies. This

---

16. Aquinas, *Summa contra Gentiles*, 2, 54. A passage from his early writings illustrates Aquinas's thought on this point, which never substantially changed. "Note that although [first] matter in its nature is *neither* formed nor formless (as bronze in its nature is neither shaped nor shapeless, *it never exists stripped of form and lack of form*, but sometimes takes on one form and sometimes another. By itself it can never exist for it has no form of its own and so—because actual existence comes with forms—matter *by itself* never exists actually but only potentially. Nothing actually existent then can be called first matter" (emphasis mine). All quotations in this work from *Summa contra Gentiles* are taken from the translation at The Jacques Maritain Center, http://www.nd.edu/Departments/Maritain/etext/gc4_81.htm.

17. One qualification is important. For Aquinas, the "heavenly bodies" were not made of the same kind of matter as the physical bodies of earth. Things of which the matter is the same are mutually interchangeable and mutually active or passive, as is said (*De Gener.* i, text. 50). But heavenly and earthly bodies do not act upon each other mutually. Therefore, their matter is not the same.

18. Copleston, *Thomas Aquinas*, 95.

analytical proposition significantly shapes Aquinas's epistemology in *Summa Theologiae* in which the concept of abstraction plays a central role.

> The object of every sense faculty is a form existing in corporeal matter, and so, since this sort of matter is the principle of individuation, *all the faculties of the sense part of man know only particulars* .... it is proper for [the human intellectual capacity] to know *forms which, in fact exist individually in corporeal mater*, yet not precisely as existing in such or such individuated matter. Now to know something which in fact exists in individuated matter, but not as existing in such or such matter is to abstract a form from individual matter, represented by sense images. Thus we have to say that our intellect understands material things *by abstraction* from sense images ....
>
> I claim that whatever pertains to the definition [*rationem*] of any species of material reality, for instance stone or man or horse, can be considered without individuating conditions which are no part of the definition of the species. And this is what I mean *by abstracting* the universal from the particular ....
> (*Summa,* Ia 85, reply and ad 1)

While he does not suggest a dualistic view of things, Aquinas nonetheless believes that the two *principia entis* (principles of being) are distinct, when considered as metaphysical antecedents necessary to account for the *singular and unified* existence of a primary being. So, a second clarification is needed for understanding Aquinas. The universal forms as secondary substances that define and determine *species* do have an extra-mental, real existence (contra nominalism). When our intellects abstract out of the data presented from the particulars in the field of sensory experience, because our minds are comprised of two powers—one passive (sensory experience) the other active (reflection upon the sensory data)—we recognize that matter and form are both real and distinct as principles. Based upon this conviction about the human mind, Aquinas seems to want to assert something like the following about the relationship between form and matter in the essence of particular beings: we recognize them by way of rational abstraction to be necessarily distinct as determining principles but not ontologically independent. We do not create the concepts; rather we recognize their reality. This is reflected in his description of what it means to be mistaken or have a false understanding regarding the relationship between form and matter.

> Therefore when it is said that that understanding is false which understands a thing other than as it is, the statement is true if 'other than' refers to the thing understood. For if the understanding is false whenever one understands a thing to be other than it is; hence *the understanding would be false if one should abstract the species of stone from matter that he would understand it to exist apart from matter, as Plato held.* The proposition would not be true if 'other than' were taken as referring to the one understanding. For there is not falsity if the mode of understanding in the one who understands is different from the mode of existing in the thing—a thing understood is in the one

who understands in an immaterial way, according to the mode of the intellect, and not in a material way, according to the mode of material reality. (*Summa Theologicae*, 1a, 85, ad 1)

With this in mind, we see clearer what Aquinas means in *De Ente* when he says that the principle that makes an *ens* to be an individual is designated matter or matter "considered under determined dimensions" (*De Ente* 2 [4.]). To grasp more clearly Aquinas's terminology here, we can note the way his technical metaphysical language changes in regard to designated matter. Armand Maurer observes that while Aquinas uses the word 'determined' to qualify 'matter,' following Avicenna in *De Ente*, he adopts a different concept in later works (*In II Sentences.*, d, q. 1, a. 4 and *In Boethius de Trinitate*, IV, 2, ad 3) written shortly after *De Ente*. In these works, he chooses Averroes' concept 'undetermined dimensions' over the idea of 'determined matter' to account for individuation.[19] The difference in these two descriptions seems to be a semantic clarification that does not change Aquinas's fundamental position in *De Ente* but does enhance it. The concept "undetermined" allowed Aquinas to acknowledge that matter could be designated (in the sense of being specific and particular, rather than prime matter in general) without needing to be limited to a specific quantity or arrangement in its dimensions. One of the reasons for this change would seem to be the recognition that growth and change in primary substances entail a change in dimensions. Aquinas would not want to deny continuity of the primary substance's *essentia* as an individual once its dimensions had changed, as in the growth of a baby into an adult or a seedling into a giant redwood.

Aquinas's analysis on this matter clarifies how, if matter is truly a part of the essence of, say, Socrates, then the matter of which we speak has to be a specifically designated material organization that, nonetheless, is not ontologically determined in scope. Socrates' physical existence has definite boundedness at each stage, even as that existence grows larger or diminishes in relation to other things around it. Furthermore, if matter is essential to Socrates' identity as a living, breathing, and rational *ens*, then the material that Socrates is as a rational and living being must itself be uniquely identified with Socrates. It is a part of his *essentia* which delineates the extent of his spatial existence. Aquinas seems to be thinking that if it one posits prime matter generically, the distinction between the material Socrates and other material humans becomes unclear or, at least accidental and not a matter of substantial identity. Thus, even the material stuff that makes Socrates uniquely Socrates must be differentiable from all other material beings, not in kind, but extent and arrangement, if Socrates *is*, in fact, a specific "what," or a *quiditas*. Socrates does not have a specific *kind* of matter but has the same material substrate of other material things, since it is after all out of prime matter that designated, undetermined matter arises. But, in Aquinas's hylomorphism, the material stuff which is Socrates is unique to him, so the Athenian

---

19. Cf. Maurer, *On Being and Essence*, 37n12.

philosopher must have "this particular bone and this particular flesh" as part of his essence. (The material body that is him would be Socrates and not Xenophon.) True and specific physical identity for primary beings is a metaphysical principle.[20]

More fundamentally, however, Aquinas's emphasis on signified or designated matter seems to develop in his metaphysics because he somewhat deviates from Aristotle concerning the nature of matter and its relationship to form. The departure is not radical but is a further development that makes the distinction between the two more fully apparent. Designated matter is the only kind of matter that we can really experience and know, because only designated matter actually exists. More fully than Aristotle spelled out, Aquinas clearly taught that prime matter is purely a logically necessary metaphysical conclusion we draw and posit through the process he calls "precision" or abstraction; however, it does not (indeed cannot) exist as a particularized entity. What actually exist are material particulars and the informed matter that makes them up.[21] In *Boethius de Trinitate*, Aquinas asserts that "form is not individuated in that it is received in matter, but only in that it is received in *this* or *that* distinct matter, and determined to *here* and *now*."[22] The notions here and now are Aquinas's ways of referring to the individual, primary being.

They indicate "*hæc caro et ossa*." And they are only possible by reason of (informed) matter, the ground of divisibility and location in space. Still, it must be noted that "*materia signata quantitate*" is not to be understood as primordial matter having an aptitude towards fixed and invariable dimensions. The determined dimensions that are found in the existing subject are to be attributed, St. Thomas teaches, to matter as "individuated by *indeterminate dimensions preunderstood* in it.[23]

This Thomistic distinction, while perhaps not lost on Aristotle, is one that is no doubt rooted in the Christian doctrine of creation *ex nihilo*. Matter was eternal, in Aristotle's view, and so was conceived as the uncaused and independent substance that is the foundation of all physical reality, which of course was an assumption rooted in the long tradition of Greek philosophy. Aquinas, on the other hand, could not embrace this conceptually for theological, as well as philosophical, reasons. In the *Summa*

20. This has important implications for the question of personal identity in Aquinas's hylomorphism, especially regarding human individuality.

21. At this, one might call to mind Spinoza's later claim that what exists are Substance and its Modes. The Attributes (Thought and Extension) do not exist. While this point of Spinoza's philosophy is hotly contested by his interpreters, the view that Extension as an Attribute of Substance does not exist except in its Modes has real resonance (possibly) with Aquinas's view of Prime Matter, i.e., that it is a proper and necessary abstraction from nature of the world, but it does not exist, because no matter ever exists unformed in some way.

22. Aquinas, *Boetheius de Trinitate* Q. iv, a. 1. Aveling, "Matter," para. 12, my emphasis. (Boeth. de Trin.," Q. iv, a. 2; "De Nat. Mat.," vii.)

23. Aquinas, *Boetheius de Trinitate*, Q. iv, a. 1. The concept of "preunderstood" means, for Aquinas, something like the observation that certain material elements are predisposed to become part of specific kinds of organisms. For instance, carbon, rather than silicone, is a designated kind of matter that is appropriate for organismic life on our planet.

Theologiae, I a, Q 66, a 1, he contends that prime matter was created together with the principle of form to be the metaphysical constituents of concrete entities that God would create. Prime matter, therefore, theologically requires a Creator. Philosophically, on the other hand, it is in some sense merely conceptual for explaining things. Therefore, its actual metaphysical status is murky, for Thomas. Because it is nothing particular until something else makes it an actual physical entity, prime matter is not a strong candidate for real existence. Thomas seems to be saying that there must be some principle that unifies physical reality by being able to become the particular physical designated matter that things are made of, but that principle is not a concrete reality in itself, for if it were there would be no true individuation between things, only "accidental" arrangements of the primal principle. Therefore, each material entity that receives form would have as its material constituent not prime matter but a specific kind of matter appropriate (designated matter) for the essence that it would be. This idea of appropriateness is what Aquinas means by "preunderstood." An example might be, that biological life could be made through the combination of specific forms, say the form of an owl, with carbon as a basic prefigured material component, but not silicone.[24]

All our understanding, according to Aquinas's epistemology, begins with the real concrete particular beings which undergo change (even continual changes) in the expression of their essential existence. As an explanation for this, he infers the coexistence and coinherence of matter and form—the determinable and determining—as the essence of any entity. The conception of designated matter as the physical principle of material elements, while arising from prime matter as the physical (or extended) stuff that is the necessary principle for materiality in general, is an irreplaceable one, even though we may, as Aquinas does in *De Ente,* 2 [11], "prescind"[25] from the existential situation of real entities in our endeavor to analyze their composite existence. By so doing, we "bracket" the material particularity of the entity under consideration and strip matter, by abstraction, from this or that determination. In other words, we may by analysis consider the material element apart from all its determinations. However,

24. When one thinks of the "Big Bang Theory" of the origins of the universe, one recalls that scientists tell us that almost immediately following the "bang" the stuff that was produced in the explosive force began to coalesce into the basic building blocks (prefigured matter?) of the universe. However, there is some basic principle of material existence that underlies as an antecedent reality all these basic building blocks. The same can be said when one turns his attention to quantum theory and the atomic physics. Quarks and fields and strings are (theoretically, at least) components that are in some sense physical but are not exactly anything in particular. Hence, their existence is perhaps a necessary component in the theories, but of indeterminate nature. Cf. Koons, "Multi-Scale Realism and Ontological Escalation."

25. The term translated in the referenced passage as 'precision' is the Latin *praecisio.* Maurer comments on the significance of this term in Aquinas: "[*Praecisio*] Precision is a mode of abstraction by which we cut off or exclude something from a notion. Abstraction is the consideration of something without either including or excluding from its notion characteristics joined to it in reality" (Maurer, *On Being and Essence,* 39n15).

if we achieve abstract consideration of matter apart from that formed material specificity by which we know it, then there is, in Aquinas's view, nothing about which we could be speaking, because have we stripped it mentally of the potentiality of definiteness in union with form. Hence, for him, even prime matter exists only insofar as it is *essentially* the potential to be concrete physical ordinary particulars.[26] Francis Aveling has noted regarding Aquinas's doctrine of matter:

> Matter is neither realizable nor thinkable without its correlative. The proper object of intelligence, and likewise the subject of being, is *Ens, Verum*. Hence St. Thomas teaches further that primordial matter is "a substantial reality" (i.e., a reality reductively belonging to the category of substance), "potential towards all forms, and, under the action of a fit and proportioned efficient cause, determinable to any species of corporeal substance" (In VII Met., sect. 2); and, again: "It is never stripped of form and privation; now it is under one form now under another. Of itself it can never exist" (De Princip. Natur.). What has been said may appear to deny to matter the reality that is predicated of it. This is not the case. As the determinable element in corporeal substance it must have a reality that is not that of the determining form. The mind by abstraction may consider it as potential to any form but can never overstep the limit of its potentiality as inexistent (cf. Aristotle's *ti enyparchontos* (Phys., iii, 194b, 16) and realized in bodies without finding itself contemplating absolute nothingness. Of itself matter can never exist, and consequently of itself it can never be thought.[27]

Because prime matter is not in itself truly existent, *materia signata* has tremendous metaphysical significance for Aquinas. His view of the ontological particularity and identity of primary substances is made clearer when we consider how he deals with the idea of, what he calls, species form in relation to the individual. "It is clear," Aquinas says, "that the difference between the essence of Socrates and the essence of man lies solely in what is designated and not designated" (*De Ente* 2 [5]). This concept is rooted in the view that all things that exist in the realm of sensible objects are, by definition, "informed" material. However, since a particular kind of form is what makes Socrates to be a particular man in the designated matter that is appropriate for the existence of his specific human body, Socrates the individual shares something with all other human beings. A metaphysical antecedent exists upon which all people as particular human essences are dependent in their organized and operationally endowed physical lives. In this all are "identical" in kind. Individuality of human persons,

---

26. Aquinas, *De Princip. Naturæ*, i, 4. Prime Matter, Aquinas teaches in this treatise, "*has its being by reason of that which comes to it,* since in itself it has incomplete, or rather no being at all." Emphasis mine. So, the essence of Prime Matter is to become specific individual material things, but this very essence implied an identity, in his analysis. Therefore, one is justified to say that Prime Matter has a nature, but one of pure potentiality. This analysis allowed him to square, he thought, Aristotle's doctrine with his Christian commitments to the doctrine of God as Creator of all things.

27. Aveling, "Matter," para. 4.

therefore, requires that designated matter be recognized as that which differentiates between members of the human species. While species form is a real feature of the world that our minds recognize, no species is an existent reality in the fullest sense (that is reserved for individuals). Nonetheless, the concept that we have of individuals as members of a class of entities that share certain features is a true concept of the real world and not simply a nominal classification. Even if the concept species has no specifically independent existence beyond its individual members, it exists in the mind only because the human intellect has discovered via abstraction a real feature of being.[28] The mind does not make things out of nothing.

Socrates, for instance, is the informed, designated, yet undetermined, matter that one could point to and name "Socrates," but Socrates is also a specific kind of thing as Socrates. That he is a member of a kind is a defining aspect of his individuality. The thing that makes him to be the *quiddity* that is Socrates is the form of humanity, the rational form, or the form that instantiates rationality. This form establishes and marks the difference between human beings and other beings. "Humanity is a term signifying a certain form, called the [*forma totius*] form of the whole [species]" (*De Ente* 2 [9]). Individually, however, the material aspect of the identity of Socrates specifically as the human being 'Socrates' includes a specific arrangement of matter and a particularized material organized organism—"this flesh and bones."[29] Recognizing the necessity for designated matter establishes, for Aquinas, a certainty that no *ens* (being) can share its particular *essentia* (essential identity) *qua ens* with any other *ens*, not even one that has the exact same *forma totius*. Socrates essence, then, is the form of humanity *and* the designated matter he is.

Aquinas engages in *bracketing* the question of Socrates's particular physical existence in order to describe how Socrates could share features of existence with other entities of his kind, even though he is a distinct, incommunicable *quiditas* as Socrates the human being. Performing this act of bracketing, Aquinas says we can acknowledge the species form that is the nature of humanness arranging the designated matter that *is* Socrates, making it to be a man instead of his being some other *kind* of entity. This species form thus establishes physically and mentally the proper operation(s) in which Socrates engages as a particular man, i.e., as an individual and particular

---

28. Copleston, *History of Philosophy*, 2:328, notes: "St Thomas did not think of forms as first existing separately and then being individuated, for the forms of sensible objects do not exist in a state of temporal priority to the composite substances; but the idea of individuation is certainly due originally to the Platonic way of thinking and speaking of forms . . . it would not become an historian to turn a blind eye to the Platonic legacy in Aristotle's thought and consequently in that of St Thomas."

29. Aquinas's views on prime matter in relation to form distanced him from the prevalent Augustinian idea of his day that within matter was embedded *rationes seminales* as some sort of vague preliminary force that allows matter to be self-arranging (within the providence of God). Copleston notes: "St. Thomas certainly employed the term *rationes seminales*, but he meant thereby primarily the active forces of concrete objects, e.g. the active poere which controls the generation of living things and restricts it to the same species, not the doctrine that there are inchoate forms in prime matter" (Cf. *Summa Theologiae* I a, 115, 2; *De Veritate*, 5, 9, ads 8 and 9).

"rational animal"[30] (*De Ente* 2 [4]). Socrates is not, however, identical with or simply the humanity per se that makes him to be human. Neither is the humanity that makes him human identical to the essence of being Socrates. So, Aquinas asserts, "If the nature of the species is signified with *precision* from designated matter, which is the principle of individuation, then it [the nature of the species] will have the role of a part"[31] (*De Ente* 2 [11]). The individuality of an entity involves it being a *kind* of thing, so both matter and form are necessary for its *quiditas*.

In other words, if we analyze the essence of any entity such as Socrates and bracket for the sake of philosophical analysis the material that he is, then we are able to see that something must make him to be the particular *kind* of physical entity he is. And yet, even recognizing that a *form* is cause for Socrates's species identity, we nonetheless realize, Aquinas argued, that form cannot be the principle of individuation. Many individuals share in the human form (rational soul) that makes Socrates a human being, so his human particularity and incommunicability must be is instantiated by some other feature of his existence. Designated matter is the only other aspect of the composite being Socrates that is left as a possibility, but only in union with the form of humanness. Other beings can share the form of humanity, but no other human beings can share his human identity because of the boundaries designated matter establishes. The material limits of Socrates's body, in union with the form of humanness, is his personal identity—his essential, unique, incommunicable nature as an *ens*. (We will deal with the issue of continuous existence across time in the next section.)

The matter that is Socrates can be so established as Socrates because it is "prefigured" to be able to be capable of being designated to be a human being through the organizing influence of the form of rationality. This form, as it co-inheres with prefigured matter, establishes for the designated matter a proper operation as a kind of thing. Speaking of a proper operation identifies the activity that the material entity performs *qua* a human being (which includes rationality as expressed in the physical human being), whereas the term "designated matter" denotes the specific, incommunicable human being so acting out the proper orientation of his humanness. The implication of this, then, is that the being (*esse*) of a being (*ens*) is incommunicable, because the *ens* is a particular essence (*essentia*) as a unique body with a species of operation proper to it. Hence, by this dynamic, Socrates is an expression of *rational animality* or humanness. This is what Aquinas means when he says that matter is the principle of individuation.

---

30. Quoting Averroes approvingly, Aquinas agrees that "Socrates is nothing else than animality and rationality, which are his quiddity" (*De Ente* 1 [24]).

31. Emphasis is mine.

MATERIA DESIGNATA AND DIACHRONIC
IDENTITY IN A COMPOSITE BEING

As individuated in designated matter, any essence obviously undergoes many changes to its material make-up. This is not only true in cases of radical outward change as we see in the acorn-to-oak tree scenario. It is just as true in cases involving less radical, but nonetheless real changes, as in the growth, maturity, and aging of an animal. What does it mean to say that something is the same entity, if its changes materially (when the matter is part of its essence) and even functionally? In other words, material change raises for Thomas's metaphysics the question how one can speak of designated matter being part of the essence of a primary being, if the matter over time changes not just its shape, but the actual material stuff that is involved in its essential existence.[32]

Earlier it was noted that Aquinas changed his way of formulating the concept of *materia designate,* replacing the concept of *determinate* dimensions with *indeterminate,* so that he might more easily account for the question of diachronic identity. In *Summa contra Gentiles* we find Aquinas addressing this in a passage that is concerned with how to explain the Christian doctrine of the continuing identity of persons upon the resurrection from the dead. He argues there that the answer starts with a metaphysical rather than theological premise.

> In a man's body while he lives, there are not always the same parts in respect of matter, but only in respect of species. In respect of matter there is a flux and reflux of parts: still that fact does not bar the man's numerical unity from the beginning to the end of his life. We have an example in a fire, which, while it goes on burning, is called numerically one, because its species remains, though the wood is burnt out and fresh wood supplied. So it is in the human body: for the form and species (kind) of the several parts continues unbroken throughout life, but the matter of the parts is dissolved by the natural heat, and new matter accrues by nourishment. But the man is not numerically different by the difference of his component parts at different ages, although it is true that the material composition of the man at one stage of his life is not his material composition at another. So then, for numerically the same man to rise again, it is not requisite for all the material that ever entered into his composition throughout the whole course of his life to be gathered together and resumed, but just so much of it as suffices to make up his proper bulk and stature. (*Contra Gentiles* 4, 81)

Identity across time is not dependent upon the specific *materia signata/designata* that comprises the primary being *at a given moment or duration.* Rather, the thing that instantiates and maintains identity in the face of corporeal difference is the living form

---

32. Such a question drove pre-Socratic reflection, as is obvious in Heraclitus's famous embrace of the dictum that change is all there is, i.e., that there is no diachronic identity. However, this also a topic of philosophical reflection that raised metaphysical concerns among the early modern Rationalists, as well as the Empiricists.

(*anima*) that gives to the living entity its proper operation and its material organization. In Aquinas's theory, any living thing engaged in the operations proper to it is manifesting its essence. A living being is primarily an action (process) of being alive in a specific way. It is the process of being alive as a specific entity that maintains diachronic identity of the living essence. Diachronic identity through outward changes does not attach to inanimate things, per Aquinas, because if a statue, for instance, were not always the same matter, it could not be the self-same statue.[33] Its identity as that particular statue is tied not only to the form it has but also the specific piece of granite from which it is chiseled. In other words, one must say about a particular stone icon: that granite thusly shape just is that granite statue, which one can still affirm even if time or accident causes loss.

Living entities are profoundly different, he thought, because the material of a living entity may change and be completely different across time. For this reason, designated matter is not a candidate for establishing diachronic identity. We also require more than merely our knowledge of a traceable history of material existence to explain the metaphysical continuity of identity of a living entity, for Aquinas, since that traceable history would be dependent upon our knowledge as the tracers. This idea of traceable history would be a nominal, rather than ontological. For example, a toddler and the old woman she becomes share a continuous essence which accounts for our ability to trace her history. Phenomenologically and character-wise these manifestations are drastically different. Yet, we intuit there is an identity relation of some kind. How are the two the *same* being? Identity requires—to borrow Aquinas's distinction in a different context—a real relation, not a relation of reason. This realness of the relation is the intrinsic relationship between form and designated, but undetermined, matter. The size of an organism's body and some features of its shape, as such, are accidents that exist only in the primary being. A living entity is granted dimensional limits, even limits on any "accident," that are strictly determined through the organizing influence of form which causes matter to exist by granting it a particularized unique nature as a primary being. Features such as quantity and shape result in corporeal substance because of matter, because as was discussed above matter has a potentiality to change, but the limited changes possible for any designated matter arise from matter's relation to form.[34] This process or relation is what Aquinas refers to as "inseparable concomitants that determine it in time and place."[35]

Earlier in this chapter we discussed the semantic changes Aquinas embraced regarding the dimensions of *materia designata*. Having dropped the Avincennian notion of determined dimensions for that of undetermined dimensions, his later works present the identity of a primary being qua material in terms of its matter

---

33. This observation does not apply to inanimate objects that merely lose parts.
34. *De Nat. Mat.*, iv.
35. *De Princip. Individ.*, referenced in Aveling, "Matter," para. 10.

being "individuated by indeterminate dimensions preunderstood in it."[36] To better understand this concept of preunderstood dimensions, consider the analogy offered in the last chapter describing the information and instruction that are conveyed to the material components of a person's body via the DNA molecule as the medium. Take an individual person such as Shaquille O'Neal the famous retired professional basketball player. From the moment of his conception his body was, all things considered, going to be far larger than the average human given his genetics. Thus, under the right conditions of proper nourishment, rest, and exercise his seven feet and one inch frame carrying more than three hundred pounds was a "preunderstood" potential dimension "written into" his cellular structure. However, the potential in him to grow was/is not limitless.[37] As O'Neal grew from a small baby to the huge athlete he is, the substantial form (DNA information?) granted the dimensional potentiality unique to him as a primary being in material terms, but the nature of the matter prefigured for the human body established ultimate limits. His physical living existence as the primary being he is always entailed the capacity for the changes because of the nature of matter, but the specific changes were granted through the principle of its substantial form. Hence, his and any living thing's diachronous identity is preserved by the life-process enabled by each essence's substantial form.

This same substantial form accounts, as well, for the arrangement of all the various material structures of which a living being is made. As a composite being the living being is still only one thing in its operation, even though various bodily parts make-up the human body, i.e., soft tissue, blood, bone, mucous, as well as heart, lungs, stomach, and brain, etc. All are distinct as entities, but each is part of the operation of the singular living being. Aquinas argues that the rational soul as the substantial form of the human person is what makes the human body to be human in all its parts functioning together. And the *forma totius* grants identity and function to all the individual parts. In an argument to establish that Christ had to have a human soul he says, "For *flesh and the other parts* of man receive their species through the soul. Hence, if the soul is absent, there are no bones nor flesh, except equivocally, as is plain from the Philosopher (*De Anima* ii, 9; *Metaph.* vii, 34)" (*Summa* III, Q 4, a 3, reply). The designated material that is appropriate for organismic life and allows for the dimensional aspect of a living being's existence is not simply a general sense of boundedness of existence. Rather, the substantial form is directly responsible for a complex of organized entities and the complex relations that all these organized entities have to one another in the "proper operation" of living bodily life. And in the case of a human being, all this is oriented to serve the purpose of enabling the existence of the rational animality of human nature.

36. *In Boeth. de Trin.*, Q. iv, a. 2; *De Nat. Mat.*, vii.

37. Research suggests that humans may have reached the limits of our potential for size, weight, and longevity, which would confirm the Thomistic concept of prefigured dimensions. See Marck, "Humans at Maximum Limits."

ONLY ONE SUBSTANTIAL FORM

Just as Thomas insisted in his more mature teaching that an *ens* is/has an *essentia* that is a singular, incommunicable reality, so he came to argue that each *ens* is made to be the essence that it is because the *materia signata* is organized with its proper operations by a single substantial form.[38] He rejected the view of some of his time with regard to the nature of composite living substances, who argued they were the result of a plurality of organizing substantial forms organizing their concrete existences. Many of his day argued that *forma corporeitatis* is the *first act* that organizes the material entity's fundamental dimensions that establish the boundedness of an organism's physical existence and marked its identity. This form could then be receptive of further "perfecting," defining forms. Aquinas viewed this way of thinking about the constitution of primary beings as fraught with philosophical confusion. The concern that shaped his thinking in this regard had, once again, to do with the concept of essence and the attendant notion of the definition of a being. His reasoned conclusion was that the plurality doctrine undercut the singularity of identity of a primary being. Contesting the coherence of the plurality doctrine, he asserts in the *Summa*:

> If we suppose, however, that the soul is united to the body *as its form*, it is quite impossible for several essentially different souls to be in one body. This can be made clear by three different reasons.
>
> In the first place, an animal would not be absolutely one, in which there were several souls. For nothing is absolutely one except by one form, by which a thing has existence: because a thing has from the same source both existence and unity; and therefore things which are denominated by various forms are not absolutely one; as, for instance, "a white man." If, therefore, man were 'living' by one form, the vegetative soul, and 'animal' by another form, the sensitive soul, and "man" by another form, the intellectual soul, it would follow that man is not absolutely one. Thus Aristotle argues, Metaph. viii (Did. vii, 6), against Plato, that if the idea of an animal is distinct from the idea of a biped, then a biped animal is not absolutely one. For this reason, against those who hold that there are several souls in the body, he asks (De Anima i, 5), "what contains them?"–that is, what makes them one? It cannot be said that they are united by the one body; because rather does the soul contain the body and make it one, than the reverse. (*Summa* I a, Q 76, a 3, reply)[39]

38. In his early *Commentary of the Sentences* (2, 18, I, 2) he accepts the standard theory of *forma corporeitatis* as the first substantial form in a corporeal entity that then includes other forms. However, in *Summa Theologica* 1 a. 47, reply 1, his rejection of this idea is indubitable. "The natural agent acts *by the form* which makes it what it is, and *which is only one in one thing; and therefore its effect is one only*" (emphasis mine).

39. Aquinas here is criticizing a theory that has some affinity, it could be argued, with the contemporary theory of supervenience, where the physical organization of an entity is prior to the mental life that supervenes upon the physical so organized, but not reducible to the physical operations.

By the plurality of forms doctrine, polyformal specifications in the make-up of entities would require us to deny, Aquinas thought, the absolute oneness of essential identity in primary beings. For example, to think of being alive as one distinct property of a human being, and then add rationality as another disparate, higher aspect resulting from a different formal cause fails to account for *how* these different *animas* could be related and function in unity as one essence. So, he presses his argument for singularity of the formal principle.

> If we have one form by which a thing is an animal, and another form by which it is a man, it follows either that one of these two things could not be predicated of the other, except accidentally, supposing these two forms not to be ordered to one another—or that one would be predicated of the other according to the second manner of essential predication, if one soul be presupposed to the other. But both of these consequences are clearly false: because "animal" is predicated of man essentially and not accidentally; and man is not part of the definition of an animal, but the other way about. Therefore of necessity by the same form a thing is animal and man . . . . (*Summa* I a, Q 76, a 3, reply)

Regarding his own earlier acceptance of the idea of *forma corporeitatis*, Aquinas came to reject this because it implies that essential predicates would have to be considered subsequent, accidental forms accruing to or being added to the originating essence. So, he rejected the doctrine of plurality, with its ideas about a *forma corporeitatis* as the cause of the corporeal essence, which would then receive or accrue subsequent forms as *hoc aliquid in actu* (a specific already existing thing).[40] If something accrues in an already existing thing which is defined in its existence by its essence, how can one say that the addition is not an accident (in the Aristotelian sense). If, however, further accruals or added aspects are not accidental, but essential to the entity's nature, then some principle must be recognized to account for the process of such accrual and harmonious linking of forms. Some organizational power or principle (form) would have to be involved to "direct" this process of accrual; and this governing form would have to be the most basic organizing principle enabling the accrual. Thus, it would have to be conceived as the true substantial form that *informs* and enables the process of acquisition of "more perfect" forms. Instead, Aquinas insisted that the essence of an organism is given to it (including everything that makes it what it is in every way), at the same moment that its being (*esse*) as a substance is made actual as it begins to exist.[41]

Aquinas argues that without this idea of a unitary substantial form as the single organizing principle of a corporeal substance, one could not maintain the synchronous identity of things. Furthermore, only in this way could one account for unity of all of the diversity of elements and powers of an entity. Consider what he says in *De Ente*:

40. Again, we can note the affinity that the plurality doctrine of Aquinas's day has to modern-day theories of supervenience.

41. *Quodlibet*, II 5, 5.

In the genus of substance we give the name 'body' to that which has a nature such that three dimensions can be counted in it; but these three determined dimensions themselves are a body in the genus of quantity. It does happen that something having one perfection may also possess a further perfection, as is evident in man, who has a sensitive nature and, besides this, an intellectual nature. So, too, over and above the perfection of having a form such that three dimensions can be designated in it, another perfection can be added, such as life, or something of the kind. (*De Ente* 2 [6])

This statement, taken by itself, might fit into a pluralistic metaphysics of forms in individuals, but Aquinas qualifies what he has in mind when he says a few lines later:

The soul [*anima*—that which makes alive in a certain way] *is not* a form different from that which gives to the thing three determined dimensions. That is why, when we said that a body is that which has such a form as allows the determination of three dimensions in it, we understood this to mean any *form* whatsoever: animality, stones, or any other form. In this way the form of animal is *implicitly* contained in the form of body, inasmuch as body is its genus. And such also is the relation of animal to man. (*De Ente* 2 [7])

Aquinas's metaphysics rejects the plurality doctrine because of the way he conceived the relations between the hierarchy of forms—vegetative, sensitive and rational—in relationship to the unity of existence and *teleological* function in living things. He contends that between these levels of form there is both continuity and superiority of organizational causation manifest in the processes of being alive. The "higher" form that grants sense experience and self-motion (which animals have over flora) entails the life-giving principle of the vegetative form that grants life to plants, even though being an animal is a distinct, more complex way of being alive—but life is life. Likewise, humans are more complex than other animals, because we are physically/materially rational or rationally/thinkingly physical. Our physical life is distinguishable from our rational or mental life, but we are only one *ens*. Aquinas argues, all human beings are made alive by the species form of rational animality, which includes the power of sensation and movement, even as this same form accounts for their individuating and speciating difference rationality. This rationality is the *telos* of the lower forms as the definition of human nature, not an addition or supervening capacity. So, in Thomistic doctrine, human beings are made alive by a form of existence that is vastly more complex and powerful organizationally than that of the animals, much less plants. Humans share the same basic life force that plants have and the same capacity for sensation that animals enjoy, but each of these expressions of life (*anima*) both have rationality as their purpose. One cannot, except conceptually, separate the lower powers of human life from the highest, because a human being is *one* entity with *one* telos, namely rational self-conscious understanding. Humanity, both definitionally and existentially, assumes the following formal features under the one substantial form: 1) life, which Aquinas sees as a fundamental rather than an emergent phenomenon; 2) a capacity, therefore, for sensory engagement with the world; 3) growth and mobility as a result of life and sensory engagement; and 4) rational understanding of the experiences we have as the *telos* of them all and the *governor* over the lesser powers. Being capable of rational thought does not accrue onto the lower powers, rather it determines the specific operation that these powers have in human beings (when engaged in the operation *proper* to them). The crux of the issue and its implications in Aquinas's metaphysics is that a single organizing principle accounts for all the essential attributes that one might discover to be a part of the nature of a primary substance, and therefore of a human person. This principle is its substantial form. There is, however, in addition to hylomorphism as a fundamental metaphysical principle, a further level of philosophical analysis that must be applied.

ESSE AND "PARTICIPATING" *ESSENTIAE*

The distinction named in *De Ente et Essentia* is a necessary differentiation, Thomas argues, between what a thing is (its essence) and the actual existence of an entity. For him, a primary being's essence composited by form and matter does not entail or explain its existence. In fact, it cannot do so, because nothing about essence per se necessitates the actual being of the essence, even though *essence* in the most basic sense is used for something that does exist. However, the concept *existence* is not, per Aquinas, reducible to the fact that we have conceived a particular essence.[42] This concept is developed even further in the *Summa*. In a passage addressing the "simplicity" of God, he analyzes the dependent nature of contingent essences.

> First, whatever a thing has besides its essence must be caused either by the constituent principles of that essence (like a property that necessarily accompanies the species–as the faculty of laughing is proper to a man–and is caused by the constituent principles of the species), or by some exterior agent–as heat is caused in water by fire. Therefore, if the existence of a thing differs from its essence, this existence must be caused either by some exterior agent or by its essential principles. Now it is impossible for a thing's existence to be caused by

42. While it is conventional in philosophy to consider that Kant's argument that *being (existence) is not a predicate* is in someway a knock-down argument against Christian ontological claims, it appears to me that Thomas's distinctions drawn at the beginning of *De Ente* address this quite nicely. There, you will recall, he tells us that a being can be considered to refer: 1) to an actually existing thing and 2) to something about which a true statement may be predicated, even if the thing predicated does not exist in any positive sense. Whereas Kant's critique is directed at definitional considerations, Aquinas's rejoinder could well be that in the real world of our experiences we indeed encounter two types of entities. Kant's reference to 100 taulers and 100 existing taulers being tautological is only so in the analytic sense, but in the existential sense the difference is quite real, Thomas could say. The predicate "existing" does not add to the taulers as an "accident." Either they are or they are not. Further, the conceptual taulers are only conceivable because we have encountered real, existing (even if phenomenologically, as in Kant's ontology) taulers prior to conceptualizing them.

its essential constituent principles, for nothing can be the sufficient cause of its own existence, if its existence is caused. Therefore that thing, whose existence differs from its essence, must have its existence caused by another . . . .

Secondly, existence is that which makes every form or nature actual; for goodness and humanity are spoken of as actual, only because they are spoken of as existing. Therefore existence must be compared to essence, if the latter is a distinct reality, as actuality to potentiality.

Thirdly, because, just as that which has fire, but is not itself fire, is on fire by participation; so that which has existence but is not existence, is a being by participation. (*Summa* I, a, 3, 4, reply)

As has been demonstrated, for Aquinas, a thing's identity is its *essentia*; it is what it is as itself. "Because we use the term 'a being' absolutely and primarily of substances, and secondarily and with qualification of accidents, it follows that essence is in substances truly and properly . . ." (*De Ente* 1 [5]). As regards a being's existence, however, no essence can be said to contain its own *esse*. The fact that a thing has actual existence is quite a different concept from the essence that it is. Such a medieval way of stating the relationship between the activity of existing and the defining essence that the thing is might strike some as odd. So, we must look at what Aquinas means when he says that a being is not its own act of being.

In the question of the how we understand the relationship between a thing's essence and existence, Aquinas moved well beyond the metaphysical framework of Aristotle's views. To see the further developed logic of his metaphysics of existence, we will be helped by briefly rehearsing Aristotle's doctrine. Gilson has noted that for Aristotle the demonstration of the truth of an essential definition was the same as demonstrating its being, its reality or existence as an essence.[43] The Stagirite analyzes this relationship as follows in the *Prior Analytics*:

The being (existence) of anything as fact is a matter for demonstration, and this is the actual procedure of the sciences, for the geometer assumes the meaning of the word triangle, but that it is possessed of some attributes he proves. What is it then that we shall prove in defining essential nature? Triangle? In that case a man will know by definition what a thing's nature is without knowing it exists. But that is impossible.[44]

43. This Aristotelian doctrine is an ancient statement anticipating Kant's claims that existence cannot be considered as a predicate. But, such an assertion rooted in a particular epistemological framework is only a failure to consider whether an existing essence exists necessarily or not. And if it is most reasonable to assume it does not, then the Thomistic discrimination *de ente et essentia* is far from unnecessary.

44. Gilson, *Elements of Christian Philosophy,* 138. Cf. *An. Pr.,* II, c. 7, 92 B 14–17.

Because Aristotle conceived of the universe as necessary and eternal, he drew no distinctions between essence and existence as metaphysical principles.[45] Furthermore, the demonstration of fact about an entity or state of affairs was, by Aristotle's lights, the result of knowing the cause(s), therefore all statements about the truth of an essence had to be statements about its actual being. His epistemological commitments about how we know things by empirical experience (rejecting Platonic idealism) shaped his ontology, and his ontology gave rise to his logic. Joseph Owens comments about Aristotle's intertwining of logic and metaphysics: "To ask whether the moon is eclipsed or not, is . . . precisely the same as asking whether *A* (i.e., the eclipse) has a defining condition (*logos*), and if this condition actually exists, we assert that *A* also actually exists."[46] While this might apply immediately to the accidents of substances, in Aristotle's account of the relationship between essence and existence, it further applies because the relationship is one of identity: a thing exists as what it is, because it just is. No distinction between essence and the fact of being is necessary, desirable, or possible.

Whereas Aristotle did not analyze the *act* of being (existing) that a thing evinces as we encounter it by our sensory engagement with the world, Aquinas saw this as the most fundamental of all relationships. The existence of an essence only contingently applies to the essential concept of the thing, for him, because there is no metaphysical necessity for it to exist at all in any extra-mental sense. For the Greek logician, on the other hand, a contingent relationship would be a *per accidens* relationship. He was "dealing with the universal and necessary connections between the elements of definition and demonstration."[47] Couple this framework with his embrace of the radical distinction between Being and non-Being, then the questions posed by his medieval follower about the distinction between essence and existence could not arise for Aristotle. Ironically, however, it was Aristotle's own reasoning regarding potency and act, which were developed to answer the pre-Socratic dilemma of Being, non-Being, and Becoming, that implied for Aquinas the necessity to examine the distinction between *esse* and *essentia*. An essence, he argued, entails the *possibility* of its existence but it not the *fact* of its existence. In *De Ente*, 4 he follows Avicenna's insights:

> Whatever does not belong to the notion of an essence or quiddity comes
> from without and enters into composition with the essence, for no essence is

---

45. Contemporary observations that have produced the cosmological understanding of the non-eternality of the universe—the "Big Bang Theory"—have, of course, diminished the truth of such a starting point of conviction. Hence, as the Kalam Cosmological Argument that has been reintroduced by William Lane Craig argues: 1) anything that begins to exist has a cause of its being; 2) the universe began to exist; therefore 3) the universe has a cause of its existence (Craig, *Kalam Cosmological Argument*, 69–149). Such an argument does not only apply a demonstration of the reasonableness of believing that a God exists, but it further can be applied to the claim that a thing's essence (which is a part of the universe of things and essences that came into being) does not have its existence proper as part of the essence that it is.

46. Owens, *Doctrine of Being*, 291.

47. Owens, *Doctrine of Being*, 291.

intelligible without its parts [the form and matter that make comprise it]. Now, every essence or quiddity can be understood without anything being known of its existing. I can know what a man or a phoenix is and still be ignorant whether it exists in reality. From this it is clear that the act of existing is other than essence or quiddity, unless, perhaps, there is a being whose quiddity is the very act of existing. And there can be only one such being, the First Being.

We need to understand that this does not mean that existence is *added to* an essence, such that the fact of a thing's real existence is accidental to the thing that it is. When Aquinas argues that a thing's essence is identical with it, and that the only things that really exist in themselves in the material world are primary beings, this implies that existence and essence *in a thing* are not separable when one considers the existing thing itself. In other words, a being (*ens*) is a being only because it has existence (*esse*). (To this extent "being is not a predicate.") However, one can, in the end, make a logical distinction between the act of existing and the things in which or by we encounter the act of existing, because the essences do not exist necessarily. His metaphysics see that *esse* is the highest principle of the being (*essentia*) of a primary being (*ens*) that has real existence. But since its existence is not contained in its essence it can only exist by participation in *esse*. So, existence can be abstracted from its essence.

This aspect of Aquinas's thought is better understood when we consider his view of how a thing can come to exist in the first place. In the *Summa Theologica* Thomas Aquinas famously argues for the existence of God.[48] The "Third Way" is his expression of the distinction between essence and existence in terms of a demonstration of the existence of a First Cause—Being—as the source of all other beings.

> We find in nature things that are possible to be and not to be, since they are found to be generated, and to corrupt, and consequently, they are possible to be and not to be. But it is impossible for these always to exist, for that which is possible not to be at some time is not. Therefore, if everything is possible not to be, then at one time there could have been nothing in existence. Now if this were true, even now there would be nothing in existence, because that which does not exist only begins to exist by something already existing. Therefore, if at one time nothing was in existence, it would have been impossible for anything to have begun to exist; and thus even now nothing would be in existence—which is absurd. Therefore, not all beings are merely possible, but there must exist something the existence of which is necessary. But every necessary thing either has its necessity caused by another, or not. Now it is impossible to go on to infinity in necessary things which have their necessity caused by another, as has been already proved in regard to efficient causes.

48. Davies, *Thought of Thomas Aquinas*, 31 has noted that the "existence argument" is granted special emphasis in Aquinas's philosophy as a demonstration of God's reality. "It appears again and again in his writings, and it is often presupposed in contexts where it is not given explicitly. It is fleshed out in *De potential* 7 and *Summa contra Gentiles*, 1. 22, and 2. 52. But it is particularly concisely stated in *Summa Theologiae*, I a. 65. 1."

Therefore we cannot but postulate the existence of some being having of itself its own necessity, and not receiving it from another, but rather causing in others their necessity. This all men speak of as God. (*Summa* I a, 2, 3, reply)[49]

Aquinas's argument is that some Being—by which he means some self-contained act of existing—that is not dependent upon anything else must be that upon which all other entities depend for their actual existence.

If things that differ agree in some point, there must be some cause for that agreement, since things diverse in nature cannot be united of themselves. Hence whenever in different things some one thing common to all is found, it must be that these different things receive that one thing from some one cause, as different bodies that are hot receive their heat from fire. But being is found to be common to all things, however otherwise different. There must, therefore, be one principle of being from which all things in whatever way existing have their being, whether they are invisible and spiritual, or visible and corporeal. (*Summa* I a, 65, 1, reply)

In other words, some source of existence upon which all else depends is needed to account for why any nonnecessary being exists. His analysis of the absolute contingency of everything in our experience suggested to him that no existent thing in our world could be the source of its own existence; nor could any property that is involved in its existence be the cause of existence. Even the universe, since it is simply a way of speaking about the sum of all the existing properties, entities, and powers, does not have necessary existence as part of its essence.[50] Any contingent being exists,

---

49. It can be noted that with "Big Bang" cosmology, even apart from considerations about God, physicists note that *whatever* was the existent reality that was the precursor of the eruption of the universe with its physical laws this something was such that the laws of physics as we know them do not apply to it. Perhaps it was only some physical (not material) reality, as many physicists would want to argue. However, an exclusive and reductionist commitment to materialism causes, in my view, materialist physicists to stretch the notion of "physical" far beyond what we have any notions to fit. How could there be anything material that produced itself if the laws of physics and matter do not begin to exist except attendant with, or subsequent to, the beginning of material/physical stuff? It could be that God is a better explanation, but at the very least we have to say that the something that preexisted the "bang" was both necessarily existent and radically distinct from anything that we know.

50. It falls outside the parameters of this book to deal with the various objections that have been proffered as refutations of this argument for the existence of God. It should be noted, however, that Aquinas is not here arguing for a sequential chain of causes back to a cause that is the very first cause in the chain. Such a notion would not let him posit a truly first and necessary cause. Rather, he is arguing here that the existence of any particular and obviously contingent being is dependent for its existence upon a prior condition of some kind. Also, any contingent chain of events or beings can exist only if some prior condition is the ground upon which the capacity for existence evidenced by that chain of contingent events or beings depends. Some foundational something must be posited as the metaphysically prior condition or state in which other things exist via participation. Hence, when he argues above that "we cannot but postulate the existence of some being having of itself its own necessity, and not receiving it from another, but rather causing in others their necessity," he is establishing that something has to be thought of as the foundational prior condition. This is not unlike, it seems to me, Spinoza's argument that the one Substance exists in itself, and all other things exist in this

therefore, only if it participates in something else which has its Being as its essence. Based on this reasoning, plus the additional conclusion that God must be defined as self-subsisting,[51] Aquinas puts forth the following conclusion about the relationship between God and all beings:

> It must be said that every being in any way existing is from God. For whatever is found in anything by participation, must be caused in it by that to which it belongs essentially, as iron becomes ignited by fire. Now it has been shown above (3, 4) when treating of the divine simplicity that God is the essentially self-subsisting Being; and also it was shown (11, 3,4) that subsisting being must be one; as, if whiteness were self-subsisting, it would be one, since whiteness is multiplied by its recipients. Therefore all beings apart from God are not their own being, but are beings by participation. Therefore it must be that all things which are diversified by the diverse participation of being, so as to be more or less perfect, are caused by one First Being, Who possesses being most perfectly. (*Summa* I a, Q 44, a 1, reply)

This means, among other things for Aquinas, that only God can create; and the notion of creation is a profoundly unique idea: "Hence it is manifest that creation is the proper act of God alone" (*Summa* I a, 44, 5, reply).

However, for Aquinas the act of creation is not merely a reference point in the past, i.e., the starting point at the beginning of a chain of events. Rather, the idea of creation entails that all creatures (primary beings, forms, matter—prime or "signified"—as the principles of that account for all specific essences, plus the laws of nature, mathematical principles, spiritual beings, etc) exist in some way as a 'participating' expression of God's own act of Being. Brian Davies comments on Aquinas's thought regarding creation as an ongoing action of the Divine: "This means that all things depend upon God for their *continued existence*. In saying that God is the Creator of something, Aquinas is not just saying that God just got it going at some time past . . .

Substance as temporal modes, even if logically necessary in their temporality. Of course, Spinoza's method of demonstration is "geometrical," i.e., a priori. Aquinas proceeds a posteriori from the beings encountered in the world and the world as it is given to us in experience. The conclusion that Aquinas draws above that a necessary prior condition all men call God is a true postulate is his endeavor to demonstrate that Christian belief in God is not irrational. We can demonstrate the philosophical appropriateness of introducing God-language into metaphysical discussion, Aquinas would argue, even if we cannot establish a knock-down proof of the Christian God. Spinoza would have agreed, even if he proceeded from the opposite direction.

51. *Summa Theologica* I a, 3, 1. "The first being must of necessity be in act, and in no way in potentiality. For although in any single thing that passes from potentiality to actuality, the potentiality is prior in time to the actuality; nevertheless, absolutely speaking, actuality is prior to potentiality; for whatever is in potentiality can be reduced into actuality only by some being in actuality. Now it has been already proved that God is the First Being. It is therefore impossible that in God there should be any potentiality."

the conservation of things is, for Aquinas, closely related to their first coming into being. Both depend upon God's activity."[52]

God is the ground of all being (to utilize Paul Tillich's phrase), because God is the prior condition in the ultimate and ultimately necessary sense. However, contingently and dependently existing things do so only by way of participation in God as God shares with them God's act of existing. As the Uncreated Creator, as Aquinas conceives God, who is reliant upon nothing and defined by nothing, God is transcendent. God's creatures, allowed a share in the divine power of existing, cannot be considered to be God properly speaking, or even modes or emanations of God. Rather, they are created participants in an act of Being that transcends them (since they are contingent) but which is shared with them. Hence, participating things exist in a way that is distinguishable from God's own essence as Being itself.

> God is in all things; not, indeed, as part of their essence, nor as an accident, but as an agent is present to that upon which it works. For an agent must be joined to that wherein it acts immediately and touch it by its power; hence it is proved in Phys. vii that the thing moved and the mover must be joined together. Now since God is very being by His own essence, created being must be His proper effect; as to ignite is the proper effect of fire. Now God causes this effect in things not only when they first begin to be, *but as long as they are preserved in being*; as light is caused in the air by the sun as long as the air remains illuminated. Therefore as long as a thing has being, God must be present to it, according to its mode of being. But being is innermost in each thing and most fundamentally inherent in all things since it is formal in respect of everything found in a thing, as was shown above (7, 1). Hence it must be that God is in all things, and innermostly. (*Summa* I a, 8, 1, reply)[53]

Primary beings, as created participants in Being, thereby do not have in themselves their own individual act of existing. That can only be had via God's sharing of the divine power to be in them. To reiterate: the act of existing belongs to God alone. Thus, Aquinas would say, God simply *is*. Ontologically, for anything that has been created by the act of God's enabling it to participate in God's power of existing there exists a relationship of dependence (for creatures) and independence (for God), or createdness and transcendence, which obtains, in Aquinas's view, even if the cosmos were conceived of as eternal.[54] An eternal cosmos would be made up completely of contingent beings and would not, thereby, account for its own existence as the sum of

---

52. Davies, *Thought of Thomas Aquinas,* 35, my emphasis.

53. Emphasis mine. It should be reiterated here that for Aquinas God is simple, not composite in any way, which implies that God's acts as *agent* are ultimately not separate ontologically from God's being. Thus, God's creative act involves God's essence. But as the only Uncreated, God cannot create something that is a part of God's own being—by definition.

54. Aquinas is willing to entertain the notion that "temporal origin" of the universe is not demonstrable. However, temporal beginning and metaphysical dependence are distinct concepts in his mind. Cf. *Summa Theologica*, I a, 46, 2.

all contingent things. This view of God's relationship to creatures is one that notes the distinction (although in a different way) which Spinoza would later observe between that which exists only in or through another and that which exists in itself.[55]

SUMMARY

Aquinas's doctrine of hylomorphism requires that individual essences and entities have existence only via participation in the Being of God. Aquinas defines God's Being as Infinite, Perfect Act containing no potentiality. However, in recognizing this kind of substantial dependence for existence, Aquinas argues that the individual entities that participate in God's Act of Being cannot be confused with the ultimate identity of God, because as Being Itself God's "essence" is not communicable to any single entity that is composite in any way. So, participation in God's existence grants reality to essences (particulars, both substantial and accidental), but these particulars are always understood to be something other than and certainly less than God, even when the realm of particulars is taken as a whole (the Universe). In Aquinas's view, a chain of contingent composites—even an infinite one taken as a whole—would not be self-explanatory, or self-causing. Both their compositeness, which indicates complexity and therefore dependence upon something to account for the compositeness, as well as their contingent essence that does not exist by necessity, make them dependent upon something other for existence.

Making these created, contingent, and composite things essentially what they are, the dynamic interplay of form and designated matter establishes individual essences. Form gives a proper organization, orientation, and operation to the designated matter that is arranged and structure to be a primary being in actual existence (an *essentia*). Since both matter and form are created things that exist via participation in God's act of Being, as well as the composite *ens* that exist because of the union of matter and form, every individual particular being in the sensible world has its materiality inherently tied to its essence along with its form. But the principle (form) that grants to them a particular physical existence cannot be conflated with the material that they are, because the material *qua* material does not and cannot be the source of its own organization. This implies that form is distinct metaphysically from designated matter, even if form cannot "exist" apart from the matter so informed. The import of this is that form as the proximate principle of existence as the organizational influence that

---

55. *Ethics* I, defs. 3 & 5. "By substance I mean that which is in itself and is conceived through itself; that is, that which does not require the conception of another thing from which it has to be formed. By mode I mean the affections of substance; that is, that which is in something else and which is conceived through something else." It is interesting that Aquinas's view about God's necessity and the dependence of all other things for their existence upon the Being of God—not just God's first instantiation of stuff in creation—has some similarity to Spinoza's views. This is not to say that their metaphysics are the same, but to note another potential point of comparison between Aquinas as a Medieval Christian Scholastic and the Modern Rationalist.

"acts" not merely upon matter but acts in concert with *designated matter* to constitute, and by participation in God's act of Being to cause, a particular essence to be what it is. But the matter, by the same lights, as the second principle of existence is passive and receptive, only there as a cooperating stuff that the organizing principle, form, establishes as a definable and specific *ens*.

Only one form in each individual primary organic being can be viewed as the foundational cause for an organism to exist the way that it does. This is its substantial form. As a singular essence, all features and functions that express themselves in the individual must be thought of as governed by the organizing presence of the substantial form. Life itself, sensory abilities, auto-motive abilities, and rational understanding are all caused in human beings by the *rational soul*. There is no supervenience of properties that are added to this basic principle. Further, changes in the shape, color, size, and relationship to other entities are conceived of as the reception of accidents. These accidental forms do not change the essence of the primary (human) being, even though they are expressions his or her actual existence at a particular moment. They are, therefore, incidental ontologically speaking , i.e., they are caused effects and subordinate in significance or nature, so occurring as a chance concomitant or consequence. These incidental accidents are dependent upon the humanness of the individual.

However, the unity of a primary being's body is a different and more complex subject, metaphysically speaking. Its unity is essentially the proper operation(s) of the primary being, which are the result of the way that it is organized *as a body*. The operations of a primary being's body depend upon the organizational interplay of bodily parts and the functions of each and all together. And further, the designated mater of which it is physically made is crucial to the proper operation being fulfilled, as in the case of organisms on earth being carbon-based (the designated matter) life forms. So, the entity is what it is physically because the body's parts function together as an individualized and specific unity. This specific operation happens because the form that organizes the designated matter and enables and governs the function of all it component parts has formed the physical, complex organism to be capable of performing certain operations specific to that organism's essence (and its species essence). Strictly speaking, however, these functions and operations are not those of the form per se but are the acts of the physical, living organism that is the composite "product" of the interplay of the basic antecedent influences—matter and form.

Maintaining the proper operation particular to it (and its kind), an animated primary being's identity as an individual is maintained diachronically in spite of the fact that changes in the material make-up take place (perhaps many times) over the course of its life. This is because it is the living, materially differentiated process of the organism's existence that establishes its identity in the first place and that maintains continuity of identity across time, regardless of physical changes. This living process is, in the final analysis, *form*-dependent, but not reducible to the form. In this living process, form grants to the organism the boundaries of what *kind* of changes it may undergo or produce in its material existence, but there are limits upon the matter that are "prefigured" as to its potential dimensions that are not determined by the form.

Aquinas utilizes Aristotle's hylomorphism and develops his own theory in important ways that distance him from his Greek predecessor. The distinction he draws between essence and existence proper is the most radical example of how he drives the act/potency distinction to do work it did not do for Aristotle. Aquinas's concept of the "oneness of the source of Being" as a transcendent source of existence in which all things must exist by participation may provide an example of a philosophy that, while fundamentally different in its understanding of God's relationship to all else, can be in dialogue with Spinoza's arguments about the "oneness of Substance." However, it is worth bracketing a comparison on this matter until we have opportunity to consider the doctrine of Spinoza in a later chapter.

Now we must turn our attention to an area where many commentators insist Aquinas parts company with Aristotle in a fundamental way that makes his metaphysics incoherent, namely the medieval doctor's conception of the human soul as not only a *substantial* form of the body, but as itself having *subsistence* as a feature of the world.[56] As we shall examine in the next chapter, the distinctions that Aquinas draws between from and matter and essence come together in his focus, regarding the relationship between mind and body, on the concept person: "an individual entity of a rational nature." Specific attention will be given to the idea of *person* in chapter 5. This is the crucial point in understanding Aquinas's real doctrine of mind-body identity. As we shall see, he would perhaps have understood what Spinoza meant when he said that "mind and body are one and the same thing; conceived now under the attribute of Thought, now under the attribute of extension."[57]

---

56. The issue of subsistence will prove to be vital to a proper interpretation of Aquinas in the next chapter.

57. Spinoza, *Ethics*, III, 2, sch.

4

Mind-Body Identity in Aquinas

On Being Composite and Being One

IN THIS CHAPTER WE turn to the question of human mind-body identity. As we consider Aquinas's metaphysics of *unity* in a human being's existence involving body and mind, we will see his hylomorphism produces a kind of "identity theory" regarding the relationship between mind and body. The "identity" does not prioritize body or mind but allows him to think of the mind and body as dual aspects of a single entity that is more than either and at the same time both, namely, a human being. This analysis of Thomas's doctrine will set down an important foundation for our consideration in chapter 6 of Spinoza's own metaphysics. There we shall show how Spinoza's doctrine of mind-body can be interpreted as a post-Cartesian expression of a framework with much affinity to Aquinas's. No dependence by Spinoza upon Thomist thought is suggested, rather simply a recognition of a striking similarity. While the philosophical terminology and analytical approach they utilize are quite different, reflecting the historical, cultural, and personal contexts in which they lived and thought, these differences notwithstanding it will be argued that Aquinas's way of seeing the issues involved provides us with a helpful interpretive framework for understanding Spinoza's own cryptic statements describing the mind and body as "one and the same thing, considered (expressed) under two distinct modes." This will allow us to address the much-discussed issues surrounding various interpretations of Spinoza's theory of mind-body identity. Doing so, a new and more adequate way of understanding Spinoza's own doctrine will be on offer. Therefore, advances can be made in understanding the great modern rationalist's concepts. But, before we begin to suggest how looking backward in time could help us understand Spinoza, let us look further into Aquinas's own metaphysical position regarding the unity of identity that mind and body entails.

INTERPRETIVE DIFFICULTIES IN AQUINAS'S THEORY

Aquinas's metaphysical theory on the bi-composite nature of being human is a challenge for his interpreters. Parts of his doctrine are particularly difficult. He claims, for example, the soul is a substantial form, but also subsists in its own right. This means that the soul is *both* a principle granting certain form and function to the human body *and* has, as well, its own subsistence, so that the soul's existence is not *completely* dependent upon the existence of the body it has enlivened and enabled to function. Bodily death does not entail the death of the soul. Given Aquinas's incorporation of Aristotle's thought, this presents many contemporary readers with the challenge to understand what he could possibly mean. How is the soul both *part* of a primary being and something that has its own distinct subsistence? Perhaps a Platonist or Cartesian might argue this, but not someone so self-consciously Aristotelian. As if this difficulty of understanding his idea of subsistence were not enough, he also presents other challenges.

A second, related obstacle to understanding Aquinas is the way he describes the metaphysical status of human beings in two different ways which seem mutually exclusive, not complementary. Guyla Klima describes very precisely what is at stake in the tensions presented to us by Aquinas's doctrine of soul-body unity.[1] Regarding the Angelic Doctor's descriptions of human beings, Klima notes that Aquinas argues that a particular human being is both (A) a *specific kind of body*—a singular rational, sensing, and living corporeal entity—and, at the same time, (B) a composite being that *consists of* a soul united to a body. These two descriptions will not co-exist easily, at least at first glance, Klima observes, because to *be* something (a body) is not the same thing as *consisting of* something (a body) as a part of one's being. Indeed, by this second definition (B), the whole human being cannot simply be (A) *this* body, because a part, no matter how integral it is to the whole, cannot be the same as the whole.

As if that confusion were not enough, when contemporary readers of Aquinas consider his doctrine of the soul, the claim that the rational soul is the one and only substantial form of the human body is difficult to understand in contemporary terms. Aquinas's argument in the *Summa* insists that there is only one soul and one substantial form of human existence—the rational *anima*. In I a, Q 76, a 4, ad 1 he contends: "And so it is said that the soul is the actuation of a body and so on, meaning that due to the soul it is a body and is organic and has power to live." This description is a response to an objection against his theory that only one form accounts for all of human bodily life. The objection he was answering proposed that the life animating a living body (when that life is considered as an activity) should be thought of as something "added to," over and above the matter that is alive. This view Aquinas is rebutting has something in common with modern theories of life as supervenient upon or emergent

---

1. For the following analysis I am indebted to Guyla Klima for pointing out the semantic difficulties in Aquinas's theory, especially Klima, "Man = Body + Soul," 179–97.

out of matter. His doctrine of single-form causation raises the question for Aquinas's hylomorphism: How can we conceive the same form to be both the essential cause of the life (animality) of a human being as well as the formative principle that gives spatiality to the organization of the human body? How are biology and physics related? In much contemporary thought, the doctrine of supervenience is the preferred way of envisioning the relationship between the presence of life and the chemical and atomic structure of the bodies of living things. Hence, the doctrine of supervenience would describe the organization of the material body as sufficiently complex to allow life to supervene or emerge epiphenomenally. This means that contemporary philosophical paradigms consider the material make-up of a living being to be one thing and the presence of life which makes the living being alive another, subsequent thing. (The pluralists, who Aquinas debated, had their own version of supervenience by positing a plurality of souls.)

But even more critical for the claims I want to make is the further Thomistic assertion that a human being's humanness (*rational* animality) is the result of the very same form that makes him be a living animal in the first place. A third disconnect between Aquinas and contemporary thought comes to light. How can the property of rationality (having a mind) be made possible by the self-same principle that grants life and biological function and spatial boundaries in human beings? In typical contemporary supervenience theories, this way of construing the issue is challenging to understand and probably smacks of *vitalism*. Yet, he insists that the power of consciousness and rational thought are not *over and above* life itself in human beings but are *the* specifically instantiated form of life that is a human being.

A fourth hurdle is encountered, because Aquinas's articulation of this doctrine is misleading, at least apart from a careful analysis of his claims. While he asserts the unity and singularity of form in a human being's existence, because a human being has a single essence, Aquinas seems to hold that the essence of a human being and the soul of a human being are not actually the same thing, since the soul and body composite is the *essence* of the human being. How could the form not be the essence? Again, Klima gives a good description of the challenge that a modern commentary on Aquinas must deal with, one that it seems might run afoul of the metaphysical essentialism that hylomorphism entails.

> Aquinas also argues that a man's humanity or quiddity is what he calls the 'form of the whole' [*forma totius*], as opposed to the "form of the part" [*forma partis*], which he identifies as the soul, and the form of the whole differs from the form of the part because the form of the whole contains both matter and form. So the form of the whole, the quiddity of man, contains the soul as its part, so it obviously cannot be the same as the soul. But if it is not the same as the soul, and yet it is a form of the human being, and it is clearly not an accidental form, then it seems that we have at least two substantial forms here,

one of which is a part of the other, and which, besides the form of the part, also contains matter![2]

Klima's observations suggest only a part of the difficulty faced by anyone who wants to take Thomistic metaphysics seriously. Other of Aquinas's formulations, which at times seem to conflate the soul (*anima)* and the intellect (*intellectus*) or mind (*mens*), introduce a fifth confusion into the mix. Aquinas argues that we can say that intellect and *anima* are both principles by which a living human being has biological life. His discussion in the Reply of question 76, article 1 of the *Summa*, regarding the nature of *anima* as the life-giving and the intellectual principle in human beings, brings out the importance of carefully reading what he says there:

> The intellect, as the source of intellectual activity, is the form of the human body . . . And the reason for this is that what a thing actually does depends on what it actually has to give; a thing acts precisely by virtue of its actuancy. Now it is obvious that the soul [*anima*] is the prime endowment by virtue of which a body *has life* [*vivo*]. Life [*vita*] manifests its presence through different activities at different levels, but the soul is the ultimate principle by which we conduct *every one of life's activities*; the soul is the ultimate motive factor behind nutrition, sensation, and movement from place to place, and the same holds true of the act of understanding. So that this prime factor in intellectual activity, whether we call it mind [*intellectus*] or intellectual soul [*anima intellectiva*], is the formative principle of the body [*forma corporis*] . . . .

But then he quickly appears to retract this claim when he asserts:

> Should anyone wish to maintain that the intellective soul is not the form of the body, he would have to find some way of making the act of understanding an act of this particular person. For each is conscious that it is he himself that understands . . . So we must either say that Socrates understands through his whole self, as Plato held, saying that man is an intellective soul, or else we must say that the understanding is a *part* of Socrates. Now the first of these is untenable . . . on the grounds that one and the same man perceives himself both to understand and to have sensations. Yet sensation involves the body, so that the body must be said to be part of man. It remains, therefore, that the intellect whereby Socrates understands is a part of Socrates, in such wise that the intellect is in some way united to the *body* of Socrates.[3]

Aquinas certainly seems to be saying that intellect (*intellectus*), which he acknowledges is a *mental activity*, is the actual *form* of the human body. This way of speaking implies that mental activity is something more than an activity. While it would be clear how mental activity could be a feature of a human being, it is far from clear exactly how understanding or knowing as an act in which the human being

2. Klima, "Man = Body + Soul," 181.

3. Emphasis mine.

engages could also be described as the *form* that enables the same human being to perform the activity of knowing. At the very least it is unclear how Aquinas could employ this kind of description, if he is indeed serious about being an Aristotelian, rather than a type of Augustinian Platonist. How could an activity (thinking/knowing) ever be conceived of as a substantial form (much less a subsisting one), if one is beginning with Aristotle and not Plato?

Our dilemma grows more confounding, because in this very same passage he contends that "the understanding is *a part*" of the human knower's existence, seeming to imply the same thing that Klima described in terms of the soul generally, namely, that the intellect is (comparable to) a *forma partis*. Aquinas insists that the fullness of the act of knowing in sensation and intellect involves the body, which is itself informed, presumably, by the very principle of "intellect" which is an activity of the knower *qua* bodily. Hence, we have a description of the intellect as simultaneously both a result of the *forma totius*—or soul-body union—and at the same time the "formative principle" of the self-same union.

REPRESENTATIVE INTERPRETIVE SOLUTIONS

One can survey briefly various commentaries and interpretations of Aquinas to see the conflict that his locutions create, since quite disparate readings of the metaphysical implications that his doctrine has for understanding the nature of human beings are on offer. On the one hand there are those who focus on Aquinas's contention that intellect is the *activity* of an embodied knower. G. E. M. Anscombe and Peter Geach are an excellent example of this reading of Aquinas, arguing that if we take the whole of Aquinas's treatment of human beings into consideration, we must see Aquinas's view of human beings in essentially physicalist terms. Aquinas views a human being as "an animal, an animal is a *body*; so [a human being] is a body, not a body plus something else."[4] Contra such a reading, Anton Pegis interprets Aquinas's doctrine to be a refutation of Aristotle's description of a human being as a physical substance—a body formed by the soul as its enabling principle. Aquinas instead prefers, Pegis argues, to describe a human being as an "incarnated intellect."[5] Obviously, Pegis is focused on the terms of Aquinas's doctrine that highlight the intellect itself as a form and not merely an activity. At least one scholar has posited an interpretation of Aquinas's ostensibly bifurcated rhetoric about the nature of human beings that goes beyond either Geach's or Pegis's appraisals, perhaps even harmonizing them. Linda Jenks's interpretation, however, is likely to make Aquinas difficult for contemporary nontheologians to consider seriously. In her view, due to his account of the uniqueness of the human soul *qua* form, "Aquinas assigns man a correspondingly unique ontological status

4. Anscombe and Geach, *Three Philosophers*, 98.

5. Pegis, *At the Origins*. I am indebted to Linda P. Jenks in *Aquinas on the Soul* for pointing me to Pegis's reading of Aquinas, as well as Geach's.

which is intermediate between spiritual and corporeal creation."[6] While it is not the focus of this current exploration to critique Anscombe and Geach or Pegis or Jenks in the readings of Aquinas they represent, in the rest of this chapter an interpretation is offered that makes choosing between Anscombe and Geach's "physicalist" Aquinas, Pegis's "intellectualist" Aquinas or Jenks's "intermediate" Aquinas unnecessary. This is done by taking his hylomorphism and the doctrine of mind-body identity that follows from it in the strongest sense.

Because of interpretive issues such as those presented above, some conclude that Aquinas's metaphysical scheme regarding human beings is woefully, irreparably confused. Getting clarity about Aquinas's doctrine and its implications is crucial, therefore, if Aquinas's doctrine is to be offered as a possible ally in interpreting Spinoza's own difficult doctrine. Therefore, we must wrestle with Aquinas's metaphysics regarding human beings. It will be demonstrated that Aquinas can be accurately designated as one who holds a type of dual-aspect identity theory. This analysis is not important simply to understand him adequately, but also to set the stage for the part of this project that shows how Spinoza's own description of can mind and body as "one and the same thing" might best be understood in light of Aquinas's metaphysical doctrine of human nature. To those ends we will specifically consider five crucial metaphysical claims that Aquinas defends. We will first consider them following, in order.

1. A human being is unitary in essence, yet composite.

2. A human being has an essential unity of identity on this basis that involves dual expressions or aspects.

3. The soul is rightly called "intellect" or "mind."

4. The composite of soul and body is rightly called a *person*, which is a foundational metaphysical concept for Aquinas.

5. The human soul can survive the bodily death of a human person.

The first two of these will be treated in this chapter with three and four examined in chapter 5. (This final claim will be discussed in the eighth chapter where we take up at the same time Spinoza's doctrine on the same issue.)

Analyzing Aquinas's use of Aristotle, we shall be in a much better position to understand both why he believes and how he arrives at the belief that human beings are an irreducible psycho-physical singular entity, neither of which (mindedness and bodilyness) can be reduced or incorporated into terms that explain the operations and existence of the other, i.e., mind cannot be described in physical terms simply

6. Jenks, "Aquinas on the Soul," 29. Her interpretation may not be acceptable to nontheologians, but this is not a critique or dismissal of the view on offer. It might very well have that theological implication, but metaphysically it is not an immediately necessary description of how Thomas views mind-body identity. I find Jenks's insights attractive and helpful as a Christian philosophical theologian but think there is more to say regarding the way that soul *qua* form in union with the body creates the possibility of *human* rationality and the human mind.

or vice versa. Also, we shall better see why he claims the rational *soul* is the principle that enables both. For Aquinas, and as Spinoza would contend later regarding all of human existence, the mind and the body are *one and the same thing,* even though they are radically distinct. This kind of unity, I contend, Aquinas is seeking to articulate in seminal fashion in his "Treatise on Man" in *Summa Theologiae.*[7]

HUMAN "BEING"—SOUL AND BODY COMPOSITE

In question 76 of the *Summa,* Aquinas takes up directly the question of human beings as *comprised* of the union of soul and body. Here he is forthright in his contention that there is only one soul (proper operation-giving principle) that is associated with the animated human body, namely, the intellectual soul. Aquinas's focus in this passage is to establish that the *activity* of rational living is the form of a human being's life, and such activity is not a feature added to human biological life. Rational activity is the definition of a human being, a human being *is* essentially a rational animal. This definition provides the foundation upon which Aquinas built his argument against the pluralists of his day, discussed in the previous chapter. As already noted, some singular principle must be adduced to account for the unity of human existence, which the medieval pluralists could not provide. Humans manifest various "powers"—growth, locomotion, sensation, and reason—but Aquinas contended (per Aristotle) there could only be a single form at work as the organizing, operation-giving principle that accounts for all human powers. Absent such a singular principle organizing the essential nature of a human being, he argued, the definitional elements in question (the essence)—rationality and animality—only exist as accidents (additions to something more basic) in a human being. That would mean, he believed, that the essential definition of a human being, as both rational and animal—mental and biological irreducibly—would have to be sacrificed.

The problem that Aquinas had with the plurality theory seems to be just this: how does one determine which of the three souls is most specific to humans? A multiple-souls theory implied an accumulation of powers—life, movement, sensation, rationality. But at what point and how does a human being become actually human.[8] For Aquinas, the dual aspects of rationality and animality are not merely "higher" ways of being alive, but are together, immediate as essential features of human nature, whether active or potential. In the *Summa* Q 75, a 1, reply, we can glimpse Thomas's logic where he argues for the unitary nature of a human being:

7. Suttor, *Thomas Aquinas,* xv–xvi describes Aquinas's treatise on man as one of the three "highly technical" treatises that shaped the theoretical orientation of Western culture. "The other two are Aristotle's *Categories* and Boethius's theological works . . . One is struck by how little he repeated his predecessors, and how radically he reorganized the material they had left . . ."

8. Neo-Darwinian evolutionary theories present a similar conundrum in attempting to account for the qualitative distinction in being human from all other animals.

The nature of a specific type includes whatever its strict definition includes, and in things of the physical world [*rebus naturalibus*] this means not only form, but form and matter. Thus materiality is part of the specific type in physical natures; not this determinate matter here, which individuates a thing, but materiality in general. For as it belongs to the very conception of 'this man' that he have this soul and this flesh and bone, so it belongs to the very conception of 'man' that he have soul, flesh and bone.

But we could [take the statement "the soul is the man"] to mean that "this soul" is "this man." And this indeed could be maintained, if we postulated that the activity of the sense-soul belonged to it apart from the body. For all the activities attributed to a man would then be attributable to the soul. For that *is* a thing which does what the thing does, and so that is man which does what man does. But it has been shown [in article 3 of this same question] that sensation is not an activity of the soul alone. Sensing is an activity of the whole man, even though it is not peculiar to man [since all animals have sensation]. And hence it is plain that man is no mere soul, but a compound of soul and body. It was because Plato held that sensation belonged to the soul as such that he could speak of man as a soul using a body.[9]

THE ESSENTIAL UNITY OF A HUMAN BEING

Once he has argued for the essential definition—compound of soul and body—of being human, he is then able to develop further his argument for the essential unity a human being. He contends the soul, therefore, is not, as with Platonism (and to an extent Augustinianism), most essentially the human in question. Therefore, per Aquinas, the soul is "part" of Socrates in the sense that Socrates *is not* his soul, for "man is no mere soul, but a compound of soul and body." To be a human being is to be a compound entity. Being compound, does not undercut the unity of the singular thing *made singular* by a single form. So, Socrates's identity is dependent upon but not synonymous with his soul. As a *rebus naturalibus* a human being (Socrates) is a physical, particularly informed, and specifically defined biological entity. The rational soul of Socrates is what makes the living body of Socrates to be a human body, rather than some other type. Socrates, therefore, is the *unity* of the two principles, a body formed and enlivened by rational soul. Socrates's body has life not in the generic sense, but as a human being with all the powers and potentialities of being human. One cannot, in Aquinas's view, legitimately differentiate his being alive and his being human, except through abstraction from actual existence. The soul is the source of the life itself, as well as the ordered biological functions and potentialities and the capacity for rational consciousness. Aquinas asserts that the soul is not the essential Socrates (or any man).

9. In this passage Aquinas is addressing the critical issue that was much discussed in his day regarding the relationship between specific entities and universals.

It is the principle or part of the compound entity that makes all the essence (*Socrates*) possible. This sets him against the kind of neo-Platonic view that would claim that the "*soul* is the man."[10] The point: the soul is a component of the very essence, without being the essence, of the existent compound entity in question. This means that the soul is not the existent man *per se* but is the organizational reality without which his existence as a man cannot be.

Aquinas's arguments in question 76 about the soul's union with the body are rooted in Aristotle's contention that each existent entity has only *one substantial form* that makes it what it is.

1. A thing exists only as a particular concrete expression of a specific kind of existent essence, not generically.

2. A concrete existent is what it is because of the substantial form that makes it be what it is.

3. A living entity is the result of an *anima* that gives it life.

4. The life the entity lives is not distinct from its essence.

5. Therefore, there can only be one substantial form/soul in any living entity.

By Aquinas's lights, one can think about the question of what makes a human being a human being as follows. If the defining essence of a human being (by 1) is to be an animal that has the specific difference *qua* animal of being intellectual/rational,[11] then (by 2 and 3) there is a human *anima* which is the form that makes the being under consideration to be human. It follows, thus, that (by 4) the soul that is productive of rational thought and understanding must be also the *sole* animating principle in a human being. In his view, it makes no sense to say humans exist first as physical bodies of a particular type, then as animals in a generic sense, and only in the last level of analysis as human. Aquinas acknowledges the continuity of life between human beings and other organisms *qua* animals, but he cannot conceive of how one could define the *life* of the human animal by any term that does not include the essential definition of a living human being.[12] Hence, for Aquinas, the animality of a human

10. The parallel between neo-Platonic, Augustinian, and Cartesian thought is obvious regarding the question of identity. When the *soul* is conceived of primarily in terms of consciousness (and therefore almost strictly equivalent to the mind) the idea that one's identity is anchored, either primarily, at least, or exclusively in the *soul* is the logical conclusion. However, neither Aquinas nor Spinoza would so conceive of the soul.

11. The terms "intellectual" or "rational," when used by Aquinas as adjective qualifiers of the term *anima,* have a synonymous use. Hence, I shall use them interchangeably. What he means in either case is the organizational form or essence of human existence that gives to an individual the quality of being a rational animal.

12. This account, of course, flies in the face of strictly naturalist theories of human evolution in which the powers that make humans distinct somehow become added to the living essence that preceded the evolution of their human distinctiveness. Whether one believes the onus is on Thomists or on evolutionary theorists is beyond the scope of this present chapter. However, for problems

being is a part of the definition of human being, namely rational *animal,* but neither rationality nor animality can be thought of as ontologically prior to the actual creature (the primary substance) that expresses in the world both animality and rationality.[13] Any other way of thinking would be, in Aquinas's view, an abstraction from actual existence and amount to the idea that a human being is not really one existing thing, but an accumulation of essences. The only animality that human beings have is always specifically *rational* animality.

Thomas's main concern in this analytical position is that we avoid attempting to posit any existential or ontological real distinction between the rationality of a human being and his animality. Following his peripatetic mentor, he concluded that if one conceived of the distinction between the two as a distinction between ontologically different substances, a human being's rationality would be something over and above his actual, physical existence in the world. He was convinced that, philosophically, we cannot divorce the rational from the biological in human beings or consider the former as an attendant or emergent addition to the latter. To allow for more than one animating principle would suggest that there is no essential oneness of a human being's existence. On this basis, Aquinas asserts in the strongest terms that there can only be what he calls the single *intellectual or rational soul* making a human biologically rational and rationally biological simultaneously. So, rational insight, reflection, consciousness, and even choice is never something over and above the other features of human life.

In a human being, other powers (life, growth, locomotion, and sensory powers) caused by the *anima* all exist for the sake of the ultimate expression of the intellectual principle (the human mind) that is, as well, caused by the self-same *anima.* This is the *rational soul,* as Aquinas calls it. Also, once the body and all the powers it has is so informed, the mind is immediately related to the functions of the lower powers, although not in the sense that it causes them to be what they are. So, Aquinas says in Q 76, a 4, reply: "We must affirm that the rational soul alone informs man so as to give him existence, no other form does so. And just as it contains within its capacities all that the sense-soul and the nutritive soul contain, so it contains all the more elementary forms and of itself effects what they effect in other cases." Hence, the "lower" (in the medieval sense) aspects of biological life—the fact of being alive, sensory perception and motive life and growth–have very specific and unique manifestations in human

---

associated with the theory that humanness evolves (as an additional feature) out of, or in addition to, a preexistent living thing, see Meyer, *Signature in the Cell.*

13. To conceive otherwise would run afoul of the Aristotelian in Aquinas, because he affirmed what Aristotle contended: what is primary in existence are the individual members of species, not the species. A *biological kingdom* genus such as animal exists in the abstract sense only because there are organisms that can be called animals, and one kind of organism is the human animal. In fact, one could say that the "kingdom" destination animal is many removes from the species "human." Of course in Aristotelian terms even the species designation is itself a secondary substance, since it only exists in the sense that each and all human beings share in this common nature. Apart from the individuals, the "species" does not exist anywhere.

life. The soul that grants life grants a form of life that involves and enables living consciously with understanding and reason. This rational life gives a distinct expression to the other features of the animated (animal) existence of a human being that are shared with other animals. Our actions in movement have a volitional component, just as our sexual drives are informed by our reasoning and even our eating and drinking is guided by our intellectual intuitions and insights.[14] We choose our movements, organize our sexual relationships by reason rather than brute strength, and discern what foods or drinks we should consume. Yet, it would not be precise enough to say that the mind in itself is the cause of the ways we live.

The definition of irreducible unity with which Aquinas works in this section of the *Summa* is further revealed when one considers how the intellectual soul must be understood as only a "part" of some other entity. In Q 76, a 4, *ad* 1, he explains what he means by this: "[The soul] is the *activating part* of an organic physical body that has the power to live."[15] Aquinas is arguing that something other than the physical elements and principles compositing the material body must be posited to account for the fact that the "physical body" has, in the first place, "the power to live." Matter is not, by Aquinas's lights, self-organizing, much less capable of being the explanation (cause) of the existence of the life a particular entity manifests.[16] In the case of a human being, the matter that is organized to be alive is a made a living reality in a very particular way. The life that is being lived is a physically rational (or spiritual) life; or one could call it living rational (or spiritual) physicality. Such an intrinsic connection between rationality and bodily life, according to which the intellectual soul is the *part* of a human being that operates as the *single* formal cause of a human being's humanness, is what drives Thomistic hylomorphism of essential oneness. In this unity, mind and body are distinct from one another as modes of existence and powers of life in the unified essence and existence of the "one and the same thing," namely a human being.

Thomas still must provide a specific account for each human being's individuality as a particular composite human, since rational soul is a shared reality by all humans, otherwise they could not be human in the same way or be members of a single species, but neither can a single human being be equated definitionally to the form of humanness. To illustrate we can note that Socrates cannot exist apart from the rational form of humanness that gives him life as human being, but he is not *identical* with the human *anima* that makes him human, nor is the *anima* alone what makes him specifically Socrates. The human *anima* makes him human, but what makes Socrates to be "Socrates?" In Aquinas's hylomorphism, Socrates is distinguished from Plato

---

14. Consider that human beings have very few instincts when compared to other animals. Cf. Adler, *Ten Philosophical Mistakes*, 158–64.

15. Emphasis mine.

16. In so arguing, Aquinas is not suggesting the need for some radically occult explanation, such as immediate reference to God's power. His view is perfectly consistent with the doctrine of hylomorphism which we traced in chapter 2.

only by the fact that the humanness of the one is present in *this* arrangement of matter and the humanness of the other in *that* arrangement of matter. The material boundaries of the body of each individual (Plato and Socrates) are what distinguished Plato from Socrates ontologically. There is no other way to understand the unique identity of each, in Aquinas's estimation. The essence of human beings is composed of matter (generically speaking) and a specific kind of form (rational animality), and all humans share this definitional essence of being human. Such a metaphysical definition (matter formed by rational soul) does not, by itself, account for how they differ from one another. Yet, each most certainly is distinct.[17] But what could Aquinas mean by saying that the arrangement of matter makes humans individuals?

Aquinas argues that Socrates is made to be an individual, and therefore *Socrates*, by the particular material stuff—*materia signata*—in the composite entity named Socrates insofar as the rational human-making soul gives it dimensions, function, and potentialities in keeping with human nature. This doctrine is a simply an application of his general theory of matter as the principle of individuation within species. The spatial dimensions of Socrates' body defining him in space and in relationship to all other things are what individuate Socrates from all other human beings, not to mention all other entities. In part three of the *Summa*, Aquinas describes the way that dimensions work to make specific the individuation of an entity. In III, Q 77, a. 2, while discussing the Eucharist, Aquinas argues that "dimensive quantity in itself has a certain individuation; we can imagine many lines of the same kind, but all different because of their position; and this position is part of the very idea of this quantity. For it is of the very definition of a dimension to be a quantity having position."[18] What is interesting here is the role that *position* plays in Aquinas's account of individuality. As Andrew Payne notes, "Rightly understood [Aquinas's account of] the nature of dimensive quantity includes position, so that whatever has dimensive quantity will also be made of parts having position in relation to each other and will therefore occupy a determinate place."[19] So, the material things like organs, bones, muscles, et al are given

---

17. This way of discussing the matter would seem to be entirely consonant with contemporary science of DNA. The encoded information that humans share is not the thing that makes them distinct from one another, even if issues of height and pigmentation and other features that are expressed in the physical makeup of a particular human being are also in the DNA information, for there is no real distinction between the humanness of human beings simply on the level of DNA, since the DNA has a shared "formal" essence and is analogous to information. The distinction is, rather, only real when actual spatial differentiation occurs. An interesting question to pursue, but which is beyond the present focus of this project, would be whether or not a Thomistic metaphysics or the metaphysics of Duns Scotus, with his doctrine of the *haecceitas*, more closely approximates the modern science of DNA and the way that the information encoded gives expression to each specific person's humanness.

18. For an excellent discussion of Aquinas's theory of individuation, see Payne, "Garcia and Aquinas on the Principle of Individuation," 545–75. A substantive criticism of Aquinas's doctrine is found in Gracia, *Individuality*, 246–72.

19. Payne, "Garcia and Aquinas on the Principle of Individuation," 568.

an arrangement in relationship to one another in an organism which arrangement together accounts for the "determinate place" in which that organism exists.

One could add that Aquinas's view of identity further includes the notion that being a unique, singular human by individuation and being given defined dimensions further involves the particularization of that individual's "place" *in relation to* all other entities in relation to which that individual exists. This is inherent in the idea of place, especially considering the argument presented in the previous quotation, according to which all the lines are individuated from one another because "of their position." Hence, the individuality of someone, say Socrates, is ultimately comprehensible regarding the place and position he fills only in relation to *other* individuals who are also similarly individuated by arrangement of parts and relative location. So, Socrates is made to be "Socrates" both because designated matter has received form and because in so receiving form the matter takes on the "dimensive quantity" of Socrates in relation to all other material entities.[20] Individuality in human identity involves relative relationality, at least spatially; and it is the rational *anima* that orders the matter, even as the properties of matter establish individuality of the material being spatially related to other bodies whose forms organize them materially.

What this does not help us with, however, is understanding how the mind of an individual (Socrates) is individuated from other minds, nor does it specifically address the *one and the sameness* of mind and body. In Thomistic terms, individuation of the body is not the *cause* of the mind's existence or particularity; neither is mind just a way of describing some physical/material process or a power that emerges from the body. Whereas the soul is the form that informs and organizes the designated matter into the arrangement of parts and their relations and creates the "position" and limits of Socrates *qua* physical body, how does the soul as the principle of intellect individuate Socrates *qua* mental consciousness and distinct rational creature? In *De unitate intellectus contra Averroistas (On the Uniqueness of Intellect Against the Averroists)*, Aquinas wrestles with the question of whether each individual human being's intellect (mind) is distinct from all others or is an expression of a singular universal act of knowing which involves all people having ontologically one intellect.[21] This was the position of the Averroists. In this treatise, Aquinas is addressing specifically the nature of what Aristotle termed *possible intellect*, which involves the particular and unique sense experiences and attainments of knowledge of specific knowers (individual minds). Aquinas takes great pains to refute Averroes's position that all human beings participate in the knowing of a single mind, because he saw that this implied there is no distinct existence for an individual human, except materially. Such a position led to the denial of perspectival knowledge and the continuing existence of human conscious existence after the death of the body, which his Christian orthodoxy would not

---

20. See chapter 3 for the discussion of Aquinas's ideas about signate matter.

21. *De Unitate Intellectus.*

countenance. He builds his rebuttal by arguing that Averroes and his disciples have woefully misunderstood Aristotle, not by asserting a biblical argument.[22]

In addressing the Averroist position, Thomas is intent on showing "that the above-mentioned position is no less against the principles of philosophy than against the teachings of the Faith."[23] For Averroes and his Latin interpreters, the implications of their reading of Aristotle's *possible intellect* was that this intellect is a substance which exists separately from any particular body of any specific human being. Among other things, this entailed, as Robert J. Dobie has noted, "every act of understanding on the part of the human being [each individual] would constitute a miracle, since, on their account human knowing is the work, ultimately, of an extrinsic and, indeed, supernatural principle."[24] This is due to there being, on Averroist principles, no true knowing subject related to the body of a human being—no mind.

The human mind is the result of the causative power of the soul as the principle of human existence (its form); this causative power of mind is co-extensive the to order, complexity, and potentiality of the human body. This is not a form of parallelism *per se*, for the hylomorphism on offer is creating an ontologically singular reality, namely the human person.[25] In Thomas's metaphysical analysis, human persons do not so much produce or manifest rational powers as they *participate in the reality of rationality* as created beings. Human rationality is ultimately grounded in the nature of God as *Logos*. However, the rationality of which we are capable is not a purely immaterial intellect. That kind of rationality is only for angels in the created order. In the act of creating, God established in humans a specific kind of rationality, one which is experience-dependent and discursive and obtains knowledge by reflection upon sensory experiences from the physical world acting on the body's sensory organs by the *intelligible forms*, which are expressions of the essence of all physical entitles in the material world. Because material things have properties, potentialities, and powers of expression and action, which are their essences, when the body, which is in its complexity and powers of operation capable of being acted upon by things in the physical world, the actions of these entities are received through the bodily organs of sense via *intelligible forms*. These actions are received by the body as purely physical actions. However, because human beings are physical, organic creatures in the material world endowed with the capacity for understanding, the intellect, which is immersed you might say in the body, by *its own powers* receives these actions from the material world as intelligible *sensations* expressing the essence and powers of the primary beings acting upon the body materially. While the mind needs these data that become available to it as the body's sensory apparatuses are engaged, this does not mean that the body

22. *De Unitate Intellectus*, proem., n.2.

23. *De Unitate Intellectus*, proem., n 2.

24. Dobie, "Incarnate Knowing," 498.

25. In the next chapter, Aquinas's understanding and utilization of the concept of *person* is explored.

is "causing" the mind to know. The soul that grants the form of receptive sensitivity of other things' actions out of their essences to the body also enables mind as the activity of engaging and receiving the actions the body receives as sensory data. As Dobie notes, ". . . the human soul is the form of a body *not despite but because of* the nature of its intellect as akin to prime matter in the order of intellects: *informing* a body allows the possible intellect [a potential individual mind] to receive the sense data that gives it specific content and make *it* truly the 'place of forms' and actualize it as intellect."[26] When presented with the sensory data from bodily interactions with other entities, the intellect is *actualized* in the sense that it now has obtained data upon which its nonbodily dependent powers of understanding and contemplation rely for actualization. The body does not cause the activity of mind, but it is a participating "partner" in the human person's knowing as mind-body composite.

It should be added that the human mind is granted by the informing power of the soul with a dual set of powers that always operate together. The one is passive sensation apt and capable of receiving intelligible forms, but the other is the abstractive power (the 'agent intellect') that can collect the sensory data and reflect upon it in such a way that it understands the essences and identities of things that act upon the body by their intelligible forms.[27] So, it is not the soul that is the intellect *per se*, but it is the soul that enables not only the mind to be expressed and active but to be expressed as the unique kind of "incarnate knowing" that is proper to a human being. The mind is neither separate from the body, nor supervenient upon the body, nor an emergent power out of the body. The mind and the body are one and the same thing—the human being—whose existence is expressed in both modes of being.[28] That *one and the same thing* is the human person who is physically moving in the world and being acted upon by other bodies, as well as understanding his or her own actions and the essences of the world in which he or she exists as both body and mind, because the multiple, complex powers of the soul grant this kind of identity.

Individuated physical humans are what exist primarily in the material world, but their ontological primacy as entities shares a specific *way* of being with other beings of the same kind as themselves. In the *Summa*, 1–2, Q 17, a. 4 he concludes that: "Many individuals that are one in genus or species are many absolutely speaking [when considered as particulars], and one with respect to something, for to be one in genus or species is to be *one with respect to reason*."[29] This means that Socrates and

26. Dobie, "Incarnate Knowing," 513, my emphasis.

27. *De Anima*, q 4.

28. *De Anima*, q 4. "Nothing in the principles of nature or of metaphysics prevents there being a form that is partially immersed in matter and partially transcendent of it . . . In fact, the whole reason Aristotle posited an immanent formal cause in things is because he noticed how the various properties and operations of material substances transcend more and more their constituent elements the more complex they become. It therefore stands to reason that there would be at least one material substance with an operation [the immaterial mind] that transcends matter altogether."

29. Emphasis mine. By reason Aquinas means our intellectual grasp of the truth of their similarities, which are understood to be real and, therefore, "substances" in a secondary sense.

Plato can be considered to be one *kind* of thing (human), in a conceptual sense, but ontologically they are distinct in their specific essences *qua* Socrates and Plato.[30] Just as each thing that exists only exists as a specific *kind* of thing, the only way that specific *kinds* exist is as the particular thing(s) that exist concretely as expressions of a kind in the world. Even though the individual essence of each of the similar particulars only exists by way of the species form to which each of them gives expression, in the activity of knowing all human beings have their own individual acts of understanding and awareness. Those acts, when exercised adequately and clearly, all achieve knowledge of the same reality that passive intellect receives and agent intellect comprehends. Such is the case, for Aquinas, because of his hylomorphism regarding human nature as existing as part of the material world. In *Summa* I, q. 85, a. 1, he asserts that human beings understand "material things by abstracting from the phantasms; and through material things thus considered we acquire some knowledge of immaterial things." While there are many distinct human beings who exist in the world, because they all exist in the same world and are acted upon by the same intelligible forms of material things in that world, and because all human minds share the same powers of receiving and abstracting there is a unity of knowledge that disparate, ontologically separate human minds can grasp individually and together. "And so, for the human intellect, the diversity of intellects according to the diversity of bodies does not hinder universal [shared] knowledge, but it ensures that each act of our knowing is *our individual act* of knowing, what at the same time opening us out onto universal being."[31]

Soul (form) and body (matter) are terms for the ontological principles of rational animal existence. In their composite unity they instantiate an entity called a human being. As principles that together are the unity, they are not substances, but are, respectively, active and passive attributes of being. Soul is the "active" factor in that it grants specific *kind* of existence to the physical entity that lives because of the union of soul and the matter that becomes the *informed* body. This specific kind of physical existence involves the capacity for relating to mind and participating in the activity of rational understanding, although the body itself is not doing the knowing. The body is the passive dynamic in human existence because it is only capable of being formed, but it grants particularity and individuality in its passive capability of being formed. Reference to both principles is necessarily involved in descriptions of the singular act of *being* human. Soul, therefore, is not an immaterial thing that occupies its own realm. Neither is soul the mental, "thing" that is the aspect of human existence that does the knowing. When Aquinas says, as quoted above, that the soul is *in* the body, he means that it is "in" it in such a way as to make the body what it is and enables the *being*

---

30. But, as was argued in chapter 3, that does not mean the existence of the concept is not real. The existence of the concept is the product of the abstract reasoning powers of a human knower who is capable of recognizing similarities between ordinary particulars. Such similarities are not nothing, even if they have no concrete existence except in the ordinary particulars that share the manifested similarities.

31. Dobie "Incarnate Knowing," 521.

(existence) of the body that is a human being, because the soul is source of organization in the specific material of that same being. Still, the soul can be loosely and rightly termed the knowing power, in abstraction from the material conditions of the being so organized, because in the *rational soul* understanding, consciousness, and contemplation are the highest powers it produces when actualized in union with matter.

The intricacy of Aquinas's theory that the soul and body are one *qua* human person in *act* (in the Aristotelian sense) is made more obvious when one considers the reciprocal relationship that exists between the human body and the soul. In his metaphysical appraisal, not only does the soul establish a bodily existence as a particular kind of essence in act, but only a particular kind of matter can be adequate for expressing the form of the human *anima*. Because of the kind of intelligence that a human being exhibits, the human soul must cause matter to become a very particular kind of body. Hence, not just any matter will do as the receiver of the information by the human *anima* gives form (literally) and function to the human body. He describes the reciprocity in I a, Q 76, a 5, reply.

> Since form does not exist for the sake of matter but rather matter for the sake of form, the form explains the character of the matter, not the other way around. Now the intellective soul [as he has argued in I, Q 55, a 2] is the *lowest grade of intelligence* in the hierarchy of nature, in that it does not have the angelic being's inborn knowledge of the truth but *has to gather it* from quantified things *through sensation* . . . . the intellective soul needs the power of sensation as well as the power of understanding. But there can be no sensation except through a body. Therefore, the intellective soul has to have a body *which is a suitable organ* of sense.
>
> Now all the other senses build on touch. And the organ of touch needs to embrace contraries within its range, hot and cold, moist and dry and so on, the things touch comprehends . . . And the more it occupies a sort of middle position between such contraries, the more *touch-perceptive* the organ will be. So that the body to which an intellective soul is *joined* has to be a compound body occupying a sort of middle position as regards objects of touch. For this reason man is the most touch-perceptive of the animals and intelligent men the most touch-perceptive of men. For instance, sensitivity and insight go together.

Whether or not Aquinas's assessment of the relationship between one's physical sensitivity and one's intellectual prowess is accurate is open to question, but it is clear, from this passage, that Aquinas is deeply indebted to Aristotle's claims in the *De anima*. Aristotle's argument in that work regarding the dependence of mental sensory awareness upon the physiological conditions of the body informed Aquinas's philosophical anthropology. In his commentary on the *De Anima* the Angelic Doctor acknowledges that human emotions can be described, at least in part, by decidedly physical categories. For instance, he thinks that Aristotle's contention that anger is "inflammation of blood around the heart," should not be neglected as a part of the analysis of what anger itself *is*. Of course, Aquinas thought that this would not fully describe the nature of anger and suggested that much of what Aristotle theorized about this matter is (understandably) undeveloped.[32]

Furthermore, Aquinas says that the soul does not merely actuate the body, but as the principle of animate existence of the living human being is "included *in* that which the soul is said to actuate, just as we say that heat actuates something hot and light something luminous—not as if it would be luminous apart from the light, but that the light makes it luminous" (Q 76, a 4, ad 1).[33] This illustration entails, what has been stated earlier, that the *intellective soul* is the principle of organic life of the human being: ". . . so it is said that the soul is the actuation of a body and so one, meaning that due to the soul it is a body and is organic and has power to live. But the first actuation [being a body] has a relation of potentiality to the second [being organically alive], which we call activity;' there is no such potentiality apart from or excluding the soul."[34]

The essential unity that Aquinas attributes to a human being is further emphasized elsewhere in this same Question in the *Summa*. In article 3, Aquinas addresses the question of whether there are other souls, not simply other forms (principles of biological organization) besides the "intellectual soul." Aquinas lays out the objection that he wishes to address:

> Aristotle says that genus stems from matter, while the differentiating features stems from form. But rationality, the differentiating feature constituting humanity, comes from the intellective soul, while man is said to be an animal because he has a body animated by a sense-soul. Thus the intellectual soul is related to the body animated by the sense-soul as form to matter. So the intellectual soul is not the same as the sensitive soul in man, but presupposes it as the matter it energizes.[35]

As he replies to this assertion in the negative, we have here another example of Aquinas overturning the plurality of souls theory of his day, which as I have already indicated made intellect life and mind a state supervening upon lower organic states. He answers those who objected to the idea that the intellectual soul was the only

32. This being the case, Aquinas would presumably not be dismayed by the discoveries of contemporary brain science, namely, the detection and demonstration of associations between psychological/mental states and physical events in the brain. More important, however, it might indeed be the case that he would have at the very least understood, if not have been able to affirm at least in part, Spinoza's argument in Book Three of *Ethics* that there is a fundamental physical "part" of the very being of human emotions.

33. Emphasis mine.

34. Klima, "Man = Body + Soul," 184.

35. The assertion that this is a medieval version of supervenience theory is based on the implication in this argument that the "intellectual" soul needs the "sense-soul" in the same way that form, generally conceived, needs matter. Hence, the conclusion that the intellectual soul "presupposes" the sense-soul strikes me as a kind of supervenience doctrine, which contends that the mind supervenes upon a physical-organic state of affairs that is necessary for, even if not productive of, the mental supervenience.

source of life in human beings in a way that is crucial for understanding his general position on the issue of the absolute oneness of body and soul in the singular entity called a human being. He begins by noting that we can and do make logical distinctions between certain concepts such as sensory life and intellectual activity in human beings. In his rebuttal, he maintains, however, that the distinctions are logical, not ontological—that human reason actually "can grasp *a single existing thing* [*unum et idem*—one and the same] in a variety of ways."

His rejection of these distinctions as real divisions of being is based on his conception of the intellectual soul; he conceived of the reality of souls in the world as entailing a concept of a hierarchy of life. In Aquinas's understanding of this issue, every aspect and power associated with the material existence of any being is actuated by the exact same *anima*. The more complex the organization of a biological entity that results in increased powers of operation, however, the more formal (informing) capacity the soul enabling such complexity of organization has. So, in an animal which has sensory life but not self-moving powers (think of a jellyfish), the *anima* that informs the matter and makes these creatures alive carries in its formal operations the power of life (such as the vegetative soul evinces) along with the sensory establishing powers that these sensing but not self-moving animals have. And animals that have life plus sensory powers plus auto-locomotive capacity are informed and organized by a soul that includes the organizational properties of making-alive and making-sensitive in addition to the greater power of giving locomotion. The chain of formal operations of *anima* ascends to the rational soul, which involves not only the more complex form (consciousness, intellect and volition) of its own level but contains, as well, the kind of existence that the less complex life forms exhibit. Recognizing that the more specific powers of a creature have an incorporative aspect to them regarding the less advanced powers, Aquinas saw no need for adding souls to account for the way of human existence, because a single organizational force (*anima*) *gives* life, function, a drive to flourish, rational understanding and anything else essential to being a human being.[36]

---

36. This particular way of arguing for the substantial unity of entities and insisting that the human soul was hierarchically capable of subsuming within itself all the powers of the lower vegetative and sensory soul of plants and animals was thought to be a dangerous innovation by many of his day and afterward. Copleston, in *Aquinas,* comments about this doctrine's controversial reception. "It was combated at a debate in Paris, before the bishop, about 1270, Dominicans and Franciscans, especially the Franciscan Peckham, accusing St. Thomas of maintaining an opinion which was contrary to the teaching of the saints, particularly Augustine and Anselm. . . . The chief ground of complaint being that the Thomist doctrine was unable to explain how the dead body of Christ was the same as the living body, since according to St. Thomas there is only one substantial form in the human substance and this more, the soul, is withdrawn at death, other forms being educed out of the potentiality of matter . . . .on March 18th, 1277 [Thomism was condemned] at Oxford, inspired by Robert Kilwardby, O.P., Archbishop of Canterbury, in which figured among other propositions the unicity of substantial form and the passivity of matter. . . . Kilwardby's condemnation was repeated by his successor, the Franscian Peckam, on October 29th, 1284, though by that time Thomism had been officially approved in the Dominican Order" (Copleston, *Thomas Aquinas,* 153–55; Cf. Suttor, *Thomas Aquinas,* 255).

This means, in Aquinas's view, that those who, based on mere ordinary observation of behavior, posit a plurality of souls really do not fully comprehend the way that a single human *anima* provides for complexity of organization in a being who is essentially one, and only one, in the most basic sense. It is not the case that one needs to posit a different organizational principle, he argues, to account for various human capacities. The single rational soul grants the very capacity for sensory life upon which it is itself dependent in order to be able to reason discursively in the first place. In the relevant observation of behavior, our minds merely identify distinct operations, rather than disparate forms of life, in human experience and action. As he puts it in the same passage of the *Summa* in question 76, "Those features of the intellective soul which are beyond the power of *sense are seen by the mind* as shaping and completing and *thus constituting* that which makes man different."[37] By contrast, doctrines involving a pluralistic hierarchy of supervenient souls go hand in hand with the suggestion that each of them, including the highest, is something over and above the material nature of human existence. Aquinas could not see how this would fit the point of the essential definition, "rational animal." The doctrine he proposed was simpler and more consistent, he thought, only needing to posit a single informing *anima* to explain the organizational complexity of a human being.

This in turn leads to a reconciliation of the claims that the soul is "in" the living human being and that it is at the same time "one and the same" as that being. Aquinas observes, as a part of his proofs, that the departure of life at the death of a person was both the end of rationality in that bodily entity and the beginning of the disintegration of the body *qua* spatial, biological entity. In Aquinas's mind, just as the initial unity of soul and body means that rationality is part of the nature of the new entity so informed, so in even the most initial forms (embryonic life in the womb) early in the process of human development, when all the powers are not operative, rationality is still part of the definition. That is why the cessation of life is evidence of the departure of the intellectual soul.

> Substantial form enables a thing simply to have existence, so that when it is there we say the thing is there, and when it is not there we say the thing has disintegrated . . . . If it were the case that *as well as the intellective soul* some other substantial form already existed in the soul's subject material, so that it came into something already existing, it would follow that the soul did not give precisely existence and was consequently not a substantial form. Its embodiment would not generate existence nor its departure bring on disintegration simply speaking, but merely as regards some particular aspect. This is clearly untrue. We must affirm that the intellective soul informs man so as to give him existence; no other form does.[38]

37. Emphasis mine.
38. Suttor, *Thomas Aquinas*, 75–83.

The singular human *anima* that Aquinas calls the rational soul, enables the complex body needed to be a *rational animal*. By this measure, Aquinas argues that the mental activity that a human being engages in because of the in-forming principles of the rational *anima* is not the product of the soul alone. Rather, the matter, which is informed by the soul, to be the organic human being capable of rationality provides the individuation of a human essence. The humanness of this essence is that which the rational soul brings to the material stuff that becomes the human body. But the soul does not account for the particularization of the essence; that is the function of the matter that is informed. Since Thomas's hylomorphism focuses on primary substances as the fundamental existents of reality, rather than essences or natures, he concludes that without the body that is produced in the union of soul and matter the organizational information that the soul provides to the material stuff goes unexpressed and, therefore is not truly existent. Soul, in other words, as the organizing principle, requires body in order to exist strictly speaking. The human being that is the singular composite and primary substance is his bodily life; and that bodily life is produced in the union of soul and matter. Both individual existence and human nature, generically named, is communicated to the matter of the body by the grounding that the rational soul bring.

5

Persons in Aquinas's Metaphysics

THE *KNOWING* SUBJECT: THE SOUL AS "INTELLECT" OR "MIND"

BEYOND WHAT WE HAVE already discovered, we must ask what Aquinas's argument means when he, in certain passages, utilizes the nouns "mind' and "intellect" as a reference to the soul of a human being. This was briefly noted in the previous chapter, but it deserves further exploration, and a further unpacking of it will enable us to understand why the category *persons* is a metaphysical one in Aquinas and why it is the key to understanding how mind and body can be understood as "one and the same thing," namely, the human person. However, his willingness to use the term "mind" to describe the soul, along with his insistence that the soul is subsistent and incorruptible, may imply that he is—all protestations aside—really a kind of substance dualist. At least it could be argued that if he holds to a doctrine of incorruptibility of the soul and he uses "mind" to name the soul, it makes no sense to interpret him as holding that mind and body are *one and the same thing,* for that would seem to suggest that "mind" is a kind of thing-in-itself (a Cartesian, therefore unspinozistic, concept). This would undercut irreparably the idea that he sees mind and body as coterminous descriptions of one thing. Hence, we need to ask what alternative meaning there could be when Aquinas says we can characterize *anima* as "intellect" or "mind." Without this alternative reading, we may find that Aquinas not only is unhelpful for understanding Spinoza but gainsays his metaphysical commitments already outlined. If he uses these terms to refer to the soul, insofar as they might be interpreted as saying they point us to an actual thing as their shared referent, that would be remarkably unaristotelian. Yet, Aquinas thought of himself as unpacking Aristotle's doctrines for the Christian church in a manner that was consonant with Christian orthodoxy and faithful to Aristotle's intentions.[1] But even if it is not the case that Aquinas holds to a quasi-substance dualism, if one thinks that Aquinas conceived of mind as some power or feature that is not only distinct from the matter of the body but is in a distinct realm of existence, the suggestion that Thomistic hylomorphism is a helpful interpretive category for understanding Spinoza would be weakened beyond all hope of rehabilitation.

In order to analyze how Aquinas develops his argument that the soul can also be called the mind, we will benefit by considering a recent "Cartesian" reading of Aquinas's doctrine, that of Anthony Kenny.[2] He argues that a strong case can be made for considering Aquinas's notion (mind) as a categorical entity. Considering Kenny's interpretation, and showing how it fails, my assertion that he conceives of mind and body as one and the same thing will be strengthened. According to Kenny, Aquinas would agree with Descartes's judgment that human beings "have" minds, because they essentially are minds. The Thomistic mind, by Kenny's definition, is a single power in itself that is a "knower" constituted by the two capacities of (1) intellect and (2) the desire for the good *that corresponds to* the nature of the mind, i.e., will.[3] Kenny attributes this position to Aquinas, because he interprets Aquinas as defining the mind as "the capacity for acquiring linguistic and symbolic abilities" that exists along with *will* as an additional power.[4] The import of all this for Kenny is that he believes that a mind in Aquinas's view is a power that is metaphysically distinct from the biological considerations that science deals with in its analysis of human life, which is certainly not a controversial interpretation. While he quite rightly, in his interpretation, describes the mind as a power of the soul, but which is not identical with the soul, Kenny's way of describing Aquinas's doctrine is, nonetheless, fraught with inadequacies as an interpretation of a Thomistic philosophy of mind.[5] As Kenny interprets Aquinas's metaphysics, the soul could not possess sensitive powers as part of the "mind."

1. Of course, Aquinas might be wrong about this. Suttor points out, for example, that in the Treatise on Man Aquinas's "argument for Aristotle's [harmony with Christian] orthodoxy is tenuous, and he can be understood [in the sense Aquinas interprets him] only if we can overcome several grave difficulties cf *De generatione animalium*, 736b 273." Suttor, *Thomas Aquinas*, 163n.

2. Kenny, *Aquinas on Mind*.

3. Kenny, *Aquinas on Mind*, 18. "The will, too, is part of the mind, as the Aristotelian tradition maintained, but that is because the intellect and will are two aspects of a single indivisible capacity."

4. Kenny, *Aquinas on Mind*, 17.

5. Kenny's treatment of Thomas's doctrine sounds, as O'Callaghan also notices, very much like his own notion of the nature of mind. In *The Metaphysics of Mind*, Kenny argues that human beings alone have minds, but they share features of life with other animals. In Kenny's view, Thomistic *anima* is fundamentally possessed of two powers, what he calls "psyche" and "mind." He offers this distinction: "We may wish to have a word to refer to the *cluster of sensory capacities* in the way in which 'mind' in my usage refers to the cluster of capacities whose major members are the intellect and will. The most appropriate word seems to be 'psyche'. If we adopt this usage, we can say that whereas only humans have minds, humans and other animals have psyches" (*Aquinas on Mind*, 19, emphasis original).

Kenny's interpretation seems to accept as a given a methodological dualism that, as O'Callaghan says, "separates the philosophical study of mind from the scientific study of everything else, including the animal life of the human body."[6] This acceptance is apparent when he describes an "Aquinas in whose philosophy there is some power called 'mind' that exists in as some irreducible core amenable *only* to philosophy."[7] This Aquinas would, in the methodological dualism Kenny offers, seem to run afoul of the medieval Aristotelian's own insistence that the one *anima* that organizes the biological life of a human being also establishes in the human being the vegetative and sensory elements of life. While Kenny recognizes and accepts this aspect of Aquinas, he nonetheless undercuts it by making Aquinas sound like the very pluralists that he stood against. As noted by O'Callaghan in an essay critical of Kenny: "Kenny preserves that plurality in a weaker sense, by his emphasis upon a strong distinction within the soul between the set of powers of vegetative and sensitive life on the one hand, and mind as a thoroughly different power of the soul on the other."[8]

If Kenny's account is lacking, how will we progress toward understanding what Aquinas, in fact, does mean where he calls the soul "mind or intellect?" We may begin with the foundational focus Aquinas provides in his treatise on man in the *Summa*. The discussion of the mind he provides later is built first upon his discussion of the nature of the soul and then secondly upon his view of human beings as composite beings who each have in themselves an essential unity in the integration of soul and body. In *Question 75, a 2* of the *Prima Pars,* he presents his argument about the soul's nature and argues that the form of the human body (the soul) is "the principle of the *act* of understanding" and this act is incorporeal and subsistent.[9] He continues on to say that "the principle of understanding, which is *called* mind or intellect, has its own activity in which body takes no intrinsic part." It seems odd that Aquinas would name the soul "mind or intellect" when it is clear from his other discussions that the human *anima* has further powers that are not describable as intellectual or mental in any reasonable sense (growth and motion). Intellect or mind is but one of the powers of the rational soul. Aquinas, however, is thinking of mind as the principal power of the soul: "the intellectual soul *sometimes* gets named from the intellect *as its principle power*" (Ia, Q 79, a 1, *ad* 1). But intellect (*intellectus*) is still only "a power of the soul and not the very essence of the soul" (Reply). So, the soul is *called* mind or intellect in an equivocal sense, naming the most unique feature that it enables human life to manifest, i.e., the specific difference of being a *rational* animal.

6. O'Callaghan, "Aquinas Rejection of Mind," 21.

7. Kenny, *Aquinas on Mind,* 5.

8. O'Callaghan, "Aquinas Rejection of Mind," 19. O'Callaghan's article is an excellent analysis of not only Aquinas's mature doctrine of the soul and mind-body relations, but also an insightful exposition of how his later theory articulated in the *Summa* relates to, and grew out of, his earlier work in his commentary on *De Anima,* through the *Summa contra Gentiles*.

9. Emphasis mine.

If *intellectus* is not "the very essence of the soul" in Aquinas's doctrine, then he is effectively distancing himself from Augustine's authority, who considered the process of thought and understanding as the ontological nature of the soul.[10] In Augustine's theory, the mind is distinct from the body and the soul is essentially the mind. Sensation is not part of the mind, for this earlier Christian theologian, because the mind is essentially one thing that has three acts it performs: memory, intellect, and will.[11] The result is, of course, dualism in Augustine, reflected in his description of the "inner" and "outer" man.[12] The former acts to understand eternal truth and the latter focuses on the sensory data the body experiences; and the result of this kind of thinking means, for Augustine, that the mind is an immaterial thing with its own special unity of operation. Aquinas, while needing to distance himself from Augustine's brand dualism, had to square himself with Augustine's authority as a theologian. Aquinas cites this Father of the Church in the first point of Question 79 where he is interpreting Augustine. There he says that we *call* the human soul the mind or the intellect in the same sense in which we speak of the souls of lower animals as *sense*-souls. "And likewise, the intellectual soul sometimes *gets named* from the intellect as its principal power, in the way, as the *De Anima* remarks, that *the intellect is a substance*. And in this way Augustine says that mind is spirit or essence."

The import of the above exposition is that in the *Summa* Aquinas says the terms "mind" and "intellect" are *only* a shorthand for describing the rational soul, because they signify the highest activity of the human being's embodied life that results from the organizing principle of a human being's existence *qua* rational animal. The act of intellection takes place in the life of a human person as a rational animal because of the influence of the soul. Since mind names the highest *act* of the human being, the terms mind or intellect refer to the soul in respect to its highest power. Only for sake of convenience and to make sure his rhetoric is reconcilable with the authority of Saint Augustine, the Dominican theologian says we can *call* the soul the mind, while at the same time not conceiving that the soul *is* the mind. In this sense, for Aquinas, it is not the terms mind or intellect (which is a power of the human person) but soul, understood as referring to the informing or organizing principle of bodily existence, that has a substantial referent. We must understand correctly this idea of the mind as a

---

10. Augustine's most important, influential, and sophisticated statements on the mind come in *De Trinitate*, in which he uses the example of the human mind to endeavor to establish the possibility of plurality in the Godhead. He posits the mind as a foundational existent but then suggests that the self-knowledge that the mind can have and the love that the mind can feel for the knowledge it has of itself are three substantive distinctions that do not imply ontological division. "Love and knowledge are not in the mind as in a subject, but they too are substantial, just as the mind itself is; and even if they are posited relatively to each other, still each of them is its own substance. . . . The mind therefore and its love and knowledge are three somethings, and these three are one thing, and when they are complete they are equal" (Augustine, *Trinity*, 273–74).

11. Augustine, *Trinity*, 298–300.

12. While Augustine is careful to insist that the body is an intricate part of the human person, he nonetheless, with his doctrine of the inner and outer man, posits a dualism.

power made possible by the soul, if we are going to understand Aquinas. O'Callaghan's exegetical observations in this respect are on the mark:

> The intellective part of the soul consists [for Aquinas] in the powers closely associated with intellect or mind. No suggestion is made [by Aquinas] that they form a potential whole that is itself a power . . . . Now 'intellective part' is nothing more than a phrase for the classification of powers associated with the intellect. Most importantly, 'mind' is uniformly associated with 'intellect' alone [with no intimation of will as a part of the 'mind'].[13]

At the heart of Aquinas's concerns is not the Cartesian problem of how to define the mind per se or to describe the ontological status of consciousness, but how to understand human existence as one whole entity that is essentially the act of rationality incarnated as an aspect of a physical being. He presents us with a dual aspect philosophical anthropology rather than a philosophy of mind *itself.* For Aquinas, mental acts are not the acts of a Cartesian mind, or even an Augustinian one (with its inner and outer man). Rather, he thinks of mental acts as the acts of a being that is as essentially material as it is mental, because they are ultimately the acts of a rational *animal*–the composite human person. As shall be argued below, this allows Aquinas to avoid the associated problems of causation and origination that attended and attend various dualisms. With respect to the question of the connection of mental acts with human bodies, he sees mental acts as the actions or experiences of a biological creature whose mental and bodily acts are involved—in distinct ways—in the life of a human person who is exercising and achieving understanding. (The same can also be said about the nature of physical motion.) Knowing is the act of a human being's bodily life, at least in the sense that it is not something that takes place apart from the actual bodily life of the human being. But since knowing and understanding constitute the highest level of that complex biological life made possible in a human being through the organizational principle of the human *anima,* the human knower is, to that extent, but no further, a mind just as he or she is a body.

This failure of *mind* to be a genuine referent in the sense in question is underscored by keeping in mind Aquinas's insistence that the human intellective soul bears in its informing properties the kind of intellect that can perform its operations only in relation to a body, which is the lowest in the hierarchy of intellects.[14] In the *Summa* (I a, Q 77, art. 3) Aquinas makes the case that the powers of the soul are distinguished

---

13. O'Callaghan, "Aquinas Rejection of Mind," 38.

14. In his doctrine of the immortality of the soul, Aquinas argues that certain powers of the soul are kept operable after death, namely, intellect and will. But these incorruptibly operating powers would not have become operable in the first place prior to the body's relationship with the soul. We shall look at the logic of Aquinas's view of the incorruptibility of the soul in the succeeding sections, but for now we can observe that this way of stating the issue underscores the fact that Aquinas thinks of soul and body in union as enabling actual existence and real "expression" to an entity that is neither body nor mind, strictly speaking, and yet, in some sense, is in fact both.

from one another by their acts, and these acts in turn are distinguished according to their objects. "Object" is to be understood in the medieval sense rather than in terms of our contemporary metaphysical currency. It can refer to a thing that is the objective or purpose of a passive power of the soul, for example music would be an object of hearing, or of the active (agent) powers of the soul—the object or the aspect of reality that is the goal or the end for which that active power exists. Just as health is the object of medical arts, so truth is the object of the rational soul.[15] But again, remember that this truth is the object of an incarnated rationality.

What then is the object of the mind, if the mind is understood to be the act of understanding that is manifest in a human being *qua* rational animal? Whereas for the Empiricist school it is our impressions and mental constructs only and for the Rationalists it is some sort of innate foundational ideas upon which other rational concepts can be formed, Aquinas's epistemology can take us some way toward understanding how to answer this question. First, as was indicated previously, he conceives of the human intellect as requiring the body to perform its acts of understanding. This does not mean that the body *causes* the mind to attain or receive knowledge. Instead, he argues, the issue that needs to be analyzed is *how* a rational animal is both animal and rational, because the activity of knowing is one that involves the whole being of a human person. To analyze this process, Aquinas offers a theory of how sensory perception provides the mind with the material that it is to understand. For Aquinas, the proper immediate object of the human mind (at least in this life) is the nature of the material world. The mind is not endowed with innate ideas. Instead, "the first thing which is known by us in the state of our present life is the nature of the material thing, which is the object of the intellect . . ." (*Summa* I a, Q 88, a 3). This comes to us through the body's being acted upon by other material objects in the world. While it is beyond the present scope to interpret or analyze Aquinas's epistemology in detail, we can observe how he understands the term "mind" by noting the general way he describes the process by which human beings come to attain knowledge of any kind. We discussed above how Aquinas viewed the necessity for a certain kind of body to be the effect of the human soul's organizational power in the material stuff of the human animal. In the *Summa* he maintains consistently what he says in his answer to the third objection posed in question fifty of the *prima secundae partis* of the *Summa*: "a man is made apt of understanding by the good disposition of the interior powers [of the organism], in the production of which the good dispositions of the body have a part to play." It is through the bodily organs of sense, that the intelligible and sensible forms of things first present themselves to the human being. In fact, the organizational principle of the rational soul, because it is the body's *form*, enables the development of certain physical sensory organs of perception to serve the purpose of knowing:

15. O'Callaghan observes, "Aquinas uses color as the object of vision for an example of a passive power, and physical maturity as the object of an active power like growth" ("Aquinas Rejection of Mind," 40).

The powers [of sensation, which are rooted in the soul] do not exist *for the sake* of the organs [of sensory perception], rather the organs exist *for the sake of* the powers. Hence it is not that different organs give rise to different powers but that nature establishes diversity to go with the diversity of the powers. Likewise different senses naturally use different media, depending on what the powers need in order to act. As for knowing the *natures* of sense qualities, that belongs to the intelligence [*intellectus*].

[A natural change] occurs when the form of the source of change is *received* into the subject of change in a physical way, as *heat is absorbed* by something being heated. [A "spiritual" or nonphysical change occurs] when the form of the source of change is received in the subject of change supra-physically, the way that the form of a colour is in the eye, which does not become the colour it sees.

[When] the *intention* [of the sensible form that is sensed] comes to be within the sense organ . . . [in sense other than sight] there is a physical change as well, either on the object's part only, or on the part of the organ also . . . Natural change of place on the part of the object occurs in the case of sound, the object of hearing, for sound is caused by impact and movement in the atmosphere . . . Touch and taste involve physical change in the organ itself; the hand touching something hot *gets hot*, and the tongue dampens through the moisture of what it tastes. The organ of smell or hearing, on the other hand, is physically affected only *per accidens* [*Summa Theologiae* I a, Q 78, a 3].[16]

Knowledge begins to develop from our initial experience of sensory awareness, which is an act of the human being as a whole person. However, our obtaining knowledge implies much more. Sensory knowledge is not (contra the Cartesian theory) the result of a solely mental power. Neither is it an act of the "outer man," as Augustine argued. Rather, sensory awareness for Aquinas is the achievement of the entire human person—body as well as mind. For Thomas, sensory knowledge—when considered in mental terms—involves not just an awareness of actual changes to the physical body, but a real engagement of the mind with those changes as the body's sensory organs are acted upon by another entity, which acts out of its essence upon the body and thereby "providing" a "communication" of its nature and essential properties. This communication, furthermore, is an expression of the *intelligible form* of its existence. This is what the mind of the human person experiences, not the physical changes *per se*. Thus, as "a change" occurs in the sensory organ of the body (for example, the eye), the *intention* of the entity is communicated to the eye as the form of the object, say the redness of an apple, is "received into" the organ of sight.[17]

16. Suttor, *Thomas Aquinas*, . (emphasis mine).

17. Such a way of speaking, it is worth noting, would be entirely consistent with the argument that the apple's redness is not strictly *in* the apple *qua* the redness that one sees. That would not in the least attenuate recognition of the fact that something from the apple's own existence is communicated to the sensory awareness. It would simply mean that the organs of sense are geared in such a way that the

According to Aquinas, as some entity is acting upon the body out of its essential powers, the mind of the human person, who is one and the same thing that has the dual aspects of body and mind operating in harmony, is aware of this. He defends this view in I a, 84 a 1, Reply, of the *Summa*.

> Even in sensible things we observe that the same form can be in different sensible objects in different ways; for instance, whiteness can be more intense in one thing than another, and whiteness can be associated with sweetness in one thing but not in another. Furthermore, the same is true of the form of a sensible object: *it exists in a different way in the thing outside than it does in sense knowledge*, which receives sensible forms without their matter—for instance, the color of gold without the gold itself. Similarly, the intellect receives material and changeable species of material things in an immaterial and unchanging way, in accord with its nature; for things are received in a subject according to the nature of the subject.

Each thing acts in certain ways and is individuated in relation to other things specifically because it is materially organized in certain ways by the form that makes it what it is. It acts or is acted upon in accordance with its essence. Hence, when the sensory apparatus of a human being is acted upon, the acting entity is conveying something of its actual objective essence to the specific part of the body that is receiving the action. Copleston describes Aquinas's view of this in a similar way.

> Our organs of sense are affected by external objects, and we receive sense-impressions. The eye, for example, sees colours or colour-patches; but it would not do so unless it were affected by its object acting on it through a medium. It receives an impression, therefore, *and undergoes a physical alteration.* The process of sensation cannot, however, be reduced *to mere physical change . . .* Sensation is a *psycho-physical process* in which a sensible "form" is received.[18]

While the human soul has the "power of sensation," per Aquinas, his hylomorphism requires that this power of sensation is a principle of the very same soul that *qua* rational soul informs the human body even before it is actually exercised in the process of sensation. Only with the body so informed can *human* sensory experience that results in cognitive understanding take place. The "intellect" requires objects of sensory experience in order to engage in its own proper work of understanding. Only through these sensory obtained objects can the rational capacity of the human being begin to operate to develop knowledge of reality or being. In other words, if all knowledge begins with sensory experience via the body's engagement with the

objects acting on them can act on them in certain ways. Just because the redness of the apple could not act upon the eye of, say, a honey bee in the same way does not negate the claim that the apple is acting out of its own essence upon the eye of a human being in such a way that redness is "received" as a result. The same thing could be said of the hardness of the apple, or its sweetness, or its crunchiness in relation to the appropriate bodily parts.

18. Copleston, *Thomas Aquinas*, 179, my emphasis.

material world, then knowledge, while much more than a physical phenomenon, is not a feature of a Cartesian "thinking substance," but is the activity of a being that is irreducibly a rational biological organism.[19] Because he conceives the relationship between mind and body that results from the integrated union of soul as form and the matter of the body in these terms, Thomas declares in the *Summa* I a, Q 98, a 1, that it is clear that it is good for the rational soul to be united with a body. And again, in *Quaestio disputata de anima*, 2, *ad* 14, he pronounces a conclusion that is fully consistent with his doctrine as it is described in the *Summa*: "Origen thought, like Plato, that the human soul is a complete substance, and that the body is united to it accidentally. But since this is false, as has been show above, it is not to the detriment of the soul that it is united to a body, but for the perfection of its nature."[20]

For Aquinas, the first *object* of the mind is the essence of many material ordinary particulars through their forms *qua* sensible. To say that these material things are known through their forms *qua* sensible is another way of saying that these particulars "act" according to what they are in relation to the human body's organs of sense. As he contends in the extended passage quoted above, the sensible forms cause some nonphysical change in the various sense-organs of the body. However, the changes are what he calls "supraphysical." The physical organs of sense remain exactly what they are *physically speaking* but still undergo changes in themselves through being acted upon by the properties and powers of the sensed entities. Aquinas seems to mean the following: the sensory capacity *qua* intellectual power of a human being which relates, say, to the retinal tissue of the eye, when receiving via light refraction the sensible essence of a rock, is changed in the sense that both the retina and the sensory capacity that is retina-related now contain within themselves the essence of the rock that can be conveyed visually. (Something similar would follow from the sense of touch.) The sensory organ of the retina, prior to the reception of that sensible form, was not acted upon by the essence of the rock, but now it has been acted upon and, while not changed physically, has encountered a change from not being engaged to being engaged by the visual presence of the reflected light. In the same way, the intellectual sensory capacity that is inherently tied to the changes that take place in the retina when reflected light acts on it is engaged and "becomes" the thing experienced through the changes the retina underwent. The presence of the sensory image communicating the intelligible form of the rock now entails that this change has occurred

19. See *Summa* Ia, 77, a 8, for Aquinas's discussion of how the soul, when "separated from the body," loses some of its capacity for knowledge. Again, it is outside my scope in this project to deal with Aquinas's doctrine of the soul exhaustively. But consider what he says in the reply of this article: "Certain powers, namely, understanding and will, are related to the soul taken on its own as their subject of inhesion, and powers of this kind have to remain in the soul after the death of the body. *But some powers have the body-soul compound for subject*; this is the case with all the powers of sensation and nutrition. Now when the subject goes, the accident cannot stay. Hence, when the compound corrupts, such powers do not remain in actual existence. They survive in the soul in a virtual state only, as in their source or root" (emphasis mine).

20. Quoted in Copleston, *Thomas Aquinas*, 163.

in the sensory capacity of the intellect. But neither the matter of the retina or its structure nor the metaphysical essence of the sensory capacity that relates to the sense of sight have altered. They are still, the one physically and the one nonphysically, exactly what they were in themselves.

Such various types of change in the physical organism, then, are what the sensory powers of the soul have as their object. And since all knowledge begins via a human being's full engagement with the material world through the changes that occur in the sensory organs, it is the changes in those that are the first objects of the mind.[21] One might put it in the following manner. The body itself (as it is acted upon by the intelligible forms that communicate the essences of things) is the first *object* of the mind; and the mind of a person is in the first instantiation the intellectual awareness of the body's interaction with the world.[22] This does not entail a causation of the mind's activity by the body, since the mind is an active, knowing agent in relation to the body's changes.

Aquinas even contends that the rational soul's awareness of itself in the human person is the product of the engagement with the objects of sensory experience and the intellectual activity that is prompted by that engagement. Since the mind is not an entity that exists on its own, Aquinas could not conceive of the human mind knowing itself and its existence via Cartesian introspection. Aquinas would most likely have pointed out such introspection must assume the presence of ideas that are not

21. We cannot in the confines of the present study adequately analyze Aquinas's epistemology, which posits a "possible intellect" and an "active intellect" in human life. Yet we can at least point out that in his complex theory the "possible intellect" is a power of the soul to receive the information that comes through the sensory organs. One possible way to interpret this is to say that for Aquinas the sensory data are communicated to the sense organs via the changes that the essence of a thing produces in the state or condition of the sensory organ. In turn, the receptive intellect, which is part of the power of the intellective soul, which is the form of the body that has the sensory organs, is aware of the changes. But, *qua* intellect, the changes in the sensory organs do not "cause" the knowledge. Rather, the receptive intellect is a process involving immediate awareness of the information provided. This information is what the active intellect works with to abstract universal knowledge of essences, natures, accidents, substances, and, ultimately, being itself. But neither can this active or agent intellect be construed as a cognitive power all its own. Rather it is a part of the human being complexly organized so that rationality can attend biology; and it is the power to abstract, from the "objects" already otherwise known, a fuller and deeper kind of knowledge. Indeed, for Aquinas, the actions of the senses and the receptive intellect are ordered to serve the activity of the agent intellect through the informing presence of human *anima* in matter. For an excellent discussion of these concepts, see Davies, *Thought of Thomas Aquinas*. Also see Copleston, *Thomas* Aquinas, 178–84. For a critique of Aquinas's complicated and "naïve" theory of knowledge and intellect, see Kenny, "Aquinas," 78–95.

22. The possible parallel between this way of putting the process of knowledge and Spinoza's own articulation will be discussed in the next chapter. But consider, by way of anticipation, Spinoza's statement in *Ethics* II, p 16, proof & corollary 1: "All the modes wherein a body is affected follow from the nature of the body affected together with the nature of the affecting body. Therefore the idea of the modes will necessarily involve the nature of both bodies. So the idea of any mode wherein the human body is affected by an external body involves the nature of the human body and the external body. Hence, it follows that the human mind perceives the nature of very many bodies along with the nature of its own body."

identical with the act of thinking about them. The mind's foundational awareness is awareness of something other than itself. This thing is its object—the body. His doctrine is a kind of medieval version of intentionality in which thought is always thought about *X*. But, in his view, thought about *X* always necessitates, subsequently, awareness of the subject knower involved in such an act of knowing *X*. So, while there is, first, an object of the mind's awareness (*X*), the very act of being aware of something creates the possibility to encountering oneself as the subject of the knowledge of the act of knowing. Aquinas puts it as follows in *De Veritate*, 10, 8:

> The soul is known [by the human person] by its acts. For a man perceives that he has a soul and lives and exists by the fact that *he perceives that he senses and understands and performs other vital operations of this kind* . . . No one perceives he understands except through the fact that he understands *something*, for to understand something *is prior to understanding that one understands.* And so the soul comes to the actual realization of its existence through the fact that it understands or perceives.[23]

Ultimately the body itself is the object of the mind's awareness because only by the body can the concrete, nonmind-dependent world be experienced. The mind is really, for Aquinas, a term that captures the whole human being's (the person's) capacity for knowing things and abstracting understanding from his engagement with the world. Those objects can be material entities engaged through the sensory experience or truths about the world that are realized through acts of reasoning; it can even be the embodied-self experienced as subject of the thoughts and experiences. However, what is clear is that the mind is an aspect of a human being that requires an object that is nonmental in order to be instantiated. The thing that "knows," therefore, is not the mind, or even the soul, because the rational soul's capacity for knowing is instantiated by the engagement with sensory experience via the body's sense organs being acted upon and the body acting. "It has been shown that sensation is not an activity of the soul alone. Sensing is the activity of *the whole man*, even though it is not peculiar to man" (*Summa* I a, Q 75, a 4, reply).

It must be emphasized, however, that knowledge is not being thought of here as caused in the mind by the passive receptivity from the bodily organs, much less by any action that the bodily organs might exert on the mind. The *Summa* in I a, Q 76, a 1, reply, is where Aquinas asserts his Aristotelian credentials and commitments on this issue.

> The activity of a moving agent is attributed to the thing it moves in one case only, when it uses it as an instrument, as when a carpenter imparts his motions to his saw. There if understanding were to be attributed to Socrates on the

23. Here Aquinas is using the term "soul" in a very ambiguous way, one time for something that a human being "has," and then again for the knowing human being itself. In any case, what he is saying is that self-consciousness is dependent upon the knowledge of objects that are, in some sense, intentional. This distances his view of self-consciousness from both Augustine and Descartes, for who self-awareness is the most fundamental type of knowledge.

ground that it was the activity of some agent acting on him, it would follow that he was said to understand because being used for understanding. This is incompatible with the Philosopher's contention that *understanding takes place without physical instrumentality.*[24]

The mind performs its act of understanding as a result of the soul's informing power in the human being, the same soul that makes the human body apt to be acted upon by other sensible things. Our act of understanding, then, has no dependence upon the physical functions of the body, even though knowledge starts with sensory experience. But, that negative way of stating Thomas's doctrine does not get a far down the ontological path as he wants to take us. One must also say that the mind's understanding is the act of a human being who, while being essentially physical, is capable of rational insight. Such insight is itself the expression of a human power that, while indeed present in the physical body, is not a physical power of the body. The intellect engages the objects of sense—as we described above—but neither the act of engaging the objects nor the act of understanding what is engaged is *caused* by anything bodily in Aquinas's theory of mind and its knowledge.

In fact, this contention is the foundation of Aquinas's doctrine of the immateriality of the intellectual soul, as well as its incorruptibility. Aquinas describes the state of affairs in the following way in *Contra Gentiles*, 2, 49: "If the intellect were corporeal, its activity would not reach beyond the order of bodies. So, it would understand only bodies. But this is patently false. For we understand many things (such as universals and mathematics and the natures of species) which are not bodies. Therefore, the intellect is not corporeal." The logic of Aquinas's argument is built upon a supposition common in his day (and even in the early modern period) that only things that are like one another can interact. One could describe this as a kind of explanatory barrier that exists between thought and the body that is the location of a thought, because there is a real difference between the material and the immaterial. Hence, as we said above, the act of knowing is one which is not reducible to the physical body's activity. Rather, it is a power of the soul that enables the physical body of a human being to be the kind of body that is capable of being part of knowing as a human person.

This concept of the mind's relation to the body via the soul's informing power, plus the argument that the intellect or mind can actually know things that are far beyond the scope of material reality or sensible form (differential calculus, geometry, universals, God, and, again, the natures of species), leads Aquinas to the conclusion the true nature of the mind must be noncorporeal. However, the intellect's awareness of sensible form does not violate the principle that only like can know like and thereby refute or confuse Aquinas's claim that the soul is immaterial, since the sensible (intelligible) form of an entity is an actual feature of the essence of that entity. As a feature of the essence of the entity, the sensible form is the way that the essence acts upon the

24. Emphasis mine.

sensory apparatus of animals in such a way that it can be engaged by them and known by the intellect as the object of sensation. We could say, in this regard, that Aquinas would allow that the sensory organs are really acted upon as physical entities when the sound waves produced by a piano strike the eardrum and activate the physical process involved in hearing. But, the essence of the musical sound is heard and comprehended, not in the way that the sensory organs receive the sensible form, but as music in its essence as it is given expression through the piano and the sound waves it produces. The process has a decidedly physical component, but the event of hearing and comprehending is not, itself, reducible to the physical.

The above analysis of Aquinas's doctrine has been described so redundantly, because it is critical to understand the centrality of the concept of *person* in his metaphysics. Understanding itself is an act of the human person in Thomas's doctrine, i.e., it is something that is exercised by a human being *qua* rational animal. Hence, Aquinas's pronouncement that it is not the soul (or mind) that knows, but the "man" that knows.[25] A human person is an agent, acting in the world to know it, and that act is made possible only by the organizing information that the soul brings to the matter of the human person's body to make it *apt* for relating to the mind. Engagement with the changes that the sensible forms cause on the body's organs of sensation provides the intellect with items of experience upon which the active intellect works—with no causative determination from the body at all. Such knowledge is not caused by the body; it could not be, Aquinas maintained, because knowledge is not material, but its lack of materiality is very different from the sort of lack of materiality involved in a Cartesian view of knowledge and mind.[26]

25. Aquinas's discussion of the soul in *Quaestio disputata de Spiritualibus Creaturis,* which he wrote in 1269, probably after the "Treatise on Man" in the *Summa* was written, further illustrates his conviction that the soul is not a *set of powers* but contains "powers" that can activate a body to be human and capable of knowing as a person. In article 11, he demonstrates this negative conclusion. None of the soul's powers are its essence, hence intellect could not be the soul's essence. "The soul's abilities are called essential characteristics *not because they constitute its essence* but because *they derive from* [*its essence*]" (my emphasis). Furthermore, he rejects the idea that the ability to understand is the soul's essence, which would entail that the soul is mental activity. "[The human soul], being essentially body's form, gives body existence (being the form of its substance) and that sort of existence we call life (being the sort of form we call soul) and that sort of [human] life we call understanding or intellectual (being the sort of soul we call intellectual). For "understanding" sometimes names an activity (and then its source is an ability or disposition), and sometimes names our very existence as creatures of an understanding nature (and then its source is the very essence of our intellectual soul)." McDermott, *Aquinas,* 121–29.

26. It seems reasonable to suppose that the reason that Aquinas thought that human *anima* could be described as "mind" or "intellect," and even be referred to as a "subsistent entity," is related to his broader views about the universe as a whole. He does not conceive of reality in Cartesian terms where an otherwise extended substance is coincided with individual "thinking things." Rather, his willingness to call the soul "mind" is the result of his belief that the act of knowing (quite apart from any particular knower) is part of the very make-up of the universe. Quite apart from the question of individual knowers, Aquinas saw the *form* of knowing to be a subsisting reality that is a fundamental feature of the universe. Knowledge is not something, for him, in addition to the material world. No! The material world, since it is intelligible, is itself part of the same world *qua* rational knowledge.

He did not conceive of the act of knowing as a supervenient addition to a world filled otherwise material objects, because the form of intellect that results in knowing is part of the one reality that exists. So, neither is any kind of parallelism or even representationalism an accurate description of Aquinas's theory. Just as life is a principle of the world which we cannot really explain but can only acknowledge as inherently present in the world, so thought for Aquinas was a feature of reality that could not be reduced to material causes that would explain it. At the same time, Aquinas would presumably not be shocked at findings in current brain research that show various correspondence between cognitive and biological processes.

Considering the foregoing, it is arguable that Aquinas's Latin term *intellectus*, which some translators simply render intellect, is better translated, in the context of the Angelic Doctor's thought, by means of the gerund "understanding." This is the practice of the Blackfriars edition of the *Summa* that I am utilizing. It is better translated in that way, I would argue, insofar as intellect or mind, for Aquinas, is simply the act of knowing a human being exercises. It is a power of the soul in the sense that the soul provides the grounding principles for the possibility of this act by a rational animal, but intellect or mind itself is not a power; and the soul does not do the understanding. That is the act of a human person. In the *Summa*, *mind* is simply a synonym for *intellect*: "the human soul, which is called intellect [*intellectus*] or mind [*mens*]" (I a, Q 75, a 2, Reply). Since this act of knowing or understanding is what Aquinas means by intellect or mind; and since this activity is the result of the organized complexity of a human person as a composite being; and since this complexity is the result of the "informing" nature of the rational soul enabling the highest power in can produce, Aquinas says that the soul can be called (equivocally) the "mind." However, for him the act properly speaking is the result of a rational animal performing an act that is not itself bodily, because the human *anima* informs a material being in such a way that rational understanding can be present in the physical human person.

PERSONS ARE METAPHYSICALLY FOUNDATIONAL

Aquinas's contention is, as I have been suggesting above, that we must focus attention on *the person* as the one and the same thing that is mind and body in union. The person acts to obtain knowledge, even as the person is engaged in physical actions. The term "person" provides him with a category that allows him to discuss the act of knowing as the act of a particular mode of intellectual being (since in his view angels and even God are higher intellectual beings)—an act that can be understood as the act of a thing that is both body and mind.[27] Following the authority of Boethius, he

---

Thought is thought about the world and it is the world that is thought. Hence, rationality is precisely a possibility that is a part of the essence of rational *animals*.

27. In his refutation of the Latin followers of Averroes, Aquinas utilizes the concept of "person" to provide a different metaphysical foundation for the individual acts of intellectual activity contra

defines a person as "an individual substance of a rational nature" (*Summa* 3a, Q 2, a 2 reply.)[28] A person is also a "supposit" in Aquinas's terminology, which means an entity that expresses a particular essence, as well as being the substantial (rather than accidental) subject of other acts of being. A person, therefore, is a primary substance, in the Latin that translates Aristotle's own term *proto ousia* (primary being).

Thomas's most critical discussion of the concept of a person takes place in the part of the *Summa* that deals with his defense and philosophical demonstration of the logic of the doctrine of the Incarnation. There he distinguishes between essence and person; and it is not essences (universals) that exist but persons, for only individual substances exist in the most precise sense[29] Human persons are supposits that exist through the formal cause of human nature (the union of matter with human-making rational soul as form). Made an actual human being by this formal cause, each person is still more than the essence of human nature that makes his or her existence actual. All persons have additional, incommunicably unique existences and characteristics that cause them to be distinguished from all other particulars that are formed by that same formal essence. Recall the above discussion of the individuating role of matter. Hence, Aquinas claims that "in things composed of matter and form the *nature* is not predicated of the supposit; we do not say for example that this man is his humanity" (3a, Q2, a 3, Reply).[30]

Person, therefore, is a different metaphysical concept than essence or nature; it is a primary concept for Aquinas because a person is a primary being in the Aristotelian sense. As "an individual substance of rational nature," a person is essentially rational. As was shown above, however, the bodily existence of a human being is essential, as well, for the true expression of human rationality in the *human* personhood of that

---

Averroism. By linking the term "person" to the definition "a substance of a rational nature," following the authority of Boethius on the matter, he utilized an important Christian theological concept to refute the doctrine—mentioned in Q 76, a 2, 1, as well as in the reply to this same article. Although he does not utilize the term in article 2, for he is arguing a different metaphysical response to Averroism there, it could not have been far from his mind. By ultimately linking the act of knowing with a human person, which he defines as mind and body in integrated material-rational life, Aquinas would have formed a base upon which Averroes's monopsychism would have been made problematic for a Christian audience. The concept of person was developed in Christian theology in the West to address the doctrine of the Trinity without denying the oneness of God. *Persona* was taken up for the Greek term *hupostasis*. In Christian theology the idea of the "persons" of the Trinity entailed the notion that each person is distinct without being separate. This concept could have allowed Aquinas a foundation upon which to discuss, against Averroism, the distinctness of each act of knowing (because it is the act of a person), given that the Christian dogma contends that human beings are made to be persons in the image of God. That would have provided Aquinas with a strong position to insist that Averroism was doctrinally untenable for Christian believers, even as he endeavors in Q 76, a 2, to refute the doctrine via the logic of his philosophical theology.

28. For Aquinas, person is, in a qualified and derivative sense, an allowable synonym for "human being," since he believed that human beings were made in the image of the Trinity.

29. In an Aristotelian philosophy, essences (or natures) only exist (as we saw in chapters 2 and 3) in concrete beings that express those essences.

30. Emphasis mine.

human being.[31] He asserts this strongly in *Summa* I a, Q 75, a 2, reply, where he argues that the soul *per se* only has substantiality in a highly qualified sense of substance, since it is, in his description, an incorporeal and subsistent *principle*. In other words, as he puts it in ad 2 of this question, the soul is itself something that is real, but it is not strictly speaking "this *particular* thing," for the concept of a particular thing can have two applications. One is what we might call a "weak" reference, i.e., that any real feature of the world can be called a particular thing. We might refer to the DNA "code" that makes my bodily and mental existence possible as a particular thing without positing it as an actually existing thing or primary substance in the Aristotelian sense. The soul, Aquinas argues, can be called a particular thing, in this "weak" sense.[32] On this basis, Aquinas argues in Q 75, a 4, ad 4, "Not every particular substance [understood in the weak sense] is a hypostasis or person, but rather, that which has the full nature of the species. Thus, a hand or foot cannot be called a hypostasis or person. Nor, likewise, can the soul, as it is *a part* of human nature." The concept person captures for Aquinas the substantial existence of a human being as a primary substance and expresses the full nature of the entity produced in the hylomorphic integration of the rational soul and the human body. Since the intellectual soul is the form of the human body, it is subsistent as a real particular thing (in the weak sense described above).

The form-giving reality of the soul does not need something else to grant it reality *qua* form-giving principle. When Thomas denotes it a substantial form, he means it has its own essence, i.e., to give essence or form to a primary substance. The essence of the soul as a particular thing (in the weak sense) is to make possible the existence of a different thing (in the strong sense), namely the primary substance—the person. From these two aspects of the nature of the soul, it follows that the primary substance that is created in the union of the soul with the matter of the body is a substance in the "strong" sense), but the soul alone is not. Only in the existential integration of

31. Again, when utilized in reference to human beings, "person" must entail the idea of a body, since the definition of a human being is "rational animal." Animality is, therefore, part of personhood and being human itself becomes a basic concept in philosophy of mind. Cf. page 49, where Williams is quoted: "A strength of hylomorphism, particularly in its more materialistic version, is that it does point to human being as a basic concept in the philosophy of mind, and, consequently, in ethics."

32. Suttor's comments on this passage help in grasping what Aquinas is doing by providing an ambiguous usage of the idea of the soul. "Thomas is concerned with a far-reaching rectification of names. Because 'soul' is a noun, we tend to think of it as a thing. We can hold a man's hand, and say by metonymy, 'This particular thing has an existence of its own,' e.g. meaning the man has, not the hand. Now the same is true of the soul: properly speaking it is man who comes into existence, and has an existence of his own" (Suttor, *Thomas Aquinas,* 12).

intellectual soul in the matter of a body does one find a true hypostasis.[33] This is what Aquinas means by his more epigrammatic assertion: a soul is not a person.[34]

The metaphysical importance of Thomas's notion of a person is emphasized when one considers his ideas about the incorruptibility of the soul and what that doctrine entails for him. Substances are what really exist fundamentally as the subjects of all other categories of being. The subsisting soul, while a reality on its own, is not, for Aquinas, a substance. Yet, he argues that it can continue in existence beyond the death of the body. As a substantial principle of rational life, but not a substance in the strong sense, the rational soul is by its very nature meant for union with and existence *in* the material body that it informs. While this issue will be discussed more fully in the eighth chapter of this work, we may observe a few things here. The soul's separation from that body, while allowed by Aquinas's philosophical conception of the soul as immaterial and demanded by his theological commitments, is nonetheless, in that state of separation, continuing to exist in a state that Aquinas viewed as *praeter naturam* (beyond what is natural). It is unnatural in the sense that the soul *qua* informing and organizing principle is meant to be in the matter that it informs. In the union with matter for which it is meant, the soul *causes* a person to exist. This means, then, that the rational soul apart from the body is not strictly a human person, because the term person signifies the complete primary substance that expresses human nature.

It could be objected, that if it is the knowing subject is a human material person, then perhaps the distinction that Aquinas is attempting to draw between soul and body is a merely nominal one. In other words, Aquinas's radical emphasis upon the unity doctrine might be regarded as supporting the conclusion that, in the words of

---

33. This is unquestionably a complicated theory, but perhaps no more truly complicated than the current scientific understanding of DNA information. In the current science of DNA, we have two notions that are quite distinct, philosophically speaking, which could not be reduced one to the other except by a rather bald assertion of materialism or idealism. One the one hand there is the material stuff (the proteins, amino acids, chemical interaction, and molecular structure) that carry the genetic information. But that which is carried is not itself thereby to be regarded as material. Rather, it is, as was argued in chapter 2, something (at least arguably) quite other than the matter by which the information is communicated and instantiated in its incipient form. This information *in* the matter in question is the source of a particular living thing's life *qua* the particular kind of thing that it is. Hence, as we understand by the light of contemporary microbiology and organic chemistry, the feature of the universe that grants life to a human creature (its DNA in the sperm-egg union) is the same principle that makes the person to be a *rational* animal. The same information encoded in the DNA that makes me have brown eyes and produces my heartbeat and orders every cell of my body to be productive and reproductive of life, in order to sustain my existence and enable me to pursue certain "ends" toward which I am naturally ordered [oriented] as a human being, is also the information that enables my rational awareness of the world and my own life. Thus, these potentialities inherent in the DNA code are not potentialities for various sorts of activity on the part of DNA itself. Rather, they are potentialities for the human beings of which that DNA is a component. And yet, the information is, itself, something (in the weak sense).

34. An intriguing insight about Thomas's formulation of the idea of person and the import of maintaining the integrated union of soul and body is offered by Suttor. "Thomas was seeking to replace [the common, more neo-Platonic claim that the soul used a body] with something more in accord with the doctrine of the Incarnation" (Suttor, *Thomas Aquinas*, 19n).

Klima, "the concepts of soul and body provide us merely with different aspects *for considering* the same, essentially *materially* entity."[35] But as our preceding discussion should have made clear, such a view would be built on a misapprehension Aquinas's doctrine. Klima has commented on Aquinas's thought about the real distinction that must be posited. "But since these [the human body and the *life* the body manifests] are obviously distinct perfections, whose distinction is given regardless of the intellect's considerations, the parts of the whole accounting for these perfections, each of its own sort, have to be parts that are really distinct, again, regardless of the intellect's consideration."[36] There is a real distinction that exists; and it is a kind of explanatory barrier. The form that gives life and specific properties cannot account for the body's materiality *per se*, even if it does account for the kind of organization that the material body has received. In the same way, the body as a material thing cannot "explain" the information that is integrated into its very existence and without which it has no concrete existence apart from the informed body. And again, as Klima has demonstrated regarding Aquinas's theory:

> What this means, then, is that in line with St. Thomas's general conception of the analogy of being the whole and its essential parts, while they are denominated beings on account of the same substantial act of existence, are not denominated beings in the same sense. For the whole substance [*the person*] is denominated a being in the primary, unqualified sense of being, in the sense in which only a complete, self-subsistent entity can be called a being, existing on its own. The essential parts of this being, namely, its matter and substantial form, however, can be called beings only in some derivative sense of the term. And this is because for a form to exist is nothing but for the thing to exist, or to have existence, *in respect to the form,* which makes it clear that the sense in which existence is attributed to the form is obtained by adding some qualification to the sense in which existence is attributed to the substance, which is said to exist in the primary, unqualified sense. Obviously, similar considerations apply to the body, in the exclusive sense of the term, insofar as it is the other essential part of a living being.[37]

Aquinas's view of *person* as a metaphysical fundament helps us to understand how he views the issue of mind and body interaction, while maintaining a kind of explanatory boundary. In his discussion of the will in I a, Q 82, a 4, Reply, Aquinas points us toward how he conceived of bodily movement in relationship to mental powers. In this passage he closely associates will with understanding; it is certainly not treated as an immaterial entity that has a realm of its own from which it acts upon other things. Aquinas discusses the activity of the will in terms of the functioning of a whole *system*. As a rational animal, a human being is oriented towards certain, particularly human

35. Klima, "Man = Body + Soul," 195, my emphasis.
36. Klima, "Man = Body + Soul," 195.
37. Klima, "Man = Body + Soul," 198, my emphasis.

ends. The pursuit of those ends—physical and nonphysical—is engaged in rationally, which entails awareness of ones needs and deliberation about how best to meet those needs. Deliberation and choice, in this scenario, are not acts that are merely mental, however, in the Cartesian or Augustinian senses of being solely immaterial acts absolutely speaking. Aquinas argues the point like this:

> One thing can set another in motion in two ways. First as an aim, and this is the way its fulfillment moves an agent cause and also the way that the *understanding* moves the will. For a good understood is will's object and moves it by being *something to aim for*. But secondly, one thing can change another by its activity, as in chemical or physical change. And it is after this fashion that the will moves the understanding and all the other powers of the soul . . . .
>
> The explanation is that *in a system* of active powers the one that concerns the perfection *of the whole* moves those that have more particularized objectives. This is just as clear in physical nature as it is in political society . . . Now the object of the will is *goodness and fulfillment* in general . . . So the will *actively moves* all the soul's powers to their acts, except for vegetative powers, which are not subject to our decisions.[38]

This concept of the will is consistent with Aquinas's hylomorphism and its implication that neither one of the aspects of human existence (body or mind) can be conceived of as having a reductionist causal relationship to the other. This conclusion follows from Aquinas's assertion that it is the person who acts and wills and knows, not the mind that directs the body nor the body that effects the workings of the mind. Since the person is the "one and the same thing expressed in two aspects (modes), Aquinas's treatment of the relationship between mind and body is analogous to the descriptions that one finds in various dual aspect theories of mind and body in human life. This is why he contends that our reason can grasp *a single existing entity* in a variety of ways" (Q 76, a 3, *ad* 4). The highlighted phrase "single existing entity" can be translated by another idiom, namely, "one and the same thing" (*unum et idem*). This would imply that such terms as "will," therefore, do not name some entity, or even some ultimately isolatable power (as Kenny tries to find), in a Thomist metaphysics. The human person is what acts and causes action; and the human person is the mind-body composite caused by the informing presence of the rational soul. Hence, the problem of the interaction of the immaterial mind and the material body would seem to be mitigated (at least). Mind or will do not refer to any immaterial thing that would be analogous in relationship to the body to the captain of a ship or motor of a vehicle. Rather, both are simply terms that name the *human person's* capacity to make informed, reason-guided choices regarding how best to achieve human flourishing. Bodily acts, then, are not caused by the will, in Aquinas's view. Rather, they are the actions of a person who is acting volitionally (i.e., in a goal-directed way), pursuing

38. Summa, I a, Q 82, a 4, Reply

an action or goal that is perceived to be a good. For example, when I reach for a piece of apple, rather than a donut, as a snack, it is not my will (or for that matter my mind) that lifts my arm. As a material being, I am lifting my material arm in my conscious pursuit of my material end, eating. My immaterial awareness of my material situation and that material situation is one reality not two because I am one and the same thing—mind and body—as a human person.

Thus, Aquinas is not inconsistent to insist there is a real distinction to be drawn between the aspects (mind and body) of the human person, all the while denying strict dualism. First, the mind, as we have seen, is not the thing that understands and chooses, for the soul, not the mind, is the source (but not the cause) of the relevant activity in the composite human person. But, by naming the highest potential that the human soul brings to the human person, he can use the convention "mind" to refer to the soul. Secondly, since the soul grants the power of mental activity to the person, and since the soul is not the body, but is the organizing principle of the body, we are correct to call the distinction between mind and body a real one. So, thirdly, Aquinas could hold that the mind *qua* immaterial entity, strictly speaking, does not cause the body to move by some occult power of interaction. Yet, the motion of the body cannot be accounted for unless one acknowledges that the person who moves and acts bodily does so in a goal-oriented way; and that goal-oriented way is rational and purposive in intent. Finally, the motion of the body is distinct from the mind's awareness, but both are aspects of the person who acts.[39]

The preceding discussion shows that Aquinas's hylomorphism sets the question of mind-body interaction on a different footing. His commitment to the unity of human life in the soul-produced *person* is the distinct contribution he makes to the philosophy of mind. Conundrums would seem to be mitigated, at least over how the so-called immaterial mind, with its ostensibly, nonlaw governed acts, could interact with or act upon the material body that subject to deterministic physical forces and laws. To advert, in our discussion of human acts, to the intellectual or even the volitional feature of human experience does not provide us with an additional causal explanation for, say, a man swimming that must be appended to the otherwise merely physical description. Bodily acts, then, are *not* best described or conceived of as *caused* by the acts of the mind, such as belief and will. That way of putting the matter posits an ontological distinction between the two aspects of the unitary human life

---

39. Here we come to a way of conceiving the relationship between mind and body that points to a solution to the Cartesian problem of mind/soul and body interaction, one which does not make the mistakes of eliminative or reductionistic theories of mind and body. Since the power and action of knowing, deciding, willing, and bodily actions or movements can only belong properly to a being that is real in the primary sense, the problem of interaction simply does not present itself. Rather, the mind, strictly speaking, is the result of an activity that is taking place in, or by, the entirety of a human person. The body is not "causing" the mind to know, but the whole person is doing the knowing. Hence, mind is not some*thing* that can be described as acting or causing to act, except in a qualified analogous way. The mind is the person's power of rational, conscious understanding.

that, in Aquinas's view, is wrong. Rather, both the acts of the mind and the acts of the body reveal to us that to be human is to be a physical being that makes informed, reason-guided choices regarding how best to achieve human flourishing. All the acts of a human being's life (both the volitional and the nonvolitional) are, ultimately, acts associated with a person, who ultimately lives in a goal-directed way, pursuing things or resultant actions perceived to be a good. Indeed, on this view, even acts of the autonomic nervous system or the cellular processes that sustain life would still be regarded as acts of a person, but merely nonconscious acts. As life sustaining acts, they too would be part of the rational *anima's* (soul's) gift of orientation toward a particular end—the living of the life of a rational animal—a human person.

If we speak of beliefs, intentions, desires, choices, and reasons we are not, in the hylomorphic theory of Aquinas, introducing mental concepts that have no relationship to the material world as immaterial mental states. For Aquinas, our life is that of a material agent, capable of awareness and understanding *qua* a material agent, who lives in the law-governed and ordered material world. But to provide an adequate portrayal of human acts as *human* acts these mental states must be brought into the discussion. Nonetheless, the mental acts have involved in them physical conditions, as well. As a single entity, a person chooses as we do, because we are oriented, toward the good, including the goods for our physical existence (of which we are conscious). Aquinas argues in *Summa* II a, Q 8, a 1, Reply: "The will is a rational appetite. Now every appetite is only of something good . . . . Since, therefore, everything, inasmuch as it is being and substance, is a good, it must needs be that every *inclination* is to something good."

That which is understood by the mind in union with the body as *the good*—we choose. This realization is, of course, linked to our experience in the material world.[40] Hence, the man (described above) who is swimming may be swimming to escape a sinking ship, or to save a child, or to impress a young woman with his athletic prowess, or to improve his health. Each choice is informed by the physical state of affairs that we consciously understand to be relevant. The fulfillment sought is not divorced from the material set of conditions. But since the rational awareness (deliberative or not) that leads to an action is not caused by the material set of conditions, even when

---

40. "For since every agent or thing moved, acts or is moved for an end, as stated above (1, 2); those are perfectly moved by an intrinsic principle, whose intrinsic principle is one not only of movement but of movement for an end. Now in order for a thing to be done for an end, some knowledge of the end is necessary. Therefore, whatever so acts or is moved by an intrinsic principle, that it has some knowledge of the end, has within itself the principle of its act, so that it not only acts, but acts for an end. On the other hand, if a thing has no knowledge of the end, even though it have an intrinsic principle of action or movement, nevertheless the principle of acting or being moved for an end is not in that thing, but in something else, by which the principle of its action towards an end is not in that thing, but in something else, by which the principle of its action towards an end is imprinted on it. Wherefore such like things are not said to move themselves, but to be moved by others. But those things which have knowledge of the end are said to move themselves because there is in them a principle by which they not only act but also act for an end" (*Summa*, II a, Q 9, Reply).

the mind's acheived knowledge is of a bodily need or condition, then in Aquinas's doctrine of human action of the body, corporeal action always includes intention. The problem that we face regarding belief, judgment, intention, choice, etc. is not how to conceive of these being deterministically caused by the physical or material. Neither is it to explain how an immaterial mind, alien to the physical world, can cause bodily actions. Rather, the issue at hand is how the person who believes, judges, etc. develops, as Aquinas contends in his reply in I a, Q 19, a 3, adequate knowledge of the good and so orders his acts and thoughts in order to make proper and good choices.[41]

AQUINAS'S HYLOMORPHISM AND CONTEMPORARY MIND-BODY THEORIES

The preceding discussion of Aquinas's arguments regarding his doctrine of hylomorphic unity and the metaphysical importance of *person* indicate why he embraces a theory of mind-body "identity." Such identity is understood as mind and body expressing duals-aspects of the more basic underlying entity, i.e., the human person. This is the relevant source of the "identity" of the mind and body. He developed his own nuanced theory of hylomorphism from an Aristotelian starting point, but the permutations he introduces to Aristotelianism place him in a distinct philosophical category.[42] As we have seen, his locutions sometimes make reading him confusing. However, as we have shown, by positing form and matter as fundamental "causes" of the existence of all primary substances, including human beings, Aquinas looks beyond the problems that are associated, even in his own day, with the confounding status of mind and body interaction. Focusing attention on the existence of primary substances (beings) as the true ontologically concrete expressions of being, his doctrine of the relationship between mind and body is a consequence of this starting point. When considering the relationship between mind and body metaphysically, Aquinas's paradigm looks to the human person as a unitary whole as the primary substance that is ontologically

41. ". . . the goodness of the will depends properly on the object. Now the will's object is proposed to it by reason. Because the good understood is the proportionate object of the will; while sensitive or imaginary good is proportionate not to the will but to the sensitive appetite: since the will can tend to the universal good, which reason apprehends; whereas the sensitive appetite tends only to the particular good, apprehended by the sensitive power. Therefore the goodness of the will depends on reason, in the same way as it depends on the object." Also, see his discussion in the entirety of this Question, especially articles 3–6, for a fuller picture of his view of the relationship between reason and the will.

42. Suttor claims that Aquinas's treatise on man "probably did more than any earlier document, and perhaps more than any later document, to confirm Christians in the realization that ensoulment (active) and embodiment (passive) are the same process looked at from different angles." It is my conviction that this estimation is essentially correct regarding Aquinas, who utilizes concrete nouns to name the various angles of vision upon the process being described. "Yet, the usage," as Suttor also acknowledges, "leaves its mark on his text, in sentences which do not do sufficiently delicate justice to the reciprocal and co-relative intelligibility of the nouns 'soul' and 'body,' which are better thought of as gerunds . . . He recognized that concrete terms better expressed than abstract terms the conditions of actual being" (Suttor, *Thomas Aquinas,* xv–xvi).

foundational. As is the case with all primary substances in Aquinas's hylomorphic metaphysics, the human being must be considered as the subject *in* which all other features or aspects of that substance exist.[43] Seeing the relationship between mind and body from this starting vantage, Aquinas offers to philosophy of mind a metaphysical scheme in which "mind" and "body" are understood to be distinct linguistic terms that describe for us the two very real modes of expression involved in human existence. But human beings do not exist in these modes; rather these modes express the complexity of human life as an organic unity.

Aquinas's insistence that the mind and the body are both equally modes that give expression to the essential nature of unitary human existence means that he is not reductionistic in the way of many modern identity theories. These theories attempt to make mental statements reducible to or translatable into statements about physical states (or at least into statements about various sorts of relations involving states of human beings, where those relations are neutral as to the existence of anything ultimately "mental" in character). However, in Thomas's judgment (as was discussed in chapter 3) the very concept of being physical itself requires some explanation. For him, in a world such as ours that has in it both physical states and mental states, being physical would be no more self-explanatory than is being mental. So reductive materialism that dismisses the mental as a real, irreducible feature of our world, preferring to claim that the mental is in the final analysis only a physical epiphenomenon, would be woefully inadequate.[44] In his estimation, the hylomorphism that he develops from Aristotelian principles, enables philosophy to begin to understand that the mental and the physical each require some other category besides themselves to account for each conception. Further, for Aquinas, neither can be ontologically prior to the other, because *anima* informing matter is productive of both.[45] Because his hylomorphism allows him to explain the nature of the physical bodies that exist *qua* informed entities, as well as explain how the mind must be understood to be distinct from the physical, he would understand the epistemological objections to reductive physicalism posed by Barbara Montero:

> Indeed, since most think that the mind *must* be physical, the project they are engaged in is not so much arguing that the mind is physical, but, rather, trying to show how the mind could be physical (given that it is). And so, whether the account of mentality that physicalists propound is expressed in terms of reduction, realization, identity, supervenience, explanation or even elimination,

43. Recall from chapter 3 that, for Aquinas, *Being* is in some sense an even more fundamental ontological category than substance. This makes his view of substance somewhat different from that of Descartes. Aquinas's use of the term "substance," while carrying the metaphysical freight that Spinoza would want it to carry, is not the same concept. *Being* is perhaps closer to Spinoza's *Deus sive Natura Naturans* than *Natura Naturata*.

44. See Montero, "Body Problem," 183–200 for a good discussion of how the presumptions of physicalism are not adequate for understanding even what it means to be physical, much less mental.

45. See chapter 3.

the goal is to provide a plausible theory of mentality (or, as the case may be, a theory that accounts for what we mistakenly took to be mentality) that is compatible with the view that the world is fundamentally physical. For example, if one thinks that it is incumbent on physicalists to *explain* mentality then the explanation, it is thought, must make reference exclusively to physical phenomena; if one thinks supervenience suffices for physicalism, then the supervenience base must be entirely physical; and so forth. But what does it mean to be physical? It seems that those who take the central concern of the mind-body problem to be the relationship between mental properties and physical properties—and if Kim is right, this is just about everyone—should have at least a rough idea of what it means to be physical, not necessarily a strict definition, but at least a notion of the physical that excludes some, if not actual, then at least possible, phenomena from being physical. For if we cannot even conceive of something being nonphysical, it is difficult to grasp what physicalists could be arguing for—to say nothing of what that they could be arguing against.[46]

Rejecting reductive materialistic explanations for the mind and body relationship, Aquinas is just as adamantly anti-dualistic, except in a *highly* qualified sense. He acknowledges that the soul is distinct from the body and can survive the death of the body, but this does not entail dualism of the Cartesian or Augustinian variety. In Aquinas's ontology, while being a "thinking thing" or a mind is part of the definition of a human being (rational animal), his definition requires us to acknowledge that being human involves a form of intellect, as was shown earlier, that is essentially biological. The allowance Aquinas makes for the survival of the soul after physical death is built on the combination of two intellectual commitments. The first is his rejection of any reductionist account of the world in which we live. By philosophical analysis we realize the world contains minds that are engaged in acts of knowing that are ontologically quite different from any physical states with which they correspond. The second is his theological belief that the soul and the rational self-consciousness that results from the operations enabled by the soul are both expressions of God's life and nature in human beings and are, thereby, as immaterial expressions of *Logos* capable of being kept, by the power of God, in (some form of) existence in an intermediate period following physical death and then be reunited with the matter of the body in the resurrection.[47] Yet, Thomas's hylomorphism keep him quite distinct from

---

46. Montero, "Post-Physicalism," 62–63.

47. This theological proposition is, of course, incredible to many philosophers. However, while its intelligibility will not be defended or critiqued in this chapter, it is worth noting that the belief in the resurrection of the body in Aquinas's theology is a further proof that calling him a dualist is wide of the mark. To be human is, for him, to be a corporeal being endowed with the image of God and living a rationally biological life, even eschatologically. We shall explore Aquinas's doctrine of the incorruptibility of the soul as opposed to the idea that it is immortal (as Spinoza puts it) in the eighth chapter of this work along side Spinoza's own claim that the mind is immortal.

contemporary versions of human mind-body relations that are on offer by Christian philosophers such as Richard Swinburne.[48]

Nor would Aquinas be a proponent of various nonreductionist theories of physicalism such as supervenience or emergentism. The first of these, supervenience, is an attempt to allow for mental states, without necessarily accepting the ontological reality of mind as something that engages in the mental activity that those states would involve. Supervenience does not insist on, in the strictest sense, the dependence of mind upon the body. It does not argue, for instance, that mental states are simply physical states described differently. And yet, there is, for the philosophers who hold to supervenience, a primacy of the physical. As Kim notes:

> According to some philosophers, mind-body supervenience gives us the right kind of physicalism: It respects the primacy of the physical by giving a clear sense to the idea that the physical determines the mental. Without the instantiations of appropriate physical properties, no mental property can be instantiated, and that particular mental properties are instantiated depends wholly on what physical properties happen to be instantiated. And yet . . . mental properties remain distinct from their physical base properties.[49]

However, many philosophers who embrace supervenience as an account of mind and body in human beings do regard it as "affirming a relation of *dependence* or *determination* between the mental and the physical; that is, what mental properties a given thing has depends on, or is determined by, what physical properties it has."[50] In the case of supervenience as a description of the relationship between mind and body, this theory does not suffice, in Aquinas's judgment, because as he saw it the acts of understanding and reasoning cannot be intelligibly described as causally dependent upon any underlying physical substrate. For Aquinas, even though the mental acts of a human being cannot be done without the physical substrate (the body, he would say), they are acts radically distinct from the material conditions which underlie and correspond to the human activity of abstraction, understanding and reasoning.[51] Even if one posits (as supervenience doctrines do) thought as a thing over-and-above a brain-state, but nonetheless insists that the brain-state is necessarily causal of the mental act, in Thomas's judgment that one fails to appreciate how understanding is something qualitatively distinct from any set of physical conditions. The very nature

48. Swinburne, *Are We Bodies or Souls?*
49. Kim, *Philosophy of Mind*, 149.
50. Kim, *Philosophy of Mind*, 11.
51. *Abstraction* is a power of the agent intellect whereby the intelligible forms that are present in the actions of things acting on the body's sensory organs are understood in the actions of those things so acting on the physical structures of the body. Hence, the ability of the mind to know is not dependent upon the body, even though the body is involved in the process of the human person's knowing.

of rational insight necessitates, he argues, that thought be conceived as nondependent *qua* rational *insight* upon physical states of affairs.[52]

It would also be incorrect to place Aquinas in the so-called emergentist school. This perspective is committed to the reality of laws of emergence at work in the world such as the following: "When appropriate [material] 'basal conditions' are present, emergent properties must of necessity emerge."[53] Emergentism attempts to protect the integrity of mind as an existent reality in its own right. The properties themselves, although still "physical," would be a special sort of physical state, not reducible in terms of the sorts of states out of which they emerge. However, against this theory of mind-body relations, Aquinas would argue, I think, that such a commitment to laws of emergence entails a granting of metaphysical priority to the physical as ontologically foundational without giving an account for how the physical organization of the "basal conditions" it posits are possible in the human body in the first place. He would argue, in good Aristotelian fashion, that the physical basal conditions cannot account for themselves, since matter is not self-organizing or self-enlivening. Therefore, the organizational form (information) that enables the existence of such basal conditions must be ontologically different and distinct from the physical states that are organized in such a way so to make possible the existence of those states as basal conditions from which mind can emerge. Here, as with every other point of comparison between Aquinas's doctrine and contemporary theories, his hylomorphic understanding of the soul is critical. Something makes the biological entity capable of rationality through a particular mode of physical organization capable of life and awareness. This same something is the source of the mind as an aspect of human existence that is radically distinct from the body and not created by the body. This is, of course, the soul.

Aquinas's hylomorphism positions his theory of mind-body in relation to other philosophical discussions as an important alternative way of expressing the nature of the question in our quest to envision the mind-body relationship. And as I have been arguing, his perspective has at first blush much in common with so-called dual

---

52. Aquinas would find common cause with the perspective of William Hasker regarding the nonmateriality and, therefore, independence of rational acts. "Now let us suppose that all human thinking is physically determined in the following sense: (1) Every thought or belief accepted by a person is a result of that person's brain being in a corresponding state. (2) We assume, provisionally, that the physical indeterminacy which exists at the quantum level makes no perceptible difference in the overall functioning of the brain. So that the brain functions, in effect, as a [materially or physically] deterministic system. It follows that (3) every brain state, and therefore every thought and belief of the person, is fully determined by the physical functioning of the brain in accordance with the deterministic laws of physics. Is it not evident, on this supposition, that rational thinking is an impossibility? It cannot be true, on this assumption, that anyone's thinking is guided by rational insight; rather, it is guided entirely by the physical laws which govern the brain's functioning, which proceed with no regard to whether the thought processes they generate correspond to principles of sound reasoning. . . . [To hold this, one] must admit that our belief that we are capable of rational thinking is an illusion which would, of course, undercut the claim that such a theory, itself, is true in any sense that we define the concept of being true" (Hasker, *Metaphysics*, 48–49).

53. Kim, *Philosophy of Mind*, 228.

aspect theory. But there is a difference, even in this positive comparison. Dual aspect theory is for the most part content to describe the paired phenomena of mind and body without pursuing an account of the reason why any entities might in fact be doubly aspected in this way. We have demonstrated that if we acknowledge Aquinas's doctrine to be a kind of dual-aspect theory, then employing the term "dual-aspect" need not cause us to think of mind (being rational) and body (being animal) as distinctly separated aspects of a human being's life, in the sense that they have nothing to do with each other. Were that false interpretation allowed, we would be placed, as we endeavor to interpret Aquinas, in the difficulty that faces the parallelism interpretation of Spinoza's doctrine, namely, that we now have a functional dualism no better for understanding human existence than the ontological variety is.

As has been shown in Aquinas's judgment a human being *qua* mind and body is a primary substance—the person—whose essence can be defined as the unitary *process* of living rationally the life of a biological entity. For analytic reasons, Aquinas considers mind and body as something like two modes that express the single act of being of an entity that is ontologically irreducible and inseparable in its rational animality. However, even calling mind and body *modes* is an abstraction from an actual act of human living, because the mindedness itself is the mindedness of a living physical entity, i.e., a person.[54] Hence, Aquinas provides at least the beginning intuitions of an account of *how* a human being can be described as a singular entity yet be regarded simultaneously as irreducibly mental *and* physical in his existence. He offers us in medieval and Aristotelian terminology a theory of the relationship between the organic complexity of the human body, which formed by the in-formational powers of the soul, that accounts for the presence of the mental in biological beings as an aspect of their material life. Aquinas grants to us in his hylomorphism a philosophical analysis of the nature of the mind that provides what Jonas claimed for Spinoza's metaphysics, i.e., "a speculative means is offered for relating the degree of organization of the body to the degree of awareness belonging to it."[55] The Angelic Doctor, therefore, provides us with a reason to think a dual-aspect theory is true, not just as a description of the state of affairs, but as the metaphysical situation of a human being's existence. He gives, in his doctrine of *anima* and its relationship to both mind and body, a way to

---

54. This is captured in Aquinas's definition of a person, when considering a human being. A person is, in his metaphysics, an individual substance of a rational nature. Such a definition can apply to the "persons" of the Trinity. But a human being is called by Aquinas both person and rational animal. Hence, a good Thomistic definition of "human person" would be something like, an individual primary substance of a rational nature whose rationality is rooted in its biology and whose biology does not exist separately from its rationality. We shall address in the final chapter how the last part of this way of envisioning the human person is reconcilable with Aquinas's claim that the act of reason is not dependent upon the body and is, thereby, separable from the body at death. Suffice it to say at this point that I am addressing Aquinas's doctrine of the identity of the "thing" that is a rational animal, not the distinction that must be posited between the principles (form and matter) that in unity instantiate a particular rational animal.

55. Jonas, "Spinoza and the Theory of Organism," 271.

recover the unitary nature of human existence that both dualistic metaphysics and those that grant ontological priority to the physical fail to do. What Jonas says of Spinoza can also be said of Thomas: he gave to philosophy a way to describe the "intrinsic belonging-together of mind and matter, which gave causal preference neither to matter, as materialism would have it, nor to mind, as [dualistic] idealism would have it, but instead rested their interrelation on the *common ground* of which they were both aspects."[56]

In his metaphysics, the mindedness of a living body is not simply to be the mindedness of something that is, *in one of its aspects*, a living body; or the mindedness of something that *also has* a bodily aspect. Rather, the singular act of existence that is a human person *expresses* itself in two aspects, but these aspects, while distinguishable in their own powers, are always involved not only alongside one another, but *in* one another. The physical act of human existence is essentially manifested in the act of living rationally. Likewise, the mental activity that is the specific difference in the definition of a human being is the activity of a physical entity that is a living body.[57] So Aquinas refuses to think of the mind (and the acts of understanding that we associated with it) simply as an immaterial aspect of a being that is also physical, but precisely as the nonphysical activity of a being that is physical. But the being itself is in the final analysis not reducible to either. Mental acts and physical acts are both the acts of a subject and agent—a person.

Fundamental, as well, to Aquinas's metaphysical theory, is the supposition that the intelligibility of the world and the intellect's capacity for intelligence about the world are the way the universe is; thought is not alien to the otherwise material world. And the rational structures we come to understand about the world of our experience are not an imposition of our minds upon an unknowable *noumenal* reality. Spinoza will later in his own way agree with that, as his doctrine of Thought and Extension as Attributes of *Deus sive Natura* indicates. So now we will turn our attention to reading Spinoza's cryptic and complicated claims about *conatus* and about "mind and body as one and the same thing" in the light of the Thomistic framework that has been developed in the last two chapters, and then eventually return to questions concerning the "subsistent" and even "immortal" status of the human soul.

56. Jonas, "Spinoza and the Theory of Organism," 272.

57. The import of this kind of unity of existence, without diminishing the distinction that actually exists, will be explored more fully in the next chapter where we take up our consideration of Spinoza.

6

Reading Spinoza Afresh
Thomistic Hylomorphism and Spinozistic Conatus

SPINOZA'S DOCTRINE OF MIND and body has spilt an ocean of ink;[1] so much so that we cannot undertake an exhaustive survey of the various interpretations offered in the secondary literature. In much of the commentary, however, a common difficulty confronts his interpreters, i.e., the meaning of his statement in II, P 7, sch.:

> Thinking substance and extended substance are one and the same substance, comprehended now under this attribute, now under that. *So, too,* a mode of Extension and the idea of that mode are *one and the same thing*, expressed in two *ways* . . . And so, whether we conceive Nature under the attribute of Extension or under the attribute of Thought or under any other attribute, we find one and the same order, or one and the same connection of causes—that is, the same things following one another.[2]

In this argument he builds on the conclusions of Book I of *Ethics* that there is only one Substance, namely God or Nature, and the God is Substance qua Thought and Substance qua Extension.[3] While Spinoza's argument in the scholium involves his conception of a single substance, of which Thought and Extension are attributes, it is not necessary for the present argument that we critically evaluate the logic Spinoza employs to reach this conclusion. We can bracket the *way* that Spinoza arrives at his monistic supposition, simply acknowledge that he does, and proceed with an analysis

---

1. A brief survey of some of the literature on this subject includes: Sprigge, "Spinoza," 164–67; Balz, *Idea and Essence in Hobbes and Spinoza*; Curley, *Spinoza's Metaphysics*; Broad, *Five Types of Ethical Theory*, 16–23; and Wolfson, *Philosophy of Spinoza*, 33–70. Add to these R. J. Delahunty, Jonathan Bennett, and Michael Della Rocca, who are cited below.

2. Emphasis mine.

3. We could, perhaps, just as readily put this in participle terms, that Thought is Substance as "thinking" and Extension is Substance "*being*" physical.

of how exactly Spinoza conceives of the *one-and-the-sameness* of the mind and the body. Of more immediate relevance for the topic of this book is Spinoza's use of this conclusion that he posits in this scholium. It is the foundation upon which Spinoza later seems to be clearly asserting (III, P 2, sch; emphasis mine) mind-body identity. He says, "mind and body are *one and the same thing,* conceived now under the attribute of Thought, now under the attribute of Extension." Interpreting Spinoza's contention that mind and body are one and the same thing is made further difficult, however, by what many have called his explanatory or causal barrier between thought and extension, as indeed between modes of any distinct Attributes. In Book III, Proposition 2, Spinoza claims that "the body cannot determine the mind to thinking, nor can the mind determine the body to motion or rest, or to anything else." Such a proposition would appear to contradict, or at least make confounding, the claim he makes (which we have already alluded to) in the scholium of this same proposition. If mind and body are in fact *the same thing* how, one can ask, can these two sorts of Modes not be causally related in some way? Hence, what he means by mind and body being "one and the same thing" and how this idea relates to the prior statements of II, P 7 is a subject of no little controversy.

As we exposit and analyze Spinoza's metaphysical commitments about mind and body, the interpretation that follows will show how the concept of mind-body oneness he presents is comprehensible in light of the concept of *conatus,* which is, I contend, a much more foundational concept in his metaphysics than has previously been appreciated. In the course of demonstrating the importance this concept has for Spinoza, the similarities between *conatus* in his metaphysics and Aquinas's particular hylomorphic understanding of *form* will be highlighted. What will be demonstrated by this approach is *why* Spinoza's doctrine is cast in the form it is, namely, mind and body as one and the same thing. His doctrine is an important and particularized form of the "identity theory" of mind and body that is best captured by seeing mind and body as two differing *aspects* of a single entity that is neither mind nor body *simpliciter,* but is essentially, inseparably, and irreducibly both. What follows will not attempt to tame Spinoza's monism or radicalize Aquinas; rather, it will show that the distinctive terms that express the former's ontological commitments regarding the oneness of human existence do much of the same work in his metaphysics of mind and body that Aquinas's Christian-Aristotelian categories do in his philosophy.

SPINOZA AND "IDENTITY THEORY"

As we consider Spinoza's cryptic statements about the identity between mind and body, we should be aware of some issues that bemuse his commentators regarding this issue. There are essentially only two basic approaches that Spinoza affords us. The first is to deny that there can, in Spinozistic terms, be an identity relation between mind and body. R. J. Delahunty is an example of one who claims, quite forcefully, that

Spinoza's metaphysical statements are self-contradictory. The other option is to take Spinoza seriously, and then try to explain how the identity in question can be understood. Two of the more engaging recent treatments of Spinoza that take the identity approach seriously are those of Jonathan Bennett and Michael Della Rocca.

Bennett sees Spinoza's theory as asserting an actual identity, but in a highly qualified sense that does not entail the numerical identity of mind and body. He argues that the concept that mind and body are one and the same thing considered under different attributes rests on Spinoza's notion that for any given mind there is a numerical identity between the "fundamental mode" in which that mind in some sense *consists* and the fundamental mode in which some particular body consists; and vice versa.[4] By contrast, Della Rocca is critical of Bennett's reading of Spinoza and argues that Spinoza's metaphysical doctrine and his accompanying epistemology require that a full-blown, strictly applied view of the numerical identity of mind and body be attributed to Spinoza. This identity, Della Rocca emphasizes, is rooted in so-called "parallelism." The distinction between these two approaches will be addressed below and shown to be closely tied to how one interprets three issues: (1) the relationship that the Attributes have to Substance; (2) whether there can be, in Spinoza's thought some type of Modes that are not Modes of the Attributes; and (3) the place that parallelism plays in Spinozistic metaphysics.

First, a world about parallelism will serve us well as a backdrop to the issues that will concern us in this chapter. Both Bennett and Della Rocca, in different ways, see the notion of a psycho-physical parallelism as playing an important role in Spinoza's thought. Typically, however, a discussion of psycho-physical parallelism is brought into a discussion of Spinozism as an alternative to an interpretation of his mind-body identity theories. Instead, parallelism views Spinoza expressing a more Leibnizian theory of the relation between the physical and the psychic worlds. On this view, given that there can be no interaction between mind and body, because they are dissimilar in essence, it is simply held that there must be no more than a kind of isomorphism or mapping between the physical world and the way that world is represented in the mental realm. Parallelism generally fails, I contend, as an explanation of Spinoza's own doctrine. Such unexplained mapping activity does not fit his system well. Psychophysical parallelism eschews interactionism on the grounds that events so totally dissimilar as those of mind and body must in some sense not only be distinct but "substance-like" in their own essences. However, parallelists simply accept, without real explanation, the idea that every mental event is correlated with a physical event in such a way that when one occurs, so too does the other. This does not seem, in my estimation, to be consistent with Spinoza's treatment of the way that mind as a location of thought and emotions relates to the body as the location of physical activity

4. Bennett's view is thus indeed a kind of numerical identity view, even though he does not himself put it in those terms, and chooses to present it as in opposition to "numerical identity" approaches to Spinoza. This issue will become clearer as we proceed.

and changes which are, in some sense, the objects of the mind. Parallelism, if it wants to be an adequate explication of Spinoza's doctrine, ought to try to provide us with an explanation of how the parallelism could work.[5]

Parallelism fails, in part, because it misses the importance of an aspect of Spinoza's thought that, I contend, is the *central* issue in his theory, namely the concept of all things as being *alive* [II, P 13, sch]. While panpsychism is the label that this aspect of Spinoza's doctrine often receives, panpsychism is not going to enter in any substantive way into my treatment of Spinoza. However, it should be noted that the actual argument in the second part of *Ethics* is not just saying that all things are "minded," but that Natura Naturata is imbued with life through and through.[6] I take this to mean, for him, that life is a *fundamental* aspect of the way Reality is, not a supervening property. Seeing the matter this way opens the possibility that for Spinoza the identity of mind and body is ontologically rooted in the identity of a *living* entity that is one with itself; mind and body, then, are essentially dual aspects of such a single thing. Where parallelism rejects dual-aspect theory on the grounds that no "third" entity could be responsible for such vastly different effects as those of mind and body, the interpretation I offer will show that Spinoza's doctrine attempts to describe just this kind of situation. My own eventual proposal will attempt to ground the duality of aspects in an underlying unity in a way that can explain the unity of mind and body as resulting from the influence of what Spinoza calls *conatus*.

DELAHUNTY, DELLA ROCCA, AND BENNETT ON SPINOZA

I will begin by considering the arguments of R. S. Delahunty, Jonathan Bennett, and Michael Della Rocca, as a way of putting the issues that must be kept before us in clear relief. Beginning with Delahunty, we find a quite serious assault on Spinoza's formulation of his doctrine of mind-body identity in *Ethics*.[7] Delahunty focuses his criticism on Spinoza's insistence that there is a causal barrier between thought and extension.

> Whether we conceive Nature under the attribute of Extension or under the attribute of Thought or under any other attribute, we find one and the same

5. Parallelism is, in my view, an example of the functional Cartesian divide in philosophy of mind. This prevailing attitude was mentioned in chapter 1.

6. Feuer has commented about this aspect of Spinoza's thought. "Panpsychism . . . was born as a mystical, social revolutionary doctrine in the seventeenth century, but it was remarkably reinforced by the science of the time. The last half of the seventeenth century was the age of microscopy . . . Spinoza was indeed one of the Dutch microscopists, reveling in the magnifications which revealed the variety of minute living things, and fitting his observations into his philosophy. As Colerus narrates, 'He observed also, with a Microscope, the different parts of the smallest Insects, from which he drew such Consequenses as seem'd to him to agree best with his Discoveries.' . . And Spinoza in explicating his grounds for believing that 'each part of Nature accords with the whole of it' made full and explicit use of the new physiology and microscopy of blood and its constituents" (Feuer, *Spinoza and the Rise of Liberalism*, 236–37).

7. Delahunty, *Spinoza*.

order, or one and the same connection of causes—that is, the same things following one another . . . . God is the cause—e.g.—of the idea of a circle only in so far as he is a thinking thing, and of a circle only in so far as he is an extended thing . . . . as long as things are considered as modes of Thought, we must explicate the order of the whole of Nature, of the connection of causes, through the attribute of Thought alone; and in so far as things are considered as modes of Extension, again the order of the whole of Nature must be explicated through the attribute of Extension [II, P7s].[8]

In a later section, Spinoza unpacks this metaphysical claim. Building on this scholium in III, P2, he flatly asserts the barrier to interaction mentioned above: "The body cannot determine the mind to think, nor can the mind determine the body to motion or rest, or to anything else (if there is anything else)." The proof offered for this proposition is the ontological distinction between the Modes of the Attributes that Spinoza believes is implied in the distinction he posits between the Attributes of Substance.

All modes of thinking have God for their cause *in so far* as he is a thinking thing, and not in so far as he is explicated by any other attribute. So that which determines the mind to think is a mode of Thinking, and not of Extension; that is it is not a body . . . Now the motion-and-rest of a body must arise from another body . . . and without exception whatever arises in a body must have arisen from God *in so far* as he is considered as affected by a mode of Extension . . . .

Because of this insistence by Spinoza, Delahunty rejects the coherence of Spinoza's claims that mind and body are actually one and the same thing. The reasoning he employs in his refutation is in the following form:

1. If mode of thought (T) 1 is identical with mode of extension (E) A and

2. If EA causes another mode of extension EB, then

3. T1 has caused EB.

This result would be contrary to the obvious ban stated in III, P2; so Delahunty concludes that Spinoza, although he does say that mind and body are the same, *should not have said* this. He contends, therefore, that Spinoza himself is confused in his conclusions, because his claims about mind and body sameness transgress against his own ban on causal interaction between the Attributes of Substance.[9] This would seem to be quite a strong objection against the notion of numerical identity between the Modes.

8. This passage has been seen by those who have insisted on calling Spinoza's doctrine "parallelism" as a main pillar of that interpretation. The problems inherent with parallelism were discussed in chapter one, namely that it presents us with a kind of functional dualism in Spinoza that does not do justice to Spinoza's further treatment in the *Ethics* of the relationship between mental states such as will and bodily states. The functional dualism implied by the parallelist reading of Spinoza might as well be ontological. This will be discussed below.

9. Delahunty, *Spinoza*.

A response to Delahunty's critique of Spinoza on mind-body identity is found in Della Rocca's work. He contends that Delhunty's arguments fail because he does not see that Spinoza's system, far from being incoherent, requires us to posit identity between mind and body in the strongest and the strictest sense. Della Rocca refutes the former's objection, noting that his criticism of the mind-body identity reading of Spinoza "turns on the view that causal contexts are referentially transparent."[10] Della Rocca instead insists that one can read Spinoza as holding that causal and explanatory contexts are referentially opaque.[11] Following Quine on this matter, he says that "a context is referentially *opaque* if the truth value of the sentence resulting from completing the context does depend on which particular term is used to refer to that object."[12] With this general principle in hand, he points to Spinoza's own stated sensitivity to the description-relative *opacity* of truth statements. Della Rocca rightly reminds us that Spinoza insists any statements about God's causality will be true only if we describe God with specific and limited consideration of the Attribute of Substance under which we are describing that causality. Since Spinoza considers God to be the *immanent* cause of each finite mode (1p18), a finite mode would be the *transitive* cause of another subsequent finite mode. Quite clearly, then, whether it is true to say that God is the *immanent cause* of a finite mode depends on how God is considered. "The modes of each attribute have God for their cause only insofar as he is considered under the attribute of which they are modes, and not insofar as he is considered under any other attribute."[13]

Undaunted by Delahunty and others who have insisted that the "barrier" between the various attributes makes a "numerical identity" view impossible, Della Rocca argues "that it is in part *because* of the explanatory barrier (and *not* in spite of it) that Spinoza holds the numerical identity view."[14] For Della Rocca, the opacity of causal contexts is the key to understanding Spinoza's dual insistence, namely that (1) Modes of completely distinct Attributes can have no causal relationship, and the claim (2) that Modes of different Attributes can be in fact *numerically* identical. "Spinoza thinks that the truth-value of certain immanent causal claims is sensitive to the way in which the immanent cause is described."[15] Della Rocca believes that his own reading avoids violating "the conceptual [and causal] separation between the attributes,"

---

10. Della Rocca. *Representation*, 121–23.

11. Della Rocca, *Representation*, 121–23. This observation is significant. However, my concerns are different from his, although the reading I will offer is consistent with Della Rocca's claim that not all causal contexts need be referentially transparent in a Spinozistic system. What Della Rocca does not provide is a *metaphysical* explanation for why referential opacity might be a part of Spinoza's view about certain causal contexts.

12. Della Rocca, *Representation*, 122.

13. Della Rocca, *Representation*, 122–23.

14. Della Rocca, *Representation*, 118.

15. Della Rocca, *Representation*, 123.

without denying the proper ontological relationship that the Attributes have to Substance.[16] The secret to this is twofold for Della Rocca: the opacity of causal relations and Spinoza's (purported) parallelism. The doctrine of parallelism is the foundation for Della Rocca's interpretation of why Spinoza asserts mind-body identity in the first place. Commenting on Spinoza's statement in II, P 7, which says "the order and connection of ideas is the same as the order and connection of things," Della Rocca takes this to mean not only that there is a one-to-one correspondence between ideas and extended things, but that, for Spinoza, "the fact that the order and connection within the two series is the same entails that certain neutral properties are shared by parallel modes."[17]

But for Della Rocca, parallelism alone cannot *account for* the identity statements that it allows. On his reading, Spinoza had a unique view of identity in which the identity between two modes requires only they have all their *extensional* properties in common. By "extensional property" Della Rocca means a property that is *neutral* regarding whether the property in question is one of Extension or Thought (or one of the other Attributes). The reason that only extensional properties are relevant for the question of how Spinoza argues for mind-body identity regards what is involved whenever we recognize nonidentity. In Della Rocca's view, any statement of the kind "a is not b," can only be true if there is "some difference between a and b that explains their non-identity."[18] He thinks that Spinoza insisted that any facts about nonidentity could only be true if they could be explained by property difference between the items under consideration. He bases this interpretation of Spinoza's reasoning on proposition 4 of Book I, which Della-Rocca sees clearly implying "that there must be a way to distinguish two distinct things."[19]

> Thus, since Spinoza regards the properties of being extended and being thinking as intensional, these properties can be left to the side for the purposes of the argument here, and so can all the particular properties that presuppose one or the other of these general properties. Any conclusion about the identity of a mode of thought and a mode of extension will have to be reached on the basis of a relatively impoverished class of properties.[20]

Since intensional properties (those that are Attribute-relative) are irrelevant, in Della Rocca's opinion, for deciding the issue of identity between mind and body, he contends that there must be a class of extensional properties that is small but

16. Della Rocca, *Representation*, 158.

17. Della Rocca, *Representation*, 133.

18. Della Rocca, *Representation*, 132.

19. Della Rocca, *Representation*, 132. Shirley's translation of this proposition reads: "Two or more distinct things are distinguished from one another either by the difference of the attributes of the substances or by the difference of the affections of the substances."

20. Della Rocca, *Representation*, 132.

nonetheless important for Spinoza's logic.[21] These properties are ones that Spinoza *assumes* in the *Ethics*; and they are comprised of properties that Spinoza utilizes during his offering of various proofs and explanations. The property of having X number of effects would be a neutral property, for example, in that more than one Mode could share the property of having X number of effects. Also, there would be the property of being temporal or having duration in existence. A final extensional property that Della Rocca thinks is important is the property of being a complex individual. These neutral ways of describing Modes does not commit one to a point of view regarding the type of Attribute in terms of which one is describing them, since such descriptions can apply across Attributes. Hence, on this level a similar description could be given of Modes of different Attributes that would allow for these different Modes to share *extensional* properties. For Della Rocca, as I have noted, Spinoza's identity theory is based on the centrality of parallelism in his thought.

This parallelism, by Della-Rocca's reading, entails the presence of neutral properties and not Attribute-relative properties. He argues that if there is a neutral property F that is a neutral property of a certain Mode of extension (E1) that contributes to the order and connection of the extended series, then (by parallelism) there must be a parallel mode of thought (T1) that also has property F. "If there were no parallel mode of thought that had feature F, or if the fact that feature F is present at that point were not explained by a certain feature of another mode of thought, then," Della Rocca asserts, "the order and connection of the mental series would be different in a certain respect from the order and connection of the physical series."[22] That would violate the parallelism that Della Rocca thinks is the foundational premise of Spinoza's ontology and epistemology. Since there must always be, in Della Rocca's reading, an intra-attribute modal explanation for all causes and since he believes parallelism always holds in Spinoza's metaphysics, he concludes the existence of shared extensional, Attribute-neutral properties explains identity. However, Della Rocca wants us to understand that things need only share *certain critical* neutral properties in order that identity-statements hold regarding what modes are parallel to each other. Such a qualification about the necessity of sharing extensional properties means that, relevant to parallelism, it follows that a Mode of extension and a Mode of thought will share *certain* extensional properties that are Attribute neutral. By focusing on *certain* extensional properties only, then Della Rocca believes that the proper distinction

---

21. Della Rocca claims that Spinoza held a version of what Della Rocca calls Leibniz's Law. "a = b if a and b have all their properties in common. As Leibniz himself and others have recognized, however, this principle does not hold in complete generality. There are certain kinds of properties that are such that the fact that a has a property of that kind, and b does not, does not by itself undermine the claim that a = b. The properties included within the scope of the above principle are, of course, intensional properties. Since intensional properties are not covered by Leibniz's Law, we can formulate a version of Leibniz's Law that is exceptionless: a = b if a and b have all their extensional properties in common" (Della Rocca, *Representation*, 130–31).

22. Della Rocca, *Representation*, 135.

between Modes of Thought and Extension can be maintained, without denying identity between mind and body. Since only a certain set is critical for identity to be asserted, then we can, based on other extensional properties, allow for distinction. This reasoning allows Spinoza, Della Rocca insists, to rightly claim that "mind = body, without treating distinction between the two as *merely* nominal."[23]

Della Rocca's view of parallelism in Spinoza attempts to posit identity of mind and body in the strictest possible form, but without denying duality in Spinoza's doctrine. For Della Rocca, "the *duality* in Spinoza's parallelism is not one between distinct things but between distinct descriptions or ways of conceiving things"; it is a semantical parallelism.[24] This idea of semantical parallelism is, in part, rooted in the "relativity" of explanatory contexts. Thus, parallelism is strict as concerns identity, but is relative regarding ways of considering the things that are identical. An object has, for example, the property of being physical only *relative to* a certain manner of conceiving or describing it.

> This conception of description-relativity of mental and physical properties in general is additional to the *mind*-relativity of content in particular [Spinoza's insistence that things are "known" differently in different minds] . . . Thus, the general notion responsible for much of what is most intriguing and important about Spinoza's theory of [mental/ideational representation] is also the notion that provides the key to understanding his position on mind-body identity. This is the notion of *relativity*. That different kinds of relativity should be so significant in Spinoza is not a surprising fact about a philosopher whose favorite locution is, perhaps, "insofar as" ("*quatenus*"). Since . . . mode identity results from parallelism, we can see how this identity stems from Spinoza's theory of representation and, ultimately, from his explanatory barrier between thought and extension.[25]

Della Rocca offers a view in which the mind is a complex set of organized ideas that not only precisely parallels the body but is at the same time one thing essentially with the latter. But how could this be? On Della Rocca's reading, when Spinoza says that, "the object constituting the essence of the human mind is the body, or a certain mode of extension which actually exists, *and nothing else*,"[26] [II, P 11] we must understand Spinoza to mean by "object," something like the following: the mind is a *representation* of the things that are going on in the body that as the representation parallels the body exactly and essentially.[27] Della Rocca seems to suggest that as a

23. Della Rocca, *Representation*, 135.

24. Della Rocca, *Representation*, 19 (emphasis mine).

25. Della Rocca, *Representation*, 139 (emphasis original).

26. Della Rocca's translation (emphasis original).

27. Della Rocca, *Representation*, 18–19. "Spinoza's use of the traditional term *objective* [when describing how things follow in God formally from God's infinite nature from his idea in the same order and connection] indicates that he is speaking of a representation relation between the items in the causal chain of things and the parallel items in the causal chain of ideas" (emphasis original).

representation, the mind can be the same as the body for Spinoza, because of Spinoza's contention that an idea of X (at least unconfused ones) always involve the idea of X's *essence*. The idea, as Della Rocca puts it, represents the objective essence and not a mere Humean-style impression of the states of the body. Since the *essence* of the body is what the body is, and since the mind's *essence* is simply to be the ideas that are the full representations of that essence diachronically and synchronically, then the mind and the body are one and the same. But the *presence* of the essence in the mind is not caused by the body; rather the mind is always active in its knowing. Parallelism allows then for there to be an essential oneness of mind and body as these two Modes share specific extensional properties without being the cause or explanation of each other. So, the mind is numerically identical with the body in the sense that the mind is just the essence of the body relative to the way that the essence is considered under the Attribute of thought, rather than the Attribute of extension wherein the essence is "located" *qua* extended Mode. In conjunction with the thought that all causal contexts (and therefore explanatory barriers) are opaque, Della Rocca holds that the mind is the body, because it is constituted in its essence by the essence of the body; hence it is identical with the body.[28]

Contra Della Rocca's subtle reading of Spinoza, there is another and better way to interpret the meaning of parallelism in a Spinozistic system. It can also deal with Delahunty's objections and is more straightforward in its reading of Spinoza. It requires taking a closer look at II, P 7, sch, cited by Della Rocca, which is, according to Spinoza (in III, P 2, sch), what we are to consider so that the denial of causality between mind and body might be "more clearly understood." But here, I contend, Spinoza is introducing only an *explanatory* limit rather than a *causal* barrier between modes of thought and extension. While Spinoza does hold to a causal barrier, the specific focus in this passage is on explanations, not causality. He focuses attention on the impossibility of *explicating* a mental state by reference to a physical event or state. Concomitantly, he instructs us that neither can a physical state be *explicated* in terms of concepts that apply to the mental. He is essentially arguing that we cannot translate (or reduce) explanatory description of states of affairs involving modes of a given Attribute in terms of language referring to a different attribute.[29] Similarly, what Spinoza's proposition 2 of Book III is arguably meant to do is not to deny mind-body interaction, but simply establish that we have no proper way of explaining such

---

28. This seems to be the import of Della Rocca's chapter entitled, "The Essence Requirement on Representation" (Della Rocca, *Representation*, 84–106).

29. This should, I think, be a hint to those who would like to make Spinoza into a reductionist (of sorts) that they should take pause. See as examples of those who want to reduce mind to body: Odegard, "Body Identical with the Human Mind," 579–601, who contends that Spinoza's theory, i.e., that the human mind is identical to the body, can only be true if it is a human body; Matson, "Spinoza's Theory of Mind," 568–78, where Matson's Spinoza has no true theory of mind, because the mind is explained functionally, not causally; and Donald Davidson, who endorses this kind of interpretation in, "Spinoza's Causal Theory," 95–112.

interaction. So, Spinoza denies to us *knowledge* about causal interaction only *in the sense* that we lack the ability to understand such interaction, because the categories by which we experience Substance and its Modes (and modes) are such dramatic binaries. This does not, thereby, need to deny that interaction takes place in some other, more ontological sense.[30] As I will argue below, the notion of *conatus* provides Spinoza precisely a kind of oneness of action on the part of a singular organism needed to eschew the difficulties he sees involved with describing interactionism between mind and body when conceived as distinct modes.

Axioms 2 and 4 in Book I show that conceptual and explanatory descriptions are closely related in Spinoza's theory. I take it that he means something like the following in these two statements.[31]

A. (Axiom 2): If one thing cannot be conceived through another then the thing must be explained through itself.

B. (Axiom) 4: Knowing causation requires us to understand and be able to describe the relationship an effect has to a cause.

If the interaction cannot be "explained" then, for Spinoza, epistemically the interaction is nil. Absent an explanation, there is no causation attributable between mind and body as distinct modes. Della Rocca explicitly argues, however, that a distinction such as the one I am drawing fails to interpret Spinoza correctly. Hence, we are parting ways. He contends: "such a separation of causal relations and explanatory relations is a possible position and, indeed, a popular one in contemporary philosophy. But, although it may be tempting to read Spinoza along these contemporary lines, there is no evidence for doing so. *This interpretation must attribute to Spinoza the view that a claim of the form 'mode of thought 1 causes mode of extension B' can be true, even if the corresponding explanatory claim is false.* However, . . . for Spinoza, the truth of a causal claim depends on its explanatory value."[32]

Such remonstrations notwithstanding, I think there is strong support for the way I am suggesting for understanding Spinoza's actual position. In the latter part of the scholium to III, P 2, he focuses on this very issue of *explanatory* agnosticism:

> . . . (1) the order and the linking of things is one, whether Nature be (2) *conceived* under this or that attribute, and consequently (3) the order of the active and passive states of our body is *simultaneous in Nature* with the active and passive states of the mind. Yet, although the matter admits of no shadow of doubt, I can scarcely believe, without the confirmation of experience, that men can be induced to examine this view without prejudice, so strongly are they convinced that at the mere bidding of the mind the body can now be set

30. For those who hold that mind-body identity is finally conceivable within Substance itself, this concept should be obvious, but I believe we can argue for such identity before that.

31. The following is my translation of the Latin put in more colloquial terms.

32. Della Rocca, *Representation*, 124.

in motion . . . . (4) Again, *no one knows* in what way and by what means mind can move body, or how many degrees of motion it can impart to body and with what speed it can cause it to move. Hence it follows that when men say that this or that action of the body arises from the mind which has command over the body, *they do not know* what they are saying, and are merely admitting, under a plausible cover of words, that they are *ignorant* of the true cause of that action and are not concerned to discover it.[33]

I have numbered the steps of Spinoza's argument so that we might be able to set down the flow of his logic very clearly. Following the inserted numbering, we can see what Spinoza is claiming:

1. There is only one order of "things"

2. This order can be conceived under either Attribute

3. So, there is simultaneity of occurrences in Nature in the states of the extended mode EA and the states of the mode of thought T1.

4. And attributing mental causation upon body or physical causation of mind is epistemically indefensible (and therefore nothing of substance).

What we are allowed to say (according to III, P 7), then, can be cast as follows (where E is Extension and T is Thought).

1. If EA causes EB (by the law of Mode of Attribute causation)

2. Then T1 attended EA's causation of EB and caused T2

3. And the nature of T1's relation to EB is opaque.

4. Hence, there is no causal interaction attributable, because [on my reading—"in the sense that"] there is no explanation of it.

At this point it might be useful to note the ambiguity of a key concept in Spinoza's discussion of the oneness of mind and body, namely, that of res (thing). The role that this concept plays (ambiguously) in Spinoza's thought will allow us later in this chapter to articulate a perspective on mind-body identity that is distinct from Della Rocca's emphasis on representation, relativity and shared neutral properties. While *res* is a general term, it seems to function in at least a quasi-technical way at times. Spinoza's locutions that say mind and body are one and the same *thing* are examples.[34] He claims that Substance and the affections of Substance are all that really exist—and he equates affections of Substance with Modes [I, def. 5]. But arguably, he may be taken as at least committed to the view that there are things which exist and are not

---

33. Emphasis mine.

34. See above in chapter 3, note 8, for a discussion of the way that *res* functions in Latin as one of the *Hertzworter*—heart words—for the Latin tongue, in which is concentrated something of the genius of the language.

precisely modes of Extension or modes of Thought, and not substances either. Rather, these things are real and can be alternatively *considered as* extended modes or modes of thought in the light of the two distinct Attributes whereby Substance *expresses* itself of which we can be aware.

The *things* in which mind and body are the same are necessarily *expressed* by (or as) the various Modes of the Attributes of Substance. So, the they must be expressed in different ways *relative to* the Attribute in question. (To that extent I agree with Della Rocca.) Stating the matter this way, then it can be argued that Spinoza conceives of these concrete particular things as necessarily expressed, and therefore understood, as a mode of extension and the idea of that mode—as the body and the mind. The thing that is expressed via these modes is what is identical to itself. *As modes* whereby the thing is expressed, mind and body are not the same. Rather, they share identity as the one thing each mode *expresses,* but as modes body and mind only express distinct aspects of its existence. This interpretation differs from Della Rocca's, where there is presumably a set of *properties* (F 1 . . . . . . 10) that are Attribute neutral that are shared by a Mode of thought and a Mode of extension.

The question, however, is how these things are, in fact, shared. Here, I think, the ambiguity of the term *res* (thing), in Spinoza's thought, comes into play. The parallel sharing of Della Rocca's neutral properties can make better sense if these properties are *in* a particular something. If so, one could then grant that bodies and minds do not causally relate to each other strictly speaking or much less explain one another. Yet, *qua* whatever properties are involved in regarding things as either bodies or minds in the first place, bodies and minds do indeed, after all, relate to one another *in* the particular something of which they are aspects. (The advantage of this approach will be filled out below, as we consider how Spinoza viewed the integrity of complex organisms.)

Reading Spinoza as I am suggesting at this point has at least some affinity with that of Jonathan Bennett, whose view is not only distinctive in the way that he posits the identity between mind and body, but it is possibly the most sophisticated in the literature.[35] Bennett offers what he calls the *mode identity* thesis as the best way to account for Spinoza's insistence that "mind and body are one and the same thing." Just as I have suggested, Bennett argues that the identity of mind and body is not rooted in the sharing of neutral properties, as Della Rocca has contended. Nor is it determined by parallelism (he thinks that mode identity explains parallelism). Rather, there is some *something* that is present in Spinoza's identity equation, but this something is neither a mode of thought nor extension precisely speaking. In order to offer his interpretation, however, Bennett must contend that a distinction in Spinoza's metaphysics is found between what he calls Attribute-involving Modes and trans-Attribute Modes.

On this reading, it is the Modes that are the most properly basic features of Substance. They are the way that Substance exists most fundamentally in concrete reality. Such Modes, Bennett argues, are not essentially Modes of thought or extension or

35. Bennett, *Study of Spinoza's Ethics.*

of any other of the Attributes. Instead, the truly, properly basic Modes are, in some sense, entities that are neither, because "they lie deep enough to combine with both attributes."[36] Bennett asserts that this way of construing the matter is critical if we are to see Spinoza's claims as coherent; it is the price one must pay to allow Spinoza to mean that mind and body can be the same thing. It must be read into Spinoza's metaphysic, Bennett contends, because for Spinoza the Attributes of Extension and Thought, while not merely nominal distinctions about God or Nature, are not "really fundamental properties, although they must be perceived as such by any intellect."[37] In Bennett's view, these Attributes are best understood as qualitative *ways* that things exist; but as *ways* they are not basic properties that make a Spinozistic mode a mode.

When Spinoza says, "whether we conceive Nature under the attribute of Extension or under the attribute of Thought, . . . we find one and the same order, or one and the same connection of causes—that is, the same things following one another" [II P 7, sch], he knows that something has to be able to account for this psycho-physical parallelism.[38] Bennett, as he interprets Spinoza's doctrine, embraces parallelism and contends, furthermore, the modes of thought should be described in their relationship to the modes of extension in such a way that recognizes mentality to be an irreducible psychological state of existence, contra interpretations such as Balz and Curley offer who conceive of the parallel "identity" between mind and body in a way that negates the psychological nature of ideas.[39] But one can ask Bennett, nonetheless, *how* his brand of psycho-physical parallelism is to be accounted for, since it is not clear how, in Spinoza's system, a Mode can be something that has its Attributes stripped off.

Bennett proposes a seemingly radical a solution to this problem involving what he calls a *differentia*.

36. Bennett, *Study of Spinoza's Ethics*, 146.

37. Bennett, *Study of Spinoza's Ethics*, 147. Cf. Shmueli, "Thomas Aquinas' Influence," 61–72. See chapter 1, where Shmueli's interpretation is presented. He argues that one can discern an influence of Aquinas (indirectly) on Spinoza's concept of Attributes.

38. Bennett, *Study of Spinoza's Ethics*, 127–56. The concept of parallelism, as I suggested earlier, is an interpretation of Spinoza that could have difficulties as an expression of Spinoza's system. It all depends upon how one conceives the parallelism. It could be seen as implying the same order, but on parallel planes of existence that would seem to entail a kind of dualism that is more than conceptual, but actually a dualism of activity. That conclusion would not be amenable to Spinoza's thought. For example, where he says, ". . . we find one and the same order, or one and the same connection of causes—that is, the same things following from one another" [II, P 7, sch]. Bennett is right in his version of parallelism, however, to dismiss Curley's "logical" interpretation of Spinoza's "parallelism" as simply meaning that an idea is reducible to truths about each particular event, since "ideas can scarcely be regarded as individual psychical entities" (Curley, *Spinoza's Metaphysics*, 118). The question is not whether ideas can be so regarded, but what it means to be *an idea of* a Mode of Extension in the first place in Spinoza's ontology.

39. Both Balz and Curley seem to view the "ideas" of the body as propositions that mirror the way that reality itself is. Hence, our ideational life is the same as our physical life, because the propositions are true propositions about real states of affairs.

[Spinoza's] thesis is rather that if P_1 is systematically linked with M_1, then P_1 is extension-and-F for some differentia F such that M_1 is thought-and-F. What it takes for an extended world to contain my body is exactly what it takes for a thinking world to contain my mind . . . .Spinoza usually takes it that a mode 'involves the concept of' an attribute (2p6d), so that entailments run upwards from mode to attribute; but in our present context I must suppose him to be thinking of modes—or 'things,' as he calls them—as having their attributes peeled off, i.e., as consisting in the F which must be *added* to extension to get my body or to thought to get my mind.[40]

By allowing for the existence of such *differentiae* in Spinoza's thought, Bennett claims that we can make sense of Spinoza's claim and allow him actually to mean that "physical state P_1 = mental state M_1." However, the identity of these states necessarily involves the *differentia* as the unstated member of the identity equation: "if P_1 is systematically linked with M_1, then P_1 is extension-and-F for some *differentia* F, such that M_1 is thought-and-F." Bennett describes the general implication of this way of reading Spinoza as meaning that what it takes for the extended world to contain a certain body is exactly what it takes for a thinking world to contain the mind of that body

For Bennett, the cryptic nature of Modes *per se* in Spinoza's system is best understood by his (Bennett) description of the nature of extended modes.[41] Bennett describes Spinoza's understanding of the nature of a mode of extension as functioning descriptively (qualifying or quantifying) as "adjectival" or "adverbial" with respect to space (extension).[42] This is a rather odd sounding way to put it, but what Bennett means is fairly straightforward, if one thinks about extension (space) in terms of quarks, as does contemporary physics.

> Contemporary particle physics depicts fundamental particles . . . not as little lumps of matter, but rather as spheres of influence; and their unsplittability is not remotely like the end point on a line running through water drops, marshmallows, billiard balls, diamonds and . . . fundamental particles, quarks. This may make quarks unsplittable in a manner which satisfies the strongest demand that Spinoza could reasonably make [that they have true particularity in substance]. But it deprives them of substantial status in a different way, by making them adjectival upon space: the existence of a quark in a given region, according to this way of looking at things, is the region's having certain *qualities* . . . . [it] is a *version* of Spinoza's own position . . .[43]

40. Bennett, *Study of Spinoza's Ethics,* 141.

41. "As for Spinoza's thesis that all particulars—minds as well as bodies—are modes: I have to suppose that he started with a sound doctrine about the modal nature of extended particulars and then stretched it over mental ones as well on the strength of a *general* thesis that the extended world is mirrored in detail by the mental world" (Bennett, *Study of Spinoza's Ethics,* 94; emphasis original).

42. Bennett, *Study of Spinoza's Ethics,* 95.

43. Bennett, *Study of Spinoza's Ethics,* 84 (emphasis original).

Bennett labels this concept "field metaphysic," and utilizes it to interpret the meaning of Mode *qua* modifications of substance (i.e., ways that Substance is "qualified" and "quantified"). "A complete Spinozist account of the world would have to provide replacements not only for quantifications over regions but also for mentions of individual regions . . . . we can replace [the substantial language] 'Region R is F' by 'Space is F there' while pointing to R, or by 'Space is F here' while occupying R . . . ."[44]

By Bennett's account, Spinoza's view regards extended modes as ultimately resting on properties whose instantiation by space amounts to the existence of what we ordinarily refer to as distinct regions of space. The Modes that Bennett offers us, then, are real states or properties of Substance. But ultimately, Spinoza's one Substance would have to be regarded as somehow the totality of all the various ultimate "fields" that there are—that of space simply serving as the model for how we are supposed to think of the latter in general. Building upon this general thesis about the nature of Modes, Bennett develops his interpretation of Spinoza's insistence on the *identity* of mind and body.[45] He argues that, for Spinoza's metaphysic: "If my mind is a mode and my body is a mode, and my mind is my body, it follows that my mind is the same mode as my body . . . . [Spinoza's] thesis about the identity of physical and mental particulars is really about the identity of *properties*."[46]

Applying this general description to Modes of all the Attributes, we can say that, for Bennett, for every Mode of any Attribute there must be a *fundamental mode* that is itself not a Mode of any Attribute and this fundamental mode is strictly speaking identical to each Mode involved in any ascription of identity across the Attributes. One can say this fundamental mode is in a certain way the two distinct Modes, which are thereby identified with one another. Indeed, the latter modes of thought and extension might even be said to exist *in* (each in its own way), and therefore express, that fundamental mode. And this fundamental mode, per Bennett, would not be reducible to either what we mean by mind or body. The relation of those *fundamental modes* to Substance, to say again, is simply that of a property to something propertied by it. Thus, the fundamental mode that is expressed *as* (in) some mode of thought is numerically identical with the fundamental mode expressed *as* (in) some mode of extension, and vice versa. This way of understanding Spinoza means, for Bennett, that

44. Bennett, *Study of Spinoza's Ethics*, 95.

45. Bennett interestingly says about Spinoza's theory: "It is a metaphysical speculation which I suppose is not true, and it is not even philosophically useful as an object lesson. But I care whether I am right in attributing it to Spinoza, since it displays his basic metaphysic as more coherent and better thought out than any previous commentator has found it to be" (*Study of Spinoza's Ethics*, 140–41).

46. Bennett, *Study of Spinoza's Ethics*, 141. While it is beyond our scope to argue this point in Bennett's views critically, I want to point out that, if there is some plausibility in it, then, as has already been suggested earlier in this work, one might be able to read Spinoza's view of Substance in relation to its Modes as having interesting parallels with Aquinas's view of God as *pure Act of Being*. Just as God's own being, for Aquinas, is the only real source of being, in which *qua* the only source of being all other things participate, so Spinoza's Substance (especially if one considers *Natura naturans*) is the source in which all other things exist *qua* modes.

we can take Spinoza seriously, when he insists that Substance and Modes are what really exist. Further, we can also account for how Modes can be understood as involving finite modes as having reality *qua* particular entities.[47]

Bennett wants to maintain the *conceptual* distinction between Attributes (that I suggested above is the focus of the relevant scholium) intact. What Spinoza cannot be saying, Bennett concludes, is that "physical P1 = mental M1."[48] To say that would violate the conceptual/explicative distinction between the Attributes, argues Bennett. And he thinks his view of the *fundamental modes* as the source of the identity relation between the mind and the body keeps this inviolate. The fundamental modes, because they are certain properties of Substance that are in a certain sense in the Modes of thought and extension, may, in turn, themselves be regarded as true *modes* (and indeed must be, given Spinoza's view that all that exists are Substance and its Modes). We are simply viewing them as ways in which the one Substance is propertied. For this reason, but also in order to distinguish his approach from the more familiar versions of the identity thesis, he calls his view the *mode identity* thesis. One need not transgress the conceptual barrier, he concludes, because the explanation of identity in terms of *differentia* means that identity is rooted in the *differentia* and not the Attributes, since it is the *differentia* that combines with all the Attributes. The explanatory barrier is kept intact.

Unlike the view of identity of the Modes as it is more ordinarily put forth—and which requires some form of relativization of identity for its formulation—Bennett's is not, strictly speaking, a view according to which Modes of thought and extension are identified with one another as modes. Again, the identity relation concerns only certain (fundamental) "modes" that are in a special way "in" modes of thought and extension. One can say, as well, that the attribute modes "consist in" the differentia. However, one might ask what these fundamental modes or *differentiae* might be in Spinoza's system? This question is especially important, since Bennett describes *differentiae* as something that "consists in the F which must be *added* to extension to get my body or to thought to get my mind."[49] Again, the *identity* that Bennett has

---

47. Cf. Bennett, *Study of Spinoza's Ethics*, 94, where he quotes appreciatively Curley's observations: "Spinoza's modes are, prima facie, of the wrong logical type to be related to substance in the same way Descartes's modes are related to substance, for they are particular things, not qualities. And it is difficult to know what it would mean to say that the particular things inhere in substance. When qualities are said to inhere in substance, this may be viewed as a way of saying that they are predicated of it. What would it mean to say that one thing is predicated of another is a mystery that needs solving." Bennett goes on to claim that his reading has "solved the mystery."

48. Bennett, *Study of Spinoza's Ethics*, 94. Also see Bennett, "Eight Questions about Spinoza," 18.

49. Bennett, *Study of Spinoza's Ethics* 142. Bennett admits his reading has to "credit Spinoza with having this change of tune: it is the price for letting him mean that a certain mental mode is a certain physical mode, rather than dismissing those texts as lapses or rescuing them through 'relative identity' manoeuvre." I think Bennett is essentially on to the right track, but he does not account for what such a *differentia* might be in Spinoza's system. In fact, he thinks that it cannot be found and must be implied in Spinoza's logic. Later, as we consider the role of *conatus* in Spinoza's thought, we may find a helpful intertextual way of making sense of Bennett's notion of *differentia*.

in mind is strictly speaking an identity relation involving the fundamental modes *in* (ordinary) particulars.

Two questions must be asked of Bennett's interpretation. First, what could it possibly mean for Spinoza to think of modes or things as having their attributes "peeled off," but able to be *added to* the Attributes. Does he mean this merely conceptually or as a metaphysical given? This idea of a thinking Mode as being T + F is, to say the least, a difficult way of constructing the relationship that a Mode has to itself. While the idea that I suggested earlier—that in Spinoza's thought there are some entities (things) that can be "expressed" in two Modes—is itself consistent with Spinoza's own statements, Bennett's claim that there are things (*differentiae*) that get "added" to Attributes is a confusing and perhaps unnecessary locution. For instance, if my body is E + F and my mind is T + F, then what am I? Am I ET + F? Or am I (E+F) + (T+F)? Or am I F in the most basic sense? Della Rocca recognizes the difficulty in Bennett's formulation and argues that the theory does not give him mind-body identity.[50] There would seem, however, to be an even more pressing existential problem. Bennett's view does not account for how I (and so, for that matter, how anything) would be in actuality one with myself (or itself). As I shall presently suggest, however, there is a different way to understand how Spinoza utilizes and develops the idea of things (*res*) such that they are not Modes of extension plus thought, but rather are that which is *expressed through* the Modes.

A second problem for Bennett is this. Does it not follow from Bennett's suggestion that these stripped-down fundamental modes, at the very least, have an ontological priority over the Attributes that are supposed to make them conceivable and intelligible in the first place? How do these *differentiae* then avoid being *nothing* within the confines of Spinoza's system? Perhaps something like this is what Spinoza means, but it is an open question whether such a reading of the concept of Mode is fully reconcilable to Spinoza's system.[51] In Spinoza's account, the Modes prima facie must have properties that reflect the primacy that he grants (in some sense) to Attributes of Substance. For the Attributes of Substance are the essence of Substance. Since the Modes are modifications of Substance, how do the *differentiae* "somehow" relate to substance as properties of it without the Attributes being involved in *that* relation at all? Bennett seems, in his interpretation, to turn Spinoza's ontological ladder upside down from the rather hierarchical view that Spinoza suggests, i.e., that Substance is foundational, manifesting or manifested in (according to how one reads Spinoza's view of the Attributes) infinite Attributes that themselves are expressed by or in infinite and finite attribute-expressing Modes. Reversing this conceptual scheme, Bennett argues:

---

50. Della Rocca, *Representation*, 158–60.

51. Della Rocca, who will be considered below, thinks Bennett's *kind* of reading is "Spinozistically unacceptable." For Spinoza, "all modes are modes of attributes" (Della Rocca, *Representation*, 121).

Now, according to my 'mode identity' interpretation, there is a good sense in which the most basic properties of the one substance are not the attributes but the modes, since they lie deep enough to combine with both attributes. Of course, extension is more basic than squareness; but to be square is to be extended and F, for an F which does entail extension because it is also combinable with thought. Given that there are such Fs, Spinoza rightly won't say that an attribute is an essence = most fundamental property, but only that it must be conceived or perceived as basic, since to get deeper we would have to think of finite modes in abstraction from either attribute, which is impossible.[52]

While I think that Bennett's basic insight here is on target, namely that there is another *something* that must be at work to account for the identity in question, his description of his "*differentia*" as being *added* to extension or thought is an unfortunate formulation. In fact, although I have spoken of his fundamental modes F as if they are simply "in" the ordinary Modes in question, when we are concerned with the relevant identities, isn't it really the case on Bennett's view (though he denies it)—or at least so one might argue—that the ordinary Modes *are* F? Namely, isn't the Mode of thought in question simply F as differentiating Thought and the mode of extension in question that same F as differentiating Extension? Now, of course, Bennett can *insist* that F as differentiating Thought and F as differentiating Extension are not identical in any way; they simply both *contain* something that is identical. But is it really so clear? After all, given the model taken from the field metaphysics, isn't the specific thing or entity in question simply some way that the substance-field is propertied? And that is F. The (distinct) Modes of thought and extension in question are then simply *that F*: in one case *qua* differentiating Thought and in the other case *qua* differentiating Extension. So, it turns out, after all, that Bennett should have to resort to relativization of identity, in order to maintain his position that the identity relation in Spinoza doesn't hold between ordinary modes, but only on the level of the Fs. This interpretation requires that some Mode of thought is identical with some Mode of extension, *qua* the fundamental Mode that the two of them are, but with the identity statement relativized so that neither is identical with it *qua* ordinary Mode.

Furthermore, why would one not be allowed to conclude from Bennett's description that we would, in some sense, have an F whose existence is dualistically divided. If this F combines with the Attribute of extension and the Attribute of thought, and if Spinoza imposes a causal barrier between the Modes of the Attributes, how would the same F be able to be the cause of all its own acts, since it would have acts that are *qua* thought not its own acts in terms of its existence *qua* extension plus F. This F would have to have two different existences, in some sense, if it exists as E_1 (extension and

52. Bennett, *Study of Spinoza's Ethics,* 146. In this portion of his argument, Bennett contends that in Spinoza's definition of Attribute in I, def 4 "there is something in the nature of an illusion or error or lack of intellectual depth or thoroughness in taking an attribute to be a basic property."

F) in one way rather than T1 (thought and F).[53] Any attempt to describe the acts of F would, it seems to me, be liable to the charge that the act of a Mode of Thought (if F combined with Thought makes F a mode of a particular Attribute) would explain the acts of a Mode of Extension (if F added to Extension makes it a mode of a different Attribute). Perhaps the impulse behind Bennett's idea of *differentiae* might be salvageable if we can find a better way of putting the issue.[54]

In the case of both Bennett and Della Rocca, their accounts of Spinoza could benefit from taking a different look at what the significance of *conatus* might be in Spinoza's metaphysics. The mind seen as integrally one with the body, and vice versa, can be understood more clearly by considering that the *conatus* of an entity is not merely a way of describing the *striving* to maintain existence, but is a metaphysical principle that grants both organizational material complexity along with mental capacity.[55] The key hint to this better way of interpreting Spinoza is found where he asserts: "From the above we understand not only that the human Mind is united to the Body but also

53. Bennett, *Study of Spinoza's Ethics*, 141. Bennett contends (146) that for Spinoza the ordinary Modes of our cognitive awareness are the most basic properties of the one Substance, since they lie deep enough to combine with both attributes. But Bennett's view requires that there be something even more fundamental than the ordinary Modes, i.e., the *differentia*, because these are capable of combining with the Attributes to make the Modes of those Attributes possible. But what could such a thing be? He denies in the passage on 146 that "essence" could mean anything more than the "fundamental property of a thing." It cannot mean, he contends, "something deeper and more general." What Bennett means by deeper is not clear. And by denying the more general, is Bennett contending Spinoza has no place for universals?

54. Chantal Jaquet has provided an intriguing interpretation of Spinoza's views on mind-body identity in *Affects, Actions, and Passions in Spinoza*. Per this reading, the key to understanding mind-body unity is in his conceptual use of *affectus*. Jaquet claims, quite rightly, that interpreting Spinoza in terms of parallelism distorts his conception of the relation of mind and body (as I have argued). Rather, mind and body should be described as equal (*aequalis*) and the same (or "at once," *simul*), regarding both the power of acting and in the order and connection of modes under the attributes of thinking and extension. There is a unity of identity in that both mind and body "share" in the same effects because Spinoza conceives of body and mind as different expressions of an underlying unity. This reading is consistent, I think, with my own, but, as will be shown, understanding the wider meaning of *conatus* as essence in his system, as I argue, provides a Spinozistic foundation for this underlying unity.

55. Della Rocca, *Representation*, 33–38 develops an argument for the importance of conatus in understanding the nature of individuality. "Spinoza's discussion of the conatus, or striving, of all things fits nicely with and indeed corroborates this reading of Spinoza's account of physical individuals. According to this doctrine, each thing—complex physical individuals, complex mental individuals, and also not-complex things, if there are any—by its very nature strives or tends to persist in existence" (35). The troublesome portion of this assessment of Spinoza's doctrine, from my vantage, is that Della Rocca interprets conatus to imply that "complex physical *individuals*" (CPI) and "complex mental *individuals*" (CMI) (emphasis mine) are both types of "things" that strive to persist. Such a reading, while it fits well with Della Rocca's insistence that parallelism is the key to understanding Spinoza's identity doctrine, suggests that the striving of the mind (CMI) and the striving of the body (CPI) are two different acts of striving. Della Rocca attempts to put the issue of the constitution of individuality in "attribute-neutral terms" as a way to avoid this implication. However, as he develops this idea he argues that the CPI is constituted by a feature that is relevant to it (the tendency to preserve their proportion of motion and rest), but that the CMI has its own relevant feature that constitutes it (the feature of affirming the existence of the body). It seems, however, that these are still two strivings, not one.

what is to be understood by the union of Mind and Body. But nobody can understand this union adequately or distinctly unless he first gains adequate knowledge of the nature of our body" [II, P 13, sch.].

In the next chapter I will demonstrate that Spinoza's concern in *Ethics* is to offer a view of the nature of a human life as that of a complex individual; what Jonas calls "an organic individual . . . viewed as a fact of wholeness."[56] This reading can pick up where Bennett leaves us with his concept of the *differentia* and Della Rocca with his concept of Modes as also bearers of *extensional* properties. My reading, however, also provides a much more dynamic understanding of the central place that Spinoza gives to *Life* as an irreducible feature in his metaphysics, which involves mindedness and bodiedness. The benefit of my exposition and interpretation will be the realization that the concepts of *anima, conatus,* and *essentia* work together in Spinoza's metaphysics as he analyzes the nature of the existence of ordinary concrete particulars and provides us with a helpful concept—the living conatic essence that a thing is. It will be demonstrated that this concept could very well represent the door that must be opened if we are to view Spinoza's doctrine adequately. Aquinas-style hylomorphism, it will be argued, is a key to that door. Before this, however, one glaring difficulty must be addressed that faces anyone who would want to compare Aquinas's and Spinoza's ontological commitments. That hurdle is Spinoza's monism.

SPINOZA'S "SUBSTANCE" COMPARED TO AQUINAS'S "BEING"

No concept is more central to Spinoza's philosophy than his complementary claims that there is only one Substance and all else that either is an Attribute or a Mode of Substance.[57] The demonstration of this is the main theme of the first book of the *Ethics.* Any attempt, therefore, to understand what Spinoza means by the claim that mind and body are "one and the same thing" will have to consider the way that this mind-body oneness is related to the oneness of Substance.[58]

If one were to argue (as does Descartes) that the obvious distinction between various attributes implies that they are ontologically distinguished, Spinoza's reply would surely be that this does not follow. The distinction of Attributes, whereby this one Substance is expressed, poses no difficulty for monism as Spinoza develops it, because of his conception of Substance as infinite and all-encompassing reality. He argues, therefore, that Substance must have an infinite number of Attributes and an infinite number of Modes within each Attribute by which the existence of Substance is

56. Jonas, "Spinoza and the Theory of Organism," 269.

57. I do not intend to take a position on whether the Attributes are really existent or not in Spinoza's ontology.

58. By this assertion I do not mean to suggest that I embrace the "relative identity" thesis, which contends that the oneness of mind and body as Modes of the Attributes of Substance are one because Substance itself is one. There is a different, and better, way to account for Spinoza's identity doctrine, as shall be shown.

manifest. The radical difference of these Attributes does not pose a problem, because an attribute represents in our understanding something that is a way of existence which implies something more fundamental of which it can be an attribute.[59] Attributes in Spinoza's view are (by implication from I, P 2) something that substances "have." Thus, Thought and Extension are not self-explanatory strictly speaking. They can only be "explained" or comprehended as qualitative ways that Substance exists. With this focus on Substance as the ontological ground of Attributes, Spinoza argues, then, that *qua* qualitative ways of existing, even though they seem totally disparate from each other explanatorily, Attributes and their Modes are not expressions of different Substances but are Attributes of the same Substance. Yet, because they are distinct as *Attributes* they cannot be conceived through any other Attribute.

Based on this logic Spinoza insists: "Consequently nothing can be clearer than this . . . that an absolutely infinite entity must necessarily be defined as an entity consisting of infinite attributes, each of which express a definite essence, eternal and infinite . . . in Nature there exists only one substance, absolutely infinite" [I, P 10, sch]. And this Substance must, by definitions 3 and 6 in Book I, be conceived of as nothing other than God. This conclusion is argued in propositions 11–13 and leads Spinoza to the conclusion that no other substance, other than God, can be conceived, "since God is an absolutely infinite being of whom no attribute expressing the essence of substance can be denied and since he necessarily exists" [I, P 14, pr].

Spinoza's particular way of conceptualizing the relationship of Attributes and Substance, plus his willingness to embrace the traditional term "God" as a part of his argument, leads him to proposition (15) in Book I. "Whatever is, is in God, and nothing can be or be conceived without God." Spinoza is quite aware during his "geometrical" argument that we do not experience *Substance* per se in our ordinary experience. Rather, we encounter ordinary particulars of perception and conceptualization in terms of Extension and Thought. This is the assumed background of the demonstrations of the *Ethics*. His point is to describe the necessity of recognizing that the ordinary particulars and every feature which we encounter of Nature are not self-caused. Therefore, neither are they self-explanatory. Because he takes our experience of the particularized *many* as the foundation of our daily experience, Spinoza asserts in his very first proposition that "Substance is by nature prior to its affections."[60] An "affection" of Substance is,

---

59. Again, the perspective that I am developing does not rely upon taking a side in the debate about whether or not the Attributes are real or nominal. However, I agree with the perspective of Shmueli, discussed in chapter 1, that something similar to Aquinas's concept of "the analogy of being" allowed Spinoza to develop a view of the Attributes that was neither a nominalistic view, nor strictly realist: "The basic view, then, of Spinoza [on the Attributes] is the Thomistic view of the attributes (universals) as extra-mental realities without being distinctly existent on their own, not the [nominalist/subjectivist] view of Maimonides."

60. This way of seeing the issue is not in discontinuity with the Thomistic insistence that what we know in the first instance is "primary substances." It is from these that we reason our way by abstraction to recognize species and universal concepts; and from these to realize the distinction between essence and existence until finally we demonstrate the necessity of God as Pure Act of Existing in which all things must exist via participation.

in Spinoza's metaphysics, a way that Substance exists in concrete expression that our minds can conceive. Affections of Substance, then, are best understood as the "form 'taken on' by something, a state of that thing, and therefore logically posterior to that of which it is an affection."[61] This is a broad concept for Spinoza by which he describes the ontological dependence upon Substance that everything has—both infinite features (Attributes and Modes) of Substance as well as finite features, the concrete and universal. Because there can be no existence conceivable apart from Substance (nor can it be actual), everything that has actual existence (materially or immaterially) is a Mode of God (as the One Substance). From the conclusion that all that exists is *in* God as "affections of Substance" and that God is expressed in an infinity of ways, it follows for Spinoza that the ways (Modes) by which God expresses its necessary existence and essence are themselves "in the divine nature and can be conceived only through the divine nature" [I, P 15, pr]. Consequently, we cannot conceive of anything existing in reality "except substance and modes [of substance]."[62]

This implies, of course, that singular material entities are *qua* material *parts* (modes) of God, because material reality, just as much as immaterial reality, must be part of God *qua* Substance.[63] In the scholium of proposition 15, as Spinoza endeavors to defend the implication that God is Substance *qua* extended, he presents an argument against the objectors to God's materiality who declare that the divisibility of matter rules it out as an Attribute of God. To demonstrate the appropriateness of his own conclusions, he utilizes the distinction between matter as existent in itself and the modifications which are the concrete instantiations of matter.[64] He says, ". . . matter is everywhere the same, and there are no distinct parts in it except in so far as we conceive matter as modified in various ways. Then its parts are distinct, not really

61. Feldman, *Ethics*, 24.

62. Spinoza would include in this not just finite modes, but the infinite modes as well. However, for the purposes of the present discussion, we will focus on the relationship of finite modes to the one eternal and infinite Substance. We can bracket the questions that attend the interpretation of Spinoza regarding the nature of infinite Modes. Cf. Bennett, *Study of Spinoza's Ethics*, 107–18 for a good discussion of various aspects of the infinite modes. Also see the chapter "Causality of Substance" in Horn, "Substance and Mode."

63. Spinoza's argument, by which he defends this conclusion, is found in propositions 12 and 13 of Book I. He argues in P 12 that even the *divisions (or parts)* of Substance must *qua* divisions exist *in* something. As parts of Substance the divisions cannot be conceived of as each themselves substances, nor can they be thought of apart from Substance, nor can they have some other ontological status besides existing in Substance. Hence the fact that Substance could be conceived as having parts does not imply that division as such cannot be part of the infinite Substance. Also, by P 13, the infinity of Substance means that we cannot conceive of anything as ultimately distinguishable from Substance. Even divisions exist in the infinity of Substance, hence the divisions into parts that we conceive of as being the case in the various Attributes does not imply that Substance, "insofar as it is substance," is divisible. All exists in the infinity of Substance.

64. Bennett's interpretation of how Spinoza could make the distinction that he does argues that Spinoza's view has much in common with contemporary quantum field theory. Bennett, *Study of Spinoza's Ethics*, 91–97.

but only modally."[65] Such a distinction was not unique to Spinoza when he made it. It is a distinction that was posited by Descartes. Prior to Descartes, the medieval philosophers had embraced it. As a translator and *commentator*, Shirley argues that it is the Cartesian background that is relevant.

> "... it is probably the Cartesian version of the distinction that is relevant ... [According to Descartes's dualism], a modal distinction [as opposed to a substance-distinction] is a distinction either between a mode and the substance of which it is a mode or between the various modes of substance.... Spinoza uses this philosophical terminology to express the difference between matter as divided up into individual corporeal parts and matter as pure homogeneous extension."[66]

What strikes me, however, is not the "Cartesian" comparison (which one might expect), but that such a "modal" distinction as Spinoza draws is very much like the distinction that Aquinas makes in his own metaphysical analysis between the natures of primary beings that exist materially *and* the prime matter upon which they depend for their existence *qua* material entities. (Of course, Aquinas calls them "primary substances" but let us set aside, for the moment, this important difference in terminology from Spinoza to see if we cannot draw an instructive comparison.) Spinoza insists that there are Modes of Substance that as extended things that do not contain in themselves the source of their own being, as well as maintaining that *Extension* as an Attribute is itself to be distinguished from the Modes that express the reality and nature of extended substance. It must be remembered that while the Attribute of Extension is an attribute of Substance, Extension does not precisely "exist," since what exists are Substance and its modifications. Spinoza, by regarding the nature of extended things as Modes of the Attribute of Extension upon which their existence *qua* extended modes depends, offers a metaphysical theory of dependence and existence that resonates with the Aristotelian/Thomistic ideas about prime matter.[67]

While Aquinas does not think of prime matter as an eternal principle, much less an attribute of God's essence, when thinking strictly in terms of material existence, he acknowledges that it is a principle of existence, but insists that it is primary substances in "designated matter" that actually exist materially. Some might suggest in reply to this claim that Spinoza's identification of extension as an Attribute of God

---

65. The import of the finite modes, then, is obvious in Spinoza's metaphysics. They become a part of his explanation for change and contingency and a part of his proof for the necessity of the existence of God *qua* Substance. E.g., the modes are not self-caused, but as temporal they cannot be immediately the result of Substance.

66. Feldman, *Ethics*, 42n2.

67. As was discussed in chapter 3, Aquinas views prime matter as real, but not a truly existent thing, because it is pure potentiality. While Spinoza does not describe extension in these precise terms, it would seem that his insistence that the Modes of Substance are what exist along with Substance itself could imply that the Attribute of extension is not precisely an existent thing, but nonetheless real *qua* an Attribute.

would undercut the comparison with Aquinas; and no doubt that would be troubling for the metaphysics of the latter. However, taking Aquinas's claim that prime matter is a principle *in* which material entities exist *qua* material and then reading this understanding of prime matter in terms of his even deeper claim that nothing that exists can exist apart from participation in the Being of God (but not expressions or parts of God), possible parallels between the ontological commitments of Spinoza and Aquinas begin to suggest themselves. Regarding the participation of the principle of materiality in the Being of God, the logic of Aquinas's deliberation can be found in Q 44, a 1 & a 2 of the *Summa's prima pars*:

1. No entity or principle of existence (including matter and material things) has its existence in itself but exists only by participation in God's own act of Being.[68]

2. Prime matter is a principle of existence.

3. Thus, Prime matter can only exist by participation in God's Being.[69]

The differences between Spinoza's account of Substance and Aquinas's idea/concept of God as Being and the ontological foundation of all existent things are obvious, but perhaps the ways that these concepts do similar work in the philosophical systems under consideration is not. It is worth noting, therefore, the functional and (to a limited extent) metaphysical similarities that one can find. Consider first, in this regard, Spinoza's argument that Substance (God or Nature) is infinite and compare this concept to Aquinas's contentions that God is Pure Act. In his "geometrical" demonstrations, Spinoza asserts in I, P 8 that "every substance is necessarily infinite." At this point in his argument, Spinoza has not yet proposed that there can only be one Substance, so the content of this proposition and its proofs and scholia will be employed to lead to that conclusion. In scholium 1, he contends, "Since in fact to be finite is in part a negation and to be infinite is the unqualified affirmation of the existence of some nature, it follows from Proposition 7 alone that every substance must be infinite." The thrust of P 7 is the necessary existence of Substance, because, by definition, it cannot be the product of some prior set of conditions; and there is no lack or potentiality (hence no nonbeing) in Substance. So, "its essence necessarily involves existence." Substance exists necessarily and must be infinity per se. This way of stating the issue resonates with Aquinas's belief that God is Pure Act with no potentiality. Recall the argument of

68. "Therefore *all beings* apart from God are not their own being, but are beings *by participation.* Therefore it must be that all things which are *diversified by the diverse participation* of being, so as to be more or less perfect, are caused by one First Being, Who possesses being most perfectly" (my emphasis).

69. "Therefore whatever is the cause of things considered as beings, must be the cause of things, not only according as they are 'such' by accidental forms, nor according as they are 'these' by substantial forms, *but also according to all that belongs to their being* at all in any way. And thus it is necessary to say that also *primary matter is created* by the universal cause of things . . . But here we are speaking of things according to their emanation from the universal principle of being; *from which emanation matter itself is not excluded*, although it is excluded from the former mode of being made" (my emphasis).

chapter 2 earlier where it was shown that the basis for Aristotle's distinction between act and potency is rooted in the concept of negation (not being something else). Taking this Aristotelian starting point, Aquinas argues that God cannot be conceived of as having any kind of potentiality. Hence, there is no nonbeing in God.[70] On the basis of the claim that God is the Act of Being itself, Aquinas argues for the infinity of God.[71]

Aquinas's claim that there cannot be an infinite magnitude does not create an objection to the possibility that Spinoza and Aquinas have potential points of continuity on the question of the ontological primacy of God in all things. First, it has already been acknowledged that there are significant differences that separate Spinoza and Aquinas on the metaphysical issue of God's identity in relation to the Universe. Aquinas's Christian views and Spinoza's theology are not compatible. It is worth noting, nonetheless, that the real source of their disagreement would be on the question of God's relationship to the world: (1) denial of God's volition by Spinoza, (2) the positing of necessity in Spinoza's God, and (3) Spinoza's failure to see the distinction between existence and essence as implying the necessity of God's transcendence. Replying to the objection, we must, as a second stage of our response, analyze exactly what Aquinas's rejection of the idea of an infinite magnitude specifically means. His argument against this concept is about the *conceivability* of such an entity. In I a, Q 7, a 3 of the *Summa,* Aquinas argues that we cannot simultaneously think of an infinite magnitude and a *particular* physical thing. His argument is that whether we consider the infinite magnitude as a natural body or as a mathematical body we run into the same logical problem. What Aquinas is arguing is that the concept of an infinite magnitude, considered as a particular thing, is a self-refuting concept.

1. To be a body is to be bounded by something.

2. To be infinite as a body is to be unbounded.

3. Hence, the idea of an infinite body (magnitude) is absurd.

70. Aquinas argues the point as follows in *Summa,* Ia, Q 4, a 2, reply: "God is existence itself, of itself subsistent (3, 4). Consequently, He must contain within Himself the whole perfection of being. For it is clear that if some hot thing has not the whole perfection of heat, this is because heat is not participated in its full perfection; but if this heat were self-subsisting, nothing of the virtue of heat would be wanting to it. Since therefore God is subsisting being itself, nothing of the perfection of being can be wanting to Him. Now all created perfections are included in the perfection of being; for things are perfect, precisely so far as they have being after some fashion. It follows therefore that the perfection of no one thing is wanting to God. This line of argument, too, is implied by Dionysius (Div. Nom. v), when he says that, 'God exists not in any single mode, but embraces all being within Himself, absolutely, without limitation, uniformly"; and afterwards he adds that, "He is the very existence to subsisting things.'"

71. *Summa* I a, Q 7, a 1, reply. ". . . [F]orm is not made perfect by matter, but rather is contracted by matter; and hence the *infinite*, regarded on the part of the form not determined by matter, has the *nature of something perfect.* Now being is the most formal of all things, as appears from what is shown above (4, 1, Objection 3). Since therefore the divine being is not a being received in anything, but He is His own subsistent being as was shown above (3, 4), it is clear that *God Himself is infinite and perfect*" (my emphasis).

When comparing this syllogistic form of Aquinas's reasoning with Spinoza's assertion that extension must logically be conceived as a part of God, other interesting similarities emerge. Spinoza argues that because God is truly infinite there can be no state of existence that is not involved in the essence of God as an Attribute of God. However, we must consider an important interpretive point in order to understand adequately the import of this claim. For Spinoza, the infinity of God *qua* the Attribute of Extension does not allow us to conceive of God as a particular thing *qua* extended. To posit God as infinite in "magnitude" (to incorporate Aquinas's term) does not allow us to conceive of God as an extended "thing," strictly speaking, because the only *particular* things that exist are Modes. Such a conclusion about Spinoza's view would seem consistent with his claim [I, P 15, sch] where he refutes those who aver that Extension cannot be an Attribute of God based on the divisibility of the material:

> The student who looks carefully into these arguments [against Spinoza] will find that I have already replied to them, since they are all founded on the same supposition that material substance is composed of parts, and this I have already shown to be absurd (P 12 and Cor. P 13) . . . . [Any] alleged absurdities . . . from which they seek to prove that extended substance is finite do not at all follow from the supposition that quantity is infinite, but that infinite quantity is measurable and is made up of finite parts . . . .
>
> If therefore we consider quantity as it is presented in the imagination— and that is what we more frequently and readily do—we find it to be finite, divisible, and made up of parts. But if we consider it intellectually and conceive it in so far as it is substance—and this is very difficult—then it will be found to be infinite, one and indivisible . . . . This will be quite clear to those who can distinguish between the imagination and the intellect, especially if this point also is stressed, that matter is everywhere the same, and there are no distinct parts in it except in so far as we conceive matter as modified in various ways.

Spinoza would agree, I suggest, that the extended Substance is not itself a particular entity, because being extended is an Attribute of the infinite God who is *qua* the matter of extended Substance "everywhere the same." When Spinoza argues that being extended infinitely is an Attribute of God, he is not identifying God *qua* material as some "thing," e.g., the whole of the universe.[72] Instead, he is identifying God

72. The reading I am suggesting is consistent with the self-described "radical" suggestion of Curley, *Behind the Geometrical Method*, 149n52. "The assumption that Spinoza's God may be identified with the whole of Nature is so common in the Spinoza literature that few commentators feel any need to justify it." In fact, Curley argues convincingly that Spinoza rejects "that kind of pantheism" in Letter 43. He notes that, engaging the arguments of Velthuysen, Spinoza contends that "his having said that all things emanate necessarily from the nature of God does not commit him to holding that the universe is God." By Curley's account, "the general disposition to identify Spinoza's God with the whole of Nature comes mainly from . . . a misreading of the Preface to *E* IV." Cf. Bennett, *Study of Spinoza's Ethics*, 118, where he opines that "Spinoza's terminology [regarding extended reality] is dangerous." He says that Spinoza's descriptions offered in Letter 64 in defense of his metaphysics cannot imply that "the make of the whole universe" suggests that this locution suggests that it names "the totality of particular facts about the extended world."

or Nature as the source (out of God's own essential nature as the *immanent* cause) of there being extended reality at all. But God is not *qua* extended Substance identifiable as a *particular* thing no matter how grandiose the identification. Add this observation to Aquinas's willingness to posit that Prime Matter *qua* the material principle of existence participates in the Being of God, and quite possibly the distance between Aquinas and Spinoza on this matter as might be less a problem than might be suggested by a passing consideration.

1. Spinoza—Modes of extension are not independent, strictly speaking, from extension.

1*. Aquinas—Material entities (primary substances) are not independent, strictly speaking, from prime matter.

2. Spinoza—Extension, as an Attribute of Substance, does not explain itself apart from Substance because its existence is not in itself but Substance.

2*. Aquinas—Prime Matter cannot account for its own existence, because it is essentially pure potentiality, and actualized existence is not part of its essence.

3. Spinoza—Extension as Attribute of Substance expresses as one among an infinite number of Modes Substance's necessary and infinite nature.

3*. Aquinas—Prime Matter must be an expression, by way of participation, of the power to be that is in the necessary, unbounded Being of God.

With the above issues addressed we can look at a second analogous conception in their respective metaphysical schemes. We can observe that Spinoza's "Substance" and Aquinas's "God-as-Being" in each of their particular metaphysical systems both grant existence to the things that exist because those things *qua* particular entities participate in the ontological reality of the first cause. Although any number of Spinoza commentators have asserted that Spinoza's theory of causation rules out the idea of a "final cause" because he does not grant purposiveness to things, it is difficult to argue that he would not share something of Thomas's claim that there is a "first cause" that grants existence to all else by way of its very being. Spinoza's insistence that God is the cause *immanens* and not the cause *transiens* does not separate him entirely from Aquinas. Of course, his pantheistic rejection of the concept of God as transcendent would be heretical, for Aquinas. However, Spinoza's description of God as an immanent cause is not completely alien to Thomas's own notions about the Creation's ontological dependence upon God's Being by way of participation. In chapter 3, I argued that Aquinas believed that contingent being is not a temporal issue, but an ongoing ontological relationship of dependence upon something noncontingent.

To this we can adduce further support for the present case being made for a complementary comparison between Spinoza and Thomas. In (of all places) his commentary, *Exposition of the Gospel of Saint John,* we find Aquinas describing what it means for God to be his own pure act of being and the relation of contingent beings to this pure act:

> Since, then, all the things that are *participate* in existence (*esse*), and are beings by participation, there must needs be, at the summit of all things, something that is existence itself by His own essence (*aliquid . . . quod sit ipsum esse per suam essentiam*), so that His essence is His existence (*id est quod sua essential sity suum esse*), and this is God, Who is the most sufficient, the most worthy and the most perfect cause of the whole being, from whom all that which is participates in being.[73]

Spinoza's concept of God as immanent cause is admittedly different from Aquinas's notion of participation in a crucially important way, metaphysically and theologically speaking. The immanent causal agency of Spinoza's God is not explicitly distinct from its effect(s), whereas Aquinas's idea of participation entails the distinct ontological identity of God apart from the things that exist via participation. Spinoza's cryptic use of the distinction between *Natura naturans* and *Natura naturata* does not assuage the tension between their metaphysical systems.[74] Spinoza's concept of Nature as naturing (*naturans*) does involve enough of a distinction from Nature as natured (*naturans*) within the nature of Substance itself that we could reconsider the judgment of one such as Bennett who claims that this locution is "quite without significance in the *Ethics*."[75] His is not the final word. One need not attempt to read into Spinoza's doctrine any traditional understanding of transcendence and volition in order to assert that the naturing power of Nature is something other than the natured effects of Nature. In fact, it would seem to be precisely such a distinction that Spinoza is insisting

---

73. Quoted in Gilson, *Elements of Christian Philosophy*, 328n12. Gilson interprets the significance of Aquinas's theory of participation as follows: "A new field of metaphysical prospection is here offering itself to our inquiry. Before being anything else [e.g. members of species], the objects of sense experience are so many existents. Their only possible common cause, qua existents, is therefore Existence. But what is Existence? Thomas says it is that which, being absolutely immovable and most perfect, is also absolutely simple; in short, a being that is to itself its own being" (Gilson, *Elements of Christian Philosophy*, 112).

74. Spinoza asserts that there is a difference between *Natura Naturans* and *Natura Naturata*. While we cannot undertake a critical examination of this distinction, it can be noted for Spinoza the distinction is one between (*Naturans*) the Attributes of God that "express eternal and infinite essence" and (*Naturata*) "all that follows from the necessity of God's nature . . . modes of God's attributes in so far as they are considered as things which are in God and can neither be nor be conceived without God" [I, P 29 sch]. See Wolfson's claim that Spinoza inherited this distinction from Aquinas, even as he modified it from its former use (Wolfson, *Philosophy of Spinoza*, 1:16). See Bennett, *Study of Spinoza's Ethics*, 119 for an argument that this distinction is "quite without significance in the *Ethics*. Also, see Curley, *Behind the Geometrical Method*, 43, where he claims that "given Spinoza's identification of God with *natura naturans*, and his identification of God's power with his essence, we have here a thoroughly naturalistic explanation of Spinoza's claim that God's essence, i.e., the totality of his attributes, is eternal and immutable. The eternality and immutability of God's essence is the eternality and immutability of the fundamental laws of nature."

75. Bennett, *Study of Spinoza's Ethics*, 119.

upon in his arguments about the dependence of Modes upon Substance. The ontological dependence runs only one way. It is not the case, for instance, that Substance
is dependent upon the Modes. So, Spinoza gives us a thoroughly transcendence-void
metaphysic, but it does not mean that the that distinction he asserts between *Naturans*
and *Naturata* is of no consequence.[76] There is a clear distinction logically, for Spinoza,
between what provides or accounts for the possibility of naturing and those things (or
the totality of things) that are natured (i.e., given essence and existence). Hence, we
can see that the concept of contingents having their existence *qua* existent contingents
by being *in* something that is completely independent and ontologically distinct and,
as such, the necessary prior condition of contingent beings is what informs the discussion of Substance for Spinoza as much as did for Aquinas's doctrine of participation.
Their differences cannot be glossed over, but the reality that in both views God gives
existence to all other things out of the divine existence should not be ignored either.
Whatever the oneness of mind and body *is*, for each of them it is in some way an
expression of the being of God.

76. Also, Spinoza's later insistence that the object of intellectual investigation is the "love" of God
would seem to suggest that he wants his readers to make a distinction between the naturing aspects of
nature and the natured aspects. Consider, for example, that, in Spinoza's view, the idea of loving something, when applied to our experience of the Modes of Substance, is inadequate. The implication of his
arguments in Books III and IV would seem to be that the way of beatitude is to know that love is but
a feeling we attach to favorable states of the body. It is those favorable states experienced as favorable.
The love of God which he discusses in *Ethics* V, P 32–35 is quite different from the inadequacy of this
feeling of love. Even if this love is, as would seem to be the case for Spinoza, the result of an epistemological shift (the third kind of knowledge), one need not deny that even this opens up for those who
embrace this beatitude a new *object* of love. Although it might be argued that such a realization is only
an embrace of the way things really are naturalistically, even this naturalistic interpretation would not
mitigate the distinction between *naturata* and *naturans* entirely. An appropriate distinction remains,
because what we come to love is the eternal necessity *qua* eternal necessity that makes the Universe
possible; and this *eternal necessity* is quite distinct in itself from the necessary, infinite flow of Modes
that exist because of the one Substance. *Naturans* is the infinite logical source of what exists; *Naturata*
is what exists as a *result* of that infinite necessity.

7

Thomistic Hylomorphism and Spinoza's *Conatus*

HYLOMORPHIC EXISTENCE AND CONATIC ESSENCE

THE NOTION THAT MINDS and bodies express the essence or being of God, in which all things are ultimately one, for a commentator such as Wolfson, was enough to account for the one-and-the-sameness of mind and body in Spinoza's metaphysics.[1] In Wolfson's view, the identity of mind and body is a *relative* identity. Since the Attribute of Extension and the Attribute Thought are not really distinct in God, the oneness of mind and body, he contends, is relative to the reality that there is only one undifferentiated Substance—God.[2] This, it seems to me, would suggest, on a Wolfsonian reading of Spinoza, that even the distinction between the Modes is not fundamentally real.[3]

---

1. Wolfson, *Philosophy of Spinoza*, 1:33–34. "[Spinoza] finds an analogy between the interrelation of extension and thought in God and the interrelation of body and mind in man. But there are fundamental differences between them, and the first fundamental difference which he discusses is that between the relation of extension and thought to God and the relation of body and mind to man. God is a substance in whom extension and thought are attributes. Logically then, God is the underlying subject of these attributes, without himself being composed of them. But man is not a substance, and logically he is not the underlying subject of body and mind; rather he is composed of them."

2. Wolfson's reading of Spinoza makes him a modern Neoplatonist with regard to the nondifferentiability of the One. However, Spinoza is clear in his insistence that our knowledge of the Attributes and their Modes gives us true (adequate) knowledge of God. For a strong case against Wolfson's understanding of the Attributes in Spinoza's philosophy see Geroult, *Spinoza*, 1:430. "[The understanding] produces only true ideas that adequately reflect what is the case. If, therefore, it perceives an infinity of attributes in the substance, then they are really there." Also, see Haserot, "Spinoza's Definition of Attribute," 499–513.

3. Wolfson, *Philosophy of Spinoza*, 1:154–57. Also, see 257–58: "The independence of each attribute which Spinoza insists upon is *merely* to emphasize his denial of the interdependence of matter and form in mediaeval philosophy; it is not an independence which implies the reality of the attributes

So, the Modes of Substance would be only phenomenal manifestations, perhaps in the Kantian sense, with no reality *qua* Modes, and hence no real distinction as Modes. Such an interpretation negates Spinoza's assertion that "what exists are Substance *and* Modes"[4] which seems to require that the distinction between Thought and Extension must be real as expressions of Substance. If the Modes of Thought and Extension really exist *qua* distinct modifications of the one Substance, then the distinction between minds and bodies must be genuine. Wolfson's relative-identity interpretation of Spinoza cannot solve the problem of mind-body identity except to *assert* flatly that the mind is one with the body only because everything is ultimately One in the one Substance's unity with itself. Thus, everything besides Substance is either a Kantian mental construct or a kind of emanationist epiphenomenalism. Something more needs to be said to account for the oneness of mind and body precisely because there is, in Spinoza's thought, a real distinction of some kind.

What many of the commentators endeavoring to maintain the distinction and identity of mind and body in Spinoza have missed is the deeper importance for Spinoza's metaphysics that is played by the concept *conatus*. While he does not introduce the term specifically until Book III, it is this concept that, I shall argue, makes the mind-body distinction and identity metaphysically real in Spinoza's system, and thus interpretively coherent. In III, 7, Spinoza suggests that such a reading of his metaphysical system is on target by positing the following: "The *conatus* with which each thing endeavors to persist in its own being is *nothing but the actual essence* of the thing itself."[5] What is instructive here is not simply that he defines *conatus* as something "with which each thing endeavors to persist in its own being." That was a commonplace notion in Spinoza's day.[6] I suggest that the more intriguing and helpful statement in this proposition is Spinoza's further description of *conatus* as "*nothing* but the actual *essence* of the thing itself."[7] This is, in one sense, at least a startling identification, since Spinoza identifies the essence of a thing as a property or principle upon which the thing depends for its existence.[8] This kind of identification of essence and *conatus*

---

in their relation to substance or a reality in the difference between themselves, with the result that the unity of substance can no longer be logically maintained. The relation of the attributes to each other is of the same order as their relation to substance. Just as the difference between attribute and substance is only a conception of the human mind, so the difference between the attributes themselves is only a form of conception in the human mind . . ."

4. Emphasis mine. Wolfson's argument, if the unreality of the Modes is the implication of his view, that a human being is composed of mind and body, raises the serious question: What is a human being, then, if the human being is composed of Modes that are not themselves real things? Wolfson's Spinozistic human world would be truly occult.

5. Emphasis mine.

6. Wolfson, *Philosophy of Spinoza*, 1:195. "At the time of Spinoza the principle of self-preservation became a commonplace of popular wisdom . . ."

7. Emphasis mine.

8. Cf. *Ethics* II, def 2: "I say there pertains to the essence of a thing that which, when granted, the thing is necessarily posited, and by the annulling of which the thing is necessarily annulled; or that

is confounding, unless Spinoza means something more than merely a process of tending to persist in existence. I suggest that there is an important ambiguity or complexity in Spinoza's use of *conatus* which, once it is recognized, helps us to interpret his doctrine of mind-body identity, and suggests some very intriguing parallels with Aquinas's hylomorphism.

Bennett states that the doctrine is confounded, finding Spinoza's arguments for the striving of things to persevere "disgracefully bad." He sees Spinoza's *conatus* doctrine as a confusing, subsequent account of the drive toward self-preservation in which all entities are engaged to a greater or lesser degree. And while it is certainly true that Spinoza only introduces the concept after he has offered his metaphysical arguments for the oneness of Substance and the nature of the mind, the doctrine that things are ordered in such a way as to be actively engaged in the preservation of their own existence is a doctrine that is fundamental to the very conception of modal existence for Spinoza. Unable to see this, Bennett tends to follow Stuart Hampshire's reading and views this doctrine primarily as a psychological basis for ethics, rather than a metaphysically basic hypothesis.[9]

One should ask, however, what it might mean for *conatus* to be a metaphysically basic notion, for Spinoza. Thus, we should (and shall) proceed attentively. First let us consider some exegetical issues regarding Spinoza's statements about the nature of *conatus*. Proposition 7 in the Latin text of the *Ethics* reads: *Conatus quo unaquaeque res in suo esse perseverare conatur nihil est praeter ipsius rei actualem essentiam.* Here Spinoza is utilizing *conatus* as though it points to a referent of some kind. This does not mean that he conceives of it as being thing-like. However, he does identify *conatus* by the phrase *nihil est praeter ipsius rei actualem.* Shirley translates this phrase "is nothing but the actual essence of the thing itself" and R. H. M Elwes renders it "is nothing else but the actual essence of the thing in question." These translations express very well the identity between *conatus* and the *rei actualem* (the actual thing or the thing active). This *conatus*, identified with the actual thing (or perhaps we might be able to say the thing's actuality), is also further identified with some specificity in Spinoza's Latin as the feature of a thing "*with which* each thing endeavors to persist . . ." (Shirley) or "*wherewith* everything endeavours to persist" (Elwes). The structure of the sentence in Latin would allow that *conatus* is being identified as a feature or perhaps a power that is also identical with the "actual essence" of a thing. It is described as *quo unaquaeque*

without which the thing *can neither be nor be conceived*, and, vice versa, that which cannot be or be conceived without the thing" (my emphasis). Spinoza's phrasing "neither be nor be conceived" suggests that essence is more than epistemological.

9. Bennett, *Study of Spinoza's Ethics*, 240–51. Bennett acknowledges that "the criteria for individuality, for the large class of individuals, do involve the concept of self-preservation; claims of the form 'x is an individual' can sometimes be rejected as failing certain self-preservation tests." However, he fails to see that even this way of interpreting the idea of self-preservation does not account metaphysically for the fact of the existence of the self-preservation impulse. Much less is it able to account for why the mind's self-preservation would be "one and the same thing" as the self-preservation of the body. Cf. Hampshire, *Spinoza*, 122–43.

res in suo esse perseverare conatur. The pronoun "*quo*" has as its antecedent the subject *conatus*; and the word *unaquaeque* ("each and every") refers to something other than *the conatus*. Hence, the grammar of the sentence suggests that we designate the *conatus* as a something "*by* which" (*quo*) "each single one [endeavoring thing]" (*unaquaeque*) endeavors (*conatur*) to persist. So whatever Spinoza more fully means by the notion of *conatus* he at least conceives of it as some feature or aspect or quality of a thing that *enables* it to endeavor "to persist in its own being." It is more than a description of the action of a thing striving to preserve its existence. That being the case, the term *conatus*, in Spinoza's usage, has some ambiguity because of its significance. Not only does it name the activity of striving, but it intimates something that is, in some sense, prior to the concrete action of striving of the entity, and is identified as the essence of the striving thing that determines and drives it to maintain existence.

Another important semantic consideration in Spinoza's *Ethics* involves how he understands the relationship of essences to existent things. Spinoza provides a definition that explains what he means when he utilizes the term "essence": "There pertains to the essence of a thing that which, when granted the thing is necessarily posited, and by the annulling of which the thing is necessarily annulled; or that without which the thing can neither be nor be conceived, and, vice versa, that which cannot be or be conceived without the thing" [II, def 2]. It is *prima facie* apparent by this definition that the essence of a thing is in some way to be distinguished from the thing itself. When essence is "granted" the thing is necessarily posited, but absent "essence" the thing is both inconceivable and cannot exist. But Spinoza also goes on to say in this definition that the essence of the thing "cannot *be* nor be conceived without the thing."[10] An essence, therefore, does not have existence, strictly speaking, (that would make it a Mode), because it can only exist and, therefore, be conceived by us as present in the existence of the thing that gives actual existence to the essence. The distinction between essence and existence is further drawn out by Spinoza in Axiom 1 of this same section of the *Ethics*. He predicates of human beings in this axiom that the "essence of man does not involve necessary existence [which reserved for God's essence]."

Spinoza assumes some type of ontological difference between essence and existence, throughout the *Ethics*. All that he says intimates—or assumes—throughout *Ethics* is consistent with his statement in the second scholium of the tenth proposition, where he is building his case that substantiality cannot be a part of man's essence, because he has already demonstrated that there is only one substantial reality *Deus sive Natura*. God *qua* Substance is the immanent or indwelling instantiator of all existent things. He establishes that God when truly understood will be conceived as the only Substance, but also denies the illicit implication being drawn that God's essence *qua* Substance pertains to the essence of the individuals.[11] Having argued in Book I

10. Emphasis mine.

11. Wolfson comments on Spinoza's brand of pantheism: "While indeed he considers man as well as all other beings as modes of the attributes of thought and extension of God, he does not consider them as being in the literal sense of the same essence as God" (Wolfson, *Philosophy of Spinoza*, 2:50).

that human existence cannot be conceived of in terms that name a human being a substance, he posits a real distinction between essence and existence in human beings, as well as all particular things:[12]

> All must surely admit that nothing can be or be conceived without God. For all are agreed that God is the sole cause of all things, both of their *essence* and their *existence*; that is, God is the cause of things not only in respect of their coming into being (*secumdum fieri*) [this would be existence], as they say, but also in respect of their being [their essential nature]. But at the same time many assert that that without which a thing *can neither be* nor be conceived pertains to the essence of the thing, and so they believe that either the nature of God pertains to the essence of created things [which need not follow] or that created things can either be or be conceived without God [which is impossible]; or else, more probably, they hold no consistent opinion . . .[13]

The distinction between the essence and the existence of a thing, that Spinoza accepts as a given, suggests that he thought of essences as, at the very least, *logically* prior to existent ordinary particulars. But something more than epistemology is involved, because the essence is also what makes the ordinary *res* (thing) to be what it is. However, the essence does not establish *that* it is. Something more is needed; and that something more, for Spinoza, is not only the necessary infinite modifiability of God/Substance. Some eternal necessity of the nature of God (*Natura naturans*) causes a process of coming to be—and coming to be in highly particularized and real ways—to be at work in *Natura naturata*. In Spinoza's metaphysics this must be their *essences* by which things are able to exist as the specific entities they are. Yet, those very essences cannot and do not *exist*, either conceptually (or in actuality), apart from the particular existent things that are posited by the essence given or granted to it.

With these semantic clarifications in place, we may move to a consideration of a systematic concept that we can infer from Spinoza's own analysis. It has already been noted that Spinoza defines the *conatus* as the actual essence of a particular thing; a thing's *conatus* must, as is the case with the thing's essence, be thought of as something that *qua* essence is what makes the actual existence of the thing possible existentially and conceptually.[14] The *conatus* is the feature or principle of a thing's existence that

12. Spinoza's insistence in II, P 10, sch 2, "individual things can neither be nor be conceived without God, and yet God does not pertain to their essence," implies two things: first, a human being (nor a Cartesian human mind) is not a substance; but secondly, it suggests that there is a *real distinction* to be made between God *qua* God's essence and identity as Substance and the Modes which exist only because the one Substance is infinitely modified, according to the necessity of its very essence. Perhaps this distinction is another way of expressing the difference between *Natura naturans* and *Natura naturata*.

13. Spinoza's Ethics, II, P 10, sch 2 (emphasis mine).

14. The existence of things as a result of essence being "granted" to them is what makes any particular essence conceivable. And the existence of things that are not self-explanatory, but require essences to explain them, is what makes the notion of essences as distinct from existence possible.

makes it what it is. Also, this very same principle, one could argue, is what grants to an entity its power of self-preservation, because it has been ordered in such a way through the presence of this *conatus* as the principle that gives a particular ordered existence. The *conatus*, then, as the activity of persisting, is the thing so ordered striving toward its good.[15]

We will return to analyzing *conatus* as a causative essence shortly, but at this point let us consider a particular interpretive implication that arises from my reading of the importance *conatus* plays for Spinoza. Proposition 7 in Book 2 is usually treated as a passage supporting psycho-physical parallelism as the framework of Spinoza's metaphysics. While neither essence nor *conatus* is the subject in II, P 7, it is not far afield to suggest that here Spinoza is really describing the parallel between existence and *conceivability* in the scholium of the proposition. So, this passage is epistemological in focus, not existential or metaphysical. When he contends that "the order and connection of ideas is the same as the order and connection of things," he is not speaking metaphysically, asserting the so-called psycho-physical parallelism. To interpret him this way, at this point, is to move to quickly to psychologize Spinoza's doctrine on this subject. While he might, indeed, think of the mind as a collection of ideas that in some way is a parallel to the world of which they are ideas, his concern here is not to posit a mental-physical mapping pattern. Rather, he is insisting that in the activity (*act*) of some essence concretely existing, an attendant reality (*res*) is being given as intelligible. While it is not clear exactly how proposition 7 about the parallelism of ideas and things follows strictly from axiom 4 of Book I,[16] it strikes me as very clear in Spinoza's utilization of this axiom in the proof of proposition 7 that he is thinking here epistemologically rather than metaphysically.

Furthermore, the corollary of this proposition clearly supports this epistemic reading of Spinoza: "whatever follows *formally* from the infinite nature of God all this follows from the *idea* of God with the same order and the same connection, as an object of thought in God."[17] Here he makes a distinction between that which follows "formally" from the nature of God and the idea that is an object of thought in God. What exists in God is also known in God, as well as in specific modes. This further suggests that Spinoza is speaking about the certainty of our epistemic engagement, as finite modes of God, with *Natura naturata*. His insistence later in the same scholium supports this reading: "a circle *existing in Nature* and *the idea* of the existing circle—which is also in God—are one and the same thing . . . we find one and the same order, or one and the same connection of causes—that is the same things following one another."[18] Clearly, Spinoza is thinking of the *intelligibility* of *Natura naturata*, which

---

15. Such immanent teleology does not undercut Spinoza's rejection of final causation generally.

16. "The knowledge of an effect depends on, and involves, the knowledge of the cause."

17. Emphasis mine.

18. Emphasis mine.

is all of the particular Modes and modes of God.[19] When he argues that ideas and actually existing things are the same in order, etc., he is describing how the essential (formal) existence of each thing is present to us and knowable by us in the self-same act of that thing's existing. We can know, therefore, nature/reality as it is; and a thing can be known for what the thing actually *is*. Finally, even God or Nature can be adequately known.

In order to indicate how *conatus* is related to knowability, we must consider an important point of Spinoza's epistemology, namely the intentional nature of being an idea. This suggests, I think, that in Spinoza's epistemology ideas are not the things we know (as with Hume) but are the things *by which* we know reality beyond the idea itself, about which the idea is an idea. Recall that Spinoza argues that the true objects of our minds are our bodies *as* they are affected (acted upon) by other things (this from II, P 13). He thinks that this claim stands on the merits of the previous proposition (12), where he contends for the 'being-about' nature of all ideas in the proof of P 12, arguing for the intentional nature of ideas.

> Whatever happens in the *object* of any idea, knowledge thereof is necessarily in God [II, P 9, Cor] in so far as he is considered as affected by the idea of that object; that is [II, P 11] in so far as he constitutes the mind of something. So whatever happens *in the object* of the idea constitutes the human mind, knowledge thereof is necessarily in God in so far as he constitutes the nature of the human mind . . . .[20]

That he is positing the intentional nature of ideas is clearly seen by Spinoza's use of the term *object* in proofs 9, 12, and 13 as he adduces proofs to demonstrate that "nothing can happen in [a human] body without its being perceived by the mind [of that body]." In each of these proofs the focus of his argument is that there is something beyond the idea itself, about which the idea is an idea.[21]

19. To this point a reading such as Curley's is appropriate regarding the sameness of ideas and extended things. However, his epistemological reading need not be strictly applicable across the board regarding Spinoza's doctrine. The doctrine of *conatus* can account for what is epistemic and what is metaphysical in Spinoza's treatment of ideas and objects or minds and bodies, if it is understood rightly.

20. Emphasis mine.

21. Spinoza in II P 10, sch, is, I think, critiquing the empiricism of the early modern variety which would tend to deny the "being-about" nature of ideas. Of course, he puts his argument in terms of the divine nature, but he thinks he has already established that thought and extension are one in the One Substance and in each and every aspect of reality. Hence he criticizes those who are confused in that "the things that are called objects of sense they have taken as prior to everything. Hence it has come about that in considering natural phenomena, they have completely disregarded the divine nature. And when thereafter they turned to the contemplation of the divine nature, they could find no place in their thinking for those fictions on which they had built their natural science, since these fictions were of no avail in attaining knowledge of the divine nature. So little wonder they have contradicted themselves on all sides." Spinoza's metaphysic demands that all ideas have an intentional quality that points beyond themselves and even beyond the objects about which they are ideas, when one considers the objects of our ideas in the light of the whole of reality in which we experience them and know them as objects of our ideas.

In Axiom 1 of P 13, Spinoza states explicitly the foundation regarding the "being-about" nature of ideas, which helps tie what has been exposited above with his doctrine of *conatus* as essence.

> "*All the ways* in which a body is affected by another body follow from the nature [natura] of the affected body together with the nature [*natura*] of the body affecting it, so that one and the same body may move in various ways in accordance with the various natures of the bodies causing its motion; and on the other, different bodies may be caused to move in different ways by one and the same body."

In other words, extended things affect the human body out of their own natures and that they do so in relation to the specific nature of the human body. By the general use of the term *natura* in this axiom, Spinoza is referencing the bodies' essences. He utilizes this axiom in the proof of proposition 16 to demonstrate that our ideas about extended modes involve awareness and knowledge of the nature (essence) of the body that is "external" to our own bodies. Of course, the ideas we have will be ideas that are specific to the ways that a human body can be acted on by another extended entity's nature. That does not imply our knowledge is lacking regarding the way reality is "in itself," because there is, for Spinoza, no action that does not involve every other aspect of reality (individually and in totality) in some way. Thus, our ideas of extended things as acting upon us are not merely representations, but constitute real and true knowledge of the world, because the things are acting upon our nature out of their natures.[22] What must be secured, he thought, was that we understand the oneness of Substance rightly.

We now return to consider *conatus* to show that in Spinoza's view the *conatus* of a thing is what makes it knowable to us, since the *conatus* is the essence of a thing. As we look further at his metaphysical analysis, it becomes clear that the process that makes something *knowable* to us—its acting on the body out of the active entity's *conatus* (conatic essence)—is also the principle that "formally" instantiates the acting entity's specific existence. We see this developed in Spinoza's treatment of the nature of bodies in II P 13. As I noted in chapter 1, it is instructive that Spinoza develops this analysis as a part of his discussion of the nature of the human mind. Especially in his consideration of the nature of composite bodies, i.e., those that are made up of many different components, he must have held some principle that would so organize them. Composite bodies, even as Modes of Extension, are not simply by being in Extension particular modes. While not being substantial in existence, the individuality of the Modes can only be individual, as was shown above, because each of them has an essence of its own. Having demonstrated that essence and *conatus* are synonymous in Spinoza's thinking, I am convinced the latter concept, although only introduced

---

22. Also, recall that Spinoza believes something like Aquinas's convictions about the human body. Spinoza thought of the human body as the most capable of acting and being acted upon.

later, is at work here. Here he argues that complex entities or bodies remain identical to themselves so long as the appropriate relation of motion and rest is preserved as a feature of the existence of this complexly organized Mode.[23]

> When a number of bodies of the same of different magnitude form close contact with one another through the pressure of other bodies upon them, or if they are moving at the same or different rates of speed *so as to* preserve an unvarying relation of movement among themselves, these bodies are said to be united with one another and all together to form one body or individual thing, which is distinguished from other things through this union of bodies [II, P 13, lemma 2, def.].

The idea here is focused on *preservation* of an unvarying relation of co-movement, but how is this preservation of co-movement to be accounted for in Spinozistic metaphysics? Della Rocca, following Matson and Bennett, suggests that the technical denomination "proportion of motion and rest" can be most adequately understood as "placeholder" for a concept that Spinoza "had not worked out, perhaps because it might involve a detailed anatomical and physiological theory of organisms which he knew was not yet available."[24] While he might be essentially correct, so far as it goes, once we recall Spinoza's doctrine that all things have an inherent striving that is part of their existence then a new insight can be gained into Spinoza's system. The "frustratingly sketchy" characterization of the inherent oneness of a complex being's existence, may well be less so, if we assume that Spinoza would had to have known that, by his own metaphysics, some principle is needed to posit and account for modal identity of a complex body over time. His brand of monism requires that something other than the infinite, eternal to account for this modal identity. He is clear and consistent throughout his depiction of how all things exist in the one Substance and that Substance is the immanent cause of all, but Substance per se does not directly out of Substance efficiently cause each individual mode to exist. Rather, each mode is the effect of some previous modal state of affairs.[25] We should assume that he might have had such a finite principle in mind, namely each thing's conatic essence.[26]

If Spinoza really means his definition of essence to be taken seriously, then the claim that "there pertains to the essence of a thing that which, *when granted*, the thing

23. Agreeing with Feldman's rendering of this definition, Della Rocca believes that the translation of *ut* in this passage is most properly rendered "so as to," suggesting a tendency, rather than a state.

24. Della Rocca, *Representation*, 33.

25. Jonas's observations mentioned in chapter 1 (p. 21) support this reading: "The continuity of determinateness (of a thing's identity) throughout such interactions (a continuity, therefore, not excluding change) bespeaks the self-affirming 'conatus' by which a mode tends to persevere in existence, and which is identical with its essence. Thus it is the *form* of determinateness, and the *conatus* evidenced by the survival of that Form in a causal history, i.e., in *relation* to co-existing things, that defines an individual."

26. For another reading of the import of the doctrine of *conatus* and its connection with Spinoza's views of identity and diachronic indentity, see Della Rocca, "Spinoza's Metaphysical Psychology," 192–266.

is necessarily posited," must be read all the way back to the very beginning of the instantiation of that thing's existence. There is, in other words, an *ordering* arrangement that is granted to the complex body that is something other *qua* ordering arrangement than the bodies of Extended substance (matter) that are so ordered. This ordering arrangement is how a complex organized body is established and determined in its compositeness. The seventh definition of Book II is Spinoza's precise definition of *res singulares* (individual/particular things) as having *determinate* existence. And by determinate he means us to understand that each particular entity that exists has a particular *way* that it is to be.[27] "All things," Spinoza says in the proof of proposition 29 in the first book, "are determined from the necessity of the divine nature not only to exist but also *to exist and to act in a definite way*," which is about *necessity* not God's efficient agency. Spinoza utilizes this argument in I, P 29 as a proof that there is no contingency in the universe, but the further implication of his argument is that all things do have a kind of necessary, teleological *ordering*.[28]

This ordering is the essence of a thing that instantiates its concrete existence. And that essence is, as we have shown above, the thing's *conatus*. This both *accounts for* and is the activity of its striving to be and remain what it is, and to flourish as itself. So, when a thing exists and acts in the *definite* way that it has been determined it to exist and to act, one could translate this to mean (without doing violence to Spinoza's ontology) that the thing is acting in the "defined" way. To be defined is to have a particular form of existence. Things having a defined existence, or even a form, fits nicely with Spinoza's own epistemological views (mentioned above) regarding the way that the concept of essence functions to be the source of that which makes things intelligible. However, the idea of having a definition/form need not involve the very unspinozistic concept of God as a conscious actor or 'definer.' Recognizing the crucial role that conatic essence plays in Spinoza's metaphysics, we can affirm—against interpretations such as Bennett's—that teleology is actually *not* foreign to Spinoza's metaphysical frame of mind.[29] In Spinoza's view, a thing's concrete existence is defined for it by the conatic essence that grants it particularized existence; and in this granting

27. Again, the metaphysical importance of *res singulares* is a critical issue. It seems clear that a thing (*res*) is, in some way, distinct from an ordinary mode of extension or thought.

28. To incorporate the concept of teleology into Spinoza's metaphysics is not to attempt an illicit interpretation which would claim that he really did have a doctrine of final causation. Rather, the teleological ordering is much more like Aristotle's concept of *immanent entelechy*, a sought after end (preservation and flourishing) out of the essential nature of a thing. The end that a thing seeks, in Spinoza's system, is simply to be what it is and persevere in being what it is in relation to all other things and modes.

29. Bennett, *Study of Spinoza's Ethics*, 215–17. For a reading of Spinoza that agrees that teleology need not be seen as absent in Spinoza, see Garrett, "Teleology in Spinoza." Garrett argues as his main points the following: (1) that Spinoza affirms that many teleological explanations are adequate; (2) that in two important ways, Leibniz's view of teleology is most likely less in line with Aristotle than that of Descartes; and (3) most significantly for this present work, that among Descartes, Spinoza, and Leibniz, Spinoza holds the view of teleology most in concert with that of Aristotle.

of specific existence an orientation toward certain ends and a drive to maintain itself within the world is part of the thing's existence. This conatic essence also makes the existent entity to be a particular kind of entity *in relationship* to all others that act upon it out of their various essences.

Perhaps the parallels between Aquinas's hylomorphism and Spinoza's ideas of conatic essence are apparent at this point but let me sketch these briefly. First, the role of *conatus* as the essence of a thing which grants it a particular kind of existence and an orientation to strive for preservation functions in the same way that the concept *form* does in Aquinas's metaphysics. Secondly, the idea that this essence must be something other than the bodies or matter that are given a defined existence by this essence echoes Aquinas's contention that form is itself distinguishable from the matter in which it is expressed. Spinoza's intention would seem to necessitate that this difference is a real distinction, even if one were to argue that *conatus* must be conceived of as, in some sense, a part of the infinite mode of motion and rest.[30] The principle of motion and rest would be, at least arguably, a feature of extension that is not, itself, material, but would not be conceivable apart from the Attribute of Extension. But even more to the point, Spinoza does not say simply that motion and rest account for the diachronous and enduring identity of any particular body, but the preservation of the *proportion* of motion and rest is necessary for identity to be maintained. Therefore, it is not a great leap to interpret Spinoza's *conatus* as the so-organizing principle that is not material but is the proximal, informing source that establishes the *proportion* of motion and rest keeps an entity in existence essentially in itself and in its movement among other entities. Continuing this same focus on the relationship of *conatus* to material existence, a third comparison is in order. Both Spinoza and Aquinas would maintain that the form/*conatus* of an entity cannot be conceived of as actually *existing* apart from the entity to which that form/*conatus* grants a particular kind of existence. Finally, it is the form/*conatus* that causes the entity to act in the world toward certain ends and by certain powers. The exertion of the entity toward its own ends is the essence of the entity at work in the world. Human experience of a particular entity acting out of its essence is the foundation of our acquaintance of the things that are acting. In other words, we know things for what they are, because their forms or conatic essences present themselves to us as intelligible in the activity of the entities upon our bodies.

30. Feldman, *Ethics*, 286–87. In Letter 64, responding to G. H. Schuller, a physician with philosophical interests who was the only person present when Spinoza died, Spinoza describes "motion and rest" as examples of an infinite Mode [of extension]. Spinoza never does develop this concept very clearly.

MIND AND BODY UNITY = IDENTITY

The analysis of the import of *conatus* presented above brings us to the crucial issue of mind and body identity in Spinoza's metaphysics. Della Rocca has noted the significance of this concept in Spinoza's understanding of individuality: "According to this doctrine, each thing—complex physical individuals, complex mental individuals, and (also) noncomplex things, if there are any—by its very nature strives or tends to persist in existence."[31] He does not, however, see the instantiating role that *conatus* plays in Spinoza's thought in relationship to the individuality of the particular complex entity. What I mean is he does not take sufficient note that the specific existence of the thing as a particular kind of entity is granted to it by the presence and influence of a conatic essence that makes it to be what it is. Not appreciating this aspect of Spinoza's doctrine of *conatus,* Della Rocca, like many others, views Spinoza's mind-body identity doctrine in terms of parallelism. Noting that Spinoza describes the *mind* in terms that highlights its particular *conatus*—"the most important element of our mind is the *conatus* to affirm the existence of our body"[32]—Della Rocca suggests that this entails that "the property of affirming the existence of the body is a feature of the mental collection that the mental collection tends to preserve, just as the proportion of motion and rest is a feature of the physical collection that the physical collection tends to preserve.[33]

As was demonstrated above, parallelism in Spinoza's philosophy works predominantly as an epistemological concept, not a metaphysical scheme. Della Rocca's parallelist account of the relationship between the *conatus* of the body and the *conatus* of the mind leaves unanswered a very crucial question: Why should there be such a mapping? More calamitously, I do not see how it can be coherently argued that the mind and body are one thing in identity based on parallelism. Even Della Rocca concludes, after much analysis of the way Spinoza presents mind-body identity, that the explanatory barrier erected by Spinoza between thought and extension denies the great Rationalist his claim of mind-body identity. Hence, Della Rocca places Spinoza in "the illustrious company of those who have failed to solve the mind-body problem."[34] The reason Della Rocca's account of Spinoza produces failure is that parallelism itself is the wrong metaphysical starting point. Not only must it treat ideas and the objects of those ideas as parallel but must also treat the *conatus* that enables a particular body to persist as something distinct from the *conatus* which would enable the mind that is associated with that body to persist. Della Rocca's work on Spinoza is creative and insightful, and among the best of the works on his thought. However, once one has

31. Della Rocca, *Representation,* 35.

32. Della Rocca, *Representation,* 37. He translates Spinoza's Latin phrase (in III, P 10, pr), *primum & praecipuum nostrae mentis conatus est . . . Corporis nostril existentiam affirmare,* "the first and principle [tendency] of the striving of our mind is . . . to affirm the existence of our body."

33. Della Rocca, *Representation,* 37.

34. Della Rocca, *Representation,* 151.

embraced the parallelism reading of Spinoza, the hopes of arguing for numerical identity for mind and body, in Spinoza's system, is hopelessly flawed.

Bennett's analysis is, perhaps, closer to the real issue in Spinoza's mind-body theory and has captured the important distinction between the ordinary modes of thought and extension versus the fundamental modes that are capable of combining with both Attributes. However, my reading is distinguished from his in the following ways that succeed where his fails. There is, indeed, something more fundamental than *ordinary* modes (bodies and minds) that is involved in the identity relation in question. However, Bennett's way of formulating the issue in terms of a *differentia* in relation to the Attributes leaves us with the difficult question of what such a property or principle might be in Spinoza's metaphysics. Bennett acknowledges he cannot derive his "*differentia*" from Spinoza's systematic program. But his basic intuition is correct, I believe, and the ascription of identity must be regarded as grounded in some more fundamental thing other than mind or body.

The reading I am offering allows the advantage that comes from positing mind-body identity in something more fundamental, but it can account for the existence of this in Spinoza's own terms. The ordinary Modes consist in or express the nature of this more fundamental "mode." Given the role that the idea of essence and *conatus* play in Spinoza's thought, this is the Spinozistic way of thinking. Not only do I gain the advantages of Bennett's approach to identity as being in something more fundamental, but I am able to relocate the discussion to a more "dynamic" level with respect to which we might regard Bennett's so-called fundamental modes precisely as things that exist as a result of the organizing and animating "form" or essence of an organism. The ordinary modes of body and mind being, on my interpretation, not the result of some *differentia* added to the Attributes' normal properties (per Bennett), but the necessary dual ways that the fundamental entity must *express* its existence because thought and extension are both irreducible aspects of Reality. Hence, mind and body are one and the same being essentially, as expressions of the *res* that is necessarily expressed in two modes of the Attributes (ways of being). The *res* to which the *conatus* gives concrete, ordered existence exhibits its specific essence in a particular striving. This *res* must express itself and its striving activities (at least to our minds) through the Attributes of Thought and Extension. Reading Spinoza in this fashion, therefore, we perceive how dual aspect theory fits Spinoza; and it points to an interesting affinity with Aquinas. If Spinoza was attending to a more fundamental and dynamic metaphysical question, it is arguably one which harkens back to Aquinas's hylomorphism. It is worth considering whether Spinoza's metaphysics even has a mind-body problem that Della Rocca says he cannot solve.

Instead of concerning himself with the mind-body interaction question, Spinoza's analysis points to the simultaneity involved in mental-physical acts; and the concept of *conatus* helps us see *how* a living entity can be minded as a material creature in the first place, even if we do not have the analytic tools to understand the operations of the unity. Because he was interested in the question of mind and body as a feature of living human beings, he perceived the *conatus* that makes a human being alive *qua* human being as a singular *conatus*, not a mapped pair that parallel one another. This single conatic essence is productive of both physical structure and operations, as well as the attendant mental activity. Such a co-inhering relationship is fundamental to his view of *natura naturata*, where all things are animate, albeit in different degrees. The little phrase, "albeit in different degrees," cannot be over emphasized. What Spinoza's metaphysics wants to recover is the reality of life as a part of the world of matter itself, a view obscured by the dominant interest and mechanistic view of organisms, I contend, in physics and mathematics that emerged during the late Renaissance and early modern period. (Descartes, because of his exceptional prowess in many fields, is the quintessential representative.) Spinoza, as Aquinas before him (and Aristotle in the ancient world), was attempting to show that *life* itself is an irreducible feature of the world and, therefore, should figure into our metaphysical account of things. Mechanistic thought and materialistic reductionism fail on this front and leave *life* as inexplicable in those reductionist terms. Regarding human beings, therefore, minded-ness or thought (rationality to utilize the medieval term) is consider the essential form that human life takes. At least one scholar has seen this central feature of Spinoza's thought. Jonas has rightly observed that, in contrast to Spinoza, the dominant philo-sophical/scientific point of view in the early modern period was to see the material world in mechanistic terms. He argues that Spinoza's doctrine of the *organism* as de-fined (or given determinate existence) by a conatic essence salvaged what was lost in philosophical Cartesianism, i.e., the reality of *life* in the world.[35]

Because he sees Spinoza's metaphysics as interested in what makes the living existence of particular entities possible, Jonas says of Spinoza's argument's about the origins of the mind: "From proposition XI [of Book II] onward, Spinoza deals with the soul-body problem, and in *that* context makes certain statements concerning the type of body that corresponds to a soul or mind, and the type of identity that pertains to it."[36] Jonas is clear that Spinoza's treatise is entitled *Ethics* because it is concerned to provide an metaphysical underpinning for morality and the human quest for meaning, but his further acknowledgement is even more on point. He says that Spinoza's way of analyzing the existence of entities "enabled him to account for features of organic existence far beyond what Cartesian dualism and mechanism could accommodate."[37] This applies to Spinoza's approach to the relationship between mind and body.

As Aquinas before him, Spinoza envisioned the issue of mind and body as a different query from the Cartesian problem of how a mind could be related to a body from which it is ontologically different substantially. His doctrine of the oneness of Substance, along with his identification of the Attributes of Thought and Extension as

35. Jonas, "Spinoza and the Theory of Organism," 267.

36. Jonas, "Spinoza and the Theory of Organism," 267.

37. Jonas, "Spinoza and the Theory of Organism," 263.

truly different (as expressions of the one Substance) but not distinct ontologically, are the basis of his affirmation that mind and body are expressions of one living thing's existence and are irreplaceable descriptions of our experience of our living in the world and of our living selves.[38] In Spinoza's system the mind is an irreducible feature of an entity that also has being physical as another irreducible feature, because the entity's existence is ordered and established by a conatic essence. This is a hylomorphic view of living things.[39]

Consider how this interpretation of conatic essence works to enable us to take a different approach to the mind-body "problem" in Spinoza's thought. The solution to the mind-body relationship cannot be solved, in Spinoza's system, by referring to the nature of Substance, because the *essence* of Substance *qua* Substance is to exist by infinitely expressing infinite Attributes; regarding our capacity to know Substance these are Thought and Extension. Substance, conceived as *Natura naturans*, is not an individual entity strictly speaking. Substance is infinite, and the infinite can never be thought of as an individual.[40] But individual things (*res singulares*) are, obviously, individual. These individual things exist as specific, natured entities, since the essence of the Substance upon which *res singulares* depend for existence, and in which they must exist and by which they are explained (ultimately), is to exist (in our experience of Substance) as the Modes Thought and Extension. Although the individuals in their *conatus*-organized existence only exist as mind and body, they are, ultimately, neither more basically one nor the other, but irreducibly both, because of the singular *conatus*.

The purpose of his argument is II, P 13, where he discusses at length the nature of the human body, is to make it more readily apparent to us how the human mind is united to the body. That union is not the union of different Modes whose union is necessarily parallel because of the nature of Substance. Rather, the union is due to the conatic essence that makes a body *qua* complex living organism capable of having a mind like the human mind. Not every entity is so organized; and the subtly of the human body makes it more apt to be acted upon and be apt for the mind in a unique and penultimate manner. Because of this kind of analysis of the conatic complexity of the human being is Spinoza says:

---

38. More work could be done to show how Spinoza's thought was in direct confrontation with the empiricism of his day. For an excellent analysis of recent scholarship on the relationship and contrast between Hume and Spinoza, see Maxwell, "Dialectic of Enlightenment." Cf. Hegel, "Lectures on the History of Philosophy: Locke," for a comparison of Locke and Spinoza.

39. Spinoza's assertion that all things are alive to differing degrees does not undercut this claim of his essential hylomorphism. In fact, some might see it as a glorious expansion of the concept.

40. One could perhaps argue that the Divine Mind knows itself and that there is the "face of the whole Universe," so there must be some sense of individuated identity. But it is not clear how an infinite mind knowing the infinite could be truly an individual entity in Spinoza's system, especially given that *Deus sive Natura* lacks volition and all the "actions" or events of *Deus sive Natura* occur of necessity.

> ... the mind and the body are *one and the same thing*, conceived now under the attribute of Thought, now under the attribute of Extension. Hence it comes about that the order or linking of things is one, whether Nature be conceived under this or that attribute, and consequently *the order of the active and passive states of our body is simultaneous in Nature with the order of active and passive states of the mind.*[41]

In the scholium Spinoza says that the scholium of II, P 7 is the foundation for the claims of this proposition (13): the mind and body do not have any causal determination over one another. He then says in his additional comments on this proposition that we can understand this lack of causal relation "more clearly from that scholium." Here he interprets II, P 7, sch to mean that "mind and body are one and the same thing ..." It is interesting that in that scholium his actual argument does not mention mind or body. Rather, he there speaks of a Mode of extension and the idea of that Mode as one and the same thing, *expressed* in two ways (modus). I have argued above that this statement is the basis for Spinoza's epistemological parallelism and not for his metaphysical view of the relationship between mind and body, but the context of III, P 2, sch applies this language about "Modes" to the metaphysical issue of the mind and the body. Spinoza's willingness to translate his rhetoric about modes of extension and the ideas of those modes into body-mind language does not do damage to my interpretation. Neither my claim that the focus of II, P 7 is epistemology nor my emphasis on *conatus* as the source of mind-body identity in Spinoza's metaphysics is undercut.

Spinoza, on my interpretation, utilizes the statements in II, P 1 and III, P 2 in way that implies a similarity but not synonymity. He can do this, because he does not need to think of "mind" as a referring term strictly speaking. On my reading of Spinoza, the mind could be in its essence the bounded set of all ideas that have come to exist as the experiences and understanding and insights of a particular organic individual. These "ideas" as a bounded set would not be caused by the body *per se* but would instead be understood as the results of *thought* (mind) itself engaged in (actively) the organic individual's living existence that is acting and being acted upon.[42] Active engagement of the body as the object of its engagement is what the mind does. Neither does his metaphysical description take "body" to be a referring term in the most precise ontological sense. The body exists, in a Spinozistic view, as an *aspect* of the "one and the same thing" that Spinoza insists is "expressed" in two ways (the Latin term is *modis* which is a form of the word *modus*). This "expressed" thing is the organism that has a body; and it not the body that expresses its existence is the actual existent thing. Because the organism *qua* the organized and defined *res* is the locus of the relevant essence, the body and the mind simply are the modes by or as which the essence of the organism existing in the one Substance is "expressed."[43]

---

41. Emphasis mine.

42. Spinoza is insistent that the mind is always active in its essence, never a passive receiver.

43. See chapter 1 for a discussion of the meaning of "expressed" in Spinoza's thought. "*Expressa*

This brings us to another important point, regarding the *conatus* that is the organization-granting, existence-enabling power of a thing's being. Just as the *conatus* organizes the body to be "apt" for the mind, the same *conatus* has the power to make the human "mind" that is the idea of the body "apt" for that body. But we might ask why the *conatus* is not itself conceived of as the thing that is doubly aspected. If this could be shown to be the case, then *conatus* is no more analogous to form or rational soul than it is to the body. The reply is that the concept of *conatus* has some ambiguity in Spinoza's metaphysics. *Conatus*, when we are thinking *of the total entity* that is organized and expressed in the two ordinary modes of body and mind, must be considered relative to the way we are considering the organism's life. If we are thinking of the thing that exists and is striving to maintain that existence *qua* simultaneously minded and extended, then there is a sense in which *conatus* names a single and unified yet doubly aspected striving. But *conatus* has a more metaphysically fundamental meaning, which is also its most *essential* meaning. This requires qualification of what it means to say it is doubly aspected. In this (essential) meaning, the *conatus* of which we have just spoken as the process of striving to be itself is dependent upon a more basic sense of *conatus*.

The striving entity exists, and its act of striving is manifested only because it has an informing and organizing essence by which it exists as what it is. This essence (which I have argued is identified with the *conatus* in the metaphysically fundamental sense I am now suggesting) is not an entity in itself. Rather, it is an informing *principle*—*conatus* considered to be the "formal cause" of the entity that strives as the two expressions of its existence—body and mind—but does so as a single existent *res*. If the *conatus* is identifiable with the essence that "can be granted" or "annulled" [2def2], then we can say that Spinoza was, at least, assuming that the organizational essence or form (*conatus*) that enables the complexity of the body to have a greater perfection and to be apt to have associated with it an "idea of that body" is the very same organizing form that grants to the organism a mind that is appropriate to the "more perfect" body with which it exists as one thing. In this sense, then, the *conatus* can be the "form" of the living organism and is productive of the organism in which the duality of aspects is *expressed*.

On this reading of Spinoza's metaphysics, *conatus* is very much like the rational soul *qua* form, as Aquinas uses the concept. In Aquinas's view the rational soul is not a form that merely gives a particular organization to the body. It also instantiates the existence of a particular kind of mind that will be apt for the body that is so organized. The body does not produce the mind, but the mind of a human is a kind of intelligence that is meant for union with a body, unlike the Divine Mind or "angelic" minds. The rational soul in Aquinas's view is the essence of a human being *qua* human body

---

can be taken to refer not primarily to the act of our describing or expressing something we observe (nominalism), but rather it might be seen as a function of the essence of the thing itself which is given existential 'expression' (objectivism) in distinct modes of existence."

and mind, because rationality and biology (animality) are essential to the definition of a human being. So, the essence of man is not the form or the soul. Rather, a body and intellect are the essence of a *rational animal.* Both expressions are ultimately involved in a person's existence and essence as a living entity. Spinoza's discussions seem quite similar to this. In this light, we can say that the mind and body are established in the living *res* and are mutually apt each for the other. This, at least, suggests a strong congruity with Aquinas's basic conception of the component metaphysical principles that are involved in the existence of a compound being like a human being. Spinoza's Modes then can be seen as analogous to the "*acts* of being" employed in Aquinas's description of his hylomorphic view of mind and body.

As *acts* of being, the body and mind are, for Aquinas, objectively real and not merely subjective descriptions. The same is true for Spinoza. But where Aquinas's speaks of "acts" (which perhaps suggests intention), Spinoza speaks of Modes that express necessarily the being of the one infinite Substance. Body and mind name Spinozistic (and Thomistic) ways of existing which the human being must exist *as.* These are the modal expressions, per Spinoza, of the Attributes, Extension and Thought. Hence, the interpretation of mind-body identity being offered here does not ignore Spinoza's insistence that what exists are Substance and Modes. The Modes of extension and thought are not reduced to mere nominal descriptions that get applied to the organism. They are, rather, the only ways that the organism's life can be expressed, because being extended and being minded are both fundamental features of Reality. And the same *conatus* that makes the body capable of accompanying "mind" in a more perfect way also instantiates the very mind that is "apt" to have as its "object" the greater perfection that is the human body. Therefore, Aquinas's hylomorphism gives the emphatic description to human beings as essentially *knowing* bodies (rational animals) whose biological reality and mental existence are distinct from one another as acts of being but are necessarily and essentially one thing—the human person. Spinoza recaptures this in post-Cartesian concepts.

MIND AND BODY "INTERACTION"

Still to be addressed, however, is the issue of Spinoza's rejection of mind and body interaction. Margaret Gullan-Whur has commented on the historical context in which Spinoza expressed what she calls his "cryptic" view of mind and body. She informs us further that the doctrine, utilized by contemporary Spinoza scholarship, parallelism, had evolved in the context of the theological controversies that surrounded Descartes's philosophy. Further, Gullan-Whur notes that the doctrine of occasionalism was closely related to the idea of parallelism at that time, at least by the leading theological defender of Descartes, Geulincx.[44] But, Spinoza was no occasionalist.

---

44. Gullan-Whur, *Within Reason*, 178.

And neither was he a materialist, although his statements in the *Short Treatise*, which Gullan-Whur points us to, had appeared to make the mind dependent, logically and causally, on the body: "The essence of the soul consists only in the being of an idea . . . arising from the essence of an object which in fact exists in Nature,"[45] But he removes the possibility of reading him as a materialist in *Ethics* when he posits the explanatory barrier between the mind and the body. We are left in Spinoza studies, Gullan-Whur concludes, with the realization that an unresolved tension exists in his "doctrine of mind between identity and anatomy."

> Here and there in *Ethics* Spinoza seems to suggest that mind and body are just two ways of seeing one thing. *The thinking substance and the extended substance are one and the same substance, which is now comprehended under this attribute, now under that. So also, a mode of extension and the idea of that mode are one and the same thing but expressed in two ways.* But this explanation will not do, since Spinoza would also insist in *Ethics* that extension and thought express two diverse and incompatible causal powers. The causal force within modes of extension was motion and rest, he claimed, whereas modes of thought, *ideas*, were empowered only by implication and inference. *The power of the mind is intelligence itself.* Neither power, he stated, could operate on modes of the other attribute. *The body cannot determine the mind to thinking, and the mind cannot determine the body to motion.* How, then, could mind and body be identical?[46]

Gullan-Whur's observations identify the core of the problem that any interpretation must face. To begin to address it we need to consider what Spinoza intends by his description of the body as "the object of the idea constituting the human mind is the body" [II, P 13]. Since Spinoza thinks that the idea of the body that is the mind is not caused by the body's affections and denies that bodily movements can be caused by the mind, then what does Spinoza mean when he calls body the object of the mind. As a materialist explanation of "mind" is ruled out by the explanatory-causal barrier of *Ethics,* then *object* must mean something other than the intension it is granted in much of current metaphysical discussion. Even though he states that "a definite mode of extension actually existing, and nothing else" is object of the mind, the term object cannot simply mean "thing that exists" or "value of a bound variable." Were that the meaning of object for Spinoza, then a mode of thought would be explained by a mode of extension, for *qua* object (bound physical variable) the body would be, in some way, the content that *is* the mind. Hence, we owe it to Spinoza and ourselves to see if there is not some better way to interpret his meaning.

Spinoza utilizes the term object (*obiectum*) ambiguously, just as he does *conatus.* He speaks, for instance, in Definition 4 of the second part of *Ethics* about an "adequate

45. Gullan-Whur, *Within Reason*, 179.
46. Gullan-Whur, *Within Reason*, 179.

idea" in itself without consideration of the idea's "relation to its object." Here, object seems to imply an entity to which the idea corresponds. This would fit well a representationalist interpretation of Spinoza's epistemology.[47] In the corollary of proposition 9, Spinoza also uses object in a way that seems to suggest that it is referring to some kind of "value of a bound variable": "Whatsoever happens in the individual *object* of any idea, knowledge of it is in God only in so far as he has the *idea of that object*."[48] Later in his consideration of "the nature and origin of the mind" Spinoza uses *obiectum* in a way that seems to move away from the concept of a bound-variable. In II, P 12 Spinoza says that the happenings "*in* the object of the idea constituting the human mind is bound to be perceived by the human mind . . . That is to say, if the *object* of the idea constituting the human mind is a body, nothing can happen in that body without its being perceived by the mind." In this instance, *obiectum* appears to be something other than the bound variable of which the idea is a representation or upon which the idea is dependent for its existence as an idea. Instead, the body considered as the *obiectum* of the *ideae* is described as something that events or states of affairs can occur *in* and which are perceived as states or events directly by the mind.

It seems obvious to me that Spinoza's claims that the body is the object of the *idea* that constitutes the essence of the human mind cannot think the idea is only a "representation," because the body is the mind's object directly. So, the description of the body as the object of the idea of the mind can be understood clearly as Spinoza's way of saying that the body (its affections or happenings) is the immediate *focus* of the mind's activity. (This is especially clear when one thinks in terms of conatic essence as the organization-giving, unifying principle of human life.) However, as the focus of the mind, the body's events do not cause the ideas to exist. The body as the object of the idea that constitutes the mind could be thought of as that mode which is engaged by the mental powers of an organism without thinking those powers are *caused* by that object. Even Spinoza's argument that "if there were another object of the mind apart from the body, since nothing exists from which some effect does not follow, there would necessarily have to be in our mind the idea of some effect of it," can be understood in terms of *focus* as I am suggesting. Spinoza does not seem to affirm the possibility of another object of the mind, because to have the body as its object is for the mind to be oriented toward a particular mode of extension as the finite focus of the mind's activity. This strikes me as quite like Aquinas's claim that the proper *object* of the human intellect is the understanding of material nature, especially as engaged

---

47. In the explication of this definition, Spinoza utilizes the term *ideatum* as an apparent synonym for *obiectum* in the definition. This synonymous linking suggests that Spinoza in the definition is thinking of object as that upon which an idea depends. In Platonic philosophy in its Latin form, *ideatum* had the implication of "eternal prototype."

48. Even here we see what is arguably an ambiguity. God can have knowledge of that object, but the individual object is also described as something that things happen *in*, hence the idea being *of the* object seems like a matter of knowing logically, but not as an engagement with an object.

through the intelligible forms acting on the body.[49] Spinoza conceives of the body as the proper and necessary focus of the mind.

This way of stating Spinoza's position is consistent with his claim that the idea(s) that constitute the essence of the mind are the "affections of the body." The body acts and is acted upon in the context of the world of extension and this interaction, as we saw above, involves the conatic essences of things acting out of their essences upon the body. The interaction of extended things that act out of the powers that their essences grant them means that in the world of extension a real interaction of essences is involved. A particular bodily entity so affected in its essence by this interaction with other entities' essences is the *object/focus* of a particular mind. As things act out of their essences upon the body, they produce affections in the body. These acts of "essences" produce affections or modifications of the body; and the ideas of these acts are the "thought of" or actively and consciously experienced nature of the essences. This constitutes the essence of the mind. And as a mode of thought the mind is just the organism's being aware of what has affected its body. Its *conatus* makes this possible for the material organism by its essence giving presence.[50] Thus, the mind's instantiating content is not representations but actual and adequate known engagements with the things that have affected the body.[51]

Such a situation would be possible because of the conatic essence of a human being that subtly and complexly organizes the body (P 13) to be the most apt to act and be acted upon, as well as establishing the mind to be apt to perceive and understand the acts of and upon the body. Further, this organization is one of coinherence, where mind and body are both *in* the human being's concrete existence as a living organism. Spinoza can, then, describe the mind exercising its powers only in relation to the body, but the body

49. This comparison is clearer when we remember that for Aquinas all knowledge begins with sensory data that is obtained by the activity of the mind from the action of things acting on the body's sensory capacities by way of their intelligible forms. The body is the focus of the mind's activity, it would seem, for Aquinas.

50. But whereas the Thomistic conception of the relationship between a power and its proper object was often described in terms of the power as passive until its object affected it, Spinoza's view would have been that the mind is active in relation to the body's affections.

51. The issue of Spinoza's epistemology has been referenced several times in this work, but no thorough defense of the epistemological interpretation on offer can be presented in the limits of the thesis on offer here. Given Spinoza's ontological conception of the singularity of Substance in which every existing entity is either one of the Attributes or a Mode expressing one of the Attributes, I contend his epistemology is a form of direct realism. The argument is as follows. He also insists that human beings can achieve adequate ideas about reality in which the causal and conceptual dependence and connection between all things can be conceived adequately (i.e., in a way that reflects the way things are) as modes of God's Substance. Furthermore, since all ideas are modes of God (even inadequate ones) as the Attribute of Thought, and since God's knowledge qua Thought must be perfect, then when a human mind forms an "adequate idea" of the true connection of things in God that mind has a direct intellectual grasp of reality. Hence, the mind can have a direct grasp (intuitively, he might say) of reality. So, the mind, even in its finitude and singular perspective as a finite mode expressing Thought, when it adequately knows something, knows not just *that* something is real, but *what* it is and *how* and *why* it is.

does not cause or explain the thoughts of the mind. The activities of the organism are "one and the same" activity because the *conatus* establishes the activity in the organism that is expressed in both ordinary modes of existence. The *life* of the organism, therefore, instantiates thought and extension as "one and the same thing." Thus, as the organism is the relevant focus of the identity, then (as Bennett tried to show *via* differentia) we can assert identity and not deny Spinoza's explanatory/causal boundary.

Similarly, the noncausal role of mind regarding the body's movement is secured by this same focus on conatic essence. It is axiomatic in Spinoza studies that he wanted to deny the will or desire or conscious deliberation as causes of the actions of the body. He was, as many have pointed out, unimpressed with Descartes concept of mental-physical interaction, not just the "pineal gland" explanation, but the general hypothesis. Recognizing the role of *conatus* in Spinoza's thought, we can account for his doctrine of oneness and his doctrine of noncausal relations between mind and body. First, the body *qua* mode of extension produces its own movement *qua* physical action through the operation of the laws of physics, chemistry, and biology. In the proof of III, P 2, he asserts this in seventeenth century terms: "Now the motion-and-rest of a body must arise from another body, which again has been determined to motion or rest by another body, and without exception whatever arises in a body must have arisen from God in so far as he is considered as affected by a mode of Extension . . ." Utilizing the example of "sleepwalkers" as an illustration of bodily actions that are not volitional, or truly conscious in the ordinary sense, to portray the body's purely physical powers, Spinoza argues vigorously in terms of real experience that the mind cannot be thought of as a single power that superintends the motion and rest of the body. However, the true intent of Spinoza's arguments against the mind as the mover or captain of the body is seen in the scholium of III, P 2 when he concludes:

> Now surely all these considerations [regarding how the acts we consider to be free acts of the mind moving the body to action] go to show clearly that mental decision on the one hand, and the appetite and physical state of the body on the other hand, are simultaneous in nature; or rather, they are one and the same thing which, when considered under the attribute of Thought and explicated through Thought, we call decision, and when considered under the attribute of Extension and deduced from the laws of motion-and-rest, we call a physical state.

Spinoza's argument is against a kind of Cartesian and late scholastic view of the mind's relationship to the body in which the mind is something that attends and uses the body or perhaps (to risk anachronism) supervenes upon it.[52] His concerns, how-

---

52. While not addressing mind-body interaction directly, Skirry, "Rene Descartes," sec. 5 argues convincingly that Descartes essentially followed a Scotistic scholastic line of thinking. "Although Descartes argues that bodies, in the general sense, are constituted by extension, he also maintains that species of bodies are determined by the configuration and motion of their parts. This doctrine of configuration and motion of parts serves the same purpose as the doctrine of substantial forms

ever, are fully addressable, and his doctrine made less cryptic, by reference to conatic essence as I have described. So, secondly, Spinoza's contention that "mental decision" is *simultaneous* in its existence *qua* mode of thought with "the appetite and physical state of the body" *qua* mode of extension is understandable, on my interpretation, as mental and physical actions of a single organism, determined and formed by its conatic essence to be capable of physical states that involve simultaneously mental awareness and the capacity for further reflection and understanding of those very physical states. Hence, the mind does not *cause* the body to move toward food that is desired, nor does the physical desire for food *explain* the nature of conscious awareness of food or the mind's "decision."[53] Rather, in Spinozism these acts are "one and the same thing" that can be explicated adequately and thoroughly from the perspective under which we might consider them—either Attribute of Substance. The one-and-the-same-thing that can be so explicated can be explicated *in this way*, because the *way* that the entity being explicated exists is precisely in the Modes of mind and body. But those Modes are both the thing being explicated in distinct *real* categories of extension and thought.

Spinoza was intent on avoiding not just a Cartesian metaphysical dualism, but even a methodological dualism that could treat the difference between mind and body

---

with regards to entirely physical things. But the main difference between the two is that Descartes's doctrine does not employ final causes. Recall that substantial forms organize matter for the purpose of being a species of thing. . . If Descartes did hold a fundamentally scholastic theory of mind-body union, then is it more Thomistic or Scotistic? Since intellect and will are the only faculties of the mind, it does not have the faculty for organizing matter for being a human body. So, if Descartes's theory is scholastic, it must be most in line with some version of the Scotistic theory. . . The purpose of a human body endowed with only the form of corporeity is union with the soul. Hence, the organization of matter into a human body is an effect that is explained by the final cause or purpose of being disposed for union. But, on Descartes's account, the explanatory order would be reversed: a human body's disposition for union is an effect resulting from the configuration and motion of parts. So, even though Descartes does not have recourse to substantial forms, he still has recourse to the configuration of matter and to the dispositions to which it gives rise, including 'all the dispositions required to preserve that union' (AT IV 166: CSMK 243). Hence, on this account, Descartes gets what he needs, namely, Descartes gets a body properly configured for potential union with the mind, but without recourse to the scholastic notion of substantial forms with their final causal component. Another feature of this basically Scotistic position is that the soul and the body were considered incomplete substances themselves, while their union results in one complete substance. Surely Descartes maintains that mind and body are two substances, but in what sense, if any, can they be considered incomplete? Descartes answers this question in the Fourth Replies. He argues that a substance may be complete insofar as it is a substance but incomplete insofar as it is referred to some other substance together with which it forms yet some third substance. This can be applied to mind and body as follows: the mind insofar as it is a thinking thing is a complete substance, while the body insofar as it is an extended thing is a complete substance, but each taken individually is only an incomplete human being."

53. As a critique of Cartesianism, Jonas has observed that Spinoza's doctrine addressed a central failing of the mechanistic view of the extended world. "[T]he main fault, even the absurdity, of the [Cartesian doctrine of mechanism and its attendant dualism] lay in denying organic reality its principal and most obvious characteristic, namely, that it exhibits in each individual instance *a striving* of its own for existence and fulfillment, or the fact of life's willing itself. In other words, the banishment of the old concept of appetition from the conceptual scheme of the new physics, joined to the rationalistic spiritualism of the new theory of consciousness, deprived the *realm of life* its status in the scheme of things" (Jonas, "Theory of Organism," 261, emphasis mine).

as a difference of existence. Such methodological dualism quickly becomes (or at least can) quasi-metaphysical; and then problems such as interaction and causal relations begin to plague the philosophical quest. Of course, materialism or idealism solve the dilemma by simply discounting some significant philosophical distinctions, thereby failing to capture human life empirically. By emphasizing the conatic oneness of the organism that exists essentially (and necessarily) as Modes that are in fact distinct as the "ways" that Reality itself is manifested, Spinoza thinks he has corrected the problems of early modern philosophy that had to opt for some choice between Cartesian-scholastic dualism, or Hobbesian materialism, on the one hand, and Leibniz's idealism, on the other. His perspective, here, is not far from Aquinas's argument that it is not the mind that knows or the body that lifts, but the *person* who does both.

What Spinoza wanted to do regarding the phenomena of human existence is in large measure compatible with (and therefore made more comprehensible by) Aquinas's hylomorphism. He offers, as the Books Three and Four of *Ethics* clearly reflect, a view of human existence as a unity, one which is always just as ideational as it is material. His concept of conatic essence was the key that allowed him to state in post-Cartesian terms the insights about the irreducible doubly aspected unity of human living that Aquinas's theory offered in a much earlier time. The idea of *conatus*, as I have interpreted it, while not stated explicitly in Spinoza's *Ethics*, is certainly present in his system; and it gives us a reason to think that the so-called dual-aspect theory is not only a good description of Spinoza's own views, but arguably true, as well.

8

Hylomorphism, Conatic Essence, and Immortality in Spinoza and Aquinas

THE PRECEDING CHAPTERS HAVE suggested that Aquinas and Spinoza articulated doctrines regarding mind and body that share intriguing similarities. Both regard *Thought* as an ontologically basic attribute of the same reality as material stuff. Such a conviction about Thought reflected in diverse metaphysical schemes is important for understanding two further propositions. The first has been discussed: the idea that human beings have a "composite" existence in which no dualism is involved. This concept in Spinoza will be further demonstrated in this chapter. A second and even more controversial claim—the immortality of the mind/soul—will be considered as well. Examining how their respective concepts of immortality relate to their overall metaphysical schemes is important, since the concept of the soul's/mind's immortality in both philosophers' doctrines has been criticized by commentators.[1] It is needed as well for the aim of this book: that the affinity between them regarding how we are what we are can help us recover the soul.

This chapter explores the logic that undergirds the claim that they make for the activity of thought as being unexplainable by any reference to the material or

---

1. In Spinoza's case, see Joachim, *Study of the Ethics of Spinoza*, 290–96. Cf. Feuer, *Spinoza and the Rise of Liberalism*, 224, and Bennett, *Study of Spinoza's Ethics*, 357–60. Both Joachim and Feuer claim that Spinoza's affirmation of personal immortality cannot be reconciled with the focus of Spinoza's metaphysics. Bennett attempts to provide a reading of Spinoza that allows Spinoza's own system to embrace this claim, but in Bennett's view Spinoza's doctrine is not just false but a "seemingly unmotivated disaster" (357). Regarding Aquinas's view, Kenny's treatment of his doctrine seems to capture the essence of many of the main arguments against him. Considering Aquinas's conception of the immateriality of the intellectual soul, Kenny wonders how Aquinas could possibly have thought that the soul, being a form, could exist without matter. Kenny thinks that this would only be possible for his nonphilosophical, religious beliefs. Hence, in his view, Aquinas shows "a disconcerting disdain for distinctions between abstract and concrete" (Kenny, *Aquinas on Mind*, 138).

extended. Providing further development of the claim that Spinoza's concept of *conatus* implies a view of human nature that is comparable to Aquinas's idea that humans are *composite* beings is important because I have not yet argued for this designation explicitly and still some might think Spinoza's monism could not allow this. Following that demonstration, I then will indicate how their doctrines of immortality, while quite different from one another, emerge directly out of their respective philosophical systems and are not embarrassing additions or dangling propositions unfitting for their basic metaphysical schemes. We can show how the doctrine of *conatus* shapes Spinoza's doctrine of the immortality of the mind; and we can do the same, as well, for Aquinas regarding the way that his doctrines of *form* and personal identity work in his doctrine of incorruptibility of the soul. Once this last piece of the interpretive puzzle is in place, the concluding chapter will point out some important analytical fruit that can be harvested from the hylomorphic understanding of human existence that is on offer, suggesting in a preliminary way how the interpretive work of this book's analysis might assist us in discovering a fruitful conceptual starting point for the continuing quest to explore the metaphysical nature of the mind-body relationship.

THE "COMPOSITE" INDIVIDUAL AND *CONATUS*/FORM

Aquinas's definition of human beings as "rational animals" captures the *hylomorphism* that defines how he *and* Spinoza (in an analogous way) conceived the basic principles of existence that make a human being unique.[2] While in Spinoza's view everything expresses in some way the Attribute of Thought, he recognizes distinct degrees of expression of that Attribute in human beings. Hence, for him, as well as Aquinas, when we consider ourselves in terms of our capacity for rationality, human persons participate in (Aquinas's terminology) or express (in Spinoza's) the fundamental Attribute of Thought. I have not argued (foolishly) that their metaphysics are compatible in every detail, but the possibility of such "hylomorphic" views in very disparate thinkers should seize our attention. There is no reason to dismiss hylomorphism out of hand.

As an individual, each human person has what Aquinas calls the "form" of rationality or the *rational* soul. The soul, while not synonymous with the mind, is the principle responsible for the existence of the mind. It makes the human body to be a body that is apt for "having" a rational mind (unlike other animal bodies), even as it establishes a kind of mind apt for having a particular body as the locus and focus of its activity.[3] The form of rationality is not the same thing as the *act* of rationality that

2. The term *principle* is a basic Thomist concept. Spinoza speaks of Attributes of Substance, rather than principles, because he wanted to press for substance-monism. However, when one reflects on the way that the Attributes work in individual modes and in complex organisms (see chapter 5) the analogy between Thomas's "principles" and Spinoza's "Attributes" emerges. In both cases, the respective concepts serve to point to what is responsible for (causes, in the Aristotelian sense) the existence of ordinary particulars.

3. Aquinas's contention was that human minds are the lowest form of intellectual substances, which means that he thought intellect was a part of reality quite apart from the existence of human minds.

a human being exercises when he is having thoughts or experiencing something. The form that Aquinas names "rational soul" is best understood as analogous to the set of life-enabling *information* that a specific person's particular genetics provide. The rational soul grants to each human person a species-appropriate body shape and function. It is the material body that is informed by the form that thereby instantiates a unique individual endowed with rational potentialities, since the form itself is something shared by all humans. The rational soul is a type of "rationality" in principle, but it is not rationality in act, therefore, "aptness" for a mind in material creatures is its purpose. The distinction in a human person between the mind and body entails only that the mind of a human being is only one aspect (the other being the body) of the existence of an entity whose existence is unified on a more fundamental level. This is the meaning of the distinction discussed in chapter 4.

Spinoza, as I have interpreted him, views *conatus* in an analogous way. Understood as the essence of an individual organism that organizes its specific and unified "striving," the *conatus* of a complexly *organized* human body is the self-same formal essence that establishes a mind as the mental aspect of the organism's "striving." *Conatus* in Spinoza's metaphysics is a term that he uses explicitly to refer to the *activity* of striving to remain in active existence. As was observed in the previous chapter, the activity of striving is the ordinary modes of mind and body, each exerting the drive to maintain existence, but as modes they are aspects of a more fundamental unity. So, what we have is a singular striving—expressed in two ways—by a unified particular entity that exists as the ground of which body and mind are but aspects. This *res* is the one and the same thing (*res*), which exists with a single teleological orientation to maintain its composite existence expressed in two ways. This is what Aquinas would term as "person." It is in this sense of a *single* striving with dual aspects that I argue *conatus* can be conceived of as an organizing form. Recognizing this helps address how, in Spinoza's thought, this individual *res* is established in existence to be capable of striving as an individual. Spinoza not only needs something similar to Aquinas's notion of form, but actually relies on it. As was demonstrated in chapter 6, *conatus* has an ambiguous meaning in Spinoza's metaphysics, signifying both (1) the activity of "striving" on the part of individuals possessed of both a mental and a physical side, and (2) an essence that *accounts* for the acts of striving [mental-striving and physical-striving] that present themselves as dual aspects of any such "thing" (*res*) in the first place. So, the mind and the body of an individual human are both irreducible, i.e., the mind cannot be reduced to a bodily process (materialism) and the body cannot be reduced to a mere mental construct (idealism). They are primary *aspects* of a human being's existence. They are not parallel processes or powers, but are the way a human being exists as an integrated whole. *Conatus* is the metaphysical principle.

Seeing this explanatory role that *conatus* as form plays in Spinoza's thought, we not only can appreciate the way that his and Aquinas's views have a conceptual affinity but can understand why both philosophers view the body as the *object* of particular cognitive acts that are the mind's activity. For Aquinas and Spinoza, the mind's knowledge of the world cannot be separated from the body's interaction with the world of things that act upon the human person *qua* bodily. In this action the body is affected by the things that affect it out of their own essences, and therefore the mind can know those acting essences as objects of understanding. Someone might object and say that for Aquinas cognitive acts are not purely intellectual, because the body is also the medium of those acts in a way that might not so fit Spinoza's view. However, if one looks closely at their descriptions this objection falls aside. Spinoza is clear that the aptness for thought and "perception of many things simultaneously" by a mind is in direct proportion to the "aptness of the body [that is the *object* of that mind] to act and be acted upon simultaneously in many ways" [II, P 13, sch]. Since Spinoza argues that the aptness for thought is directly tied to the aptness of the body, he must accept something like Aquinas's view that the body is involved in the process of a person knowing, even though it does not explain what the act of knowing is or cause cognition and intellection.

Furthermore, when Spinoza describes the body as the "object of the idea constituting the human mind," (presented in chapter 6) the term *object* in Spinoza's usage ascribes an intentionality to thought. Such a description suggests that he utilizes the term object in this context in a way that is compatible with Aquinas's epistemology, for it implies that the body is that to which the mind is properly oriented as the medium through which engagement with the world occurs as the physical world is engaged as things act upon the material body out of their particular essences. Again, let us be clear, such a way of viewing the matter does not mean the body's interactions causes the mind's thought *qua* Thought. Rather, we are merely observing that in Spinoza's view (and Thomas's) there is a single entity that is both bodily engaged in interaction with the world of extended things and mentally engaged in conceiving ideas about that world, as well as ideas about the ideas.

The human person is ontologically unitary, expressing mental and physical essential properties that are distinguishable one from the other and yet one and the same thing *as aspects of the person.* Precisely as such properties of a unitary human being, then, the body is where the mind is focused, and the mind is the consciousness of the body and not just "located" with the body. To conceive of the body as the location or focus of the mind's acts does not imply that the mind, *per se* as an immaterial "thing," is the cause or explanation of any of the body's movements. Such movements *qua* physical activity require a physical or material explanation in the strict sense of causation. This way of posing the issue is explicit in Spinoza. For Aquinas, it is implicit in his view that locomotion, growth, and to sensation are bodily powers granted to *physical organisms* by the rational soul, but not directly caused by *the mind.* Because of this way of conceiving the powers of the soul, and of seeing the rational soul as including all the *nonrational* powers, without negating their essence as nonrational powers, Aquinas contended that it is *the person* formed by the rational who is the source of his physical actions and movement. The body has operations of which the person is not conscious (autonomic nervous system, for example), but also the bodily movements of which the person is conscious occur as the person (and not the mind) acts with intent or choice. Since the person is the "one and the same thing" that is body and mind when one reaches out to pick something that he wants or needs, it is not the rational powers of the soul acting upon the body to move it. Rather, it is the person *qua* rational animal that is moving with a rational purpose. Similarly, for Spinoza the same follows, because the mind is not strictly speaking a thing (*res*) that could act upon the body, nor vice versa. They are both modal aspects of the more fundamental "one and the same thing" that exists because of the *conatus*-form which defines it and organizes its life *qua* organism to be both extended in a certain complex way and apt for thought in a way that is complementary to and in direct proportion to the complexity of the organized body. Since the striving to continue in existence has intentionality to it for an organism, we can say that intentional actions are part of Spinoza's system regarding the *res* that exists as "one and the same thing." So, the methodologically dualistic problem of mind-body interaction, does not arise because in their hylomorphic view it is more appropriate to think of the self-same organism as what is both acting *qua* body and knowing *qua* mind. One and the same thing is acting, in a deterministic way for Spinoza and in a limited way for Aquinas.[4]

My contention that Spinoza did indeed have a view of human existence that is congruent with Thomas's idea of "composite" being is perhaps not as clear as it could be. Of course, Aquinas's doctrine of compositeness is obvious, for he describes form and matter jointly as the "principles" involved in the existence of a human being (and all other things). His is a clear-cut, but nuanced, Aristotelianism.[5] Spinoza's understanding was not, I contend, far from this, because "compositeness," in just the same sense, was arguably his general understanding of the nature of things as well. And here again, and most crucially, I am not merely referring to Spinoza's insistence that all things have both mind and body as an essential part or side of their existence. The composite nature is the thing that expresses the two Modes of substance. That is precisely why, as I have been contending, Spinoza made a distinction between the *essence*

---

4. There is the objection that the idea of volitional action is scandalously anti-Spinozistic, and certainly he does not have any sympathy for a libertarian view of free will. Yet, Spinoza's insistence that all things are necessitated by the nature of the One Substance, does not negate volition as a feature of human existence in a weak sense. While all things happen in human experience and existence by necessity, this only means that "the will" is not an entity which is not related to the necessary chain of causes. As a mode of thinking, "the will" is subject to all the precursor ideas that bring a person to the moment of response. That need not imply that the necessitated moment of response does not qualify as a volitional response in the weak sense. Even a determined "choice" can be considered a "choice" by the "chooser" in the weak sense. The *conatus* of mind is, while necessitated, an act that is called will: "When this striving is related only to the Mind, it is called Will; but when it is related to the Mind and Body together, it is called Appetite" (III, P 9, S). For a very fine treatment of Spinoza's view of will, see Melamed, "Causes of Our Belief in Free Will."

5. See chapter 3 for a discussion of Aquinas's development of Aristotle's thought.

of a thing that grants it existence and the actual *existence* of the thing as an individual entity that is expressed via the two modes extension and thought. As was shown in chapter 6, the *conatus* is this essence. But even at that, how close is this really to the sort of doctrine of compositeness that is Aquinas's? The answer is to be found, I think, by more closely considering his doctrine of *conatus* in the light of the relationship that he says exists between Thought and Extension as Attributes.

To demonstrate further the way that compositeness functions in his metaphysics, we must look more deeply into Spinoza's account of how individual *physical* identity is instantiated. In II, P 13, he provides an extensive philosophical explanation of this, which was mentioned in chapter 7: "the *relation* of motion and rest."[6] This proportional relationship is inherently involved as complex things maintain enduring physical identity (EPI). The EPI of complex things is the way physical individuals that are made up of many simpler bodies can be seen as and can continue to exist as units (modes) of Extension. As a Mode of Extension, no EPI can "explain" itself by itself, only the extended Substance can explain the existence of the Mode. However, although the Substance extended is the ontological ground for all physical existence, the property of being extended, considered only in relation to the *Attribute* of Extension, cannot account for the *particularity* of any extended particular Modes. This is because "being extended" *qua* Attribute is not any particular thing. Whereas the Attribute of Extension is a necessary presupposition to account for extended things *qua* extended just as the Attribute of Thought is necessary to account for all that is mental, Attributes do not have *real* existence. Substance and its Modes are all that exist (I, P 28, pr.). So, Extension is only real *in* the extended Modes of Substance that express this Attribute of Substance in a concrete way. In Spinoza's system, therefore, something is needed to explain the nature of the Modes as *particular* instantiations of Extension (besides the mere *fact* of their extendedness).[7]

The proportion and relation of motion and rest necessary for the EPI of a complex individual is not itself an extended thing, even though it involves extended things. Such a relation requires extended things, but also is needed by Extension (matter) insofar as the *relation* is something by which the EPI as a Mode of Extension is given concrete expression. This proportion or relation is *something* that could be involved with the Attribute of extension, and therefore in its Modes, but which would not be reductively identifiable with the *Attribute* of Extension or of the Modes of Extension. Even thinking of this relation as a part of the physical world *qua* extended in the sense of being a physical law, or the totality of physical laws, would not make the *relation*

---

6. Emphasis mine.

7. Presumably the explanation of these things would be in the so-called "infinite modes" of Substance. However, Curley is correct when he says, "In the *Ethics* proper, Spinoza tells us precious little about these modes, and he does not have much more to say in other works. But we do learn in the correspondence . . . that motion and rest is an immediate infinite mode in the attribute of extension, and that the body of the whole universe is a mediate mode, presumably in the attribute of extension" (Curley, *Behind the Geometrical Method,* 35).

in itself an extended thing.[8] Something else is needed to identify metaphysically the reason the relation of motion is maintained so that an EPI of a complex individual endures in its existence. Spinoza speaks of the maintenance of this *relation* in Lemmas 4—7 of II P 13, but for our purposes we may consider only Lemmas 4-6.

(Lemma 4) If from a body, or an individual thing composed of a number of bodies, certain bodies are separated, and at the same time a like number of other bodies of the same nature take their place, the individual thing will retain its nature as before, without any change in its form. [*This Lemma addresses the replacement of component parts of an entity, such as the replacement of cells and tissues that a growing and aging body experiences.*]

(Lemma 5) If the parts of an individual thing become greater or smaller, but so proportionately that they all preserve the same mutual relation of motion-and-rest as before, the individual thing will likewise retain its own nature as before without any change in its form. [*This Lemma describes how an individual thing is the same from its earliest, most immature phases (think small sprout) all the way through its life as fully mature thing (think great oak).*]

(Lemma 6) If certain bodies composing an individual thing are made to change the existing direction of their motion, but in such a way that they can continue their motion and keep the same mutual relation as before, the individual thing will likewise preserve its own nature without any change of form. [*Here the focus seems to be on movement and change of place within the oneness of Substance.*]

In each of these, Spinoza asserts that the "form" of the thing is not changed. The use of this term "form" does not necessarily mean that Spinoza was thinking in any kind of hylomorphic sense of compositeness. We do not want to proceed in a rapid and anachronistic fashion; but neither should we rule it out, given that his idea of a *relation* or *proportion* of motion and rest would entail something other than the property of being extended. Spinoza was not simply making a bald assertion about the nature of things in his use of the concept of motion and rest in proportion and the idea that a

---

8. Bennett, *Study of Spinoza's Ethics*, 111 offers a different interpretation. He argues that Spinoza had to conceive of the Attributes and their Modes as being the "repositories of all causal laws." This means, in Bennett's view, that Spinoza's concept of "motion and rest is not just a system of description and classification but somehow embodies the whole of physics. The laws of physics are supposed to be part of the 'extension' package—and the extended world must obey them . . ." Bennett's reading suggests of course only that "motion and rest" is an undeveloped concept that is supposed to capture the whole of physics and all its laws of motion and order. Even with that, however, one can still argue that, with those laws in place, a *relation* of motion and rest, while being *described* by the laws of physics, would nonetheless be something other than the "laws" that are involved in motion and rest. Materialists often miss the point that scientific "laws" are not causes or explanations but are only *descriptions* of regularities observed in the physical universe. No law is the cause of what we observe. Cf. Russell, *Problems of Philosophy*, 101–5 where he contends that "relations" are something that "subsist" over and above physical reality and are, therefore, real *qua* subsistent conditions.

relation of motion and rest had to be maintained for EPI to continue. Everything in his system has a cause or explanation, even if we only know it inadequately.[9] The EPI that strives to maintain existence is dependent upon the required relation of motion and rest. Its enduring identity *as a physical entity* is maintained even as the constituent elements of its existence change. *Striving* is the essential feature of its bodily existence, but although the action of striving may begin after it is instantiated for Spinoza, something else must be involved in the maintenance of the proportional relations of motion and rest. In Lemma 4—6 of proposition 13 of Book II, Spinoza seems to use the concept of a thing's nature (which is retained across time) as synonymous to the idea of its *form*. The form of a thing in these Lemmas cannot simply describe the order of arrangement and contour structure that is maintained, for in Lemma 5 Spinoza insists that even a change of shape does not change the entity's essential identity that results from the *relation* of motion and rest being established. The striving to retain its form is the *conatus* that makes itself manifest in the physical strivings of the individual one-and-the-same-thing.[10] A change of constituent bodies (Lemma 4), a change in size of the constituent bodies (Lemma 5), and a change in place or direction (Lemma 6) all require something other than the bodies involved in the process of so changing, growing, or moving to account for the ongoing unity of existence of the EPI. What Spinoza says in the proof of Lemma 6 applies to the nature of EPI regarding all changes of bodies that constitute a complex individual: "by hypothesis, the individual thing retains all that we, in defining it, asserted as constituting its *form*."[11]

It is reasonable to conclude, therefore, that the form (arrangement) a thing has and the "informing" principle that establishes the arrangement were distinct *concepts* for Spinoza. (This is also the Thomistic way of discussing the relationship of a *form* and the entity that is formed.) Since *conatus* is "nothing but the given, or actual, essence of the thing" (III, P 7), it is best understood as the implicit source or perhaps cause of the relevant *relation* of motion-and-rest, in a Spinozistic metaphysics.[12] If we add

9. See chapter 5 for citation of Della Rocca's claim that "motion and rest" is a placeholder for a perspective that Spinoza had not fully worked out.

10. In Spinoza's case, however, we must be sure to note that the conatus qua form would function only to bring about the relationship or proportion of motion and rest of the various parts of an entity. This would not, however, deny that an individual entity does not have its own particular *conatus*/form, but only that in a Spinozistic system the way that this functions would have to be in the nature of a Mode of Substance.

11. Emphasis mine.

12. Donagan, "Spinoza's Proof of Immortality," 254–55. Donagan argues, contra the kind of interpretation I am offering, that Spinoza rejected the distinction of form and matter in its Thomistic form. However, Donagan does not explain why this is so. He asserts it. But his point seems to be (1) that Spinoza held that all essences are individual, (2) that the scholastic notion thought that each individual shared a common essence (humanity) with all others, and (3) that as an actual "essence or *conatus*" each individual man is identical with his actual essence. Donagan's arguments would rule out the possibility of affinity between Spinoza and Aquinas's distinction discussed in chapter 3 between *essentia ut totum* and *essentia ut pars*. However, as was shown earlier for Aquinas, Socrates's essence *qua* Socrates is indeed identical to him. That does not mean, however, that he did not share a common

to this conclusion the arguments of chapter 6, namely that a single *conatus* accounts for the entire identity of the organism and hence involves both the body that strives and the mind that both accompanies that body and strives itself, it is reasonable to see Spinoza as at least implicitly assuming in his metaphysics something analogous to the Thomistic concept of form. The *conatus* enables a striving mind that is apt for the body that is continually kept as an EPI by the relation of motion and rest. This body is the *idea* of the mind, even if the mind does not know that or how the EPI is kept in its integrity as body.

All that is left, then, is to show how "compositeness" is involved *Spinozistically* in the existence of each thing. Given that the Attribute of Extension does not explain the particularity of each of its Modes as instances of extendedness, some organizing information is required to instantiate the relevant *relation* of motion-and-rest that maintains the EPI and the enduring idea of the EPI (mind) of an entity. Just as in Aquinas's doctrine of compositeness, for Spinoza, the conatic information underlying an organism does not exist in the strictest sense of the word. It is real and *subsists* in some manner (as Aquinas would put it). However, organizing, operation-granting information that is the *conatus* only actually exists within the thing informed by it. It is simply the action of informing, by which a particular organism's existence is enabled. Of all the Thomistic claims Spinoza would reject, he would not be reserved about Aquinas's insistence that the person is the relevant referent (Spinoza's *res*) regarding bodily actions and conscious ideas; and this person who knows is "one and the same thing" whether considered via the Mode mind or the Mode body. This one and the same thing exists as mind and body in unity of identity, because an organizing principle has given rise both materially and mentally to a being whose physical existence is the home of rationality and whose mental existence is the form of its physical life.

Since the idea of form is closely associated in medieval Aristotelian philosophy with the concept of *idea* (*eidos* in Aristotle's Greek), some might cry foul at this point, objecting to the fact that this way of conceiving of the relationship between *conatus* and extension violates the explanatory or the causal barrier that Spinoza interposes between the Attributes of Thought and Extension. However, I think this is not the case. First, the idea of *form* is not synonymous with ideas of a *mind;* it is a principle not an idea. Second, the extended nature of the organism's existence *qua* extended is

---

defining property with, say, Plato. Neither, it seems to me, would Spinoza have denied this, although he does not argue for it and in at least one part of the *Ethics* denies the concept of universals. But that denial was an objection not, I think, to a Thomistic notion of universals as real but only objectively real as knowledge. In fact, Spinoza speaks in the introduction of Book IV of "human nature" in such a way that he has some affinity to Aquinas's conception of universals as real in the intellect: "For since we desire to form the idea of a man which we may look to as a model of human nature, we shall find it helpful to keep these terms [good and bad] in the sense I have indicated. So in what follows I shall mean by 'good' that which we certainly know to be the means of our approaching nearer to the model of human nature that we set before ourselves. . . . Again, we shall say that men are more perfect or less perfect in so far as they are nearer to or further from this model." Donagan's analysis is not, then, a defeater for my interpretation.

not being caused or explained by the "form." Rather, it is the whole organism's existence *as an entity* that has extendedness as one of its *expressions* that is established in existence. Similarly, conceiving *conatus* as an informing principle does not entail that *conatus* itself determines the Extended powers that operate as Extended to organize simple extended Modes into a complex extended entity. Rather, it acts only through any relevant operational structures related to the Attribute of Extension to establish and maintain a specific proportion of motion and rest sufficient for the bodily existence of such an entity. This way of viewing the matter is, if not essentially then very much analogously, like Thomas's hylomorphic doctrine that form and matter both explain (or cause) the existence of the *composite* thing, even though each of them is a "cause" that is *qua* cause independent of the other.[13] The formal cause does not explain the material cause *qua* "cause," nor vice versa. But *together* they explain (and cause) the existence of the primary being whose existence is being analyzed. And yet there remains an important respect in which, in the strictest sense, the formal cause alone gives a particular kind of existence to things.[14] Further, the *conatus* itself creates an integrated entity that strives to remain in existence through both expressions of the individual thing's strivings, which is also the way that the rational soul functions in Aquinas's understanding of the relationship between form and matter in a human being's activities as an organism. This is the essence of the doctrine of "compositeness," in which both principles (material/physical laws and nonphysical "information") are involved in the existence of a living human being.

LIFE AND COMPOSITE EXISTENCE

In their respective foci on form or *conatus*, Aquinas and Spinoza are interested, in their distinct ways, in the phenomenon of life in the world. They both are interested in describing and analyzing the nature of *living* human beings in the fullness of their existence and experience in the world. Neither the scholastic Catholic nor the excommunicated Jewish rationalist thought that life could or should be conceived as a supervenient property present in a world that is itself, in the most ultimate sense,

13. The Aristotelian distinction between the formal cause and the material cause implies a strong distinction, not a weak one. The distinction is just as strong as the distinction between the formal and the efficient cause. Hence, Spinoza's distinction between causes in which there is Thought and Extension and also the efficient causation of God at work in the infinity of Modes fits into an Aristotelian model, minus final causality in the universal sense. But even Spinoza's definition of God's acts as necessary can pose a certain kind of final causation, just not volitional, which I take it is what Spinoza really wanted to deny about God anyway.

14. Aquinas employed this concept that form grants particular existence to show that *qua* individuals all men could not be, contra Averroes, possessed of one intellect as the form of all. The rational soul instead makes existent individual knowing persons, who are each primary rational beings and who participate, individually in their own right, in the act of understanding that is itself an expression of, and participation in, God's own powers inherent in God's Being.

lifeless.[15] For Spinoza the fact that Thought, as much as Extension, was a fundamental Attribute of Reality, meant that *Life* was everywhere, although not in the same degree [II, P 13, sch].[16] In a parallel way for Aquinas, while the concept of all things being *animate* or of panpsychism was alien to him, life is a fundamental feature of the universe, because all things participate in God's Being and "life is properly attributed to God" in the highest sense.[17] Something of Life is at work, then, even in the "inanimate" objects of Thomas's worldview. The physical (extended) *organism*, therefore, is deemed, by both philosophers, to be *alive* essentially and not in some supervening sense. Life is a basic property, and therefore an irreducible reality that cannot be reduced down to the electrochemical properties of particles of matter. As living beings, human persons are single entities of a composite nature; hence one and the same *living* thing whether conceived in terms of body or mind.

Their unwavering focus upon the co-inhering unity of mind and body in *living* human beings, however, recognized a duality of activity without positing a dualism of existence. On the level of the individual person, this means that each person has dual aspects; the individual is irreducibly both. Perhaps then, Aquinas and Spinoza could help us begin to see that there may not really be a mind-body "problem" so much as there is a wrong focus on the whole issue of the mind-body relationship based on methodological dualism and the presumption of the priority materialistic explanations. And perhaps these things blind us to a more profound vision for understanding how we are what we are.

15. The presupposition of the material universe in mechanistic terms is just that—a presupposition. Materialistic explanations for the existence of life have notoriously failed. Not to recognize this is to be less than philosophically forthright.

16. It seems quite clear to me that for Spinoza the notion that all things are animated would have to entail for him more than the mere claim that all things are "minded." The reasons are twofold. First is his insistence that the Attributes of Substance are Extension and Thought and all the Modes that express those Attributes are Modes of one or the other. For him to have a third category, "Life" would suggest that being alive would be another Mode of existence. Hence, being animate entails being minded and extended, because all things are minded and extended and alive. Second, Spinoza was moving away, it seems to me, from the mechanistic view of "life" as merely aspects of extension because life is a biological, and therefore extended, thing (in some sense). He, along with Aquinas, saw life as a feature of reality that could not be reduced to either the physical functions of biological entities (simply) or made into a level of reality that is "tacked-on" to the otherwise bare and lifeless universe. Life for both is something of an ontological ground of being, not an emergent property.

17. Aquinas discusses this in *Summa* I a, Q 18 a 3, reply. His basic argument is that life is about self-movement or determination and that God is, by essence, the only truly self-determining or moving being. Furthermore, in article 4 of the same question, Aquinas argues: "In God intellect, the thing understood, and the act of understanding, are one and the same. Hence *whatever is in God as understood is the very living or life of God*. Now, wherefore, since all things that have been made by God are in Him as things understood, it follows that all things in Him are the divine life itself" (my emphasis).

THE LINGERING QUESTION OF IMMORTALITY

There remains for both Spinoza and Aquinas a lingering problem for their metaphysics: how to account for their similar insistence on the capacity of the mind or soul to maintain existence even after the death of the body. To this question we now turn, not to defend their substantive claims philosophically at this point, but to see how such claims might fit the context of the rest of their metaphysical schemes. We will begin with Spinoza.

Spinoza's View of Eternality and Immortality

Curley sets the stage well for our considerations regarding Spinoza's doctrine of the immortality when he admits, ". . . in spite of many years of study, I still do not feel that I understand this part of the *Ethics* at all adequately. I feel the freedom to confess that, of course, because I also believe that no one else understands it adequately either."[18] Many, if not most, Spinoza scholars have decided that his case for the immortality of a human mind is hopelessly flawed.[19] The purportedly confounding issue is his insistence that "the human mind cannot be absolutely destroyed along with the body, but something of it remains, which is eternal" (V, P 23). Perhaps the problems presented by Spinoza's claim that the "mind" survives the body's death are obvious, but a very brief mention of them will nonetheless help us see what is required if one might hope to make his doctrine internally consistent.

1. The mind and the body are one and the same thing.

2. The essence of the mind is to be the idea of an actually existing body.

3. The striving of the mind to maintain itself in existence is inextricable from the body's striving, because the mind and body are "one and the same thing."

4. Spinoza's metaphysics entails that in both infinite and eternal Attributes of Thought and Extension the Modes of Substance exist in some kind of simultaneity, so how could he allow for the eternity of the mind but not the body?

Given these four points of Spinozism, is there any way to account for what motivated him to claim for immortality as possible for the mind? Alan Donagan's work represents one attempt to allow Spinoza's doctrine to make sense on his own terms. He argues that the key to understanding Spinoza on this point is rooted in two aspects of his thought: (1) the parallel identity of the "order of ideas and the order of things," and (2) that there can be "actual ideas of the formal essences of *nonexistent things*."[20]

18. Curley, *Behind the Geometrical Method*, 84.

19. In this Bennett is the most forceful recent commentator (Bennett, *Study of Spinoza's Ethics*, 537). Calling it an "unmotivated disaster," Bennett says that he only deals with the doctrine at all, because "a little can be learned from firmly grasping what is wrong with the core of it."

20. Donagan, "Spinoza's Proof of Immortality," 254, my emphasis.

He argues that Spinoza held in the *Ethics* (the proof of I, P 11) that not only actual essences are contained in the infinite and eternal Mode of the Attribute of Thought, but also essences that are merely "possible." These later essences, because they are only possible are within the parameters of Thought alone, since they do not correspond to actual Modes of Extension, therefore are in some way Infinite Modes of Thought.

> Spinoza saw, if [Donagan's description about possible essences is true], then the very theorem that the order and connection of ideas is the same as the order and connection of things, entails that what, in the attribute of thought, corresponds to a mere possibility in the attribute of extension, must be *more than a mere possibility* [in the attribute of thought] . . . Such actual ideas of the formal essences of nonexistent individuals, since they cannot be *finite* modes of thought, must form *part of an infinite mode* of it, a mode which Spinoza referred to as "*Dei infinita idea.*" This infinite mode of thought must contain, *inter alia*, an actual idea of the formal essence of every individual body, existent or nonexistent . . .
>
> Once it has been grasped that the identity of the order of ideas and the order of things not only does not forbid that there should be actual ideas of the formal essences of nonexistent things, but on the contrary demands it, Spinoza's proof of immortality is simple. When a living human body is destroyed, the corresponding mind, as nonderivative idea of that body actually existing, perishes with it; for they are the same finite mode in two distinct attributes. However, that mind, *as actual essence*, had as a part the idea of the formal essence of that body. And the idea of that formal essence belongs to God *sub specie aeternitatis* . . . . Therefore, the part of a man's mind which consists in the idea of the formal essence of his body must be eternal: it must have preexisted his body and cannot be destroyed with it. Q.E.D.[21]

Donagan's interpretation represents what Bennett calls an "asymmetrical" explanation for Spinoza's doctrine, which is the kind that Bennett provides and believes is all that is Spinozistically warranted.[22] Bennett argues that Spinoza's suppositions in Book V rule out any possibility of interpreting his doctrine of immortality as an implication of his otherwise symmetrical account of the parallelism between the mind and body.[23] I take it that Bennett sees this as a fatal misstep on Spinoza's part. It is not

---

21. Donagan, "Spinoza's Proof of Immortality," 254–55, my emphasis.

22. Bennett, *Study of Spinoza's Ethics*, 361. He contends that Spinoza's doctrine is based on the following line of reasoning. "Take a necessary truth about the body, not (a) the corresponding truth about the mind, and then redescribe it as (b) a thought in the mind. The upshot is that you have got a single item which is at once (a) eternal and (b) contained in the mind. Q.e.d."

23. Bennett, *Study of Spinoza's Ethics*, 158–59 (emphasis original). "What Spinoza says is asymmetrical: 'the human mind cannot be absolutely destroyed with the human body, but something of it remains which is eternal.' It has been contended that he has merely underexpressed his position, and would not have minded adding that if the mind is eternal then so is the body; but that is too weak to rescue the symmetrical account. If the appearance of asymmetry is to be explained as a mere result of understatement, then Spinoza must be willing to say: 'The human body is not absolutely destroyed

my purpose to analyze Donagan's interpretation or to take up Bennett's characterization of it as the product of an "asymmetrical" procedure. Rather, I present Donagan's description at this point because it provides us a sympathetic reading of Spinoza's doctrine that is helpful background for my alternative reading. In my view, the question whether Spinoza *needs* a symmetrical or an asymmetrical account to justify his proposition of immortality does not come into play, because it does seem to me that there is a way to provide a more symmetrical account of Spinoza's metaphysics of immortality. (However, Spinoza's own formulation of it in the final part of the Ethics seems *prima facie* to imply an asymmetrical relationship between body and mind.) As I noted, Donagan's commentary is built on the presupposition that the idea of the formal essences of things provides the true basis of Spinoza's doctrine. So, a mind that is the "idea" of a particular body subsequently has the further idea of the formal essence of that body (not just its concrete existence) as a *part* of itself as the idea of the existing body. This idea of the formal essence of the body existed even prior to the actual existence of either that body or the mind as the idea of that actual body. Because the idea of the formal essence of the body in question is not simply the idea of the body as an actually existing individual, this "idea" that is *in* the mind belongs to God *sub specie aeternitatis*. Therefore, the idea of the formal essence of the body is eternal by its very nature; and per Donagan the corresponding *idea* any finite mind "contains," at least, is eternal.

I suggest a different, complementary solution to the purported tension. It is rooted in the doctrine of *conatus* and the singularity of identity that I have contended is the basis of mind-body identity. This a better starting point to help us read him as maintaining consistency in his ontological commitments. Recall that in Spinoza's thought the essence of the body is not that of a radically independent entity that exists in isolation from all other things. This cannot be, because the body as a mode of Extension is a modification of Substance as extended, which Substance is not actually divisible (as was shown in the previous chapter). Any individual extended thing is not, therefore, truly separated from the rest of extended Reality. On this proposition he builds his argument in Book IV, where he critiques the strength of human emotions produced by the wrong conception and the bondage such inadequate ideas can entail for a person.[24] In Book IV, P 2, for instance, he asserts that each individual person is "passive in so far as we are a part of Nature *which cannot be conceived independently of other parts*."[25] From this premise, Spinoza proposes in the fourth proposition in Book IV, "it is impossible for a man not to be a part of Nature [God/Substance] and not to

with the human mind, but something of it remains which is eternal,' and, indeed, 'The human body is not absolutely destroyed with the human *body*, but . . . etc.' No one has been willing to cram those sentences into his mouth."

24. Note also: it is part of his argument in Book II that we can only have inadequate ideas of particulars.

25. Emphasis mine.

undergo changes other than those which can be understood solely through his own nature and of which he is the adequate cause."

However, since every entity actively strives out of its own particular essence (*conatus*), we often, insofar as we are such striving entities, fail to understand the inherent necessity of our own acts in relationship to all other things or the acts of other things upon us. According to Spinoza's thinking, because of our inadequate ideas about our lives in Nature, we wrongly understand our own particularity, and thereby we understand inadequately things that negatively impact us bodily (or mentally). Inadequately conceptualizing, we do this because we do not perceive or conceive our lives as part of the infinite and necessary essence of God or Nature. This inadequate existential understanding, in turn, provides a false foundation for our emotional life, upon which we conceive categories of good and evil about the nature of things and actions in the world, not realizing that this way of thinking is confused and inadequate. Nothing is good or evil, he says, except as it is only relatively good or evil as it acts favorably on or in opposition to our perceived interests. Failing to see the necessity of all things, we suffer the limits of mere "imaginative" knowledge, not intuiting that our individual striving is part of the whole of *Natura Naturata*. We live, Spinoza argues, in a perspectival limit upon our own virtue and beatitude in our very existence.

This line of thought is the focus of propositions 28 through 35 in Book IV. Propositions 1–5, listed below, are all based on three previously established doctrines from Books I–III: (a) the oneness of Substance and its Attributes and Modes, (b) the identity of mind and body, and (c) the nature of our striving as individual essences. First, then, P 28 states that knowing God as absolutely infinite being is the highest good of the human mind. Then Spinoza proceeds as follows with the remaining propositions:[26]

1. Good and evil are evaluations given to things based on whether the thing has (a) some common element with us that increases our activity out of our nature or (b) some contradictory element that diminishes or checks our power to act out of our nature. (P 29—P 31)

2. Our capacity to be acted upon and the passive emotions that can attend this capacity is what accounts for our sense of "difference" in nature and causes us to believe we are, in our strivings, contrary to one another. (P 32—P 34)

3. However, reason that sees beyond the passive (and inadequate) emotions can enable us to see that our acts and all others' acts are merely the acts of our natures. Hence, we will see that we only seek what all other things seek for themselves; and reason will compel us to embrace this fact of the unity of striving that marks the universe in some fundamental sense, and lead to a conscious embrace that all things *together* are seeking the good. (P 35)

26. My paraphrased summations.

4. Because we are all part of the eternal and infinite essence of God as individual Modes of God, the highest virtue of those who act according to their own *conatus* is "common to all men and can be possessed equally by all men in so far as they are of the same nature." (P 36)

Spinoza wants his readers to understand their own lives and the nature of all things as deterministically necessary Modes (expressions) of the same Reality. If one takes his line of reasoning about the "commonness" of human endeavor in seeking happiness and fulfillment out of one's own nature, and then recalls Spinoza's claims about the third kind of knowledge (which he introduced in II, P 40), we can, I think, begin to see how he understood the mind's immortality, or at least its possession of an eternal part. In Book II (P 40, sch 2) the third kind of knowledge, intuition, "proceeds *from* an adequate idea of the formal essence of certain attributes of God *to* an adequate knowledge of the essence of things."[27] Such adequate knowledge of the "essence of things" would involve, for Spinoza, understanding them all as Modes of a single Substance, since intuition proceeds *from* the adequate understanding of the Attributes *to* an adequate knowledge of "the essence of *things*." Therefore, fully adequate knowledge perceives all things as united to one another in Substance as the Ground and Source of all things. Furthermore, in proposition 44 he asserts, "it is not in the nature of reason to regard things as contingent, but as necessary." This understanding of the necessity of all things, then, must be a part of the "third kind of knowledge." By this most adequate knowledge, each thing that exists is known to be a necessary Mode of God or Substance.

The "basic principles of reason" allow us to explain and understand things in the light of that which is "common to all things" (which Spinoza thought he had demonstrated in Book I and the first 43 propositions of Book II), i.e., that all things are simply affections of the one Substance. True reasoning will not, therefore, provide any analysis or explication of individual modes that considers the essences of those things in isolation from *Deus sive Natura*, because true reason knows these to be essentially modifications Substance. Anything that is *truly* known, he tells us in the second corollary of proposition 4 in Book II, therefore, is not conceived only in temporal terms, but "in the light of eternity." This kind of knowledge is the greatest power of the mind and is the most adequate (only true) knowledge. It is the true expression (one might dare say *telos)* a finite mind's *conatus* as a particular expression of Substance.

> The third kind of knowledge proceeds from the adequate idea of certain of God's attributes to adequate knowledge of the essence of things [see its definition in Sch. 2 Pr. 40 II], and the more we understand things in this way, the more we understand God. Therefore, the highest virtue of the mind, that is

27. Emphasis mine.

[by definition 8 of Book IV] its power or nature, or its highest *conatus,* is to understand things by this third kind of knowledge. (V, P 25, pr).[28]

Intuition seems to be an achieved, immediate grasp of reality by emending the intellect in which a person understands that all things are essentially *one* in God and necessary and inherently linked to one another, thereby instantiating a crucial state of affairs: "Whatever the mind understands *under a form of eternity* it does not understand from the fact that it conceives the present actual existence of *the* body [which is the object of the mind], but from the fact that it conceives the *essence* of the body under a form of eternity" [V, P 29]. In other words, the particular body which is known is known now in its very essence to be necessarily one part of the infinity of extended Modes that has *qua* particular essence a particular function in the whole chain of extended causes and effects. This intuited idea of the body under a form of eternity is the true conception of the body. The mind as the idea of the body is itself, *now,* understanding its object as but one part of the infinite and eternal chain of causes and effects. In fact, according to Spinoza, this way of understanding the body *qua* the "object" of the mind is the very nature of *reason:* "it is the nature of reason to conceive things *under the form of eternity.*"[29] So, when through the "emendation of the intellect" one intuits his life and all of Reality under the form of eternity (and one could add infinity), thereby the unity of All is now perceived. The mind, then, has achieved not only the greatest state of awareness possible by its very own nature, but it is being in the most ultimate sense what it truly is, namely, the idea of the eternal, universal unity of all Reality. Such knowledge is the highest expression of its *conatus* as a particular mode.

Positing this kind of knowledge as the "highest" form of understanding, Spinoza's epistemology does not negate the *particular* body as the object of the mind. Rather, the intuited *idea* of the body as united to all things means the mind, as the idea of the body, transcends the mind's finite idea of the body that is based upon sensory or imaginative rather than intuitive awareness. Intriguingly, Spinoza insists in the proof of this proposition that "the mind conceives nothing under a form of eternity except in so far as it conceives the *essence of its body* under a form of eternity, that is, except so far as the mind is eternal."[30] I take this to mean that Spinoza believes that the truest

28. Emphasis mine.

29. Emphasis mine. This epistemological claim seems to me to be related to Spinoza's insistence that there is only one Substance and that Substance is infinite and necessary. Having so defined Substance, then the nature of reason, since he thinks we can have adequate ideas of Substance, would be to understand Substance (and its Modes, etc) as infinite and necessary. Of course, an infinity of time would be eternity, if Spinoza is thinking in Aristotelian terms, rather than Platonic. And "necessity" is also a term that has connotations that could be related to eternity. So, to say that it is the nature of reason to understand things under the form of eternity is just to say that the human mind can recognize the truth about God and all things. See, Donagan, "Spinoza's Proof for Immortality" 242 for an interpretation of Spinoza's views of eternity as Aristotelian. Cf. Joachim, *Study of the Ethics of Spinoza,* 298 for a view that Spinoza's notions are Platonic.

30. *Ethics,* V, P 29. Emphasis mine.

form of self-knowledge of which an individual is capable is to understand the essential nature of the body (and, correlatively, of the mind) as I described it in the previous paragraph, i.e., to understand it as part of the great whole of *Natura Naturata*, which is the necessary, indivisible expression *Natura Naturans*.

Here we get to the heart of the matter regarding how Spinoza views of the immortality of the mind. His reasoning is symmetrical, quite so! Spinoza would say that the truest intuition that one can have of oneself is the awareness that one is a particular individual as an existent *thing* (*res*), but as such not independent from the one Substance. This immediate grasp is not just something that the mind is potentially capable of attaining, but is, in some way, "knowledge" that the mind must already *have* as part of its essence, since there is, in Spinoza's doctrine, no such thing as "potential" intellect, but only "active intellect."

We see this when we consider what is going on in the scholium of proposition 31 of Book I: "The third kind of knowledge depends on the mind as its formal cause in so far as the mind is eternal." When he speaks later of "the intellect in act," it is not because he grants "there can be any intellect in potentiality." In fact, he is careful to deny this very thing so that he is not interpreted as embracing something like the medieval notion of potential intellect. Instead, he is confining himself, in this instance, to this way of expressing the issue merely because he wants to "avoid any confusion to what we perceive with utmost clarity, to wit, the very act of understanding." Since, for Spinoza, ideas are necessarily present in us, either adequately or inadequately, our problem is that we become mistaken in our thought because of the immediacy of the mind as the idea of the body in relation to other modes. The third kind of knowledge is the ultimate ontological essence that makes the mind what it is. Without our intellect being made adequate by the measures he points us toward in *Ethics*, an individual will be noncognizant of this essential nature. Once one has attained the knowledge of the third kind, then the person knows herself under the aspect of eternity, in the sense I have been explicating. She knows herself rightly as a part of the whole of things, and yet with her own interests and ends and purposes, which can be harmonized with all other things in the ontological unity of all things as expressions of the one Substance. The more one understands his ultimate relatedness to all things in the one Substance, the more he is made capable of truly knowing his own particular existence. In knowing his own existence truly as a expression of *Deus sive Natura*, he is, Spinoza contends, becoming conscious of his life for what it really is, and is able to take pleasure in all things now that he understands his own existence through this way of true knowledge.

Spinoza's must believe that as the person comes to realize that his own existence is not ontologically distinct from all other things and, therefore, can embrace a new, more "blessed" sense of his own significance. By this new knowledge of his essence as one with all things in God, the person becomes essentially more than his temporally experienced existence bodily and mentally. For this reason Spinoza never speaks, to use Bennett's characterization, "of having a *good* eternal part of the mind, but rather of having a *large* one."[31] Because one comes to see that he is a Mode of Substance, the person begins to know himself in far "larger" terms than could ever have been possible so long as he was focused on the mere sensory awareness and passive emotions that accompanied his false beliefs about his place in the world.[32] This "enlarging" of the mind as the idea of the body qua actually existing, is the person's realization of the meaning or significance of her own body "under the form of eternity." A "large" mind is actually developed as the conscious part of the mind's essence *qua* "idea" of the body comes to realize that the very body of which it is an idea is itself intricately united to all things in God or Nature.

The mind's essence as the "idea of the body" is still the "idea of an actually existing thing, and nothing else," as Spinoza puts it in Book II, but now in the sense that the mind's object of reference is the individual extended Mode that *qua* individual is conceived as one with all things (*Natura* naturata) in the one Substance (God). In proposition 11 of Book II, Spinoza says only that the body is the *first thing* (*primum*) that constitutes the actual being of the human mind. However, in his translation of this passage, Shirley uses the term "basically" to translate *primum*. This probably obscures, unintentionally but regrettably, the deep intention behind Spinoza's qualification. Most likely Spinoza wants to affirm that, whereas the first ideas are about the body and the experience of its individual bounded finitude, when true knowledge is attained of the individuality of the body as the object of the mind, that mind knows this same body in a quite different way: not merely as an "actual being" but rather in its essence as part of the eternal and necessarily infinite nature of God. By intuition, then, the mind's domain is expanded. No longer understanding this body as an individual entity who is acted upon by and acts upon an alien "other," the body is now understood to be *one* with the whole of *Natura naturata*. And, of course, Spinoza's concept that *Natura naturata* is a manifestation of *Natura naturans* means that the understanding that is *the mind* knows the eternal nature of God is involved in its own being. So, the eternal part of the mind is that which is, from the very beginning of the duration of the organism, oriented toward the essence of the body under the aspect of eternity. This part, by the conscious use of reason by the truly reflective and understanding person, comes to be perceived to be the real nature of the person. The person discovers his truest identity by knowing himself as part of the eternal mind of God. Hence, beatitude follows in the near term and immortality in the eternal. This is what the entirety of the *Ethics* labors to demonstrate. It is not so much the case, in Spinoza's way of seeing this issue, that the mind survives the death of the body. Rather, the mind that is immortal is the mind that "in the light of eternity" has realized the

31. Bennett, *Study of Spinoza's Ethics*, 359.

32. It is clear that Spinoza thinks that one must achieve this kind of knowledge by realizing its truth. He insists in Book II that the mind exercises no real judgment over ideas; it can only be presented with true ideas. When it sees them rightly, it will then know them as true, and these ideas, then, will become the basis of what we call (although Spinoza does not use the word) "beliefs."

essential union with all things. Because that union is the mind's essence, once this is the idea that the mind *is*, a mind is made "large" enough to *be* this eternally, i.e., its immortal identity.

But what of personal identity in this doctrine? Is this a philosophical doctrine that has no real existential import regarding an individual's personal identity as a mode of Thought? The answer, for Spinoza, must lie in how one understands the idea of one's own "history" *qua* the "one and the same thing that is expressed in two ways." Spinoza would argue, I think, that even the contingent history of an individual is part of the eternality of Substance. Here, Donagan argues in a way that corresponds to my own thinking about this matter:

> We must remember that Spinoza did not think that our sense of self-identity, even in this life, depends on memory. A man knows his own identity to the extent that the primary constituent of his mind, his idea of his own body, is adequate. And, however inadequate it is, that idea is individual.

We can go further. A man's idea of the essence of his body changes during his life, and in that change there is loss as well as gain. However, God's idea of that essence, inasmuch as God constitutes the essence of that man's mind, is eternal and cannot change; hence it cannot be the idea which that man has of it at any given moment during his life. Can it be anything but the ordered totality of those ideas? If it cannot, it is reasonable to infer that Spinoza conceived the eternal self-knowledge of each man as being complete in a way in which his durational self-knowledge cannot be; for it is an idea of his body's essence through his whole life. Yet that idea not only need not be a memory-image, it cannot be, because it cannot correspond to physical traces in the brain.

> Eternal self-knowledge, while more complete than any durational self-knowledge, can contain no element that is not present in durational self-knowledge . . . That is why Spinoza thought it all-important to attain wisdom in this life. No wisdom and no virtue that a man attains in this life will be taken away from him; but neither will anything that he does not attain be added to him.[33]

I believe that the thesis I have pursued accounts for how this potentiality and process of the immortality of the mind is possible in Spinoza's system. *Conatus*—in the sense of "form," as I have presented—which establishes the individual entity and the dual Modes in which its existence is expressed, is itself part of the whole of Nature/God. And my interpretation accounts for how Spinoza's doctrine of eternity of the mind does not transgress his doctrine that Thought and Extension are always expression of Substance together, and that a mind is one and the same thing with *a* perceived body in unity of which it is an idea. On my interpretation, Spinoza assumed that a "conatic essence" establishes one's existence as a necessary particular expression of the infinite, unified nature of things. The *conatus*-enabled mind has immediate

---

33. Donagan, "Spinoza's Proof of Immortality," 257.

knowledge of the *conatus*-enabled body, and through reason's process of analysis comes to intuit the union of "its" body with all Extended Substance in *Deus sive Natura's* infinite number of manifestations. As a realization of true the nature of things, the idea now must always exist, for it encompasses all extended reality as its idea and therefore is, itself, unbounded in "self" awareness. The cessation of the body's specific duration is, therefore, a change *qua* Mode of extension into a different modification of the extended Substance. The mind that was the idea of the body while it strove to maintain itself in existence is now under the true knowledge the mind that knows that (and in a sense knows "all along") the body's existence and its striving were ultimately one with Nature and all other things. This "idea" of the individual, then, persists in existence as consciousness of its former body and now its larger body as part of the Attribute of Thought understanding rightly its relation to the Attribute of Extension.

Aquinas's Views on Incorruptibility and Resurrection

Aquinas's views on the question of postmortem survival have critical differences from Spinoza's. He speaks of the survival of the soul and not the mind and Spinoza does not utilize the language of subsistence to describe the nature of the rational principle.[34] But the most significant point of divergence is that Aquinas's doctrine of the nature of the soul's survival is not one about eternality or immortality. He focuses, instead, upon the issue of the soul's *incorruptibility* as a philosophical feature related to the Christian doctrine of the resurrection of the body as the way to understand the nature of the soul's inherent ability to survive the cessation of life in the body. Just like Spinoza's interpreters, commentators on Aquinas have claimed, as well, he cannot justify his claims of continuous personal identity, even if he shows that the rational soul is incorruptible.[35]

Arguing that the rational soul survives the death of the body because its essence as a rational principle is incorruptible, Aquinas builds his demonstration on the foundational premise that rationality, as a human activity, is an act so unique in the universe that it cannot be accounted for unless the rational soul is a power not dependent upon matter or material principles. As the highest act that the soul brings to the life of the person, human rational consciousness is incapable of demise for three interrelated reasons.[36] First, the act of understanding is by its very nature qualitatively distinct from any physical property (I a, Q 75, a 2 reply). So, it cannot be accounted

34. However, by Donagan's interpretation, one could argue that the presence of the formal essence of the body as the eternal part of the mind that is present "in" the mind from the very beginning could be a type of "subsistence."

35. See Pasnau, *Thomas Aquinas on Human Nature* for an interpretation that denies Aquinas can hold to a human being's ongoing survival after the death of the body.

36. The following analysis is a summary of Aquinas's thought based on his arguments in *Summa contra Gentiles* mainly, supplemented by his arguments in *Summa Theologiae* I a, Q 75 & Q 89. The form of reference will, therefore, be to refer to the former as *CG* and the later merely by the standard reference that has been utilized in my presentation, listing section, question, article, etc.

for by reference to any physical state of affairs: "the *principle* of understanding . . . has its own activity in which body takes no intrinsic part." This does not contradict Aquinas's contention that our initial conceptualization takes place through the physical body's engagement with sensible forms.[37] Human persons' mental engagement with the world involves a physical process, but the achievement of understanding what is engaged and what it means is not produced by a material cause or process. Furthermore, Aquinas contended that any specific act must be explained by reference to something that can be the agent of that act. Since the ability to understand and reason has no physical explanation, it must have its own nature. A material explanation for its activity being impossible, Aquinas says that the power of understanding "subsists in its own right." "For only [that which] actually exists acts, and its manner of acting follows its manner of being." Since it is not a physical state, it does not depend upon a physical state to exist.

Unlike other forms, whose essence is *only* to form matter, and therefore cannot be thought of as having its own *esse* in any sense, the rational soul is possessed of a power or property (understanding and reason) that is distinct from its relationship to the matter that it informs. Whereas other forms cease to exist when the material object that is formed disintegrates, the highest and most proper power of the rational soul is not in any way dependent upon the material object it forms. Hence, *qua* form, the rational soul must be understood as subsisting apart from the matter it informs. Its specific and proper essence is to be the cause of knowledge in a human person as the form of the human body.

> That act of being, in which it [the soul] itself subsists, the soul communicates to the physical matter; this matter and the intellectual soul *form a unity* such that the act of being of the compound whole is the soul's act of being. This does not happen in other forms which are non-subsistent. And for this reason the human soul continues in its act of being when the body is destroyed, whereas other souls do not [I a, Q 76, a 1, ad 5].[38]

Having the capacity for mind is the definition of human life. This human soul is what Aquinas calls an "actuality." It grants the capacity for mind because of the informing organization it grants to the body, but nothing besides the soul's own act of being (apart from the participation in the Being of God) accounts for the existence of the soul-form *qua* informing principle:

> . . . whatever belongs to a thing *per se* cannot be separated from it. And to form as actuality being belongs *per se*. Matter acquires actual existence precisely as acquiring a form, and its ceasing to be comes from its losing a form. But for a

---

37. See Cohen, "St. Thomas Aquinas," 193–209 for an excellent discussion of how Aquinas's epistemology is built on the conviction that the composite being resulting from the union of soul and body is involved in the process of knowing and understanding.

38. Emphasis mine.

form to be separated from itself is impossible. So, too, for a subsisting form to cease to be. (I a, Q 75, a 6, reply).

Second in the triad of reasons he gives for the incorruptibility of the rational soul is Aquinas's premise that is much like Spinoza's use of *conatus* to describe a thing's striving for permanence: "man naturally craves after permanent continuance" (*CG* II, Q 79). This is more than a mere psychological assessment on his part, for it is founded on the thesis that no "natural" condition can go unfulfilled unless something contrary to the natural orientation is introduced as a barrier to its *telos*. All things have an inner orientation to continue in existence and to flourish in their natures, but the human intellect is a special case, he contends. "While existence is desired by all, man by his understanding apprehends existence, not in the present moment only, as dumb animals do, but [understands the act of existence of things] absolutely."[39] This apprehension of existence absolutely is not possible unless the knowing power is itself participating in the absoluteness of existence, for Aquinas. The Divine, in which all things participate, grants to the world not only intelligibility but also to some creatures the power to know this intelligible world. As creatures capable of understanding and reasoning, human beings, while but the lowest type of rational beings, still participate in God's rationality. This is, Aquinas insists, not in a univocal sense, but in a limited, equivocal manner. Thus, any finite act of understanding is, in some sense, an expression of the foundational property and creative power of God's own essence *qua* Divine Mind which has omniscient permanence. Since the actual existence of contingent beings requires some prior principle to explain the fact of their finite specific existence, every contingent thing's existence is explained, in Aquinas's view, by the doctrine of participation.[40] Applying this notion of participation in God's own power to be to the act of knowing, we see even deeper into how Aquinas thinks of the act of having knowledge as a participation in that which has permanence. Just as the existent contingents that are known only exist via participation in God's act of Being, the acts of knowing those existent realities must also "exist" only as participative powers. Aquinas asserts that "[Since man can know the truth about things], man attains to permanence on the part of his soul, whereby he apprehends existence absolute and for all time."[41] The capacity to *understand* existence itself requires that the rational soul exists only as a finite expression of the absoluteness of existence. Therefore, it cannot, Aquinas reasons, be

39. *Of God and His Creatures*, 79, 4. https://ccel.org/ccel/aquinas/gentiles/gentiles.v.lxi.html.

40. The discussion of this distinction is found in chapter 3.

41. This way of casting his argument assumes what was argued above, i.e., that Thought is a fundamental aspect of Reality or Nature. Of course, an empiricist like Hume could argue that consciousness is indeed a fundamental aspect of Reality, but deny that this entails that *knowing the truth* about the way things really are is an attendant fundamental aspect of reality as well. However, here we are onto a question of such import that we cannot, in the present context, defend Thomas's (or Spinoza's) epistemological doctrine. However, it could be noted that an empiricist doctrine misses the deep intentionality involved in ideas and that ideas are always *ideas about* something. This, at least, allows for the possibility that our ideas are "in touch" or place us "in touch" with the world in itself.

corruptible and its natural striving to know is, thereby, unthwartable. To this extent, then, permanence is an intrinsic property of the contingent, created *anima intellectiva.*

Related to this is the third of Aquinas's arguments for the incorruptibility of the soul, namely that the nonexistence or cessation in existence of anything can only result from a contrary state of being that would exclude the existence of that thing. (His position about the cessation of existence being caused by something external is consonant with Spinoza's Proposition Four in the third Book of the *Ethics.*[42]) Applying this principle to the human soul explicitly in the *Summa,* Aquinas utilizes the term "soul" as a placeholder for the rational consciousness made possible by the soul qua form. He expresses this proposition as follows: "There can be no contrariety in the intellectual soul, for it receives in the manner of its own being, and there one thing does not push out another. There even our ideas of contraries are not themselves contrary, since one habit of knowledge holds them together in relationship."[43] Since there is no *contrary* state (nor could there be) that the soul could undergo *qua* principle of understanding, there is no external contrary that could be the cause of cessation of the activity of understanding that the rational soul enables for a person's existence. Hence, the soul cannot be presented with a set of conditions that could negate its existence. I take it, then, that for Thomas the mind's awareness of the demise of the body as its object, since the power of understanding was not produced by the body, is held in the "habit of knowing" that the rational soul made possible.

Based on the three arguments for the incorruptibility of our rational consciousness, being a *knower* cannot be produced by a physical process or material stuff. Although he recognizes that human cognitive processes involve two related but distinct powers—passive sensible receptive awareness and active abstractive intellection—our ideas have an intentionality to them that implies a reference beyond their own existence *qua* ideas.[44] This epistemological realism (as opposed to representationalism) is a consequence of his insistence that the world is both intelligible and intellectualizable because the world is a finite created reality that participates ontologically in God's own act of Being and Knowing. Therefore, the finite knower (whose rationality is a participatory power) is engaged in a limited but real way with knowledge of that which exists beyond the mind; and our ideas (when rightly abstracted and formed

---

42. "No thing can be destroyed except by an external cause. Proof: This proposition is self-evident, for the definition of anything affirms, and does not negate, the thing's essence: that is, it posits, and does not annul, the thing's essence. So as long as we are attending only to the thing itself, and not to external causes, we can find nothing in it which can destroy it."

43. *Habitus,* which means for Aquinas something like a condition and ongoing activity that is either given by grace or acquired through practice. This condition of acting is an exercise of agency that enables a faculty to orient itself to its proper object in a better, fuller, and more appropriate way—a way more adequate to the nature of the object and the knower.

44. Cohen, "St. Thomas Aquinas," 195–98 demonstrates that for Aquinas the mind does not receive images and have knowledge of the world "in a mental image, but in a physical likeness."

Recovering the Soul

by reason) are not the things we know, but they are "tools" by which we engage and obtain true knowledge of reality.

While it is the case, for Aquinas, that the soul is possessed of the power to enable imperishable rationality and understanding in those embodied beings informed by this substantial form, whose intellective acts are not "caused" by or emergent from bodily states, he further emphasizes that this remarkable power of the soul is not self-explanatory or self-instantiating. As indicated above, it only exists as a participatory expression of God's Being. In I a, Q 79, reply, Aquinas offers the following:

> For what is such by participation, and what is mobile, and what is imperfect always requires the preexistence of something essentially such, immovable and perfect. Now the human soul is called intellectual by reason of a participation in intellectual power; a sign of which is that it is not wholly intellectual but only in part. Moreover it reaches to the understanding of truth by arguing, with a certain amount of reasoning and movement. Again it has an imperfect understanding; both because it does not understand everything, and because, in those things which it does understand, it passes from potentiality to act. Therefore there must needs be some higher intellect by which the soul is helped to understand.
>
> Wherefore we must say that *in the soul is some power derived from a higher intellect,* whereby it is able to light up the phantasms. And we know this by experience, since we perceive that we abstract universal forms from their particular conditions, which is to make them actually intelligible. Now no action belongs to anything except through some principle formally inherent therein; as we have said above of the passive intellect. Therefore the power which is the principle of this action must be something in the soul. For this reason Aristotle (De Anima iii, 5) compared the active intellect to light, which is something received into the air: while Plato compared the separate intellect impressing the soul to the sun, as Themistius says in his commentary on De Anima iii. But the separate intellect, according to the teaching of our faith, *is God Himself,* Who is the soul's Creator, and only beatitude; as will be shown later on (90, 3; I-II, 3, 7). Wherefore the human soul derives its intellectual light from Him, according to Ps. 4:7, "The light of Thy countenance, O Lord, is signed upon us.

Since the rational soul's existence is only possible because, as an individuated act of understanding, it participates in God's own Being, the life of an individual human being, therefore, *qua* "rational animal," participates in God's Being; in the activity of understanding it is a type of analogue of God's own knowing. Such participation is for Aquinas, a purely analogous concept, because of God's aseity. Things exist *in* God's Being by being preserved and held together by God's power, but in natures other than the divine. Yet, as "ideas" these creatures share in something of God's essence, not as actual creatures but God's ideas. In the *Summa* I a, Q 18, a 4, ad 1, where he is answering the question of whether all things are "in" God, he says:

> Creatures are said to be in God in a twofold sense. In one way, so far are they are held together and preserved by the divine power; even as we say that things that are in our power are in us. And creatures are thus said to be in God, even as they exist in their own natures . . . In another sense things are said to be in God, as in Him who knows them, in which sense they are in God through their proper ideas, which in God are not distinct from the divine essence. Hence things as they are in God are the divine essence. And since the divine essence is life and not movement, it follows that things existing in God in this manner are not movement, but life.[45]

By Aquinas's further reasoning, since the human intellect is a finite, perspectival participation in God's own omniscient rational Being, God himself is the telos of the human exercise and achievement of understanding. As reason proceeds, and one grasps mentally more and more of reality, this leads to an acknowledgment of God's existence. As a gift of grace (when received by faith), the knower may come to know in a direct way even the eternal and unchanging, although in a limited manner. This capability, for Aquinas, is even more reason that human intellect could not be a physically dependent epiphenomenal act. It must be a power that is, itself, connected to the Divine in order to know the Transcendent. Aquinas rejects the notion of a universal mind in which all persons share—Aristotle's agent intellect—and insists that the active intellect is in each person in a particularized way and each person knows by a unique act of understanding.[46] Through a progression of reasoning, which is made possible by the mind's abstractive power enabled by the active intellect as a participation in God's own rational Being, a person abstracts from the particulars of experience. However, the knowledge is always "knower-specific." While the process that is engaged is the same for all people, it is obvious that not all people share simultaneously the same perspective, understanding, or ideas.

---

45. Norris Clarke describes Aquinas's notion of participation according to a three-part schema: 1) God, who is the source of Being as pure actuality, has any given reality (perfection) in an unlimited manner in virtue of the divine essence, 2) participating subjects (as mixture of act and potency) are endowed with any given perfection (including existence) in a "partial and restricted" measure (because they are created and, by definition, finite), and 3) the participating subject who is comprised of act and potency (unlike God) has the perfection from the unlimited one—the pure actuality of God's Being.

46. This finely sliced reasoning is what separates Aquinas from Avicenna on the question of whether there is one mind that is at work in all people. Aquinas believes that human knowing participates in God's power of knowing, but each person has his own power of knowing, and it is a participated power. Here again, I see a parallel with Spinoza's insistence in Book II that all Modes of Thought are Modes of God *qua* Thinking Substance, but the things that are "in the mind of God" in these Modes of Thought are not there under consideration of God *qua* Substance, but are, rather, in God insofar as these finite Modes of Thought are particular and limited by that particularity.

Aquinas's contention that while the rational soul does subsist apart from the body *qua* informing principle, it nonetheless cannot be said—as the form of the human body—to *exist* in an actual sense, as a Cartesian mind would be described. Although it does have a real essence that is not merely emergent out of or supervenient upon the embodied being that is given function by this organizing form, the knowing mind is not an entity prior to the union with matter. At the very least, the form/soul that grants function has logical priority, but the doctrine of participation in God's Being means the informing rational soul is more than logically prior but also real *as a principle of existence* prior to the existence of the rational animal, since it explains *how* the human becomes what he is. Aquinas, because of his doctrine of God as the Pure Act of Being in which all other things exist by participation, posited that the rational soul *qua* form has existence prior to being actualized in matter in the mind of God as an eternally subsistent idea. But, once God acts to create, God knows this rational soul not only as a possible existent in the Divine mind, but as an actuality of the Creator's activity. Therefore, as a principle of creation, the rational soul "subsists" and gives specific organization to certain "designated matter," but is real in itself prior to the particular entity that is so informed and organized.

Indeed, the human soul/form is part of the inherent intelligibility of the universe. Thomistically speaking, the intelligibility of the *material* universe (i.e., Thought, per Spinoza) requires that another complementary principle exist as well, what we could call the principle of knowing-the-intelligible (i.e., Thinking, per Spinoza). Both are part of the same Reality that exists apart from and potentially *in* the rational soul when it acts through the body that it informs. The rational soul, thereby, brings to the human person that is formed by it a capacity for the act of knowing-the-intelligible as a pure act of intellection, without which the universe would not be intelligible. We cannot posit any kind of rational insight about the nature of the material universe, unless the mind made possible by the rational soul is distinct from and even higher than that which is known.

> . . . we must observe that the nobler a form is, the more it rises above corporeal matter, the less it is merged in matter, and the more it excels matter by its power and its operation; hence we find that the form of a mixed body has another operation not caused by its elemental qualities. And the higher we advance in the nobility of forms, the more we find that the power of the form excels the elementary matter; as the vegetative soul excels the form of the metal, and the sensitive soul excels the vegetative soul. Now the human soul is the highest and noblest of forms. Wherefore it excels corporeal matter in its power by the fact that it has an operation and a power in which corporeal matter has no share whatever. This power is called the intellect. (I a, Q 76, a 1, reply)

Strictly speaking, the power called "intellect" that he mentions above is *in* the soul but is not a power that the soul exercises *qua* form. Rather, intellect, in this sense, is only a principle, as has been said, that the soul *qua* form produces in the entity it informs. In the *Summa* I a, Q 79, a 1, ad 1 Aquinas is clear that intellect or the act of understanding is a power of the soul and not its essence. By "power" Aquinas means it is a capacity the rational soul "communicates" or forms as part of a human person's existence as a bodily organism. Because it produces this kind of effect in a human being, the soul is sometimes referred to as the intellect by Aquinas as a short-hand designation, utilized because the intellect marks the "highest power" that the rational soul can produce in a human person. As the source that enables the capacity for discursive thought and true understanding in a human being, Aquinas argues that this rational "presubsisting" soul is an aspect of human nature not dependent upon biological life. Thus, this soul will in some sense continue to exist, even when the body ceases to live, because it subsisted prior to the existence of the body that it formed into a particular human person. Just as the material stuff of the body existed prior to being that body, the organizational information that shaped the body is in some way also antecedent. These principles not only reflect the way that God has created the world, but they also reflect that the nature of the Creation in question must *participate* in his own Being as Creator.[47] The soul thus makes intellect possible as an aspect of the human person in Aquinas's metaphysical scheme, insofar as it is itself a participation in the active intellect that is a feature of the universe's own existence.[48] Such rationality is the highest power that, *qua* organizing information, the rational soul brings to human beings.

Each individual act of being we call understanding exists as an analogue to God's act of Being qua rationality. This implies that, for Aquinas, the activity of knowing is to be understood (as it was later by Spinoza) as a principle (or an Attribute, Spinozistically speaking) that is part of Reality *per se*. The rational soul qua form of knowing, if it informs something and as a result makes it a true knower, must subsist prior to the knower because it is what enables the knowing to be possible in the human person.

47. Recall that Aquinas is insistent that in God there is no distinction between essence and existence and that God is utterly simple. So, God's act of knowing, act of creating, act of willing, act of being knowable are, in some way, all one and the same in God, while being rightly differentiated by our intellects. There is not a conflation going on in Aquinas's mind here, rather a belief that *qua* unbounded and eternal God is beyond any full comprehension by the human mind, while being, nonetheless, knowable and predicable. This is because of the doctrine of the analogy of Being that Aquinas insists upon.

48. In the following quote Aquinas's argument is not only to prove that the intellect participates in God's own being *qua* intellect, but to insist, against the Averrorists, that each human soul has in it its own particular and specific act of participation in the active intellect, not a general kind of partaking of it. Hence, he says: "no action belongs to anything except through some principle *formally inherent therein*; as we have said above of the passive intellect (*Summa*, Q 76, 1). Therefore the power which is the principle of this action must be *something in* the soul" (emphasis mine). One will have to recall, however, Aquinas's insistence that God is his own essence and his own existence in order to understand how Aquinas argues that nothing else can be a part of God's essence. God is Being and the act of being is God's essence philosophically stated, but only one act of Being can be the source of all things who do not have existence as a part of the definition of their essence. This is the basis of Aquinas's views about transcendence.

And because contingent moments of individual knowledge are not self-explanatory or self-generating, they must exist as such only because they *participate* God's power of knowing. Only perspectival and individually experienced, hence finite in understanding, a human being *qua* knower participates in God's act of Being.[49]

THE SURVIVAL OF PERSONAL IDENTITY IN AQUINAS'S THEORY

The incorruptibility of the rational soul, in Aquinas's view, is ultimately not enough to argue for, if by incorruptibility of the rational soul one simply considers it to be a formal, life-giving and function-enabling principle of existence. Aquinas is after a more robust sense of incorruptibility. He wants to demonstrate that the living personal identity of a person who exercises the noncorporeal act of understanding or knowing survives the death of the body. What Aquinas *the philosopher* had to demonstrate was how the person who is, by definition, a "rational animal" could continue in existence and exercise the power of understanding apart from being embodied. Without such an explanation, his theological belief that there is "personal" survival beyond the cessation of bodily life is philosophically untenable. He expresses the arguments against the possibility of such survival in strong terms in objections 1 through 3 in I a, Q 89, a 1: "The first point [against the idea that the rational soul could continue to exercise knowledge after death] . . .

1. It would seem that the separated soul cannot understand anything at all. For Aristotle says that the *intellectual apprehension is destroyed through the decay of some inward part.* But all the inward parts of man are destroyed in death. Therefore understanding itself is also destroyed.

2. In death the senses and the imagination are totally destroyed . . . . Therefore the soul, after death, understands nothing.

3. Again, if the separated soul understands anything, it must do so by means of species. But it does not understand by means of innate species [in the mind], since it is, from the beginning, like *a writing tablet on which as yet nothing is written* [Aristotle, *De anima* III, 4. 429b29]. Nor yet by species it abstracts from things because it has no organs of sense and imagination by means of which species are abstracted from things. Nor, again, by species previously abstracted and retained in the soul, for in this case the soul of a child would understand nothing after death. Nor, finally, by species which come from God, for this would not be the

---

49. It would be an interesting area of inquiry for a theistic philosopher to consider how the concept of God's omniscience relates to the question of individual knowledge. If God exists and is in fact omniscient, then God would have to know not only what I know, but would have to know it, in some sense, as I know it and would have to know it as adequate or inadequate and know every person's perspective and every possible person's perspective, as well as having *sub specie aeternitatis,* a knowledge of the whole and more than the whole.

natural knowledge we are talking about, but a gift of grace. Therefore the soul, when separated from the body understands nothing."

Understanding Aquinas's response to such objections requires us to consider a few issues that relate to his view of the human person's capacity for thought and self-consciousness that are essential to a human being's activity qua rational animal. First, he is clear that the state of separation that his metaphysics allows for is *praeter naturam*, i.e., it is not the "natural" state of the human soul. He describes the state of human existence he envisions: "To understand by turning to sense images is as *natural* to the soul as being joined to the body, whereas to be separated from the body is *offbeat* for its nature [*praeter naturam*], and so likewise is understanding without turning to sense images. The soul is joined to the body in order to be and act in accordance with its nature"[50] (I a, Q 89, a 1, reply). This entails that rational soul, when considered as separated from the body, cannot be considered in the fullest sense a human person. As if this were not a large enough hurdle, however, Aquinas must also, by his own definition that the *person* knows and not the soul, explain how the survival of said soul beyond the demise of the bodily aspect of the person maintains the personal identity and existence of the *knower*.

In order to demonstrate that these difficulties need not be insuperable, Aquinas offers in the same reply an analogy:

> The nature of a light body does not change, whether it is in its proper place (which is natural to it) or whether it is outside its proper place (which is besides its nature). Thus to the soul according to its mode of being when united with the body belongs a mode of understanding which turns to the sense images found in corporeal organs, whereas when separated from the body its mode of understanding, as in other immaterial substances, is to turn to things that are purely intelligible.

Such an analogy, based as it is on the medieval physics of his time, is perhaps not very helpful for us at face value, even if Aquinas and some of his readers at the time found it persuasive. But perhaps we can decipher his meaning. He is describing the true nature of the soul as a cause of the acts of understanding and reasoning that takes place in the human knower. The nature of the rational soul *qua* informing principle is to produce in a human being this kind of activity; as an informing intellectual principle, the soul's nature is to instantiate in the human person the power to know. I take it that he means by this that the organizing properties the soul communicates to the matter of the body results in a physical being capable of acts of rationality, which as acts of rationality are distinct from the purely physical properties that make him a biological creature. Because the soul qua informing principle establishes in the biological being the power to *know*, the being, insofar as we are speaking of the power to know, evinces a participation in the fundamental intelligibility of the universe that is

50. Emphasis mine.

produced by God's own act of knowing. Such a activity cannot be (as we have argued) a physical thing. Even though the human intellect is the "lowest of all intellectual substances," as Aquinas puts it, its "power of intelligence comes from the influence of divine light." The person who knows, through the power that the rational soul makes possible out of its essence, therefore, participates (analogously, not univocally) in God's knowing.[51]

The way of knowing for human beings is through discursive knowledge that develops from sensory engagement with the world and abstraction from particulars in coming to understand the nature of Reality. The soul conveys the *power* of intellectual understanding to the human person *qua* knowing agent when the soul informs matter. "Prior" to giving actual power of rationality to a living entity the soul must be, to put Aquinas's argument in contemporary jargon, something like life-giving information that orders and enables human existence to be capable of all human powers—including personal rational consciousness. The result is the soul-enabled person who is something over and above the soul qua form that has enabled the existence of a personal being capable of acts of rational insight. In this human person the power of the rational soul takes on a new meaning logically and a new existence ontologically. The exercise of the potential for consciousness and rationality was, prior to the coinherence of the soul and the body, only an inherent property-giving feature of the informing nature of the soul. It was, therefore, only a potentiality until an entity informed by the *anima intellective* was created. Now in the union this potential becomes a real property of the human person. The rational soul *qua* form has communicated its "highest power" (the potential for rationality) to the human person. But the soul is the source of this possibility; and a person is more than the soul ante-union, not less. Hence, in Aquinas's view, the knowing person is what the soul becomes in union with the body it informs. Therefore, personal experiences and insights into the nature of the world and into the existence of God become part of existence that the soul has instantiated, because the soul's informing potential is now active. Personal conscious, rational identity becomes united with the incorruptibility of the soul's nature. This is one of the meanings of *Summa* I a Q 89, a 5, reply):[52]

> But just as acts of the intellect are *principally and formally* seated in the intellect itself, but materially and in the manner of a disposition in the lower faculties [capacity for sensory awareness], so also must the same be said *of habitual dispositions [our acquired understanding and rational processes]*. Therefore as to man's present knowledge, the part that is in the lower faculties will not

51. Again, this distinction that Aquinas makes between participation analogously and univocally has a possible parallel in Spinoza. He insists that qua Modes of Thought, the ideas that a Mode has are in God, but not insofar as God is thought of in his essence. Only insofar as that Mode is a finite Mode of Thought that only exists as an "expression" of Substance is it "in God." However, it is distinct from God/Substance as an individual, and a finite and limited instance of Thought.

52. Emphasis mine.

remain in the separated soul, but *what is in the intellect will necessarily remain.* For as Aristotle says, a form [the rational soul] can be destroyed in two ways, first, in itself, when it is destroyed by its contrary, e.g., heat by cold; second incidentally, that is, by the destruction of its subject. Now it is obvious that demonstrative knowledge in *the human intellect* cannot be destroyed by the destruction of its subject, because, as shown before [I a, Q 75, a 6], the intellect is immortal . . . .

Aquinas here expresses what was described in the discussion preceding the above quote. The rational soul gives rise to an entity who, being capable of knowledge, acquires understanding and insight that once acquired become part of the essence of the person's conscious intellect. Because this soul must be understood to have a subsistence of its own that is logically prior to the person's actual existence, Aquinas contends that the subsequent thoughts, experiences, and insights that become a part of the soul-enabled person continue to exist. While the "powers" of the soul that rely on bodily cooperation (sensation, etc.) will not be operative separated from the body, the intellectual acts of human consciousness, because they do not—as intellectual acts—depend upon the body, will be maintained because they have become part of the essence of an immaterial, and therefore incorruptible, principle that itself participates in the very intelligibility of the universe that is rooted in God's own power of knowing. Thus, the personal particularity of each human being does not cease to exist, he thinks, even though the "separated soul" is not strictly speaking the full person. So, the perspectival knowledge and the individual character of the knower that is shaped in the acquisition of that knowledge becomes a part of the "presubsisting" soul in actual existence. Therefore, these cannot be lost, because perspectival intellectual true knowledge and immediate understanding, though acquired in relation to the body, never were caused to exist by the body in the soul-body *union.*[53]

As I indicated at the beginning of this section, Aquinas did not attempt to argue philosophically for the specific doctrine of the immortality of the soul, but for the closely related, yet distinct, notion of its incorruptibility. Furthermore, he did not argue for immortality, because as a philosophical theologian he embraced, analytically explained, and defended the doctrine of the resurrection of the body.[54] He did not think this doctrine, unlike his argument for the incorruptibility of the soul, was

53. One might further say that cessation of personal identity in existence is impossible because even the particularity of perspective that each person qua knower attains and entertains is part of the knowledge that is maintained in the eternal intellect of God. And since the soul *qua* form participated in God's own Being *qua* understanding, and since God's power of Thought is an inherent aspect of the universe, then personal knowledge, and even personal identity, become part of the universe of knowledge and cannot be destroyed. Therefore, even absent the body, one's personal identity is maintained, albeit in an attenuated form.

54. This doctrine is most clearly spelled out in the Bible in 1 Corinthians 15. The doctrine of an intermediate state of the soul "awaiting" resurrection is one that Aquinas inherited from Christian teaching and is found throughout the New Testament. For a good treatment of these ideas, see Cooper, *Body, Soul and Life Everlasting.*

open to philosophical demonstration *per se*. (Or as he would put it, it was not open to "natural philosophy.") It is, rather, an article of faith. So, I will not go to great lengths discussing it for our purposes. However, it should be noted that he thought this doctrine was completely consistent with his demonstration of the soul's incorruptibility and his demonstration that the rational soul is the form of the body.

We can also note that in the supplement to the *Summa's tertia pars,* he contends that the issue of how personal identity is maintained, if there is a resurrection, implies that a "new" body is going to be part of continuing personal identity. Seizing the authority of Aristotle in *Summa* III supp. Q 80 a 1, reply, Thomas argues that the soul in relation to the body is not only the formal cause of the body's existence but is, as well, the efficient cause of its existence.[55] He argues, in good Aristotelian fashion, from the example of a craftsman or artist, and describes the soul as analogous to the "art" by which an artifact or masterpiece is made. Just as everything that appears in the work of art is contained implicitly (but without explicit expression) in the "art" that guides the artist, so it is the case with the soul in relation to the body. Whatever was in the body prior to its death was (and is) contained, in a way, implicitly in the soul. What follows then is that, at the resurrection, the body will not rise again except according to the relation it bears to the rational soul. This is the same soul which originally informed the body and established the possibility of rational consciousness that now is itself informed by the identity of the human being whose existence it made possible. For a person who prior to death has received God's presence by faith in his or her existence, the immaterial intellective principle of existence (the soul now itself informed by personal experiences and knowledge) continues to participate in God's Being following bodily death and is, thereby, maintained in the Being of God. Since the soul came from God and is a participating finite expression of God's Being, in the appropriate state of "union with God," it is being "perfected." It follows that any person who by faith has been in union with God, must rise again perfected because a radically transformed soul now informs the matter of the resurrected embodied person. This is because, as Aquinas puts it, he is *thereby* repaired in order that he may obtain his ultimate perfection.[56]

55. "As stated in *De Anima* ii, 4, 'the soul stands in relation to the body not only as its form and end, but also as efficient cause.' For the soul is compared to the body as art to the thing made by art, as the Philosopher says (*De Anim. Gener.* ii, 4), and whatever is shown forth explicitly in the product of art is all contained implicitly and originally in the art. In like manner whatever appears in the parts of the body is all contained originally and, in a way, implicitly in the soul. Thus just as the work of an art would not be perfect, if its product lacked any of the things contained in the art, so neither could man be perfect, unless the whole that is contained enfolded in the soul be outwardly unfolded in the body, nor would the body correspond in full proportion to the soul. Since then at the resurrection it behooves man's body to correspond entirely to the soul, for it will not rise again except according to the relation it bears to the rational soul, it follows that man also must rise again perfect, seeing that he is thereby repaired in order that he may obtain his ultimate perfection. Consequently all the members that are now in man's body must needs be restored at the resurrection."

56. In the *Summa* III Supp, Q 79, a 2, Aquinas deals with the question of whether or not the self-same man will rise again. His argument there merely insists that it must be the self-same man

It is not my intention to defend this position, any more than I have wanted to defend Spinoza's or Aquinas's positions on immortality or incorruptibility. Rather, what I wanted to show is that his Christian doctrine is reconcilable with the larger scheme of his metaphysics. And in the final analysis, perhaps a coherence theory of truthfulness is the best we can ask of any system, given the way that competing presuppositions establish for each of us distinct starting points that lead to (sometimes radically) divergent philosophical commitments. In the final chapter, however, I want to demonstrate the explanatory power that a Thomistic-Spinozistic hylomorphic theory can bring into current philosophical discussion of human nature and existence. Explanatory power is, after all, a feature of epistemic warrant when comparing the respective adequacy of divergent philosophical answers to confounding questions.

---

that rises, but does not provide an argument for how this could be the case. It could well be that my reading of him as holding that all that is true of the person in life becomes part of the rational soul that is incorruptible could have provided him with the "explanation" that he would need. If the experiences and the history of the person are part of the "knowledge" that is maintained in the sum of all knowable things in God's intellect, and the soul continues to be a kind of information, even in the postmortem condition of separation from the body, then, once united with matter again, not only does the "same" body appear, but the same person, because the informing soul is not distinct from the history of the person that it originally informed and will (according to Aquinas) inform again. I do not think that this way of stating the matter will convince those who are not predisposed to believe in the resurrection. Indeed, it probably could not, nor should (if faith is the issue). But it might at least tie up for a Thomist a dangling existential issue regarding personal identity missing in Aquinas's treatment in the *Summa*.

9

Recovering the Soul

Insights and Implications for Contemporary Philosophy of Mind

THE OPERATING PREMISE OF this book has been that Aquinas's hylomorphism helps us interpret Spinoza's metaphysics, and that their respective theories of mind and body, therefore, have an important affinity. Such a proposal is, no doubt, surprising to most, if not all. Furthermore, I have argued, by addressing some of the critiques of their philosophies, that each respective metaphysical system is internally coherent. To that extent, I hope this volume contributes to the discipline of the history of philosophy. More crucially, however, I propose that the affinity between their hylomorphic insights be taken seriously in the dialogue and debate we have in contemporary philosophy of mind and body. Spinoza and Aquinas should not be considered members, to borrow Della Rocca's description of Spinoza, of "the illustrious company of those who have failed to solve the mind-body problem."[1] I think, instead, that they actually avoid the mind-body problem in its typical contemporary form, because they push the issue back to an even more fundamental point of philosophical exploration: how human beings exist as *living* beings the way we do in the first place. We are the result of a soul as *form,* or a *conatus* as essence, that is neither mental nor physical, but informs and enables our living existence. For this reason, we experience our lives subjectively as a unified, living, and lived reality.

Given this starting point, the issue of the mind and the body in relationship to one another is cast in a different light than the mainline functionally Cartesian categories to which Putnam alerts us. The main problem with contemporary theories of mind (and body) is that they equate (following Descartes) the soul with the mind *simpliciter.* This conclusion is avoided by hylomorphism, as it has been described. It may raise its own set of analytical challenges, but hylormorphism sets us on a different path of inquiry, and avoids the hurdles that one finds in reductionistic theories of mind and

---

1. See 177 above.

their substance dualism counterparts. Human existence is a much more complex, irreducible, and integrated reality than those options allow. The similar hylomorphism of Aquinas and Spinoza deals with this integrated complexity, because they start with Life itself as a basic feature of the world. Mind-and-body relations are a component of Life, which they treat as a first principle, not a mysterious *emergent* phenomenon out of inanimate biochemical properties and interactions. Such an embrace of Life provides another helpful course corrective for contemporary reductionist and emergentist theories about ourselves and our world. In this concluding chapter I want to point to some ways their metaphysical recognition of hylomorphism as a fundamental *living* process in the world can inform our thinking and grant us a different angle of vision by which to view, analyze, and understand our minded, embodied lives.

Putnam's claim regarding the methodologically Cartesian perspective of contemporary cognitive philosophy and science strikes me as essentially on target. This is the result of present-day approaches to deciphering our own existence that divide the discussants into two distinct epistemological camps. The natural sciences and the philosophers who take their cues from them describe human existence and our consciousness purely in terms of physical laws. Such metaphysical reductionism grants *a priori* the material world absolute priority, and hence *the* causative role in producing all else. On the other hand, nonreductionists remind reductionists that our consciousness presents data not congenial to empirical science such as qualia. Even more critically, our claims to achieve nondeterministic rational insight to truth is hard to defend on reductionist or physicalist terms. We are left with a kind of antinomy that still views our existence as described by science and analyzed philosophically as a *problem* to be solved. Further exacerbating the difficulties is the assumption that the epistemological approach of science alone deals with what is "natural." Only such a starting point would suggest to philosophers that positing any principle that is not a purely *physical* property is illicitly importing something "nonnatural," or (even worse) "supernatural." Strangely, this materialist epistemology rejects the credibility of inferential reasoning about empirical data[2] when applied contra the prevailing scientific orthodoxy. Consider the raging antipathy manifest in the declarations by many that Intelligent Design theorists are not being scientific, because only an explanation amenable to reductionist materialist terms is "scientific." This is quite an ironic claim, since the preference for scientific *naturalism* itself is not defensible, provable, or mathematically expressible by the scientific method. (Does anyone remember the demise of Logical Positivism?[3])

Mainstream scientific and philosophical reductionistic analysis unfortunately does not envelop the whole of human *Life*, nor does the question of how we are alive raise much pondering. This orientation of thought in modern philosophy finds its

2. Natural selection is, after all, an inferential interpretation, as is the concept of the metaverse (even if mathematical).

3. The claim that only empirically demonstrable statements could be meaningful itself proved to be meaningless by that definition.

roots in Descartes's original metaphysical meditations, just as the issue of mind-body dualism is the legacy of his thought. He was not the first, but his influence wedged into modern thought the possibility that living organisms and life itself are definable in completely mechanistic terms.[4] From this Cartesian mechanism of physical Life, the early years of genetic science gave it the veneer of scientific credibility, since materialists assumed that realization of DNA's role in *heredity* was the "final, killing blow to the belief that living material is deeply distinct from nonliving material."[5] This triumphalism is, however, unearned because DNA's role functions within living creatures, and apart from the Life that makes them living DNA has no function. So widespread is the materialist assumption that philosophers (and especially scientists) seem not to realize that mechanistic materialism as a starting premise of thought and pursuit of understanding is a *presupposition*, not a demonstrated truth.[6] This presupposition causes all aspects of our world to be viewed in a way that denies from the outset any nonmechanistic properties. Yet, mechanistic materialist experiments and theories have never accounted for *how* much less *why* life exists.[7] Aquinas and Spinoza, on the other hand, considered Life to be an obviously basic and foundational principle of all reality, one which could encompass the physical world of matter and bodies as well as the undeniable presence of conscious thought and reasoning.[8] It was

---

4. By defining "life" in terms of immaterial consciousness alone, Descartes (infamously?) contended that animals were merely "automata," no more than complex physical machines without experiences—and that as a result, they were the same type of thing as less complex machines like cuckoo clocks or watches. He believed this because he thought that thoughts and minds are properties of an immaterial soul. See his *Discourse on Method* (1637) and *Meditations* (1641) for his elaboration of this idea. John Cottingham has shown that Descartes couldn't quite stomach his own strict separation of man and beast ('A Brute to the Brutes': Descartes's Treatment of Animals). Descartes does speak of animals having sensations, even feeling emotions like anger and happiness. Yet, his dualism would demand that they could only do so if they possessed an immaterial soul. So, like many other philosophers (and human beings generally) such equivocations suggest that, in practice at least, Descartes saw a meaningful difference between animal life and inanimate objects.

5. Dawkins, *River Out of Eden*, 17.

6. Consider Richard Lewontin's admission: "It is not that the methods and institutions of science somehow *compel us* to accept a material explanation of the phenomenal world, but, on the contrary, that we are *forced by our a priori adherence to material causes* to create an apparatus of investigation and a set of concepts that produce material explanations, *no matter how counterintuitive*, no matter how mystifying to the uninitiated . . . for we cannot allow a Divine Foot in the door" ("Billions and Billions of Demons," 31, my emphasis).

7. Tour, "Open Letter."

8. To be clear, hylomorphism's view that life is basic does not mean that it necessarily (logically or metaphysically) was attendant with material stuff from the beginning of the universe or that it was not expressed in the universe at a later time than physical particles and material objects. One can grant matter's preliminary existence and at the same time recognize that its existence cannot explain the actualization of life on material terms. While Spinoza's "panpsychism" entails that life is and always was ubiquitous in some sense, Aquinas's Christian theological commitments would embrace that after the world of matter was established then God "infused" life into the material world. Being basic and foundational is not a temporal designation but a metaphysical one. The same applies for the presence of mind in matter.

beyond analysis—a kind of first principle. Richard Lewontin's admission of the limits of materialistic science for explaining "the evolution of cognition" apply even more to Life, since thought is a function within Life itself, hence the latter is more ontologically primary. Responding to his editor's request for a caveat to his "'unremitting attack,'" he writes:

> I have not added a last section relieving the "unremitting attack" because I cannot. It may be true that we cannot keep people from storytelling, but I cannot see that my response to that should be to tell stories. [Even developing a hypothesis to explain cognition] calling a story a hypothesis does not make it anymore scientific. We should reserve the notion of hypothesis for assertions that can be tested . . . . Finally, I must say that the best lesson our readers can learn is to give up the childish notion that everything that is interesting about nature can be understood . . . It might be interesting to know how cognition (whatever it is) arose and spread and changed, but we cannot know. Tough luck.[9]

When materialists attribute the existence of Life to hypothesized arrangements and conditions of inanimate matter arising in random spontaneity, they are simply granting mysterious, undemonstrated powers to the physical constituents of our existence.[10] As aspects of life, our thought and reasoning about our lives are reduced to physical explanations; human beings are nothing more than entities determined by the laws of chemistry and physics. This demands we ignore what is most immediately obvious to us in our own lived experience, i.e., that we live embodied lives truly "minded" and free in important ways from materialistic strictly deterministic forces. It is logically possible to consider that we might need to deny someday, as the physicalists claim, that our day-to-day experiences of having insight, being motivated, making decisions or even experiencing love are nothing in themselves but the motions of electrons and the firings of neural pathways. But logical possibility does not mean existential reality. In fact, to posit that our lived experiences are not what they seem is to engage in a nonempirical exercise of metaphysical speculation that assumes the physical is all there is and then argues that the physical is all there is. Barbara Montero has assiduously analyzed what she calls "the body problem," noting the difficulty physicalists face in describing what being physical means, if everything is physical. Her observations show the material/physical categories we have cannot divide neatly the world into dualistic categories of mind and body. Some more comprehensive scheme must be developed.[11]

Michael Morange has described the challenges for contemporary science to explain Life and living things. "Two options are open. Either the formation of the

9. Lewontin, "Evolution of Cognition," 130–31.

10. Tour, "Open Letter," para. 20. "We synthetic chemists should state the obvious. The appearance of life on earth is a mystery. We are nowhere near solving this problem. The proposals offered thus far to explain life's origin make no scientific sense."

11. Montero, "Body Problem." 183–200.

fundamental characteristics of life and of the links between them are driven by physical laws and life emerges each time favorable conditions occur, or alternatively, there is a large part of contingency in the formation of the fundamental characteristics (functionalities) and the relations between them."[12] The first solution to the question of not just what Life is but how it emerged posits that physical laws and "favorable conditions" are the causes of life, yet upon what other than *a priori* materialism should one choose option one? Alternatively, to hold onto "contingency in the formation of the fundamental characteristics" explains nothing. A movement beyond materialistic naturalism is required, which will require us to revisit the question of the nature of Reality. Though it is claimed that metaphysics is a roadblock to scientific analysis, drawing inferences to what may not be ultimately empirically demonstrable is not to give up on knowledge but to give up on undemonstrated reductionist presuppositions, since there are so many things that materialistic reductionism and reductive physicalism cannot explain and probably never will.

Thomas Nagel has brought attention to this in his work *Mind and Cosmos.* His observations are quite instructive, even if his own atheistic presuppositions cause him timidity in considering the most radical inferences to be drawn from them.[13] Noting that materialist principles will not account for life, since they cannot account for or explain what consciousness is, he confesses, "I find the confidence among the scientific establishment that the whole scenario will yield to a purely chemical explanation hard to understand, except as a manifestation of an axiomatic commitment to reductive materialism."[14] Life *and* mind are not merely physical processes nor are materialist theories of their original actualization adequate, even if they are only expressed in, through, and with the bodily existence of material organisms.

If materialism fails to explain Life and the unity of mind and body, dualistic theories of a Cartesian-style are inadequate, as well. Substance dualism depends upon introspection as the epistemic foundation of one's being essentially an immaterial soul. And substance dualists seem to assume that life is, in good Cartesian fashion, something quite mechanistic and then focus on the nature of mental substance. There exists a wide range of substance dualist approaches. So, I'll comment on two in order to indicate how hylomorphism in is a better theory. Stewart Goetz notes Substance Dualism has the advantage of being a widespread assumption in human cultures and

---

12. Morange and Falk, "Recent Evolution?," 425–38.

13. Nagel, *Last Word,* 130–31. About his resistance to theism, he states: "I am talking about something much deeper—namely, the fear of religion itself. I speak from experience, being strongly subject to this fear myself: I want atheism to be true and am made uneasy by the fact that some of the most intelligent and well-informed people I know are religious believers. It isn't just that I don't believe in God and, naturally, hope that I'm right in my belief. It's that I hope there is no God! I don't want there to be a God; I don't want the universe to be like that."

14. Nagel, *Mind and Cosmos,* 49. Earlier in the book Nagel asks, "[G]iven what is known about the chemical basis of biology and genetics, what is the likelihood that self-reproducing life forms should have come into existence spontaneously on the early earth, solely through the operation of the laws of physics and chemistry?" (6).

contends the most convincing and plausible reason for this is the experience people have of themselves as being a "simple substance that exemplifies psychological properties." This the ground of such a belief.[15] In this way, he posits it as a "basic belief."[16] Goetz's dualism contends, as well, for a kind of Kantian description in which "the soul is located as a whole in every part of space occupied by its physical body," a view termed "holistic dualism."[17] Such a version of dualism sounds quite close to hylomorphism, but is distinct in important ways, I think. It sees the *person* as a presence to or in the body—in every part—but provides little reason to see the life of the person as a fully integrated existence. It strikes me as analogous to the parallelist accounts of Spinoza that are on offer, hence suffering from some of the same shortcomings described earlier.

Richard Swinburne has also argued for a substance dualism of identity. In *The Evolution of the Soul,* we find his basic framework in which he equates the soul exclusively with what are deemed mental properties, i.e., the mind.

> "I understand by substance dualism the view that those persons which are human beings (or men) living on Earth, have two parts linked together, body and soul. A man's body is that to which his physical properties belong. If a man weighs ten stone, then his body weighs ten stone. A man's soul is that to which the (pure) mental properties belong. If a man imagines a cat, then, the dualist will say, his soul imagines a cat."[18]

Swinburne does allow that a physical body is *physically* necessary for a soul to operate. However, he contends that the body is not logically necessary.[19] Contending for such a necessary physical relationship raises big questions. The first is why the body is *physically* necessary. There are theological reasons that can be offered by a Christian philosopher such as Swinburne (or Goetz), but is this the only metaphysical account they can generate? Of course, even if the immaterial soul is "located" in every part of the body's spatial extension, the issue of how it relates to the material body is, nonetheless, still a major question. Whether we are talking about how the soul "moves" the body or how the body's sensory data processed by eyes and ears become the experiential operations of an immaterial soul it is still there. While this objection does not entail the conclusion that there cannot be an immaterial soul that is in some fashion

---

15. See Goetz, "Substance Dualism," 39.

16. Goetz, "Substance Dualism," 57. He also points out that there are non-Cartesian versions of dualism that avoid the issue of interaction.

17. Goetz, "Substance Dualism," 56. Cf. Cooper, *Body, Soul, and Life Everlasting* for a thorough development and explication of holistic dualism or dualistic holism. Holistic dualism is the proper approach for substance dualists who are also committed to Christian theism. This view is quite close to that of Augustine.

18. Swinburne, *Evolution of the Soul,* 145.

19. Swinburne, *Evolution of the Soul,* 145.

related to a material body, it does raise very substantive problems (no pun intended) for *substance* dualism.

Swinburne's treatment of Aquinas must be mentioned here, because he employs Aquinas's category *soul* in order to strengthen his own position. He says: "Aquinas's claim that we are not 'complete substances' without a body seems to me to have the great merit of bringing out just how important for human life it is that we should have a body."[20] However, his next step is to contend that while we are in some sense a composite form of life, nonetheless, we are essentially our souls. The disconnect between the soul having and using or being related to a body and being a body-mind entity because the soul has formed both and enabled both are quite different things. Swinburne's thorough arguments in *Are We Bodies or Souls?* is typical of substance dualism's view of the soul, i.e., that it is a synonym for the mind qua consciousness, rationality, and volition. This enables him to seemingly adopt a kind of emergence or actualization theory of human nature regarding the soul, so he attributes the existence of the soul to the development of the vertebrate brain structure in human beings. It is, however, a separate substance. Yet, what could possibly account for *how* the human body might so develop the capacity that the soul could emerge? Here, hylomorphism's notion of the soul as a form that actualizes life, physical organization and development of the materials of the human body, and the potentiality for mind (while not being "the mind) has greater explanatory power, while safeguarding all the claims of substance dualism.

A related, more troubling conundrum for substance dualists is how we live one life rather than two (the problem of parallelism). If the experiences of the body are different *substantively* from the experiences that the soul/mind has *of* those bodily experiences, then is this set of conscious states of awareness and understanding essentially experiences *about* those bodily events and acts? Or is it the numerically same experiences of one integrated being? It is difficult to say how the mental-soul experiences are *identically* the same as the experiences of the body. For example, is the event of birthing a baby into the world (1) the conscious experience of a human woman who becomes a mother or is it (2) an attendant conscious experience that her essential existence as a mind has of her body having an event in life. Perhaps the substance dualist will want to admit that of course she is having the experience of childbirth. If so, how are body and soul a single life, if the person is essentially her soul? Introspectively, we might sense that we are a single life (as substance dualists argue), but a philosophical account of this oneness is not immediately on offer. A "just-so" assertion is not enough. Hylomorphism, on the other hand, establishes the unity of one's consciousness and one's physical existence in foundational ways, while substance dualism (even holistic) seems to equate and reduce the soul to consciousness and volition that is present to the bodily life. Furthermore, substance dualism seems to me unable to sit comfortably with what is increasingly obvious in brain research, namely that manipulation and

20. Swinburne, *Are We Bodies or Souls?*, 84.

stimulation of regions of the brain can result in certain states of consciousness. This is not the problem of interaction or how the mind could cause actions of the body, but how we could account for the seemingly causal activity of the physical states upon the mental states. If the soul is conceived of essentially as the mind and is then considered a distinct substance and a separate entity, even if "located" through all parts of the body, why would this metaphysical relationship entail that changes in brain conditions would result is specific kinds of mental states? Hylomorphists expect to find a point of connection between the brain and mental acts. They do so while insisting that the relationship does not necessitate the conclusion that mind is the product of bodily states, because this relatedness holds as a result of the one-and-the-same-thingness of mind and body in a life instantiated by the principle of the soul.

Two other theories must be mentioned additionally: nonreductive physicalism (NRP) and emergent dualism (EmD). NRP is a denial of dualism, but insists and argues that physicalism need not entail denying that human existence has meaning, that human beings have responsibility for actions, and that human person have liberty of decision.[21] For NRP metaphysics all the "higher" activities of human persons—rationality, moral intuitions and values, religious impulses, societal/political prudence—are explainable as brain functions (as with their reductivist counterparts) but are only *in part* explainable by reference to the brain: ". . . their full explanation requires attention to human social relations, to cultural factors and, most importantly, to God's action in our lives."[22] Nancy Murphey represents a very subtle approach to this theory and contends that the way to affirm and account for these higher activities is by starting with the recognition made by philosophers of biology that the material world itself involves and forms a hierarchy of stages or ranks of complexity which has conscious, rational, moral, and spiritual human beings at or very close to the top. NRP notes, Murphey states, "that as we move up this hierarchy of complexity [from atomic physics, chemistry, and biology], we encounter genuinely new entities—atoms, molecules, cells, organisms and finally sentient and conscious organisms."[23] She and NRP also posit the concept of "downward" causation, which allows that the "higher" activities have causal effect on the physical substance that they attend.[24] However, the solutions that NRP proffers in which *causality* is two-way, while insisting that the physical is the ontological grounding of the higher activities, only solves the mind-body interaction "problem" by insisting that the microphysical events and states are not *exclusively* causal. No real explanation for how this could be so is offered, hence the nonreductive

---

21. I will use the terms "physicalism" and "materialism" interchangeably, even though some NRD theorists (especially theists) insist upon a distinction because materialism is associated with a metaphysical agenda associated with atheism, because I believe there is a critique of this theory that is not associated directly with the question of God's reality.

22. Murphey, "Nonreductive Physicalism," 116.

23. Murphey, "Nonreductive Physicalism," 117.

24. Murphey, "Nonreductive Physicalism," 115–38.

side of this version of materialism seems to be hamstrung by its own principles. The way NRP could avoid this it seems to me is by having recourse to affirming some stout and vigorous emergent element with its own proper powers that operate independently. Yet, it would have to be shown why we should believe that matter alone could be the source of such substantial emergence. Even reference to the workings of God for theistic NRPs seems occasionalistic and *ad hoc*. Hylomorphism, which takes the physical aspect of our nature's seriously and fundamentally, understands that soul is more than mind and is the formal cause of life and function in bodily life. Hence, it can account for the mind's presence with the body/brain.

Another metaphysical framework is that of EmD, which starts with the priority of the material world of atoms and molecules—just as NRP—but with an important, insightful twist.[25] William Hasker, a leading proponent of EmD, acknowledges that patently the human brain as a physical structure is simply atoms and molecules subject to the deterministic laws of physics and chemistry. He suggests, however, "given the particular arrangements of these atoms and molecules of the brain, new laws, new systems of interaction between the atoms, and so on, come into play" and play an essential role in mental activities such as "rational thought and decision making."[26] Not detectable in any arrangement less complex than that in the human brain, these "are *emergent laws*, and the powers that the brain has in virtue of the emergent laws may be termed emergent causal powers."[27] Knowing this is a provocative and debatable metaphysical claim, Hasker argues, "important facts about our mental lives cannot be explained in any other way." Further, he asserts that EmD "establishes a close connection between the mind/soul and the biological organism" which is far less robust, even shaky, in other forms of dualism.[28] The essential premise of emergent dualism is that the metaphysical appearance of the mind or soul (Hasker equates them) is the result of a level of physical complexity occurring in the atomic and molecular structure of the human animal so that the human brain can be causative of the emergence of an independent force. By this, EmD avoids the event horizon at physical death when

25. Emergentism has its dualist and monist schools. I focus on the dualism, because emergent monism strikes me as very close to nonreductive physicalism, but also because emergent dualism is quite close to, but still less successful than, hylomorphism.

26. For those who are wondering how EmD differs substantially from NRP, the description by Murphey, "Nonreductive Physicalism," 105, helps: "The difference . . . is that I am satisfied with asserting, in the case of human beings, the emergence of new causal *powers*. I would argue that he has simply gone too far . . . in postulating the mind or soul as an emergent *entity*." Emphasis mine. NRP in Murphey's case is denying the soul/mind has any essence per se that is ultimately nonphysical. Hasker wants to describe how it emerges as an essence with its own properties.

27. Hasker, "On Behalf of Emergent Dualism," 77.

28. Hasker, "On Behalf of Emergent Dualism," 78.

mental properties are always ended, which NRP does not.[29] As Hasker admits, "it is not a simple or obvious theory."[30]

It is claimed this theory harmonizes best with contemporary scientific theories of human origins, by which they invariably mean materialistic evolution. However, to simply accept that a metaphysical theory must resonate well with evolutionary paradigms is short-sighted, since there are tremendous problems that have been identified with the evolutionary paradigm as an explanation for cognition.[31] Also, emergentists simply equate the soul with the mind and contend that adequately complex material components produce the context in which the mind/soul emerges. Providing no basis for how matter and energy so-organized, EmD seems content to assume they are self-organizing in some sense. But why should we believe that about consciousness when it is not the case for Life. The view of hylomorphic soul that I contend we must recover, where an informing, life-giving principle in union with physical substrates accounts for the complexity of the body and the powers of the attendant mind, provides what EmD lacks.

Dualistic, emergent, reductive, and nonreductive approaches lack any principle, so far as I can see, to provide an analytical account adequate to explain *how* body and mind are instantiated in a living being to be what they are individually and in relation to one another. Recovering the natural principle of *form* as the life-giving, organizing influence that co-inheres in the material stuff of the body offers a new and fruitful way of envisioning mind-body relations that could be developed and move beyond the limitations of the approaches outlined above. It would, as well, I contend, be consistent with the new frontiers in genetic research, which now acknowledges there is a living process that utilizes DNA *informing* code. While providing the information necessary for all basic functions in organic life—from building proteins out of amino acids, to the folding of those proteins, to regulating the timing and expression of various processes involved with development and growth, and to the process of transcription and translation in conjunction with RNA—this information, however, is not the source of the Life itself. Although, it is irreplaceable for some entity *being* the specific kind of living organic being that it is. This code is *information,* and qua information it is not something physical, even as this information inheres in every part of our living physical existence, without losing its immaterial nature as information. However, without the living process that utilizes the DNA information it would not be information. Life needs the DNA encoded information and the DNA encoded information needs Life. This is the biological process that produces minded bodies. This entire process is analogous to

29. Murphey seems committed to the idea that our identity after death and before the resurrection in Christian theology does not need to entail any kind of ongoing continuity of personal existence (as in a soul, however understood). Rather, she argues that "God's remembering, recognizing and relating to me are essential to my post-resurrection identity" (Hasker, "On Behalf of Emergent Dualism," 187).

30. Hasker, "On Behalf of Emergent Dualism," 100.

31. Cf. Lewontin above, 226–27. See as well Nagel above, 229.

anima (the soul) that gives life and *forms* the physical material that thereby becomes a *human* body in its organized life with shape, functions, and potentialities.[32]

Three things are striking here. First, modern genetic science and biology have prescientific antecedents in the kind of hylomorphism that I have been describing in relation to Aquinas and Spinoza. Life is being manifested, but in specific, defined entities given *essential* qualities and capacities and limits through the self-same process of existence. The soul of Aquinas's metaphysics and the *conatus*-essence in Spinoza's *Ethics* describe something eerily similar. These terms name the process we now understand as vastly more complex than they could have known.

Equally intriguing is a second circumstance, namely the implications that arise from the realization that a DNA molecule is only a *medium* of information. It carries information, and along with the structure of our genes, chromosomes, and the epigenetic components communicates something analogous to instructions to our cells. This is beyond dispute today.[33] As information it is distinct from the physical structures it enables, which depend upon it. But if it is not physical, then how are we to regard it? And if the specificity of physical entities and their lives depend upon it, the physical world is not all there is. Because the information is not something that exists materially, something like Thought must be regarded as a basic principle at work in the universe and not merely a supervenient property upon an otherwise rationality-void cosmos. If Thought is, in some way, involved in the life-giving information of DNA, then just as the living process utilizing this information cannot be explained by physical properties and potentialities the process enables, the *potentiality* for rational understanding (mind) in humans that the information in this process also forms could well be directly the result of the *soul* and not the properties of matter or its sufficiently complex arrangement.[34] As was argued in chapter 2, hylomorphism is consistent with this scenario. So, one cannot really appreciate the significance of the genome without acknowledging the kind of dualism one finds in Aquinas directly and Spinoza implicitly which recognizes the "natural" presence of the soul/form or *conatus*/essence in relation to matter.[35] Aquinas and Spinoza are old witnesses to the momentousness that genetic science has for the way we should understand the *soul*.

32. That the two are mutually dependent can be seen when one realizes that even on an evolutionary model of Natural Selection there would be no survival advantage for a particular arrangement of amino acids and proteins without life being at work. But *specified* life could not be at work without them.

33. Meyer, *Signature in the Cell*, 107–11. "Although DNA does not convey information that is received, understood, or used by a conscious mind, it does have information that is received and used by the cell's machinery to build the structures critical to the maintenance of life" (109).

34. The differences in the DNA information that results in, say, a chimpanzee and its cognitive abilities and that of a human being are not simply quantitative. The nature of human abstract reasoning and self-consciousness are qualitatively different from the chimp's mental powers. Given the strong similarities between the two physically, it is a reasonable inference that the powers of human DNA information establish the mind along with the body.

35. Even nontheists could embrace this and regard DNA as containing and communicating immaterial "information." While I find his account inadequate, this seems to be the approach of Nagel in *Mind and Cosmos*.

The third salient observation is the realization that these, Aquinas's form and Spinoza's *conatus,* are conceptual bridges connecting the Spinozistic gap between Thought and Extension but do not transgress the causal barrier. While information may be *related to* Thought it is not Thought as conceived by Spinoza—the idea of a thing. The *conatus* as the organizing principle of an organism's life is also the cause of the functional drive to preserve the organism's integrity. Just as the entire process of genetic function and cellular life informs and maintains the physical life of an organism, *conatus* also equally enables and preserves the corresponding mental powers operations which attend but are not caused by the physical organization properties. In a similar way one could say that the living process that utilizes DNA forms organisms whose brains are amenable to, even if not causative of, rational thought. And *conatus* as initiating an orientation and concrete manner of an organism's existence functions precisely like the rational *form* that Aquinas asserts gives shape, function, orientation, perseverance in existence, and all physical and mental operational powers of life to a human. It involves information but is not Thought.

Perhaps this comparison of the soul to the life process that involves DNA information still does not convince contemporary thinkers that we should think rationality is not caused by a human being's *physical* brain. Here, Aquinas analyzes how we must think about this issue in a way that will do justice to a holistic understanding of human existence, which I think Spinoza might have been able to affirm.

> The *principle* of the act of understanding, which is called the soul of man, must of necessity be some kind of incorporeal and subsistent principle. For it is obvious that man's understanding enables him to know the natures of all bodily things. But, what can in this way take in things must have nothing of their nature in its own, for the form that was in it by nature would obstruct the knowledge of anything else . . . . if the intellectual *principle* had in it the physical nature of any bodily thing, it would be unable to know all bodies . . . The *principle* of understanding, therefore, which is called mind or intellect, has its own activity in which body takes no intrinsic part.

We can extrapolate an interpretation of this argument to engage current discussion about the nature of acts of cognition. He is saying that it is impossible to conceive of how understanding could be attained if we try to attribute it to be the "by-product" of any kind of physical process or property in the brain, which would qualify as what he calls "the physical nature of any bodily thing." If thought depends upon any physical process, one must conceive of mental activity, like all physical entities and their by-products, as *deterministically* produced by physical laws. If they are merely events fully describable by physics or chemistry, Thomas would argue we have lost any reason for considering our reasoning as an activity engaged in logical analysis and having a claim to truthfulness. We cannot achieve *rational insight* or "knowledge," at least insofar as we traditionally want to refer to knowledge as realizing something that is *true.* Judgments cannot be regarded as *either true or* false, if all that is involved in what we call knowledge is a physical process (brain function, considered as purely physical interactions) that operates based on strict or even nonstrict causal laws. To attempt recourse to quantum mechanics and to indeterminacy provides no relief, for indeterminacy per se cannot be a foundation for logical thought and rational insight. We are left with a self-refuting, yet unavoidable implication: Every "rational" conclusion reached would be deterministically produced, *even the theoretical judgment that all thought is a determined epiphenomenon.* There is no freedom to think, if all is physical/material. If we want to claim rational insight and understanding the mind must be regarded as rooted in something other than physical laws. Without this we find ourselves in an incoherent position. Seeing them as established by the self-same form/*conatus* which structures the brain to be amenable to rational processes in the first place has a greater explanatory power.[36]

Aquinas and Spinoza described Thought, just as they did Life, as a fundamental feature of Reality, rather than a supervenient property. In conjunction with their notions of form/*conatus* this offers us another conceptual lens through which we might view the foundation of mind and body identity. As has been noted, DNA is arguably a type of information that is analogous in modern terms to the older concept form/*conatus*. Spinoza and Aquinas would argue that the obvious nature of DNA as a conveyor of information requires us to embrace—*as a part of the philosophy of nature*—an obvious truth: that information requires an explanation of its origin, a source, especially meaningful information, the kind that can produce outcomes as is the case with DNA. Meaningful information is hard to account for, if one assumes a random, meaningless, and "thought-lacking" process to explain the development of life. And the DNA "code" is meaningful, it communicates processes to amino acids and to all other physical parts of the organism that will not exist without that information.[37] Hence,

36. If one were to suggest that a computer functions on strict laws of physics in a deterministic fashion to arrive at truthfulness, and therefore the critique being suggested fails, one could observe that a computer does nothing apart from a "software" program that establishes the principles upon which the computer will function. Hence, we can ask, perhaps, how the programming interfaces with the hardware, but we cannot deny that the program establishes the possibilities of operation for the computer. And the program plus the software is only an extension of the rationality of its designers and those who use them. As Hasker says, "it is no more an independent source of rational thought than a television set is an independent source of news and entertainment" (Hasker, *Metaphysics*, 49). This would strongly suggest that the materialistic model, which is implicitly rejected in Aquinas's doctrine of the intellectual soul as "something" that performs nonphysical operations, still does not account for insight *qua* insight. Something else must account for how our thoughts achieve rational understanding, unless we want to give up altogether the idea that we actually think.

37. The distinction between information as meaningful (semantic information) and unmeaningful (Shannon) information is noted thoroughly in Meyer, *Signature in the Cell*, 85–90. Also, see Stegmann, "Genetic Coding Reconsidered" for a description of the historical usage of the term "code" to refer to the abstract symbolism involved in the process involved in DNA. For an analysis of how proteins function, see Scaiewicz and Levitt, "Language of the Protein Universe." In it they describe biological information in language-like terms: ". . . the vocabulary (domains) of proteins is built from an alphabet of amino acids . . . a process governed by hierarchical rules (grammar), that determine the structure and

Thought qua Attribute of *Deus sive Natura* (Spinoza) or Rationality as participation in God's act of Being (Aquinas) is a fundamental aspect of the "natural" world. We need such an insight to account for how encoded information is woven into the fabric of the natural world. Additionally, the information, as Aquinas would say, subsists prior to the organism, even though it is established in actual existence in the organism. The fact that the genetic information creates the organism via previous living organisms (parents or previous cells that divide) is not a problem for hylomorphism. These are efficient causes that imply no infinite regress. So, we still face the question of the most reasonable explanation for the origin of the genetic information and the organic life involved in the process of Life and the instantiation of living creatures. Is it inanimate matter or a divine maker/source?

Many are wary of positing, to use Spinoza's terminology, Thought as a fundamental Attribute of the natural world. Yet, upon what is the *encoded* or *informing* nature of DNA logically dependent? The fear of posing such an Attribute because it implies a "Thinker" as the source of such Thought-dependent information seems to me a rather unphilosophical way of approaching the search for insight into our existence. Only someone who has in an a priori fashion assumed that physicalism or mechanistic materialism must be true or who wants it to be true would, I think, dismiss it out of hand. The question of God (or god) is quite philosophically reasonable otherwise. Science has shown that DNA carries information and the analogy of information as *form* in comparison with hylomorphism presents us with a need to reorder how we think about and analyze the universe and the living organisms that populate it. Thought is implied in the question of the source of the information of DNA and the living process of cellular transcription and translation. An honest philosophical response is "so be it," because an honest questioner should not rule out the idea from start simply because he wants to avoid bringing God into the discussion.[38] The premise that Thought should be understood as ontologically ultimate, while unsettling for some, provides a better explanatory base for contemporary mind-body discussions. And those who claim that hylomorphism is incoherent must show why it is. But I think that they would be begging the question by assuming "ontological physicalism."

This "new" way forward shows how to avoid thinking about the nature of mind in the universe and in human experience as tacking another level of reality upon an otherwise lifeless and thoughtless world. Thought, as much as Life, is a fundamental basic ontological reality. We participate in this and are, thereby, more than our bodies, but we are not other than them. Our own *experience* of ourselves that includes mind and body as "one and the same thing" is due to the kind of living things we are. There are dual

hence the biological function of proteins" (51). Most of the arguments against regarding the Intelligent Design claims of DNA as information concern whether "mind" can be inferred as the source. See Shallit's "Stephen Meyer's Bogus Information Theory" for a strong critique of Meyer's ideas.

38. Philosophy (and even science) ought to be interested in whether some concept of "God" is valid. It is not a hindrance to scientific pursuits to explain function and process. Nor does it hinder philosophical pursuits of metaphysical explanations. It is simply, perhaps, the best inference available.

aspects of our lives—body or mind—by which we might regard ourselves in any given analysis, but this does not pose the mind-body problem. Rather, it manifests for us the irreducible complexity of our existence as beings that participate in a universe in which equally Thought and Extension (as Spinoza would say) are ontological fundaments.[39]

Colin McGinn has argued that the well-rehearsed difficulty of mind-body suggests "the question must arise as to whether human minds are *closed* with respect to certain true explanatory theories [about mind-body relations]."[40] McGinn's argument is persuasive in its focus, but it could be asked whether the closure he notes is not the result of our being finite, contingent creatures, endeavoring to analyze the "system" of our own existence. Being composed by the system, even our capacity for rational insight depends upon the system. Therefore, a large dose of epistemic humility is in order. We might get a glimpse of the nature of the system if something about us can "transcend" the system. This requires the rejection of a materialistic/physicalist ontology to affirm intellect has some feature(s) not dependent upon a materialist set of conditions. Perhaps the problem for many is not just *what* we are considering in the analysis of mind-body relations, but their materialistic starting points. Kim argues that if the ontological priority of the physical is not presumed, then one must allow "that there are things in the space-time world other than physical things, *like Cartesian souls*, or at least that some things in the world have certain properties that are independent of their physical nature."[41] Yet, we have much evidence that the *natural* world (of which the physical is a part) only operates because certain "nonphysical" principles enable it. With so many reasons to doubt the adequacy of physicalist accounts to explain the nature, development, and exercise of our human mental powers, it is reasonable to suggest that the principle that makes the body possible is also what makes—in a simultaneous action—the mind a potentiality in human beings. We would do well to pursue what Edward Feser has called for—a reclamation of the "philosophy of nature." This bridges the purported chasm between scientific inquiry and metaphysics.[42] Hylomorphism is such a philosophy and grants a much better explanation for the life of the body and its functions and strivings, as well as the reality of mind that results *in union with the body* from this kind of soul.

39. While I cannot expound this here, such a philosophical perspective as that represented in my interpretation of Aquinas could, I think, be embraced by theistic philosophers, especially if they are Christians. To argue that the soul *qua* form is "natural" to the world and that all of the natural world "participates" in the Being of God, need not entail that one give up religious beliefs that are traditionally established in doctrines such as "transcendence" and "immortality." Rather, it simply would entail that they embrace a richer notion of what the "physical world" and the "natural world" are. God could always be "beyond" our world's ontology (transcendent) and the "soul" could be nonetheless seen as immortal in the metaphysics offered here. But the kind of Augustinian/Cartesian dualism that has marked much of Christian reflection might have to go.

40. McGinn, "Can We Solve?," 544.

41. Kim, *Philosophy of Mind*, 12, my emphasis.

42. Feser, *Aristotle's Revenge*, 3–11.

Admittedly, what I have presented is only suggestive of how the hylomorphism we have examined in Spinoza's and Aquinas's metaphysics provides needed tools for the philosophy of human nature and the relationship between body and mind. Recognizing the living process that utilizes the information of DNA, that alone makes DNA information truly meaningful, we might find that contemporary science has placed us, after all, closer to that hylomorphism than might otherwise be supposed. Recovering the hylomorphic "soul" is not an antiquated notion and can enable us to look with newly opened eyes at the mystery of human origins and human existence. Recognizing the need to push back the theoretical questions about the relationship between mind and body to the prior, more basic question of what it really takes for an organism such as a human being to be endowed with rationality, we have a richer journey ahead. This will require an embrace of a moderate dualism, not of mind and body, but of soul/*conatus* as *form* and matter. Aquinas and Spinoza in this respect serve well as we recognize that a human being does not *have* a mind and a body nor relates to a body as a mind but is essentially a rationally physical and physically rational single, united "one and the same thing." Interaction is no longer an issue, because the human *person* is the locus of all that occurs; and we recognize that the soul is not a synonym for mind nor is it the person, but the soul makes a person possible. From the original informing life-energy that made personal life possible in union with the body *emerges* a human individual person, who then brings development to the original life-giving principle, as the personal life made possible by the soul engages experiences and insights and character that all become part of the life that is being lived. The soul then "becomes" an embodied person, as I outlined in the previous chapter. Seeing this might help us to understand more deeply Wittgenstein's observations about a human person: "My attitude towards him is an attitude towards a soul. I am not of the *opinion* that he has a soul." And *qua* form/*conatus* the soul as it established the person is, as well, the best account of the mind's presence with the body as "one and the same thing." So, we can say, again with Wittgenstein, "the human body is the best picture of the human soul."[43]

The failure of contemporary philosophy to deal adequately with the enigma of human existence is grounded in the methodological dualism that Putnam observed, which bifurcates the wonder of being human and presumes materialism as its starting point. To embrace the broader implications of this book's comparative study of Aquinas and Spinoza and acknowledge the reality in human existence of substantial form or conatic essence as a feature of the way that living things are what they are–especially humans—will open philosophical considerations that may seem "new" but are actually quite old. The concept "person," recognized as more than a psychologically functional description naming certain phenomenal expressions, enters again into consideration as a metaphysical concept. Even more importantly, we need to jettison the fear of the Divine haunting the house. As a historical matter, the similarities between Aquinas and Spinoza are at least intriguing and perhaps helpful for interpretive

43. Wittgenstein, *Philosophical Investigations*, 178.

reasons. Philosophically, their angle of vision for metaphysical analysis of the mind-body "problem" seems to fit with current scientific observations about genetics and biological life. The questions become different, possibly harder, but more comprehensive. Recovering the soul, therefore, is the most philosophically appropriate and the most human thing we can do.

Bibliography

PRIMARY SOURCES

Aquinas's Works

Aveline, Francis. "Matter." *New Advent*. http://www.newadvent.org/cathen/10053b.htm.

De Ente et Essentia. https://isidore.co/aquinas/DeEnte&Essentia.htm.

De Principiis Naturae. https://isidore.co/aquinas/DePrincNaturae.htm.

De Unitate Intellectus contra Averroistas. https://Isidore.co/Aquinas/English/DeUnitateIntellectus.htm#

De Veritate. Turin: Marietti, 1949.

Fathers of the English Dominican Province, trans. *The Summa Theologica of St. Thomas Aquinas*. New Advent, 2017. http://www.newadvent.org/summa/.

Maurer, Armand, trans. *On Being and Essence*. Toronto: The Pontifical Institute of Mediaeval Studies, 1968.

McDermott, Timothy, ed. *Aquinas: Selected Philosophical Writings*: Translated by Timothy McDermott. Oxford: Oxford University Press, 1993.

Of God and His Creatures. https://ccel.org/ccel/aquinas/gentiles/gentiles.v.lxi.html.

Pegis, Anton, ed. *Introduction to Saint Thomas Aquinas*. New York: Random House, 1965.

The Soul (De Anima). Translated by John Patrick Rowan. London: Herder, 1949.

Summa contra Gentiles. Translated by Joseph Rickaby. https://maritain.nd.edu/jmc/etext/gc.htm.

Summa Theologiae. Blackfriars edition. New York: McGraw-Hill, 1967.

Super Boethium de Trinitate, https://isidore.co/aquinas/english/BoethiusDeTr.htm#.

Suttor, Timothy, trans. *Thomas Aquinas: Summa Theologiae: Man* vol 11. 61 vols. London: Eyre & Spottiswoode, 1970.

Spinoza's Works

Benedict de Spinoza. Translated by. R. H. M. Elwes. New York: Dover, 1955.

Feldman, Seymour. *The Ethics*. Translated by Samuel Shirley. Indianapolis: Hackett, 1992.

Meijer, R. W., ed. *Ethica ordine geometrico demonstrate*. http://home.tiscali.be/rwmeijer/spinoza.

———. *Tractatus de Intellectus Emendatione*. http://home.tiscali.be/rwmeijer/spinoza.

Works of Spinoza: A Theologico-Political Treatise and A Political Treatise. Translated by R. H. W. Elwes. New York: Dover, 1955.

OTHER WORKS

Ackrill, J. L., ed. *A New Aristotle Reader*. Princeton: Princeton University Press, 1987.

Adler, Mortimer. *Ten Philosophical Mistakes*. New York: Touchstone, 1985.

Allen, Reginald E., ed. *Greek Philosophy: Thales to Aristotle*. New York: Free Press, 1966.

Allison, Henry. *Benedict De Spinoza*. Boston: Twayne, 1975.

Anscombe, G. E. M., and Peter Geach. *Three Philosophers: Aristotle, Aquinas, Frege*. Oxford: Blackwell, 2002.

Antony, Louise. "Anomalous Monism and the Problem of Explanatory Force. *Philosophical Review* 98 (April 1989) 153–87.

Aquila, Richard E. "The Identity of Thought and Object in Spinoza." *Journal of the History of Philosophy* 16.3 (July 1978) 271–88.

Augustine. *The Trinity*. Translated by Edmund Hill. Brooklyn, NY: New City, 1991.

Aveling, Frances. "Matter." *New Advent*. http://www.newadvent.org/cathen/10053b.htm.

Balz, Albert G. A. *Idea and Essence in the Philosophy of Hobbes and Spinoza*. New York: AMS, 1967.

Bennett, Jonathan. "Eight Questions about Spinoza." In *Spinoza on Knowledge and the Human Mind,* edited by Yirmiyahu Yovel and Gideon Seagal, 2:11–26. 2 vols. Leiden: Brill, 1993.

———. *A Study of Spinoza's Ethics*. Indianapolis: Hackett, 1984.

Broad, C. D. *Five Types of Ethical Theory*. London: Routledge & Kegan Paul, 1930.

Clarke, W. Norris. *Explorations in Metaphysics: Being–God–Person*. Notre Dame: University of Notre Dame Press, 1994.

Cohen, Sheldon. *Aristotle on Nature and Incomplete Substance*. New York: Cambridge University Press, 1996.

———. "St. Thomas Aquinas on the Immaterial Reception of Sensible Forms." *The Philosophical Review* 91.2 (1982) 193–209.

Collins, Francis S. *The Language of God: A Scientist Presents Evidence for Belief*. New York: Free Press, 2006.

Cooper, John. *Body, Soul and Life Everlasting: Biblical Anthropology and the Monism-Dualism Debate*. Grand Rapids: Eerdmans, 1989.

Copleston, Frederick. *A History of Philosophy Vol. II.* 11 vols. 1962. Reprint, New York: Bantam Doubleday Dell, 1993.

———. *Thomas Aquinas*. New York: Barnes & Noble, 1976.

Cornford, Francis M. *Plato and Parmenides*. London: Kegan Paul, 1939.

Cottingham, John. "A Brute to the Brutes: Descartes' Treatment of Animals." *Philosophy* 53.201 (1978) 551–59.

Cottingham, John, et al., eds. *The Philosophical Writings of Descartes* 3 vols. New York: Cambridge University Press, 1984.

Craig, William Lane. *The Kalam Cosmological Argument*. Eugene, OR: Wipf & Stock, 2000

Curley, Edwin. *Behind the Geometrical Method*. Princeton: Princeton University Press, 1988.

———. *Spinoza's Metaphysics: An Essay in Interpretation.* Cambridge: Harvard University Press, 1969.

Davidson, Donald. "Spinoza's Causal Theory of the Affects." In *Desire and Affect: Spinoza as Psychologist*, edited by Yirmiyahu Yovel, 95–112. New York: Little Room, 2000.

Davies, Brian. *The Thought of Thomas Aquinas.* New York: Oxford University Press, 1992.

Dawkins, Richard. *River Out of Eden: A Darwinian View of Life.* New York: Basic, 1995.

Delahunty, R. J. *Spinoza.* London: Routledge and Kegan Paul, 1985.

Della Rocca, Michael. *Representation and the Mind-Body Problem in Spinoza.* Oxford: Oxford University Press, 1996.

———. "Spinoza's Metaphysical Psychology." In *The Cambridge Companion to Spinoza*, edited by Don Garret, 192–266. New York: Cambridge University Press, 1995.

Dewan, Lawrence. "Aristotle as a Source for St. Thomas's Doctrine of Esse." *The Thomistic Institute*, 2000. https://maritain.nd.edu/jmc/tioo/dewan.htm.

Dillon, Thomas E. "The Real Distinction between Essence and Existence in the Thought of St. Thomas Aquinas." PhD diss., Notre Dame University, 1977.

Dobie, Robert J. "Incarnate Knowing: Theology and the Corporeality of Thinking in Thomas Aquinas's *De Unitate Intellectus Contra Averroistas.*" *The Thomist* 77.4 (October 2013) 497–529.

Donagan, Alan. "Spinoza's Proof of Immortality." In *Spinoza: A Collection of Critical Essays*, edited by Marjorie Grene, 241–58. Garden City, NY: Doubleday, 1973.

Feser, Edward. *Aristotle's Revenge: The Metaphysical Foundations of Physical and Biological Science.* Neunkirchen-Seelscheid, Germany: Editions Scholasticae, 2019.

Feuer, Lewis. *Spinoza and the Rise of Liberalism.* Boston: Beacon, 1958.

Flanagan, Owen. *The Problem of the Soul.* New York: Basic, 2002.

Fraser, Kyle A. "Aristotle on the Separation of Species-Form." *Animus* 4 (1999). https://docslib.org/doc/3806410/aristotle-on-the-separation-of-species-form.

Garrett, Don. "Spinoza's Ontological Argument." *Philosophical Review* 88 (April 1979) 198–223.

———. "Teleology in Spinoza and Early Modern Rationalism." In *New Essays on the Rationalists*, edited by Rocco Gennaro and Charles Huenemann, 310–36. Oxford: Oxford University Press, 1999.

Garrigou-Lagrange, Reginald. *Reality: A Synthesis of Thomistic Thought.* Translated by Patrick Cummins. London: Herder, 1950.

Geroult, Martial. *Spinoza, Vol. 1.* 2 vols. Paris: Aubier-Montaigne, 1968.

Gilson, Etienne. *The Christian Philosophy of St. Thomas Aquinas.* Notre Dame: University of Notre Dame Press, 1994.

———. *The Elements of Christian Philosophy.* New York: Doubleday, 1960.

Goetz, Stewart. "Substance Dualism." In *In Search of the Soul: Four Views of the Mind-Body Problem*, edited by Joel B. Green and Stuart L. Palmer, 33–74. Downers Grove: IVP Academic, 2005.

Goichon, A. M. *La Distinction de l'Essence et de l'Existence d'apres Ibn Sina.* Paris: Desclee de Brouwer, 1937.

Goyette, John. "Substantial Form and the Recovery of an Aristotelian Natural Science." *The Thomist* 66.4 (October 2002) 519–33.

Gracia, Jorge. *Individuality: An Essay on the Foundations of Metaphysics.* Albany: State University of New York Press, 1988.

Green, Joel B., and Stuart L. Palmer, eds. *In Search of the Soul: Four Views of the Mind-Body Problem.* Downers Grove, IL: IVP Academic, 2005.

Gullan-Whur, Margaret. *Within Reason: A Life of Spinoza*. New York: St Martin's, 2000.

Guttenplan, Samuel ed. *A Companion to the Philosophy of Mind*. Oxford: Blackwell, 1995.

Haecker, Theodor. *Vergil: Vater des Abendlandes*. Frankfurt: Fischer Bucherei, 1958.

Hampshire, Stuart. *Spinoza*. New York: Penguin, 1951.

———. "Spinoza's Theory of Human Freedom." *The Monist* 55.4 (October1971) 554–66.

Haserot, Francis S. "Spinoza's Definition of Attribute." *Philosophical Review* 62.4 (1953) 499–513.

Hasker, William. *Metaphysics: Constructing a World View*. Downers Grove, IL: InterVarsity, 1983.

———. "On Behalf of Emergent Dualism." In *In Search of the Soul: Four Views of the Mind-Body Problem*, edited by Joel B. Green and Stuart L. Palmer, 75–114. Downers Grove: IVP Academic, 2005.

Hegel, G. W. F. "Lectures on the History of Philosophy: Locke." http://dbanach.com/archive/mickelsen/locke_001.html.

Heraclitus. *Fragments: The Collected Wisdom of Heraclitus*. Translated by Brooks Haxton. New York: Penguin Putnam, 2001.

Hoffman, Paul. "The Unity of Descartes Man." *Philosophical Review* 95.3 (1986) 339–70.

Holveck, John. "Aquinas' Interpretation and Use of Aristotle's Theory of Matter." PhD diss., Duquesne University, 1973.

Hope, Richard, trans. *Aristotle's Metaphysics*. Ann Arbor: The University of Michigan Press, 1963.

Horn, Walter. "Substance and Mode: A Spinozistic Study." PhD. diss., Brown University, 1978.

Jacquet, Chantal. *Affects, Actions and Passions in Spinoza: The Unity of Body and Mind*. Translated by Tatiana Reznichenko. Edinburgh: Edinburgh University Press, 2018.

Jarrett, Charles. "The Logical Structure of Spinoza's *Ethics*, Part I." *Synthese* 3 (1978) 15–65.

Jenks, Linda P. "Aquinas on the Soul: Substantial Form and Subsistent Entity." PhD diss., University of California-Irvine, 1985.

Joachim, H. H. *A Study of the Ethics of Spinoza*. Oxford: Oxford University Press, 1901.

Jonas, Hans. "Spinoza and the Theory of Organism." In *Spinoza: A Collection of Critical Essays*, edited by Marjorie Grene, 259–78. Garden City, NY: Doubleday, 1973.

Kenny, Anthony. "Aquinas: Intentionality." In *Philosophy Through Its Past*, edited by Ted Honderich, 78–96. New York: Penguin, 1984.

———. *Aquinas on Mind*. London: Routledge, 1993.

———. *The Metaphysics of Mind*. Oxford: Oxford University Press, 1992.

Kim, Jaegwon. *Philosophy of Mind*. Boulder, CO: Westview, 1998.

Klima, Guyla. "Aquinas's Theory of the Copula and the Analogy of Being." *Logical Analysis and History of Philosophy* 5 (2002) 159–76.

———. "Man = Body + Soul: Aquinas's Arithmetic of Human Nature." In *Philosophical Studies in Religion, Metaphysics, and Ethics: Essays in Honour of Heikki Kirjavainen*, edited by Timo Koistinen and Tommi Lehtonen, 257–74. Helsinki: Luther Agricola Society, 1997.

Kneale, Martha. "Eternity and Sempiternity." In *Spinoza: A Collection of Critical Essays*, edited by Marjorie Grene, 227–41. Garden City, NY: Doubleday, 1973.

Koons, Robert C. "Against Emergent Individualism." In *The Blackwell Companion to Substance Dualism*, edited by Jonathan J. Loose et al., 377–93. Hoboken, NJ: Wiley & Sons, 2018.

———. "Forms Are Not Structures: How Grounding Theory Illuminates Hylomorphism." https://www.academia.edu/33470465/Forms_are_not_Structures_How_Grounding_Theory_Illuminates_Hylomorphism.

———. "Multi-Sacle Realism and Ontological Escalation: How the Quantum Revolution Has Vindicated Aristotle," https://www.academia.edu/11327130/Ontological_Escalation_ How_Quantum_Theory_Vindicates_Aristotle.

Kulstad, Mark, and Laurence Carlin. "Leibniz's Philosophy of Mind." *The Stanford Encyclopedia of Philosophy* (Winter 2020 Edition). Edited by Edward N. Zalta. https:// plato.stanford.edu/archives/win2020/entries/leibniz-mind/>.

Levin, Dan. *Spinoza: The Young Thinker Who Destroyed the Past.* New York: Weybright and Talley, 1970.

Lewontin, Richard. "Billions and Billions of Demons." Review of *The Demon-Haunted World: Science as a Candle in the Dark,* by Carl Sagan. *The New York Review of Books,* January 9, 1997. https://www.nybooks.com/articles/1997/01/09/billions-and-billions-of-demons/.

———. "The Evolution of Cognition: Questions We Will Never Answer." In *An Invitation to Cognitive Science* 4, edited by Daniel N. Osherson et al., 106–32. Cambridge: MIT Press, 1998:

Marck, Adrien, et al. "Humans at Maximum Limits for Height, Lifespan and Physical Performance, Study Suggests." *Science Daily*, December 6, 2017. www.sciencedaily.com/ releases/2017/12/171206122502.htm.

Matson, Wallace I. "Spinoza's Theory of Mind." *The Monist* 55 (October 1971) 567–78.

Maxwell, Vance. "The Dialectic of Enlightenment: A Critique of Recent Hume-Spinoza Scholarship. *Animus* 7 (2002). https://www2.grenfell.mun.ca/animus/OLD_ SITE/2002vol7/maxwell7.pdf.

McGinn, Colin. "Can We Solve the Mind Body Problem?" In *Problems in Mind: Readings in Contemporary Philosophy of Mind,* edited by Jack S. Crumley II, 539–52. Mountain View, CA: Mayfield, 2000.

Melamed, Yitzhak Y. "Causes of Our Belief in Free Will: Spinoza on Necessary, Innate, Yet False Cognition." In *Spinoza's Ethics: A Critical Guide*, edited by Yitzhak Y. Melamed, 121–41. https://philarchive.org/archive/MELTCO-14.

Meyer, Stephen C. *Signature in the Cell: DNA and the Evidence for Intelligent Design.* New York: Harper Collins, 2009.

Miller, Jon. "Spinoza's Axiology." *Oxford Studies in Early Modern Philosophy* 2 (2005) 149–72.

Montero, Barbara. "The Body Problem." *Noûs* 33.2 (1999) 183–200.

———. "Post-Physicalism." *Journal of Consciousness Studies* 8.2 (2001) 61–80.

Morange, Michel, and Raphael Falk. "The Recent Evolution of the Question 'What Is Life?'" *History and Philosophy of the Life Sciences* 34.3 (2012) 425–38.

Murphey, Nancy. "Nonreductive Physicalism." In *In Search of the Soul*, edited by Joel B. Green and Stuart L. Palmer, 115–51. Downers Grove, IL: IVP Academic, 2005.

Nagel, Thomas. *The Last Word*. Oxford: Oxford University Press, 1997.

———. *Mind and Cosmos: Why the Materialist NeoDarwinian Conception of Nature Is Almost Certainly False.* New York: Oxford University Press, 2012.

O'Callaghan, John. "Aquinas Rejection of Mind, contra Kenny." *The Thomist* 66.1 (January 2002) 15–60.

———. Concepts, Beings, and Things in Contemporary Philosophy and Thomas Aquinas." *The Review of Metaphysics* 53 (September 1999) 69–98.

Odegard, Douglas. "The Body Identical with the Human Mind: A Problem in Spinoza's Philosophy." *The Monist* 55.4. (October 1971) 579–601.

Owen, G. E. L. "Logic and Metaphysics in Some Earlier Works of Aristotle." In *Plato and Aristotle in the Mid-fourth Century*, edited by Ingeman During, 180–200. Goteborg, Sweden: Humanities, 1960.

Owens, Joseph. *The Doctrine of Being in the Aristotelian Metaphysics.* Toronto: Pontifical Institute of Mediaeval Studies, 1963.

Pasnau, Robert. *Thomas Aquinas on Human Nature: A Philosophical Study of Summa Theologiae, 1a 75–89.* Cambridge: Cambridge University Press, 2001.

Payne, Andrew. "Garcia and Aquinas on the Principle of Individuation." *The Thomist* 68 (October 2004) 545–75.

Pearcey, Nancey R. "DNA: The Message in the Message." *First Things* 64 (June/July 1996). https://www.firstthings.com/article/1996/06/002-dna-the-message-in-the-message.

Pegis, Anton. *At the Origins of the Thomistic Notion of Man: Augustinian Lectures 1962.* Philadelphia: Villanova University Press, 1963.

Peterson, John. "Reductionism in Metaphysics: A Mistake in Logic." *The Thomist* 64.2 (April 2000) 301–8.

Putnam, Hilary. *The Threefold Cord: Mind, Body, and World.* New York: Columbia University Press, 2002.

Russell, Bertrand. *Problems of Philosophy.* Oxford: Oxford University Press, 1959.

Scaiewicz, Andrea, and Michael Levitt. "The Language of the Protein Universe." *Current Opinion in Genetics and Development* 35 (December 2015) 50–56.

Searle, John. "Searle: "Why We Are Not Computers." In *Other Minds: Critical Essays 1969–1994,* edited by Thomas Nagel, 96–111. Oxford: Oxford University Press, 1995.

Shallit, Jeffrey. "Stephen Meyer's Bogus Information Theory." *Recursivity,* January 13, 2010. https://recursed.blogspot.com/2009/10/stephen-meyers-bogus-information-theory.html.

Shmueli, Efraim. "Thomas Aquinas' Influence on Spinoza's Concept of Attributes." *Journal of Religious Studies* 6–7 (Fall 1978—Spring 1979) 61–72.

Skirry, Justin. "Rene Descartes: The Mind-Body Distinction." *The Internet Encylopedia of Philosophy.* https://iep.utm.edu/rene-descartes-mind-body-distinction-dualism/.

Sokolowski, Robert. "Formal and Material Causality in Science." *Proceedings of the American Catholic Philosophical Association* 69 (1995) 57–67.

Spinoza, Benedict de. *The Chief Works of Benedict De Spinoza: A Theologico-Political Treatise and a Political Treatise.* 2 vols. Translated by R. H. M. Elwes. New York: Dover, 1951.

Sprigge, Timothy. "Spinoza: His Identity Theory." In *Philosophy Through its Past,* edited by Ted Honderich, 145–74. New York: Penguin, 1984.

Stegmann, Ulrich E. "Genetic Coding Reconsidered: An Analysis of Actual Use." *The British Journal for the Philosophy of Science* 67.3 (September 2016) 707–30.

Swinburne, Richard. *Are We Bodies or Souls?* Oxford: Oxford University Press, 2019.

———. *The Evolution of the Soul.* New York: Oxford University Press, 1997.

Tour, James. "An Open Letter to My Colleagues." *Inference* 3.2 (August 2017). http://inference-review.com/article/an-open-letter-to-my-colleagues.

Ury, M. William. *Trinitarian Personhood: Investigating the Implications of a Relational Definition.* Eugene, OR: Wipf & Stock, 2001.

Von Dunn-Borkowski, Stanislus. *Der Junge de Spinoza.* Aschendorff: Muenster, 1920.

Wilkes, Kathleen. "Psuche versus the Mind." In *Essays in Aristotle's De anima,* edited by Martha Nussbaum and A. O. Rorty, 109–28. Oxford: Clarendon, 1992.

Williams, Bernard. "Hylomorphism." http://www.uwichill.edu.bb/bnccde/PH19c/hylomorphism.html.

Wippel, John F., and Allan B. Wolter, eds. *Medieval Philosophy: From St. Augustine to Nicholas of Cusa.* New York: Free Press, 1969.

Bibliography

———. *Metaphysical Themes in Thomas Aquinas.* Studies in Philosophy and the History of Philosophy 10. Washington, DC: Catholic University of America Press, 1995.

Wittgenstein, Ludwig. *Philosophical Investigations.* Translated by G. E. M. Anscombe. New York: MacMillan, 1957.

Wolfson, Harry A. *The Philosophy of Spinoza: Unfolding the Latent Processes of His Reasoning,* 2 Vols. Cambridge: Harvard University Press, 1934.

Zukav, Gary. *The Dancing Wu Li Masters.* New York: Harper Collins, 2001.

Made in the USA
Middletown, DE
08 September 2024

60572730R00146